THE
AUTHENTICITY OF
THE RHESUS OF
EURIPIDES

THE
AUTHENTICITY OF
THE RHESUS OF
EURIPIDES

BY

WILLIAM RITCHIE

Senior Lecturer in Greek in the
University of Sydney

CAMBRIDGE
AT THE UNIVERSITY PRESS
1964

PUBLISHED BY

THE SYNDICS OF THE CAMBRIDGE UNIVERSITY PRESS

Bentley House, 200 Euston Road, London, N.W. 1
American Branch: 32 East 57th Street, New York 22, N.Y.
West African Office: P.O. Box 33, Ibadan, Nigeria

©

CAMBRIDGE UNIVERSITY PRESS

1964

Printed in Great Britain at the University Printing House, Cambridge
(Brooke Crutchley, University Printer)

CONTENTS

PREFACE

The suspicion that *Rhesus* is not by Euripides, among whose works it is preserved, has its origin in antiquity; for in one of the ancient hypotheses attached to the play this is recorded as the opinion of some unnamed scholars. In our own era the view that the play is spurious is found as early as Scaliger, but the foundations of the modern case against its authenticity were laid some two hundred years ago by Valckenaer, Beck, Morstadt, Hermann and others. These scholars based their contention partly on an adverse estimate of the play's artistic merits, partly on the evidence of supposed peculiarities in its vocabulary, style and technique. Subsequent exponents of the same view have added especially to the arguments of the latter kind, placing less emphasis on purely aesthetic considerations, although these have never ceased to have some influence. The defence of the traditional attribution, first taken up by Vater in his edition of *Rhesus*, has been carried on by a minority of scholars.

Opinion today is still sharply divided. Some writers on Euripidean tragedy accept *Rhesus* as genuine, although few do so without reserve. More often it is either condemned as the work of an inferior poet, who is usually held to belong to the fourth century B.C., or else left out of account altogether as being of indeterminable date and authorship.

Apology might be needed for adding to the already substantial literature on the subject, if the question were one of small moment or if there were no more left to be said. I do not believe, however, that either is the case. Although no one would rank *Rhesus* among the greatest extant Attic tragedies, the question of its authorship is one to which the serious student can hardly be indifferent. For if it is not by Euripides but by a later poet, then it is historically important as a unique specimen of tragedy later than the fifth century and not from the hand of one of the three great tragedians. On the other hand, if Euripides is its author, those very differences from his other works which provoke doubt of its authenticity make it a play which the student of his drama ought not to neglect.

Nor does further progress seem impossible. There has been a tendency in the past to attack the problem piecemeal and on too small a scale. Useful studies have been made of some parts of the evidence, but taken in isolation their results are inconclusive. If a solution is to be reached, it must be based upon the aggregate of all kinds of evidence. Until quite recently there did not even exist a systematic review of the arguments accumulated by earlier scholars. This need was supplied by the able and judicious survey of C. B. Sneller, published in 1949, to which I am much indebted. His work, however, has shown how many aspects of the problem deserve closer examination. In particular, the vocabulary, style and metre of the play are potentially important sources of evidence; but only the first of these has been investigated with any thoroughness.

This book aims therefore at providing a fuller investigation of the evidence than any previously undertaken. In many respects it follows quite closely the lines of inquiry pursued by previous scholars. This was necessary in order to test the validity of their arguments. But I have tried to present the evidence in greater detail and to evaluate it by a more extensive comparison of other tragedies. Special attention is given to style and metre, and here I have sought to determine where *Rhesus* stands in relation to marked differences between Euripides' earlier and later manners. Although the inquiry arrives at a positive conclusion in favour of authenticity, it was undertaken in an impartial spirit, and I have tried to preserve this in my presentation. It must be stressed that the evidence is to be judged by its cumulative weight. For the sake of completeness I have sometimes recorded even quite trivial findings, if it seemed that they might contribute something to the total impression.

PREFACE

I have not included a detailed history of the dispute, but the Bibliography provides a conspectus of the literature on the subject, and references are given throughout to older works as well as to recent ones. I hope that in this way my debts to previous scholars, including those from whose views I differ, have been acknowledged adequately.

The present work is a revised and enlarged version of a doctoral dissertation presented to the University of Cambridge in 1957. I wish here to express my gratitude for the award of the Prendergast Studentship, which enabled me to begin research in this subject, and for assistance from Pembroke College, which helped me to continue it.

Among those from whose help and advice I have profited at some time I should like to mention particularly Professors A. M. Dale, P. H. J. Lloyd-Jones and G. P. Shipp. My thanks are also due to Mr J. H. Quincey for his careful reading of the proofs, which has led to many improvements, and to the staff of the Cambridge University Press for the skill and care which they have brought to their task. Above all I owe more than I can adequately acknowledge to Professor D. L. Page for first encouraging me to undertake this study, for guiding it with kindly and penetrating criticism and for sustaining its laboured progress by his unfailing enthusiasm. I need hardly add that I alone am responsible for the views expressed and, of course, for errors.

Finally, I wish to thank the Australian Humanities Research Council for its generous contribution towards the cost of publication.

W.R.

SYDNEY
September 1963

CHAPTER I

EXTERNAL EVIDENCE

The fact that *Rhesus* is preserved in our manuscripts of Euripides may be regarded in itself as substantial evidence that it was at least commonly accepted in antiquity as his work. Our tradition, however, has also preserved, in one of the Arguments accompanying the play in the manuscripts, a record of the fact that some ancient scholars suspected that it was not Euripidean. It is from this ancient suspicion that doubt about the authenticity of *Rhesus* in modern times takes its origin; and although today those who refuse to accept it as the work of Euripides argue principally from internal grounds of language, style and technique, an inquiry into the problem ought still to begin with a careful examination of the external evidence. What facts can be established about the history of our play? Is there any other evidence, apart from the doubt recorded in the Argument, to encourage the belief that the play has been falsely attributed? Can we discover more precisely what views were held in antiquity about its authorship?

The total amount of external evidence available to us is very small and falls far short of enabling us to reconstruct the history of our play in even the barest outline. *Rhesus* is among the plays of Euripides for which scholia have survived. Compared to the scholia for some of the other plays these are meagre in their total bulk, but they are not entirely devoid of valuable material. In addition, the Arguments prefixed to the play in the manuscripts contain a few pieces of useful information for our purposes. Our only other possible source of evidence, quotation of *Rhesus* or allusion to it in the works of other authors, yields little or nothing of value. These literary sources will be reviewed first.

LITERARY SOURCES

Rhesus is seldom cited in ancient literature. Verbal quotations are to be found only in late writers, none of them earlier than the fourth century A.D.[1] Even though these refer to the play specifically as the work of Euripides, testimony of such late date is of no value to us, since there is no reason to suppose that it is based on a greater knowledge than our own. We can, however, say that none of the writers who quote the play expresses any doubt about its authenticity. There is no mention of our *Rhesus* by name in extant literature earlier than the Christian era, nor indeed of any play so titled; nor is it possible confidently to identify any allusion to our play. There are one or two places in Aristophanes where reminiscence of *Rhesus* seems possible, but the resemblance is not nearly striking enough to establish a connection. The following passages, however, are worth recording, if only to show how far we are from being able to prove that Aristophanes knew our play:

'Acharnians' 280 ff.[2]

The Chorus fall upon Dicaeopolis crying

οὗτος αὐτός ἐστιν, οὗτος.
βάλλε βάλλε βάλλε βάλλε,
παῖε πᾶς τὸν μιαρόν.

We cannot fail to be reminded of the cries of the Chorus as they enter in pursuit of Odysseus, *Rh.* 675 ff.:

[1] The following in quoting *Rh.* name Euripides as its author: Eustathius, *ad* Dionys. Perieg. 270 (*v.* 29); Stobaeus, *Anth.* LIV, 9 (*vv.* 105–8); Marius Victorinus I, p. 2498 (*v.* 211); Schol. A *Il.* Z 479 (*vv.* 390 f.); Io. Tzetzes, *Chiliades* IV, 996 (*vv.* 510 f.); Etym. M. p. 439, 3 (*vv.* 854 f.). Other quotations and possible allusions, in which the poet is not named, are collected by Vater, *Vindiciae* (Berlin, 1837), pp. ix–xii: these have no value as evidence.

[2] Regarded as a possible parody by Hartung, *Euripides restitutus*, I, 37, Bates, *TAPA*, XLVII (1916), 7 f.; rejected as fortuitous by Beck, *Diatribe critica de Rheso suppositicio Euripidis dramate*, p. 302, Pearson, *CR*, XXXV (1921), 52, Sneller, *De Rheso Tragoedia*, p. 109 n. 2, Pohlenz, *Die griechische Tragödie* (2nd ed., 1954), p. 474.

ἔα ἔα·
βάλε βάλε βάλε βάλε,
θένε θένε. τίς ἀνήρ;

with παῖε πᾶς a few lines below in 685. There is also a likeness, both verbal and metrical, to this passage of *Rhesus* in *Ach.* 204 ff., where the Chorus first enter searching for Dicaeopolis. But such resemblance of diction as there is may result simply from the similarity of situation, and it is to be noted that παῖε παῖε and βάλλε βάλλε occur as the cries of attackers in a passage of Xenophon.[1] We cannot be sure that parody is intended here.

'Acharnians' 1190 ff.

This passage is perhaps worth mentioning, since it occurs in the same play. Lamachus returns to the scene wounded and uttering cries of distress, which may at times remind us of the pained utterances of the stricken Charioteer (*Rh.* 728 ff.). A similarity of phrase is to be remarked here and there (e.g. 1203 συμφορὰ τάλαινα τῶν ἐμῶν κακῶν: *Rh.* 731 συμφορὰ βαρεῖα Θρηκῶν; 1205 τραυμάτων ἐποδύνων: *Rh.* 750 ὀδύνη τραύματος). Here again the verbal resemblances may result from an accidental similarity of situation. Although parody of the tragic style is certainly intended, the resemblance is not close enough to prove that it is specifically parody of *Rhesus*.

'Frogs' 840

ἄληθες, ὦ παῖ τῆς ἀρουραίας θεοῦ;

Addressed by Aeschylus to Euripides this line is clearly a parody of his diction, as the scholiast confirms: εἴρηται δ' ὁ στίχος παρὰ τὰ Εὐριπίδου· 'ἄληθες, ὦ παῖ τῆς θαλασσίας θεοῦ;'.[2] If the line parodied is accurately reported, the parody is certainly not of our play. But the phrase τῆς θαλασσίας

---

[1] *Anab.* v, 7, 21 and 28: noted by Goossens, *Ant. Class.* I (1932), 124. Cf. Pohlenz, *op. cit.*, *Erläuterungen*, p. 190.

[2] Eur. fr. 885 N.² Cf. Ar. *Vesp.* 1518.

θεοῦ does occur at *Rh.* 974, and this phrase is the main point of the parody. Clearly Aristophanes thinks it typical enough of Euripides to merit a jest, and of course Euripides may well have used it in more than one place (cf. *Andr.* 17 ἡ θαλασ-σία... Θέτις). We cannot be sure that Aristophanes had our passage in mind.

Other coincidences of expression between *Rhesus* and Aristophanes are even less significant.[1] Even if these are added, the evidence does not suffice to prove that Aristophanes was acquainted with the play. If he were parodying *Rhesus*, we should expect a much more obvious resemblance to the original than anything we have here.

THE ARGUMENTS AND SCHOLIA TO 'RHESUS': INTRODUCTORY

In the absence of any certainly identifiable literary reference to our *Rhesus*, or to any play of the name, the only external evidence for our problem is to be derived from the Arguments and scholia to our play. These remnants of the work of ancient commentators contain the only clues we have to the history of *Rhesus* between the date of its composition and the date of our earliest surviving text of any part of the play (fourth to fifth century A.D.).[2] But such useful learned material as the Arguments and scholia embody derives from a shorter period than this, the age of active scholarship which covers some three hundred years from Aristotle to Didymus. We may look here then for the views held by scholars within this period about the authorship of *Rhesus*, and for such information about its earlier history as chance may have preserved from their writings.

We are fortunate to the extent that the Arguments and scholia to *Rhesus* preserve the names of several scholars and thus provide some datable evidence for our problem. But

---

[1] Pohlenz, *op. cit.*, notes 149: *Ach.* 513; 195: *Ra.* 882; 943: *Ra.* 1032. None of these is of any significance.

[2] *P. Achmîm* 4 (containing *vv.* 48–96).

4

the scholarly matter has been miserably curtailed, with the result that there is sometimes doubt about its interpretation. In piecing together such scraps of evidence as we can discover we are further handicapped by the extreme limitations of our knowledge of the tradition by which the works of the tragedians were preserved and studied during the period in question.[1] We believe, although we have no certain proof, that our text of Euripides derives from an edition produced at Alexandria by Aristophanes of Byzantium. About this important event in the tradition we may be reasonably certain, but we know next to nothing about the contributions of scholars before and after to the study of tragedy. Of the numerous works on tragedy produced by the Peripatetic scholars we have barely more than the titles.[2] About the work of the earlier Alexandrian scholars we have almost no information; the scholarship of this period in all branches of literature was consummated in Callimachus' monumental Πίνακες, the catalogue of the Alexandrian Library, whose 120 books are known to us through only some two dozen references.[3] After the Alexandrian edition came the commentators, from whose works our extant scholia are in part derived; we seldom know more about them than we can glean from the scholia themselves.

The history of the tragic texts is generally so obscure that the interpretation of our evidence for *Rhesus* must often be tentative. This should not discourage us from trying to extract their full worth from the pieces of information that can be assembled. It is fair to assume, where the views of particular scholars are cited, that we have at least the essence of what they wrote. Where more than one interpretation is possible, we may reasonably prefer that which accords with greater probability and contributes to a consistent general picture.

[1] On the history of the text of the tragedians: Ziegler, *RE*, s.v. Tragoedia, 2067–74; Wilamowitz, *Einleitung in die griechische Tragödie* (1889), ch. 3.

[2] Ziegler, *op. cit.* 2069 f.

[3] Frr. 429–53 Pfeiffer, *Callimachus* I (1949). See below, p. 10 n. 2.

The first Argument

The first of the two Arguments to *Rhesus*, in its best-preserved form, consists of a concise narrative summary of the plot followed by scholarly notes on two matters of special interest about the play, the doubt concerning its authorship and the existence of variant forms of prologue.[1] In this arrangement of its matter it has some resemblance to the first Argument to *Medea*, in which the summary of the plot is followed by notes on other versions of the myth, on Euripides' debt to Neophron and on certain aesthetic criticisms of the play. In neither case are we obliged to suppose that the scholarly material belongs to the author of the plot-summary; the two elements are quite distinct from one another and their juxtaposition may well be the work of a later compiler. The précis of the plot is similar in character to those preceding many other plays in our manuscripts of Euripides. These longer summaries are to be distinguished from the very succinct indication of the dramatic theme extant for some plays, including *Rhesus*, in the hypotheses of Aristophanes of Byzantium. It is quite probable on stylistic grounds that the majority of the narrative hypotheses, including that for *Rhesus*, are by the same hand, but we do not know by whom or when they were written.[2] Unless it can be shown to have originated at an early date, the narrative hypothesis of *Rhesus* will have no value for us as evidence.

The same summary of the plot of *Rhesus*, with some minor verbal differences, is extant also in a papyrus fragment of the second century A.D.[3] It is there followed by similar

---

[1] It appears thus in V and Harl. In L and P the plot-summary is omitted, and the scholarly notes are placed after the Hypothesis of Aristophanes. Pearson (*CR*, xxxv (1921), 60) thought that Aristophanes was their author: this is possible, but cannot be proved (see below, p. 31).

[2] G. Zuntz, *The Political Plays of Euripides* (1955), pp. 129 ff., distinguishes different types among our Euripidean hypotheses and discusses their origins. (His case for distinguishing *I Alc.* and *I Med.* from the main group of narrative hypotheses is not compelling.)

[3] *Pap. Soc. Ital.* xii, 2, 1286: first published by C. Gallavotti, *Riv. di fil.* lxi (1933), 177 ff. Cf. Koerte, *Hermes*, lxix (1934), 1 ff.

hypotheses of two other plays of Euripides, *Rhadamanthys* and *Skyrioi*, and this roughly alphabetical arrangement is evidence that the fragment belongs to a collection of narrative hypotheses for the works of the Euripidean corpus, published separately from the texts but presumably based on the collected edition of his works, which is generally held to have been made at Alexandria by Aristophanes of Byzantium.[1] It was tentatively suggested by Gallavotti[2] that the papyrus hypotheses and their counterparts in our manuscripts of Euripides might be traced back to the Peripatetic scholar Dicaearchus (fl. *c.* 300 B.C.), who is known to have written ὑποθέσεις τῶν Εὐριπίδου καὶ Σοφοκλέους μύθων.[3] If this could be demonstrated, we should have certain evidence for the existence of our play, and quite substantial evidence for its attribution to Euripides, at the end of the fourth century B.C. We ought therefore to consider briefly whether this ascription is justified.

In support of the attribution to Dicaearchus is the fact that the narrative argument to *Alcestis* has, in L only, his name at its head, and that he is besides cited by name in the notes appended to the narrative arguments of both *Medea* and *Rhesus*. But we have already observed that these notes need not come from the same source as the plot-summary, and the *Alcestis* hypothesis is not so ascribed in any of the other manuscripts. Against the attribution to Dicaearchus there is the commonly held view that his hypotheses were not narrative.[4] This, however, is by no means a necessary inference from the very meagre evidence we have about the work. The passage of Sextus Empiricus on which this view is

---

[1] On the alphabetical arrangement of the Alexandrian edition see Wilamowitz, *Analecta Euripidea* (1875), pp. 131 ff.

[2] Gallavotti, *loc. cit.*

[3] Sext. Emp. *Adv. Math.* iii, 3 = Dicaearchus, fr. 78 Wehrli.

[4] Propounded by Schrader, *Quaestiones Peripateticae* (Hamburg, 1884): accepted by Wilamowitz, *Einl. in die gr. Trag.* p. 133 n. 19; Martini, *RE*, s.v. Dikaiarchos; Raddatz, *RE*, s.v. Hypothesis; Wehrli, *Dikaiarchos (Die Schule des Aristoteles*, Heft 1, 1944), 68; Sneller, *op. cit.* p. 88. Zuntz, *op. cit.* pp. 143 f., rightly questions the validity of this assumption.

founded distinguishes various applications of the word ὑπόθεσις and in illustration of its use in the general sense of ἡ δραματικὴ περιπέτεια cites Dicaearchus' work.[1] In this broad definition of the class of dramatic hypothesis there is nothing whatever to exclude the common narrative type, such as we have for the plays of Euripides. Indeed, from the fact that Dicaearchus' hypotheses are chosen as typical, it is more natural to suppose that they were essentially of a narrative kind. Such a work need not be thought unworthy of a pupil of Aristotle; for the comic poet Antiphanes describes a contemporary, probably the Peripatetic scholar Heraclides Ponticus, as ὁ τὰ κεφάλαια συγγράφων Εὐριπίδη.[2] Work of this sort might be regarded as a useful supplement to the compilation of the *Didascaliae* undertaken by Aristotle and as a preliminary to further study of the treatment of myths by the tragic poets.

The hypotheses of Dicaearchus, whatever else their purpose, may well have included a summary of the plot. It is not impossible that they should be the ultimate source of the extant narrative hypotheses; but the evidence does not permit us to draw this conclusion.

The scholarly material appended to the narrative summary is of much more vital interest to us. The passage will first be quoted in full and then considered sentence by sentence.

τοῦτο τὸ δρᾶμα ἔνιοι νόθον ὑπενόησαν, ὡς οὐκ ὂν Εὐριπίδου· τὸν γὰρ Σοφόκλειον μᾶλλον ὑποφαίνει χαρακτῆρα. ἐν μέντοι ταῖς διδασκαλίαις ὡς γνήσιον ἀναγέγραπται, καὶ ἡ περὶ τὰ μετάρσια δὲ ἐν αὐτῷ πολυπραγμοσύνη τὸν Εὐριπίδην ὁμολογεῖ. πρόλογοι δὲ διττοὶ φέρονται. ὁ γοῦν Δικαίαρχος ἐκθεὶς τὴν ὑπόθεσιν τοῦ ᾽Ρήσου γράφει κατὰ λέξιν οὕτως·
νῦν εὐσέληνον φέγγος ἡ διφρήλατος.
καὶ ἐν ἐνίοις δὲ τῶν ἀντιγράφων ἕτερός τις φέρεται πρόλογος,

---

[1] Sext. Emp. *op. cit.*

[2] Fr. 113. Cf. Diog. Laert. v, 86; Wehrli, *Herakleides Pontikos* (*Die Schule des Aristoteles*, Heft VII), 10, 61, 123.

πεζὸς πάνυ καὶ οὐ πρέπων Εὐριπίδῃ· καὶ τάχα ἄν τινες τῶν
ὑποκριτῶν διεσκευακότες εἶεν αὐτόν. ἔχει δὲ οὕτως·
  ὦ τοῦ μεγίστου Ζηνὸς ἄλκιμον τέκος
  κ.τ.λ.

Two separate matters are here the subject of comment:
a doubt about the play's authenticity is mentioned, against
which arguments are put forward in defence of its genuineness; and evidence is cited for the existence of two different
iambic prologues, neither of which is in our text.

It has sometimes been held that all this matter is derived
by the compiler of our Argument from Dicaearchus.[1] If this
were so, it would of course mean that the controversy about
the question of authorship was to be traced back to the
Peripatetic scholars of the late fourth century, and our task
of interpreting this evidence would be greatly simplified.
But the view is not substantiated by the wording of the
Argument. From the fact that Dicaearchus is specifically
quoted on only one point it is natural to infer that his work
was only one of the sources used by the compiler. There is
nothing to be said for Wehrli's curious suggestion that the
line νῦν εὐσέληνον φέγγος ἡ διφρήλατος was quoted by
Dicaearchus as an illustration of ἡ περὶ τὰ μετάρσια πολυπραγμοσύνη. We cannot assume that Dicaearchus is the
source for any more than is specifically attached to his name,
and for the other statements must be content with what we
are actually told about their origin. The precise extent of the
quotation from Dicaearchus is a problem to which we shall
return later.

In the note on the question of authorship four statements
are made. These are not necessarily all derived from a
common source; there may be here up to four separate
contributions to the dispute, which have been brought
together by the writer of the Argument and may represent

---

[1] Kirchhoff, *Philol.* vii (1852), 563; Wehrli, *Dikaiarchos*, pp. 30 (fr. 81),
68.

the views of scholars widely separated in date. We may at any rate consider each of the four statements separately.

(1) τοῦτο τὸ δρᾶμα ἔνιοι νόθον ὑπενόησαν, ὡς οὐκ ὂν Εὐριπίδου.

ὡς οὐκ ὂν Εὐριπίδου LP Harl.: Εὐριπίδου δὲ μὴ εἶναι V.

This is a bald statement that some persons, who are not named, have suspected that *Rhesus* was spurious. From it all doubt in the authenticity of the play takes its origin. It has of course long since ceased to be a principal ground for denying Euripidean authorship, but it is none the less important that we should investigate this ancient suspicion, consider its possible grounds and try to discover by whom and how widely it was held. The answers to these questions may perhaps become clearer after we have considered the other pieces of evidence to be found in the Arguments and scholia. It is too early at this point to speculate about the identity of the ἔνιοι.

It is nevertheless possible to suggest tentatively a period when suspicion was likely to arise. Early in the third century B.C., when material was being acquired for the newly founded Library at Alexandria, those responsible for arranging and cataloguing it are bound to have inquired into the genuineness of the works that came under their scrutiny. This task of setting in order the Library's acquisitions was undertaken by different scholars for the different branches of literature; we are told that the arrangement of tragedies was in the hands of Alexander Aetolus, whose activity at Alexandria is dated between the years 285 and 276.[1] The work of these early scholars was assembled and consolidated by Callimachus (*c.* 310–240) in the 120 books of his great catalogue of the Alexandrian Library (Πίνακες τῶν ἐν πάσῃ παιδείᾳ διαλαμψάντων καὶ ὧν συνέγραψαν).[2] From surviving references to the Πίνακες it is evident that Callimachus pro-

[1] Io. Tzetzes, *in Aristoph. proem.* 1, 19 = *CGF*, p. 19 Kaibel; Knaack, *RE*, I, 1447 f.; Sandys, *Hist. Class. Schol.* I³, 121.

[2] Fr. Schmidt, *Die Pinakes des Kall.* (Klass.-phil. Stud. hrsgbn. v. F. Jacoby, 1, 1922); R. Pfeiffer, *Callimachus* I (1949), pp. 344–9 (frr. 429–53).

nounced on questions of authorship and indicated when it was suspect.[1] If any suspicion about the authenticity of *Rhesus* had been voiced before his time, the fact is likely to have been recorded in the Πίνακες. The librarians of Pergamum also produced their πίνακες, and here too opinions about authenticity, not necessarily identical with those of the Alexandrians, may have been expressed; but we know even less about this work than we do about its Alexandrian counterpart.[2]

It is of course quite possible, even if no doubt about our play's authenticity were recorded in the Πίνακες, for suspicion to have been expressed later. Our references to the Πίνακες show that later scholars consulted it on matters of authorship but did not always accept its authority as final. Nor is it impossible that the suspicion is earlier than the period of Alexandrian scholarship; in this case the record of it could have been transmitted by Callimachus or independently. Consideration of other evidence may help us to decide where the greatest probability lies.

(2) τὸν γὰρ Σοφόκλειον μᾶλλον ὑποφαίνει χαρακτῆρα.

ὑποφαίνει codd.: ὑποφαίνειν Valckenaer.

The only clue to the grounds of the suspicion entertained by the anonymous critics is provided in this brief observation. Unless we adopt Valckenaer's emendation, we are not obliged to take it as a record of the original grounds of suspicion; a later commentator, or the author of the Argument, could have added it by way of explanation. The emendation is not justified; nevertheless, in the absence of contrary evidence, it is fair to assume that this purports to represent the views of the ἔνιοι.

The assertion is a surprising one. Modern scholars have found difficulty in explaining what is meant by Σοφόκλειος χαρακτήρ, since few have been willing to see any close

---

[1] Frr. 437, 442, 444–6 Pfeiffer, *op. cit.* (= 9, 14, 18, 19, 21 Schm.). Cf. fr. 451 (= Schol. E. *Andr.* 445).

[2] Athen. VIII, 336 E; Dion. Hal. *de Din.* I (630), II (669).

resemblance to the manner of Sophocles. Gruppe's attempt to prove that Sophocles was the author of *Rhesus* has found no acceptance, but an explanation of Σοφόκλειος χαρακτήρ has been variously sought in the brevity of the gnomic expressions, in the metrical style, in resemblances to the diction of Sophocles (which indeed are few) or in supposed reminiscence of a particular play of his.[1] It has also been suggested that the ancient critics may have been influenced by the form of the play's opening, which is strikingly different from the familiar Euripidean monologue;[2] but it is no more in the Sophoclean manner. Another view is that the Sophoclean quality was found in the subject of the play and the manner of its treatment.[3] Sophocles was admired in antiquity for the faithfulness with which his plots followed their epic sources, while Euripides was notorious as an innovator in matters of mythology.[4] *Rhesus*, which takes its plot directly from the *Iliad* and keeps closely in many details to the original, might well have seemed in this respect more Sophoclean than Euripidean.

It is, however, rather doubtful whether the last two features would ordinarily be embraced by the term χαρακτήρ. In the language of literary criticism χαρακτήρ normally denotes *style*, and as it is commonly used with reference to a particular author, the *individual stamp* of his style.[5] In this

---

[1] Brevity of *gnomae*: Valckenaer, *Diatribe in Euripidis dramatum perditorum reliquias* (Leiden, 1768), p. 95; Hermann, *De Rheso Tragoedia*, p. 257; Hagenbach, *De Rheso Tragoedia*, p. 25. Metre and diction: Hermann, *op. cit.* 267; Wilamowitz, *Einl. in die gr. Trag.* p. 41 n. 81. Imitation of Sophocles, *Poimenes*: Wilamowitz, *De Rhesi Scholiis*, p. 12, and *Hermes*, LXI (1926), 284. Resemblance to Sophocles, *Ajax*: Richards, *CQ*, x (1916), 195; cf. Pohlenz, *op. cit.* pp. 473 f. These matters are discussed in the following chapters.

[2] Bates, *TAPA*, XLVII (1916), 9; others (Valckenaer, *op. cit.* pp. 90 f.; Beck, *op. cit.* p. 287; Morstadt, *Beitrag zur Kritik*, p. 69) thought that those who expressed this opinion read the play with the second iambic prologue, but the fact that this was in dialogue does not make it Sophoclean.

[3] See esp. Pearson, *CR*, XXXV (1921), 60; also Ridgeway, *CQ*, XX (1926), 11. For discussion see chapter II.

[4] For Sophocles: Athenaeus VII, 277E; *Vit. Soph.* 20 (for further references cf. Pearson, *Fragments of Sophocles*, I, xxiii f.). For Euripides: Schol. *Hec.* 3 *et passim* (*Scholia in Euripidem*, ed. Schwartz, Index, p. 404).

[5] *LSJ*, s.v. II, 5.

application the word is first found in common use in the literary works of Dionysius of Halicarnassus, but the usage may well have been established earlier.[1] With our passage we may compare a number of other places where χαρακτήρ is invoked in cases of disputed authorship. These tend to confirm that the reference is particularly to style.

(i) Dion. Hal. Περὶ Δεινάρχου 11 (Ψευδεπίγραφοι δημόσιοι), 659: ἀπ' αὐτοῦ τοῦ χαρακτῆρος εὕροι τις ἂν οὐκ ὄντα τὸν λόγον Δεινάρχου (ὑδαρής τε γὰρ καὶ ἀσθενὴς καὶ ψυχρός ἐστιν), ἀλλὰ μᾶλλον αὐτὸν ἄν τις θείη Δημοκλείδου ἢ Μενεσαίχμου ἢ τῶν ἄλλων τῶν τοιούτων τινός (cf. 660, 661).

(ii) Libanius, *Arg. Demos.* xvii, 2: ὁ δὲ λόγος ψευδεπίγραφος εἶναι δοκεῖ. οὐ γὰρ ἔοικε κατὰ τὴν ἰδέαν τοῖς ἄλλοις τοῖς τοῦ Δημοσθένους, ἀλλὰ τῷ 'Υπερείδου χαρακτῆρι μᾶλλον προσχωρεῖ τά τε ἄλλα καὶ λέξεις τινὰς ἔχει κατ' ἐκεῖνον μᾶλλον εἰρημένας ἢ τὸν Δημοσθένην, οἷον νεόπλουτοι καὶ βδελυρεύεσθαι.

(iii) *Ibid.* xxiv, 11: Διονύσιος δὲ ὁ 'Αλικαρνασσεὺς οὐ δέχεται τούτους τοὺς λόγους Δημοσθένους εἶναι ἐκ τῆς ἰδέας τεκμαιρόμενος. οἱ δέ φασιν ἐπίτηδες τὸν ῥήτορα τοιούτῳ χαρακτῆρι κεχρῆσθαι ζηλώσαντα Λυκοῦργον εὐδοκιμοῦντα παρὰ τοῖς 'Αθηναίοις....

(iv) Schol. Euripides, *Or.* 640: ἔνιοι ἀθετοῦσι τοῦτον καὶ τὸν ἑξῆς στίχον· οὐκ ἔχουσι γὰρ τὸν Εὐριπίδειον χαρακτῆρα. (The style of the lines must be meant, although the grounds of the objection are not apparent.)

(v) *Arg. Hes.* 'Ασπίς: καὶ 'Απολλώνιος δὲ ὁ 'Ρόδιός φησιν αὐτοῦ (*sc.* τοῦ 'Ησιόδου) εἶναι ἔκ τε τοῦ χαρακτῆρος καὶ ἐκ τοῦ πάλιν τὸν 'Ιόλαον ἐν τῷ γ' Καταλόγῳ εὑρίσκειν ἡνιοχοῦντα 'Ηρακλεῖ.

If then, as these passages suggest, Σοφόκλειος χαρακτήρ refers to style, did our critics wish to suggest that Sophocles actually wrote *Rhesus* or merely to give a general indication of the kind of difference they felt? The former is perhaps the strict implication of their words, but it is very unlikely to be what they meant. It would be a foolish suggestion, unless they had evidence that a *Rhesus* of Sophocles had been lost. We have no such evidence, and it is most improbable that

---

[1] χαρακτήρ in Dion. Hal.: Rhys Roberts, *D.H., The Three Literary Letters,* p. 208, and *D.H. on Literary Comp.* p. 333. Earlier uses: *LSJ,* s.v. ii, 3.

there was any in antiquity.[1] Moreover, it is inconceivable that a work of Sophocles should have been fraudulently passed off as Euripidean, and hardly less difficult to believe that such a false attribution could have been made by error.

It is more likely that the reference to Σοφόκλειος χαρακτήρ was an attempt to define succinctly the quality of the style. The differences between the styles of Sophocles and Euripides would be readily appreciated. Certainly the stylistic differences of the three tragedians were clearly distinguished by Dionysius of Halicarnassus.[2] Our critics, however, are not necessarily of so late a date. Although the Alexandrian canon of five tragedians included Ion and Achaeus, scholarship even at that period must already have been largely concentrated upon the three great tragedians. Indeed the way for such stylistic distinctions had been prepared, for Aeschylus and Euripides at least, by the parodies of Aristophanes. We have, too, the evidence already quoted that Apollonius Rhodius used the argument from style in the dispute over the authorship of the *Shield of Heracles*. It is thus not impossible that Alexandrian scholars should have expressed such a view as this.

Even if their meaning was simply that the style of *Rhesus* was like that of Sophocles, we cannot regard it as an acute piece of criticism. It is conceivable that the style might be felt to be uncharacteristic of Euripides (modern critics have thought so too), but it is hard to think of any respect in which it might be thought more like that of Sophocles. We shall see, when we examine the evidence of style, that it offers no support for this view.

If this was the sole reason of the ancient critics for doubting the authenticity of *Rhesus*, they do not deserve much respect. So far as we are informed, their doubt was based upon a purely subjective aesthetic criticism; there is no indication

---

[1] A few Sophoclean titles have probably been lost (Pearson, *Fragments*, I, p. xvi).

[2] *De imit.* 422–3 (*Opusc.*, ed. Usener–Radermacher, II, 206); *De comp. verb.* 22–4.

that they had any external evidence that the play was spurious. Finally, the reference to Σοφόκλειος χαρακτήρ does not imply either a low estimate of the play's quality or a belief that it is other than a work of the fifth century.

(3) ἐν μέντοι ταῖς διδασκαλίαις ὡς γνήσιον ἀναγέγραπται.

This statement provides a most valuable piece of evidence. The name διδασκαλίαι designates the chronological records of the dramatic and dithyrambic productions in the contests of the Athenian Dionysiac festivals.[1] It is generally supposed, with good reason, that the reference here is to the *Didascaliae* of Aristotle; for, of the several citations of διδασκαλίαι by ancient scholars, six are specifically referred to Aristotle's work of that name, and it is a safe inference that this was the source from which the ancient grammarians regularly derived their information about dramatic productions.[2]

The scope of Aristotle's work cannot be precisely defined from the few references we have to it. We can, however, form a general idea of the content of didascalic records from the surviving fragments of didascalic inscriptions as well as from the brief didascalic notices which survive, in a more or less mutilated condition, for many of our plays in the hypotheses of Aristophanes of Byzantium.[3] Aristophanes no doubt derived his material from Aristotle. The inscriptions we have, although they preserve fragmentary records as far back as the fifth century, date from the early third, and they too are thought to be dependent on Aristotle for the period which his work covered. From these sources it is clear that the *didascaliae* comprised basically a continuous list, year by year, of all those who had competed in the contests, in the order in which they had been placed by the judges, together with the titles of the works they had presented. Winning

[1] Reisch, *RE*, s.v. Didaskaliai; Pickard-Cambridge, *DFA*, pp. 69 ff., 85 ff., 110–13; Schm.–St. I, 2, 51 n. 3.

[2] Aristotle, frr. 618–30 Rose.

[3] *IG*, ed. min., II², 2319–23. Remains of didascalic notices in Arguments: Aeschylus, *Pers.*, *Sept.*, *Agam.*; Sophocles, *Phil.*; Euripides, *Alc.*, *Med.*, *Hipp.*, *Phoen.*

actors were also named. It is likely that Aristotle's *Didascaliae* provided a systematic compilation of this information from the official archives, and that this, probably the first such compilation, subsequently became the standard work of reference for information in these matters.

It cannot be taken for granted that Aristotle's *Didascaliae* were complete for the whole of the period they embraced, which was probably from the inception of the official competitions down to his own time. Official records may not have been extant for every year, and he may sometimes have depended on reconstruction from other, less reliable, sources. On the other hand, from the use later scholars make of the work we may infer that its record was held to be both accurate and complete, as the following pieces of evidence tend to show:

(*a*) Schol. *Andr.* 445: εἰλικρινῶς δὲ τοὺς τοῦ δράματος χρόνους οὐκ ἔστι λαβεῖν· οὐ δεδίδακται γὰρ ᾽Αθήνησιν. ὁ δὲ Καλλίμαχος ἐπιγραφῆναί φησι τῇ τραγῳδίᾳ Δημοκράτην.

The implication of the first sentence is that *Andromache* was not recorded in the *didascaliae*, but would have been if it had been produced at Athens, and its date would then have been certainly known. The latter part of the note is naturally taken to mean that Callimachus reported finding the name Democrates inscribed on an extant copy, or copies, of the play. Whether this is regarded as relevant to the problem of dating is not clear. It may be, as some have thought, that Callimachus wished to identify the play with an *Andromache* recorded in the *didascaliae* under the name of Democrates.[1] If so, he was not necessarily doubting the accuracy of the *didascaliae*; his suggestion was simply that the play was attached there to another name, and he was perhaps allowing for the possibility that the play had been entered under the name of its producer and not that of its author (see below,

---

[1] The view of Wilamowitz, *Anal. Eur.* p. 148 (cf. Murray, O.C.T.). But the evidence is not necessarily to be so interpreted: G. Jachmann, *De Aristot. Didascaliis* (1909), 27 f. (cf. Pfeiffer, *ad* Callim. fr. 451).

pp. 26 ff.). On the other hand, there may be no connection between Callimachus' observation and the question of the play's production. At all events the chance of an omission from the didascalic record is excluded implicitly.

(*b*) Schol. Ar. *Plut.* 385: It is decided that the Pamphilus mentioned by Aristophanes is not a tragic poet, because no tragedian of that name appears in the *didascaliae* before the date of *Plutus*. This implies a complete chronological record embracing all playwrights, as indeed might also be assumed from several other references to the *didascaliae* for information about obscure poets.[1]

(*c*) Schol. Ar. *Nub.* 552: Callimachus thought to have detected an error in the *didascaliae*, which recorded the *Marikas* (of Eupolis) two years later than the *Clouds*, although there is a reference to *Marikas* in the latter play. Eratosthenes comes to the defence of the *didascaliae* by pointing out that the *Clouds* we possess is a revised version, later than the *Marikas*, and that only plays actually produced are recorded in the *didascaliae*. This is the only place where we find the authority of the *didascaliae* challenged, and the charge is found to be groundless. It is probable that second versions of plays were recorded if they were produced at the Dionysiac festivals. A second *Peace* was apparently entered in the *Didascaliae*.[2] There is no reason to suspect a mistake in the case of the *Clouds*: its second version was probably not produced in the contest, if at all.

From this ancient testimony it seems safe enough to infer that the *didascaliae* were complete and accurate for the period they covered, which almost certainly included the whole dramatic career of Euripides. And so from the information that *Rhesus* was entered in the *didascaliae* ὡς γνήσιον we may conclude with certainty that Euripides produced a *Rhesus* in Athens, and further that the date of its production was known to all who consulted the work of Aristotle. The words

[1] Frr. 619, 620, 624, 628.   [2] Cf. *Arg.* 1 Ar. *Pax*.

ὡς γνήσιον need not mean that the authenticity of *Rhesus* was expressly affirmed by Aristotle. No such assurance would be needed unless suspicions had already been put forward. It may mean no more than that the record included an entry in the form Εὐριπίδης Ῥήσῳ.

Unfortunately the details of the didascalic notice for *Rhesus* are not preserved. There is, however, one clue about its date which should not be ignored. In schol. 528 there is the following note:

Κράτης ἀγνοεῖν φησὶ τὸν Εὐριπίδην τὴν περὶ τὰ μετάρσια θεωρίαν διὰ τὸ νέον ἔτι εἶναι ὅτε τὸν Ῥῆσον ἐδίδασκε.

Crates, the leading scholar of the Pergamene school in the second century B.C., says that Euripides is ignorant of astronomy because he was still young when he produced *Rhesus*. Crates' attribution of the play to Euripides' youth is often treated as a mere inference from the alleged ignorance in a matter of astronomy, and so discounted on the ground that Crates himself has misinterpreted the passage and has wrongly held that the astronomy is at fault.[1] This reasoning is perverse. Crates is not putting forward here a deduction about Euripides' age from his errors in astronomy; if he had been doing so, his statement would have been expressed differently. Rather, he is excusing Euripides' ignorance of astronomy on the grounds of his youth. If this is a mere guess, the note is more fatuous than we have a right to suppose. It would be idle to conjecture the date of composition when the facts were easily to be established by reference to Aristotle's *Didascaliae*. It is most unlikely that the library of Pergamum lacked a copy of this standard work of reference. But even if Crates did not have access to the

---

[1] By, e.g., Hermann, *op. cit.* p. 272; Hagenbach, pp. 12 f.; Ridgeway, *CQ*, xx (1926), 14; Porter, on *Rh.* 528 ff.; Geffcken, 'Der Rhesos', *Hermes*, LXXI (1936), 394. The contrary view, that Crates' statement is based on knowledge of the *didascaliae*, is maintained by Gruppe, *Ariadne*, pp. 313 f.; Buchwald, *Studien zur Chronologie*, p. 51; cf. Wilamowitz, *Einl.* p. 41. Grégoire, *Ant. Class.* II (1933), 95 n. 13, doubts the authority of Crates' evidence, which is incompatible with his date for *Rhesus* (424 B.C.).

Didascaliae, he would hardly make a statement which could so easily be disproved by others who did have it. The only reasonable inference is that Crates was acquainted with the didascalic record, and that it was common knowledge at both Pergamum and Alexandria that the *Rhesus* of Euripides was a youthful work. Indeed, while Crates' criticism of Euripides' astronomical knowledge is challenged by Alexandrian scholars, his statement about the poet's age is accepted without comment.

We may therefore be confident that *Rhesus* was recorded in the *didascaliae* under the name of Euripides and at a date quite early in his career. It is difficult to define the limits within which Euripides might be referred to as νέος; if, however, his birth is rightly placed in 480, it is unlikely that he would still be so called much later than 440, even in terms of his dramatic career, which began with the production of *Peliades* in 455.[1]

If then the *Rhesus* of Euripides was entered in the *didascaliae*, and their record was accurate, why should there still be a doubt about the authenticity of our play? It is not enough to argue that those who voiced the suspicion may not have been aware of the didascalic notice; for others who did know it have nevertheless seen fit to preserve a record of this suspicion, and have sought corroboration for the authority of the *didascaliae* in the internal evidence of ἡ περὶ τὰ μετάρσια πολυπραγμοσύνη. It seems then that the *didascaliae*, however reliable, are not regarded as infallible evidence of the authenticity of the play. There appear to be three possible reasons for not accepting their authority in the matter:

(i) Our play is not the one whose production is recorded in the *didascaliae*, but another play of the same name which has been mistaken for it.

---

[1] Chronology of Euripides' career: Schm.–St. III, 313 ff., 322 f. Buchwald, *op. cit.*, fixes 438 as a late limit for the composition of *Rhesus*. It is not possible to agree with Grégoire, *op. cit.*, that a work of the 420's could be said to belong to Euripides' youth as a dramatist.

(ii) Our play is the one recorded in the *didascaliae*, but the poet is another Euripides.

(iii) The author of the play may not himself have been its producer, and it may have been the latter's name that was entered in the *didascaliae*.

Each of these possibilities must be considered.

(i) This is the hypothesis most commonly adopted today by those who do not accept our *Rhesus* as Euripidean. It is generally supposed to be a work of the fourth century, which has in some way supplanted the play which Euripides is acknowledged to have written. A few have placed its date of composition even later.[1]

The adherents of this theory do not suggest exactly how or when the erroneous identification might have taken place. Let us first consider the limits of date within which this could have happened. At first sight it would appear possible for a mistake to have been made by the early Alexandrian scholars. We are told that at the time when texts were being acquired for the libraries of Alexandria and Pergamum forgery was prevalent.[2] Although we have no evidence for such practice in the case of tragic texts, the Alexandrians, who lacked not a few works of the Attic tragedians, could have been deceived either by a deliberate forgery or by the accidental substitution of another play of the same name.[3] It is probable however, as we shall see later (p. 37), that our *Rhesus* was known as the work of Euripides at least as early as 300. If then it is a substitute, it became established as Euripidean some time before it reached Alexandria.

We do hear of the production in the fourth century of spurious works purporting to be from the hand of one of the

---

[1] Morstadt, Hermann and Menzer argued that *Rhesus* was Alexandrian. Recent opponents of authenticity generally favour the fourth-century dating (e.g. Geffcken, Schmid, Pohlenz, Lucas, Björck, Lesky).

[2] Galen, xv, 105, 109 Kühn (referring to Hippocratean works).

[3] For tragedies of Euripides not extant at Alexandria see Arguments to Euripides, *Med.*, *Phoen.*; *Vita Eur.* (cf. Suidas, s.v. Εὐριπίδης). For Sophocles cf. Pearson, *Fragments* I, pp. xvi, xxi.

great tragedians. Heraclides Ponticus (*c.* 390–310), it is said, composed tragedies which he brought out as works of Thespis, and in imitation of his example his pupil, Dionysius the Renegade, wrote a play called *Parthenopaeus*, which he passed off as the work of Sophocles, deceiving his master.[1] Heraclides' compositions may perhaps later have gained currency as genuine works of Thespis, and may or may not be the source of the spurious fragments of Thespis we possess, but it is very doubtful if he intended to perpetrate a public fraud. The anecdote suggests that his practices were well known to his contemporaries. This kind of forgery would seem to have been only a form of literary exercise for the amusement of a small circle. It is unlikely that the plays were meant for the stage.

Our *Rhesus*, if it is spurious, must belong to a different category; for its possession of a variety of prologues is strong evidence that it was acted. This fact is important in considering the likelihood of a mistaken identification. If a supposititious work which was publicly performed were to be accepted as genuine, then quite certainly all trace of the genuine work must have perished. Allowing that the Athenians were much less sensitive than we to alteration and interpolation of the texts of the great dramatists, it is still unthinkable that they would have accepted as the genuine work of Euripides a play known to be wholly spurious. We should need to suppose total ignorance of the genuine *Rhesus*, and this in Athens, where the dramatic performances were attended by a large proportion of the population, would require an interval of close to fifty years from the time the play was last seen or read. The *Rhesus* of Euripides was an early work, it is true, but even so, if it had been circulated at all widely after its production, copies would be likely to have survived well into the fourth century.

Only if the *Rhesus* of Euripides was lost soon after its first production, perhaps not published at all, could another play

---

[1] Diog. Laert. v, 92.

have been mistaken for it early in the fourth century. There is no proof that this was not so, but we have no evidence that any plays of Euripides, even early works, were allowed to pass so quickly into oblivion. It seems therefore that the substitution of the spurious play could only have occurred in the fourth century and could only in exceptional circumstances have taken place in the early part of that century.

Allowing that a substitution could have taken place in the fourth century, are we to suppose that this was done deliberately or that it was accidental? Is the hypothesis to be that our *Rhesus* was brought out as the work of Euripides, or that it was first produced by its author without intent of fraud and was only later mistaken for Euripides' work? The former seems rather unlikely. There might be a motive—to ensure the popularity of the production; but how many, even if they had no memory of Euripides' *Rhesus*, would have been deceived by a contemporary forgery, and how well could the secret have been kept?

That the mistake should have been made at a later period, when the spurious play was itself old, is more credible. Again, however, we should require a considerable interval within which the play's first production under the name of its real author could be forgotten. Such an interval could easily be supposed if the spurious *Rhesus* were itself a work of the fifth century, contemporary with Euripides. But if, as is more commonly argued, its composition is to be placed in the fourth century, it becomes more difficult to fit in a sufficient lapse of time between the original production and the making of the mistake. It would however be possible for a work produced in the first third of the century, if its fame had been slight, to be mistaken in the last third for the *Rhesus* which Euripides was known to have written and of which no trace survived.

Here again the evidence of the prologues is relevant. We cannot be quite certain that both the iambic prologues attested in the Argument were already current in the fourth century, but it seems probable that they were (see below, p. 34). If our *Rhesus* was popular on the stage during the fourth century, it becomes much less likely that it was forgotten long enough for its true authorship to be mistaken.

There is one piece of evidence that mistaken attribution of the kind proposed may have occurred. The Catalogue of titles of Aeschylus' works includes the separate entries Αἰτναῖαι γνήσιοι and Αἰτναῖαι νόθοι. From this evidence it would appear that the Alexandrian scholars possessed two plays purporting to be the *Aetnaeae* of Aeschylus, of which they accepted one as genuine and rejected the other as spurious. But the fact that the latter was nevertheless retained among the works of Aeschylus suggests that it may have been a work of some antiquity, which had been erroneously identified as his work and had become established as such. In this case it is possible that a spurious work supplanted the genuine one, and that the error was discovered when the genuine play turned up. But we do not know what the circumstances were, and so cannot say whether there is any parallel to the kind of error that is suggested in the case of *Rhesus*.

We hear of numerous other plays whose authorship was regarded as uncertain in antiquity. Often the details are unknown, but in no other case of which we have knowledge is a spurious work held to have supplanted a genuine one. The work in question is accepted as the original, the issue being simply one of its actual, as opposed to its reputed, authorship. The *Life* of Euripides names as spurious three of his tragedies, *Tennes*, *Rhadamanthys* and *Pirithous*.[1] For the first two of these we know nothing further about the nature of the doubt, but concerning *Pirithous* we learn from Athenaeus that there was uncertainty whether its author was Euripides or Critias.[2] It is not suggested that there was once

[1] *Vita Eur.* p. 3, l. 2 Schwartz. Some plays of Sophocles were also adjudged spurious, but we are not told their titles (*Vita Soph.* 18).
[2] Athenaeus, XI 496B. Others who cite the play treat it as Euripidean (see *TGF*), as does Satyrus, *Vita Eur.* frr. 37, 39 von Arnim. The weight of evidence

another play of the same name by Euripides, which has been lost. Similarly, four plays of Aristophanes are named as being of doubtful authenticity, but the point of dispute is simply whether they are not to be regarded as the work of Archippus, a contemporary comic poet.[1] That such doubts often arose in the case of comedies is clear from Athenaeus, who is often unable to say for certain which of two, or even three, contemporary poets is the author of a particular comedy.[2] One reason for this was no doubt the frequent duplication of titles, especially among the comic poets of the fourth century. The records might attest the same title for two or more poets, and in such cases, if it happened that the plays were preserved without their authors' names or that not all survived, confusion might sometimes occur.[3] The case of *Rhesus*, according to the hypothesis now under consideration, would not be parallel to any of these; for we are asked to believe that the *Rhesus* certainly written by Euripides was lost, and that another play of the same name, probably of later date, was subsequently wrongly attributed to him and was then transmitted as the work of Euripides.

The possibility that our *Rhesus* has been substituted, through either accident or fraud, for the work of the same name by Euripides cannot be discarded. The substitution however could only have been made in the course of the fourth century, and for this it is necessary to suppose that Euripides' *Rhesus* was lost very early. Moreover, if our play is itself a work of the fourth century, as most supporters of this hypothesis hold, it is not particularly easy to believe either that a mistake would have been made or that a deliberate fraud would have succeeded. The apparent popu-

favours its authenticity: cf. Page, *Greek Literary Papyri*, pp. 120–5. Wilamowitz, *Anal. Eur.* pp. 161 ff., thought that Critias was the author of a tetralogy consisting of *Tennes, Rhadam., Pirith.* and the satyr-play *Sisyphus*; this hypothesis has found wide acceptance, but is not substantiated.

[1] *Vita Aristoph.* p. 13, on which see Kaibel, *Hermes*, XXIV, 42 ff.

[2] Athen. III 86 E, 92 E, 104 F; IV 140 A; IX 381 A; VII 312 C; IX 400 C; XIV 638 E; III 109 C, 123 B, 127 C; XIII 567 C, etc.

[3] Kaibel, *op. cit.*

larity of the play reduces the chances of error; nor do we have, except perhaps in the case of the *Aetnaeae*, any evidence for the replacement of one play by another of the same name.

(ii) Another way of accounting for the notice in the *didascaliae*, while not accepting *Rhesus* as authentic, is to suppose that the poet is a different Euripides. It has occasionally been suggested that the author is the younger Euripides, son of the tragedian.[1] We know that the last three plays of Euripides (*Iphigenia in Aulis*, *Alcmaeon* and *Bacchae*) were produced after his death by this son of the same name.[2] And so it is possible that he himself wrote tragedies and produced them in his father's lifetime. If so, they would have appeared in the *didascaliae* under the name of Euripides, whence confusion might easily have arisen.

The attribution of *Rhesus* to the younger Euripides is said to be supported by some similarities of style in the anapaestic prologue of *Iphigenia in Aulis*; for the anapaests have often been thought spurious, and it may be that we are to discern in them the hand of the son preparing his father's unfinished work for production.[3] This is tenuous evidence: the resemblances are not very remarkable; it is by no means certain that the anapaests are not the work of the great Euripides; and we have no proof that the son was a poet in his own right. An even stronger argument against the theory is provided by Crates' testimony that *Rhesus* was produced by Euripides when he was still young. If this information comes from the *didascaliae*, as is likely, the date given there can hardly have been a possible one for the younger Euripides. If he was a dramatist at all, he would not have been active at

---

[1] Porter, *The Rhesus of Euripides* (2nd ed. 1929), p. lii, is the most recent exponent of this view. Cf. Nock, *CR*, XLIV (1930), 173. It was suggested previously by Valckenaer, *Diatribe*, p. 94 (who referred to Delrio, *Proleg. in Senecae tragoedias*, and Boeckh, *Graecae Tragoediae principes*, pp. 229 ff.

[2] Schol. Ar. *Ra.* 67. The youngest of Euripides' three sons bore his father's name: *Vita Eur.* p. 2, l. 14 Schw.; Suidas, s.v. Εὐριπίδης.

[3] Porter, *Rhesus*, p. liii; cf. p. xliv.

a date when his father could still be regarded as νέος. It is hardly necessary to add that Crates is certainly not speaking of the younger Euripides.

Suidas gives notice of two other dramatists named Euripides, besides the great one. These two entries precede the notice of the famous poet:

Εὐριπίδης 'Αθηναῖος τραγικός, πρεσβύτερος τοῦ ἐνδόξου γενομένου. ἐδίδαξε δράματα ιβ', εἷλε δὲ νίκας δύο.
Εὐριπίδης τραγικός, τοῦ προτέρου ἀδελφιδοῦς, ὡς Διονύσιος ἐν τοῖς χρονικοῖς. ἔγραψε δὲ 'Ομηρικὴν ἔκδοσιν, εἰ μὴ ἄρα ἑτέρου ἐστί. δράματα αὐτοῦ ταῦτα· 'Ορέστης, Μήδεια, Πολυξένη.

The latter of these, it should be noted, is not necessarily to be identified with the younger Euripides just mentioned, son of the great poet, who produced posthumously his father's last works. There is no record of either of these two, who may owe their existence to a confusion in the tradition. But if the notice is to be trusted at all, they were earlier than the famous dramatist or early contemporaries.[1] If we are to attribute *Rhesus* to some other Euripides, it is easier in view of Crates' testimony to assign it to an elder Euripides than to a younger. A namesake who produced twelve plays and won two victories would be an eligible candidate, if we wished to persevere with this highly improbable theory.

(iii) If the author of a play was not himself its producer, it might be the latter's name that was preserved instead in the official records. Here is a third reason why the ancient grammarians may have thought the didascalic notice an insufficient guarantee of the authenticity of *Rhesus*. Among modern scholars however this hypothesis has found little favour.[2]

That poets did not always produce their own plays is well known. Aristophanes is a familiar example: he had his three earliest comedies produced by Callistratus, and entrusted

---

[1] Unless the second notice was originally meant to follow that of the great poet.

[2] It was suggested by Bergk, *Griechische Literaturgeschichte*, IV (1887), 497 ff.

some later works to the same producer, as well as to Philonides and his own son Araros.[1] The same thing was done not only by other comic poets, but also certainly by tragedians. The posthumous production of some of Aeschylus' works by his son, and perhaps by others, is not parallel; but it would seem that Sophocles in his own lifetime had some of his plays produced by his son Iophon.[2] In the fourth century certain tragedies of Aphareus, with which he even won victories, were produced in the name of Dionysius.[3] The *Andromache* of Euripides has sometimes been cited as another example: it may have been produced by Democrates, but the evidence, as we have already seen, is far from conclusive.[4]

It is a disputed point whether the *Didascaliae* of Aristotle gave the name of the producer or that of the poet.[5] Didascalic inscriptions from the fourth century onwards record specifically the name of the poet, but it is possible that the records of productions in the official archives, on which Aristotle would have depended for the fifth century, gave the name of the producer. It may well be that Aristotle himself made it his concern to establish the true authorship of the works he recorded: some references to the *Didascaliae* imply that he set out to name the actual poet.[6] But even if this was his policy, there was room for error so long as he relied on incomplete records.

There may then have been room for doubting the authority of Aristotle's *Didascaliae* on these grounds, and it is conceivable that such was the nature of the doubt in the minds of the ancient critics who suspected that *Rhesus* was not the work of

---

[1] For details: Schm.–St. IV, 2, 185; Pickard-Cambridge, *DFA*, p. 85.

[2] Schol. Ar. *Ra.* 78; Suidas, s.v. 'Ἰοφῶν.

[3] Plut. *Vit. X Orat.* 839 c. But Aphareus was named in the records (*IG*, II², 2325; cf. Pickard-Cambridge, *DFA*, p. 86).

[4] Schol. Euripides, *Andr.* 445 (see above, p. 16).

[5] The evidence is discussed by Pickard-Cambridge, *op. cit.* pp. 85 ff. For other references cf. p. 15 n. 1 above.

[6] Harpocr. s.v. διδάσκαλος (Aristotle, fr. 624 Rose); Schol. Ar. *Plut.* 385. Cf. Arist. frr. 619, 628, 629.

Euripides. The wording of the Argument does not suggest that our play was thought to be other than the one recorded in the *didascaliae*. At least, if the challenging critics had such a notion, the defenders seem to have missed their point. For them it is τοῦτο τὸ δρᾶμα which is attributed by the *didascaliae* to Euripides. If both parties were arguing on common ground and the words are taken strictly, it is not contested that ours is the play named in the *didascaliae*, that is, that it is a fifth-century work of known date. The only point in dispute is the authorship. If this is so, the opponents of authenticity could perhaps have accounted for the didascalic record by supposing that Euripides was named as producer of another poet's work.

It is conceivable that they thought along these lines. The hypothesis is theoretically admissible, but is unlikely in the present case. Euripides was young when he produced *Rhesus*, and we should not expect to find an inexperienced young dramatist entrusted with the production of the work of another poet (let alone that of Sophocles, if this is in fact the implication of our note). It is easier to imagine, as in the case of Aristophanes, the young poet assigning his drama to a more experienced producer.

We have examined three different grounds for disputing the authority of the *didascaliae*. It is not certain which, if any, of these the ancient scholars had in mind. Indeed their suspicion may have been only vaguely formulated. We cannot insist too closely on the wording of the Argument.

We may now turn to the fourth and last point in the Argument's note on authorship.

(4) καὶ ἡ περὶ τὰ μετάρσια δὲ ἐν αὐτῷ πολυπραγμοσύνη τὸν Εὐριπίδην ὁμολογεῖ.

To the evidence of the *didascaliae* is added a further argument in defence of the play's authenticity: the keen interest in matters of astronomy points to the hand of Euripides (for so we must interpret the phrase ἡ περὶ τὰ μετάρσια πολυπραγμοσύνη).[1] It is a rather surprising remark, because there is only one passage in the play (vv. 528 ff.) to which it is applicable. Grégoire was probably right in supposing this note to be subsequent to the dispute, which the scholiast reports, concerning the accuracy of the astronomical allusions in this passage.[2] So far as it goes, the observation is fairly made. Euripides is fond of introducing references to the stars, and several passages similar in character to this one can be cited from his works.[3] It is nevertheless curious that anyone should have thought it worth while to single this point out for special mention.

The Prologues

After the remarks on authorship the Argument proceeds to the subject of prologues, as follows:

πρόλογοι δὲ διττοὶ φέρονται. ὁ γοῦν Δικαίαρχος ἐκτιθεὶς τὴν ὑπόθεσιν τοῦ ῾Ρήσου γράφει κατὰ λέξιν οὕτως·
  νῦν εὐσέληνον φέγγος ἡ διφρήλατος.
καὶ ἐν ἐνίοις δὲ τῶν ἀντιγράφων ἕτερός τις φέρεται πρόλογος, πεζὸς πάνυ καὶ οὐ πρέπων Εὐριπίδῃ· καὶ τάχα ἄν τινες τῶν ὑποκριτῶν διεσκευακότες εἶεν αὐτόν. ἔχει δὲ οὕτως·
  ὦ τοῦ μεγίστου Ζηνὸς ἄλκιμον τέκος....

Ten more lines of this prologue follow.

Here Δικαίαρχος is Nauck's restoration for δικαίαν (VLP: om. Harl.); it has won general acceptance and may be regarded as almost certain.[4] Otherwise the readings here are from the manuscripts (variants being unimportant).

There does not appear to be any connection between this and the preceding note, and we need not suppose that the

---

[1] Wrongly interpreted by Bates, 'Notes on the *Rhesus*', *TAPA*, xlvii (1916), 9, as meaning 'the attention to lofty expressions'.
[2] Grégoire, *op. cit.* pp. 97 f. Cf. Schol. *v.* 528.
[3] *El.* 464 ff.; *Ion* 1152 ff.; *Or.* 1001 ff.; frr. 357, 779, 780. Also *IA* 6 ff., if authentic (see below, pp. 102 f.).
[4] Earlier scholars (e.g. Morstadt, *op. cit.* p. 69; Hartung, *op. cit.* p. 11) based their discussion on the corrupt text.

existence of different prologues is regarded as relevant to the question of authenticity. We may nevertheless find here some evidence of value for our inquiry.

We are informed here of the existence of two different iambic prologues, neither of which is in our text of *Rhesus* (which begins with anapaestic dimeters spoken by the Chorus as they enter) or otherwise known to us. The note is clearly intended as a comment on the text which we have. It cites the authority of Dicaearchus of Messene (*c.* 347–287), the Peripatetic scholar and pupil of Aristotle, and the reference is evidently to his work, which we have already mentioned, Ὑποθέσεις τῶν Εὐριπίδου καὶ Σοφοκλέους μύθων.[1] We considered earlier the view of some scholars that all the matter of our Argument was derived from this work, and concluded that it cannot be assumed that Dicaearchus is the source except where he is actually quoted. Our first problem here is to decide the extent of the quotation from Dicaearchus: is his authority cited for only one prologue or for both?

It is usually assumed that only the one verse νῦν...διφρή-λατος is quoted on the authority of Dicaearchus and that all that follows has been added by the author of the Argument.[2] A few scholars however have taken the view, first put forward by Kirchhoff, that the quotation from Dicaearchus extends to the end of the Argument, that is, that the knowledge of both iambic prologues is due to him.[3] In favour of this latter interpretation is the fact that the quotation is introduced by the formula γράφει κατὰ λέξιν οὕτως. In the scholiasts' idiom the phrase γράφει οὕτως commonly introduces direct quotation of an author's words, and κατὰ λέξιν, with which it is here reinforced, regularly certifies that a quotation is

---

[1] See above, pp. 7 f.

[2] So, e.g., Hagenbach, *op. cit.* p. 14; Menzer, *De Rheso Tragoedia*, p. 59; Porter, *op. cit.* p. xxxviii; Pearson, *CR*, xxxv (1931), 59 f.; Grégoire, *op. cit.* p. 98; Sneller, *op. cit.* p. 34.

[3] Kirchhoff, *Philol.* vii (1852), 563. Supported by Walda, Geffcken; also by Schwartz, who supposes that there is a lacuna after κατὰ λέξιν οὕτως, and by Wehrli, *Dikaiarchos*, p. 68.

given verbatim.[1] It would seem superfluous, if one were merely quoting one verse of Euripides on the authority of Dicaearchus, to say 'Dicaearchus writes word for word as follows'. For who would imagine that an iambic line was being quoted otherwise than verbatim? On the other hand, if one were quoting Dicaearchus' own arguments, it would be natural to emphasize that his exact words are preserved.

Against this it may very well be argued that the remarks which are prefaced to the quoted passage of the second prologue are, in both context and expression, wholly typical of a later period of scholarship. The reference to a different text to be found in other copies, the potted aesthetic judgement and the assumption of interpolation by actors all have parallels elsewhere in our Euripidean scholia.[2] So little remains of Peripatetic literary criticism that we cannot be sure that Dicaearchus would not have written like this, but the passage certainly smacks of a later era. It is credible that a prologue not in our text of *Rhesus* could have survived at a date later than the period of Alexandrian scholarship: the scholia contain evidence that the publication of the Alexandrian edition of Euripides did not prevent the circulation of a variety of texts at a later date.[3] The citation of the second prologue could therefore be due to a commentator on the Alexandrian edition; and this could have been anyone from Aristophanes of Byzantium himself to Didymus, who is known to have played an important part in the compilation of our scholia. Wilamowitz believed that many of the scholia which refer to histrionic interpolation originated from the editor Aristophanes himself; his argument is plausible, and if

---

[1] γράφει οὕτως: e.g. Schol. *Rh.* 29, 311, 346; *Hec.* 3, 131, 934; *Andr.* 32; *Alc.* 1. γράφει κατὰ λέξιν οὕτως: Schol. *Med.* 264. Cf. LSJ, s.v. λέξις II, 1.

[2] References to variant versions: Schol. *Or.* 957, 1227, 1394; *Phoen.* 375, 1075, 1225; *Hipp.* 871, 1050; *Andr.* 1254; *Alc.* 820; cf. Schol. Sophocles, *El.* 102, 232; *OC* 390. References to actors: Schwartz, *Scholia in Eur.* p. 406. Various aesthetic criticisms (not always implying spuriousness): e.g. Schol. *Or.* 640, 957, 1366, 1512, 1521; *Tro.* 14.

[3] See previous note.

we accept it, we shall be inclined to attribute this note to Aristophanes.[1] There seems to be nothing against this, but certainty is impossible.

Perhaps then we ought not to press too far the implication of a single formula in a text that may have suffered considerably in transmission. On the whole it seems easier to believe, with the majority, that the author, whoever he be, of our note on prologues refers to Dicaearchus for only the first of them and himself attests the existence of the second. Nevertheless, in view of the uncertainty, we ought to consider the consequences of both interpretations.

In either case it is certain that the first prologue is cited on the authority of Dicaearchus, and it may therefore be presumed that this prologue anyway was no longer extant when the Argument was compiled. Of it we are given only one line, and this may be all that Dicaearchus preserved. It is a reasonable conjecture that, according to a common practice, he quoted the first line of the play at the head of his hypothesis for the purpose of identification. Our papyrus fragment of Euripidean hypotheses, though not necessarily the work of Dicaearchus, provides an illustration, if one is needed, of this convention (Σκύριοι ὧν ἀρχή· ᵔΩ Τυνδαρεία παῖ Λάκαινα ⟨–∪–⟩· ἡ δ' ὑπόθεσις...).[2] This would account for the fact that there is only one line, of which there is no further discussion.[3] If this is so, it is the first line either of the only prologue known to Dicaearchus or, if he knew another, of the one which he regarded as authoritative and which he held to be the generally known opening of the play. In the latter case he may or may not have mentioned the other version.

---

[1] *Einl.* pp. 152 f.; cf. Page, *Actors' Interpolations in Greek Tragedy* (1934), pp. 109–11.

[2] Above, p. 6 and n. 3. Cf. *P. Oxy.* 1235 (Menander hypotheses); Schol. Euripides, *Med.* 693; Schol. Ar. *Av.* 281, etc.

[3] And so it is not necessary to follow either Schwartz, who supposed a lacuna immediately before the quoted line, or Wilamowitz, who proposed καὶ ⟨τ. ἑ.⟩ immediately after it.

If we now assume that only the first prologue is cited on the authority of Dicaearchus, we may offer the following reconstruction of the evidence:

(*a*) Dicaearchus quoted in the introductory lemma of his hypothesis what he held to be the genuine opening line of the *Rhesus* of Euripides; if he knew another version, he may or may not have mentioned it.

(*b*) The Alexandrians, we must suppose, failed to acquire a copy with the first prologue. If they had it and knew that it was the version approved by Dicaearchus, why was it not included in the Alexandrian edition of the play, which is the ancestor of our text? And why did it apparently not survive at the time when our note on the prologues was written, by a commentator on the Alexandrian edition, who may have been Alexandrian or post-Alexandrian but is not likely to have been later than Didymus? Presumably the copies received at Alexandria were ones having either the second iambic prologue or, like our text, none at all; indeed copies in both these states may have been received. We must be a little surprised that a prologue still known in Dicaearchus' day did not reach Alexandria, but it is by no means impossible. So many works had to be procured for the library that the number of copies of an individual work may have been small. If there had already been tampering with the text of *Rhesus*, copies with the genuine prologue may have become rare and the Alexandrians may well have obtained only an inferior version. The librarians of Pergamum probably had no better fortune: at all events the first prologue does not appear to have been cited by any commentator later than Dicaearchus.

(*c*) The Alexandrian editor of Euripides, commonly thought to have been Aristophanes of Byzantium (*c.* 275–180), finding no trace of the first iambic prologue and deeming the second (if he knew it) spurious, published his text of *Rhesus* without any. It is true that elsewhere in the works of Euripides he did not expunge some obviously spurious lines, but we need not expect his policy to have been entirely consistent.[1]

(*d*) In the period after the Alexandrian edition, when a grammarian wrote the note in our Argument, there still circulated some copies having the second prologue, and this was regarded as the work of actors.

If, on the other hand, we take the view that both prologues are cited from Dicaearchus, the evidence may be reconstructed thus:

(*a*) Dicaearchus adopted for his lemma the opening line of the prologue which he regarded as genuine, but, knowing that another version was current, he mentioned it and gave, in the words preserved in our Argument, his reasons for thinking it spurious.

(*b*) At Alexandria the opening accepted by Dicaearchus was unknown. Copies having the second iambic prologue may or may not have been extant, although we should naturally presume that they were not, since it was later necessary to refer back to Dicaearchus for it.

(*c*) Aristophanes of Byzantium, knowing no prologue or only the one already condemned as spurious, published his text of *Rhesus* without any.

(*d*) At the date when our grammarian wrote, neither iambic prologue was still extant; for it was necessary to refer to Dicaearchus for both.

The apparent failure of the Alexandrians to acquire a copy of *Rhesus* with the prologue approved by Dicaearchus may reasonably be looked upon as evidence that there had already been interference with the prologue before the foundation of their library at the beginning of the third century. And so, although we cannot say that our information about both prologues comes from Dicaearchus, it does seem likely that both versions were already current in his day. Indeed, the attribution of the second prologue to actors suggests that it

[1] On Aristophanes' editorial practice: Wilamowitz, *Einl.* pp. 147 f.; Page, *op. cit.* p. 3.

was thought to belong to this period; for the literary activity of actors was then most prevalent and most notorious.[1] We may therefore suppose, upon either interpretation of the evidence, that by the end of the fourth century *Rhesus* was known in versions having either of two different iambic prologues. There may also have existed the version without any prologue; but if Dicaearchus knew this version, he does not appear to have accepted it.

A quite different possibility must now be considered. So far our argument has been based on the assumption that the *Rhesus* known to Dicaearchus was the play we possess. The form of the note in our Argument invites us to assume this; but can we exclude the possibility that Dicaearchus had a quite different *Rhesus* from ours?[2] At first glance this might seem to offer an easy solution of the problem of the different openings. There are however serious objections to this view, which are not far to seek.

If Dicaearchus knew a different *Rhesus*, there would theoretically be three possibilities about the genuineness of the two plays. We may however be excused from considering the hypothesis that neither work was genuine, or that Dicaearchus had a spurious work, ours being genuine. The only hypothesis that it is relevant for us to consider is that Dicaearchus possessed the authentic *Rhesus*, while we have a spurious work that has taken its place.

This hypothesis requires us to reject the obvious implication of the statement in our Argument; and there are the following further objections to it:

(*a*) If the genuine work of Euripides was known and preserved down to the time of Dicaearchus, a hundred years after the poet's death, it is hard to imagine how a spurious work could then have supplanted it and all trace of the genuine work have been lost within a short space of time.

---

[1] Although it may have continued into a later era: Wilamowitz, *Einl.* p. 131; Page, *op. cit.* pp. 15 ff.

[2] Suggested by Paley, *Euripides* (1872 ed.), I, p. 9.

Dicaearchus' death is placed in 287, and the foundation of the library of Alexandria is within a few years of this date. Under the first librarian, Zenodotus, the Alexandrians were assiduous in procuring from abroad texts of all available works of the classical authors, and the task of sorting and arranging the tragedies was undertaken at this date by Alexander Aetolus (*fl. c.* 285).[1] Within so short an interval since the genuine play was certainly known it is hard to see either how the Alexandrians could have failed to obtain a copy of it or how they could have mistaken a spurious play for it. We have, it is true, already admitted that a prologue known to Dicaearchus did not reach Alexandria, but this is not so improbable, since the prologue was only in some copies of the play.

(*b*) We do not know the exact scope of Dicaearchus' hypothesis of the Euripidean *Rhesus*, but it is difficult to believe that it gave so little indication of the content of the play that it was possible to take it as relating to another work. Such a mistake is the less likely in view of the fact that Dicaearchus is known to have quoted the opening line of his play, which is quite different from the opening of ours. This discrepancy would surely have aroused the suspicions of the Alexandrian librarians and have invited them to look closely before identifying our play with that of Dicaearchus.

(*c*) If we are to suppose that there were two different plays, the problem of the prologues becomes more complex. We cannot be sure whether Dicaearchus knew both the iambic prologues or only one, but on either hypothesis we should be faced with a curious set of circumstances. For in the former case we should be obliged to suppose that there was a genuine *Rhesus* with two different prologues, one of them presumably spurious, and a spurious *Rhesus* without any prologue. This is much too remarkable a coincidence. On the other hand, if Dicaearchus is the authority for only the first prologue, then there was a genuine play with a prologue, which did not

[1] See above, p. 10 n. 1.

reach Alexandria, and a spurious play which survived in several copies, some having a prologue of inferior quality and others none at all. This obliges us to suppose that while the Alexandrians failed to get a copy of the genuine *Rhesus*, they acquired several copies of the spurious one, and these in two distinct versions;[1] and from this we should further have to conclude that the play was a quite well-known one, which had been produced more than once (though hardly as the work of Euripides, if the genuine *Rhesus* was still known in Dicaearchus' day). It would therefore be the more extraordinary that its real author was not known and that it should be possible to attribute it mistakenly to Euripides.

It is clear that the consequences of supposing that Dicaearchus possessed a different *Rhesus* from ours are not such as to attract us to that hypothesis. We may feel confident that the play known to Dicaearchus was our own, and so that our *Rhesus* was extant at the end of the fourth century, being then known as the work of Euripides. It is further probable that two different iambic prologues were then current in different copies of the play. These conclusions were anticipated earlier in the discussion of the Argument's remarks on the authorship of the play. The assumptions made there have now been justified. The information about the prologues is thus seen to throw important light on the history of the play between its composition and the era of Alexandrian scholarship.

The identification of the *Rhesus* known to Dicaearchus with our play is generally accepted. But the existence of a diversity of openings has often been accounted for otherwise than we have interpreted it. Some scholars, including both opponents and defenders of the play's authenticity, have held that we have the text in the form in which it was originally written and that the two iambic prologues were separate attempts of later writers to supply a supposed deficiency.[2] This question

---

[1] Unless we take the much less likely view that the second prologue was unknown at Alexandria and came to light later.

[2] Vater, *Vindiciae*, p. 60; Wilamowitz, *Einl.* p. 130; Grégoire, *op. cit.* pp. 98 f.; Pohlenz, *op. cit.* p. 474; Geffcken, *Hermes*, LXXI (1936), 394 n. 1; etc.

will be discussed more fully when we come to discuss matters of dramatic technique: it will then be argued on internal grounds that the play in its present state is incomplete, and that an iambic prologue was originally prefixed to the text we now have.

But assuming that there was originally an iambic prologue, are we justified in supposing that of the two cited in the Argument the first was the original and the second the spurious version? Can we accept the ancient grammarian's verdict on the latter? Although most scholars have agreed in condemning it as an inferior piece of work, a few have come to its defence; and it must be allowed that its spuriousness is not immediately demonstrated by the eleven lines quoted. To this question too we shall return later;[1] for the present argument it makes little difference which, if either, prologue is regarded as original. For if the second prologue were the genuine one, this would strengthen the evidence for the antiquity of our play. It would then be quite certain that both prologues existed before Dicaearchus' day, and we should have to suppose that the interpolation had taken place long enough before Dicaearchus for him to be deceived about the authentic version of the opening. The same would be true if the present opening were original and both prologues later interpolations.

The fact that *Rhesus* possessed more than one prologue is of course not evidence either that it is spurious or that it was once regarded as spurious. Indeed *Rhesus* was perhaps not unique among the plays of Euripides in having more than one form of opening; there may have been other plays whose prologues suffered interpolation. Among the extant plays *Iphigenia in Aulis* has been cited as an example, but it probably ought to be excluded: the unusual form of its present prologue does not necessarily mean, as has often been held, that it is a conflation of two originally separate versions.[2] The other possible cases of interpolation of prologues concern lost plays,

_____

[1] See below, pp. 111 f.   [2] See below, pp. 102 f.

38

and conclusive evidence is wanting.[1] In *Melanippe Sophe* only the opening line was changed; Euripides himself is said to have been responsible, but it may have been the work of a later interpolator. In *Meleager* and *Archelaus* there may have been greater changes. For both plays the lines quoted by Aristophanes in the *Frogs*, which we should naturally assume in the context to be the openings of the plays, differed from the openings later known to the scholiasts. In the case of *Meleager* we are told that the line and a half of Aristophanes' quotation were to be found in the prologue, but not at the beginning: either Aristophanes was not quoting the opening or the prologue had later been altered with the addition of other lines at the beginning. *Archelaus*, however, seems a more certain case of interpolation: the two-and-a-half lines quoted in the *Frogs* are different from the opening later current, of which we have the first eight lines, and in this case Aristarchus was unable to locate Aristophanes' quotation in this or any other play. It is true that the two passages could stand in the same prologue, but we must credit Aristarchus with enough diligence to have read the whole prologue of *Archelaus*.

These other instances of interpolation in prologues remain doubtful, but a parallel is hardly needed. We have abundant evidence that the texts of the great tragedians were generally treated with scant respect by fourth-century interpolators. The prologue was not the least vulnerable part. The interference with the prologue of *Rhesus* is certainly not evidence that it was regarded as spurious. On the other hand, it does indicate that the play was reproduced on the stage in the fourth century. For who else but actors can be held responsible for these changes? If *Rhesus* is really a work of the time of Demosthenes, as Wilamowitz and others have believed, it must have acquired its different versions of prologue very quickly. This is not impossible, but it must be allowed that the evidence of the prologues is strongly against a date any later than the middle of the fourth century.

[1] Details in Page, *op. cit.* pp. 92 ff., and Nauck, *TGF*.

It seems possible to go further. We may be reasonably certain from the fact of its inclusion in his work that Dicaearchus accepted our *Rhesus* as authentic, or at least that it was already firmly established as Euripidean in his day. This means that it cannot then have been by any means a new play, an inference which is confirmed if it already had two different prologues. It follows that our play must have been in existence in the time of Aristotle, a generation earlier.

This leads us back to the previous statement in the Argument, that *Rhesus* was entered in the *didascaliae* ὡς γνήσιον, the reference being, as we saw, to the work of Aristotle. We decided that these words do not in themselves imply that Aristotle himself knew a *Rhesus* of Euripides and vouched for its authenticity; they could mean simply that in the *didascaliae Rhesus* was attached to the name of Euripides, and Aristotle could have been reproducing the record of a play with which he was not personally acquainted. But now that we know that our *Rhesus* existed in his day, we may be the more willing to accept these words as evidence of his personal testimony. We should certainly expect him to have inquired in the course of his researches whether or not the known *Rhesus* was to be identified with the *Rhesus* of Euripides recorded in the public archives. It is moreover hard to believe that Aristotle did not accept our *Rhesus* as the work of Euripides, when his pupil Dicaearchus did so.

Thus, although we cannot affirm it with certainty, it is at least probable that Aristotle too regarded our *Rhesus* as Euripidean, and that, if this was a mistaken view, the error occurred in or before his day. If this is so, then the composition of *Rhesus* must be placed well before his time. The hypothesis that *Rhesus* is a spurious work of the fourth century will indeed still be tenable, but the possible date of its composition will be confined within even narrower limits.

The second Argument: Aristophanes of Byzantium

The second of the two Arguments to *Rhesus*, comprising a very concise account of the theme and brief appended notes, has in V the heading Ἀριστοφάνους ὑπόθεσις. It is thus attributed to Aristophanes of Byzantium (*c.* 275–180), the scholar who is generally believed to have produced at Alexandria a collected edition of the works of Euripides, which is the ancestor of our text.[1] The attribution is confirmed by a comparison of other tragic hypotheses which bear his name in the manuscripts. These show common features of content, arrangement and style, which are shared by our *Rhesus* hypothesis; the same features also enable us to trace his hand in other hypotheses which no longer bear his name.[2] It may be, as Wilamowitz held, that Aristophanes' hypotheses to the plays of Euripides were separate from his commentaries and were originally prefaced to the plays in the edition itself; for in this position they survive even before plays that are transmitted without any scholia.[3]

The content of Aristophanes' hypothesis to *Rhesus* leaves no doubt that it was written for our play. We therefore have in it proof, if any be needed, that he included our *Rhesus* in his collected edition of the works of Euripides. This does not in itself necessarily mean that he thought it was genuine; for the edition appears to have included the three tragedies reported to be spurious, *Tennes, Rhadamanthys*, and *Pirithous*. This is implied in the statement of the *Life* of Euripides:

τὰ πάντα δ᾽ ἦν αὐτοῦ δράματα ϙβ', σῴζεται δὲ οη'· τούτων νοθεύεται τρία, Τέννης Ῥαδάμανθυς Πειρίθους.

---

[1] Cohn, *RE*, II, 994 ff.; Wilamowitz, *Einl.* pp. 145 ff.

[2] Aristophanes' hypotheses are preserved under his name for Aeschylus, *Eu.*; Sophocles, *Ant.*; Euripides, *Med., Ph., Or., Ba.* (Verse arguments bearing his name for Sophocles, *OT*; Aristophanes, *Peace, Birds*; Menander, *Dysc.* are probably wrongly ascribed.) There are, besides, traces of the hand of Aristophanes, without his name, in the hypotheses of Aeschylus, *Pers., Sept., PV, Agam.*; Sophocles, *El., Ph., OC*; Euripides, *Alc., Hipp., Andr., Su., IT.* Discussion: F. G. Schneidewin, *De hypoth. trag. gr. Arist. Byz. vindicandis* (1856); Wilamowitz, *Einl.* p. 146; Sneller, *De Rheso Tragoedia*, pp. 93 f.; Zuntz, *op. cit.* pp. 131, 139 ff.

[3] Wilamowitz, *Einl.* p. 145 n. 37.

41

The figures presumably relate to the only collected edition of Euripides' works, which was that of Aristophanes; and, in fact, the corresponding statement in the *Life* of Sophocles actually gives its figures on his authority.[1] The νενοθευμένα were clearly among those preserved, as we should also infer from the presence of *Rhadamanthys* in the papyrus copy of Euripidean hypotheses, which is shown by its alphabetical arrangement to be based upon the collected edition.[2]

It thus appears certain that Aristophanes included in his edition works suspected as spurious, but we may be reasonably confident that *Rhesus* was not for him of that class. Indeed, it seems likely that his view is represented in the statement already quoted from the *Life*; in which case the only plays of Euripides regarded as spurious by him were the three tragedies there named and one satyr-play, as we learn from another version of the same figures.[3] If Aristophanes had any suspicions about *Rhesus*, his hypothesis, in its extant form, does not reveal them.

Our Aristophanic hypothesis is undoubtedly an abridgement of the original. Most regrettable is the omission of the didascalic notice, which was an ingredient of Aristophanes' hypotheses in their fullest form. Its absence here is not especially significant, being no doubt due to the laziness or carelessness of a scribe. Many of the Aristophanic hypotheses have suffered curtailment. We know of course that the didascalic notice for *Rhesus* was preserved and would have been available to Aristophanes.

The only point of historical interest in the Argument of Aristophanes is his statement that the Chorus speak the opening words (προλογίζουσι). This confirms that the text he published had the same opening that we possess. If he knew any other form of opening, he makes no mention of it; not that any significance attaches to his silence, since he is

---

[1] *Vita Soph.* 18 ἔχει δὲ δράματα, ὥς φησιν 'Αριστοφάνης, ρλ', τούτων δὲ νενόθευται ιζ' (ζ' Bergk). Cf. Pearson, *Fragments*, i, p. xiii.

[2] See above, pp. 6 f.

[3] *Vita Eur. Minor*, p. 4, l. 10 Schw.

merely following his usual practice of naming the opening speaker and his purpose in doing so may be to help identify the play in his own text. As we have seen, Aristophanes may well have been acquainted with the second of the two iambic prologues. If so, his omission of it from his text is perhaps a little surprising, because elsewhere in the text of Euripides he has allowed obviously spurious matter to stand. We cannot however be sure that his policy was consistent. He may well have regarded this as an exceptional case; for he had Dicaearchus' evidence that another prologue had previously been known, and the prologue that he knew was not in all copies. If his choice lay between a copy with no prologue and one with an apparently spurious prologue, he might well choose the former. There is too the possibility that our note on prologues derives from Aristophanes. As we saw, we cannot be sure about this, but if it were so, he would appear to have adopted the reasonable procedure of omitting the prologue from his text but referring to it in his hypothesis (or in his commentary). At all events Aristophanes' adoption of a text without a prologue cannot be interpreted as meaning that he held this to be the original form of the play.

The Lycurgan text

There is one tradition about the history of our tragic texts that has so far been left out of account. We are told that the Athenian statesman Lycurgus, as a measure against the corruption by actors of the texts of the three great tragedians, enacted that an official text should be made of their works, which was to be adopted for subsequent productions.[1] Another source informs us that Ptolemy Philadelphus, on a surety of fifteen talents, borrowed this copy from the Athenians, had a copy made, then sent back the copy, and forfeiting his deposit retained the original for the library of Alexandria.[2]

If we were to suppose that the Alexandrians acquired the

[1] Plut. *Vit. X Orat.* 841 F.
[2] Galen, xvii, 607 Kühn; cf. Ziegler, *RE*, s.v. Tragoedia, 2068.

text of *Rhesus* in this way, we might have to revise our interpretation of the evidence concerning its prologues. The date of Lycurgus' measure must have been about 330, certainly earlier than the date at which Dicaearchus wrote. If the official copy preserved a text of *Rhesus* approved as the genuine work of Euripides, did this include an iambic prologue or not? If it did, then we should be at a loss to account for the absence of this prologue from the Alexandrian edition. If it did not, then either we should have to suppose that Dicaearchus ignored the official copy or we should have to abandon the idea that he accepted the first iambic prologue as Euripidean. On the other hand, if a text of *Rhesus* was not included in the state-copy of Euripides' works, was its omission accidental or did it mean that *Rhesus* was not yet accepted as Euripidean? It is difficult to believe the latter, if at about the same date the work was accepted by Aristotle.

There is however much room for doubt about the Lycurgan copy. We may accept that there was such an official text, but we do not know if it embraced all known plays of the three poets (this would have been a huge undertaking). Certainly the Alexandrians, even if they had the Lycurgan text, lacked several works of each of the tragedians, although these of course may have been already lost at Athens in the fourth century. About the tradition that the state-copy was acquired by the Alexandrians we may well be a little sceptical. We have only Galen's authority for this, and his story of Ptolemy's ruse has a decidedly romantic flavour.

If we do accept in full the tradition concerning the Lycurgan text and assume that it contained *Rhesus*, we shall have to believe that no iambic prologue was received into this official Athenian copy, and this may make us less inclined to admit as genuine either of the two reported in the Argument. Apart from this our interpretation of the evidence will not be affected; for, as we saw earlier, even if neither prologue were original, the inferences to be drawn from the existence of different versions would be the same.

44

The 'Nyctegresia' of Accius

Aristophanes' hypothesis closes with the words περιέχει δὲ τὴν Νυκτεγερσίαν. The scholiasts on *Iliad* K inform us that the title Νυκτεγερσία was sometimes given to that book; it was thus an alternative name for the episode commonly known as Δολωνεία.[1] Aristophanes means simply that the plot of *Rhesus* embraces this epic theme.

The Roman dramatist Accius (170–c. 85 B.C.) wrote a tragedy called *Nyctegresia*, of which we have about ten fragments, none of them exceeding one line.[2] Some earlier scholars thought that our *Rhesus* was the source of Accius' play.[3] Even if this could be established, it would not add significantly to the history of our play; for we know already that it was extant and regarded as Euripidean at the time when Accius was writing. Let us nevertheless look briefly at the evidence.

The surviving fragments of Accius' *Nyctegresia* leave no doubt that, like *Rhesus*, it was based on the Homeric *Doloneia*; but from only ten lines it is quite impossible to prove that Accius modelled his drama on *Rhesus*. In fact, we cannot identify any fragment of *Nyctegresia* with any passage of *Rhesus*. The nearest resemblance is between *Rh.* 535 f. ἀὼς δὴ πέλας, ἀὼς γίγνεται and the line

> iamque auroram rutilare procul
> cerno.

But this fragment (*inc. fab.* xx) is not attributed to *Nyctegresia* and could hardly be assigned to it on the grounds of this likeness (and that of *Il.* K 251), even if it were more striking than it is. The fragments that are certainly attributed to *Nyctegresia* are quoted without indication of context or

[1] Schol. A *Il.* K, *praef.*; *Anecd. Bekk.* 768.
[2] *TRF* (Ribbeck), pp. 230 ff.; *Remains of Old Latin* (Warmington, Loeb Lib.), II, pp. 488 ff.
[3] Vater, *op. cit.* pp. xiii ff.; Hartung, *op. cit.* pp. 11 ff.; Christ, *Gesch. Gr. Lit.* (5th ed.), I, 357. They are opposed by Rolfe, *Harv. Stud. Cl. Phil.* IV (1893), 71; Sneller, *op. cit.* pp. 39 f.

speaker; some (e.g. frr. v, viii), without showing any particular verbal resemblance, could be assigned to situations that occur in *Rhesus*, but others (including frr. iii, vi, vii) cannot easily be interpreted except as belonging to a scene in the Greek camp corresponding to the opening scene of the *Doloneia*. Indeed fr. vi has a close verbal reminiscence of *Il.* K 243, a line not represented at all in *Rhesus*. Therefore, if Accius made use of *Rhesus*, he must have added to it, either by direct adaptation of the *Doloneia* or by *contaminatio* with another Greek play based on this source, of which we know nothing.

A different view was taken by Hartung, who, regarding our *Rhesus* as Euripidean, thought that Accius used it, but possessed it with a prologue that is now lost.[1] The fragments incompatible with our text were derived from this prologue, which therefore consisted of a scene in the Greek camp, in which the Greek chiefs met and decided to send Diomedes and Odysseus to spy among the Trojans. This would require a very remarkable change of scene, of which the audience could in no way be forewarned, between the prologue and the entry of the Chorus, with which the play now begins. The only comparable change of scene in extant tragedy is in Aeschylus' *Eumenides*, where the action is transferred (at *v.* 235) from Delphi to Athens, but for this the audience is well prepared. The action of his *Aetnaeae*, which was written for production in Sicily, was set in four different Sicilian cities, and there were four changes of scene; but we do not know how these were contrived.[2] Nothing of the kind is known for Euripides. An opening scene set in the Greek camp would seriously disturb the unity of *Rhesus*, and we should need very much stronger evidence before believing that Euripides began the play in this way, or that Accius had a prologue which the Alexandrians lacked.

Vater, who also held our *Rhesus* to be genuine, supposed that Accius took it as his model but himself added the

----

[1] Hartung, *op. cit.* pp. 13 ff.   [2] Fr. 26 Mette (*P. Oxy.* 2257, fr. 1).

prologue.[1] But a more likely interpretation of the fragments was offered by Ribbeck, according to which Accius did not follow our play, but treated the story entirely from the Greek point of view, confining the action to the Greek camp.[2] This is easier to accept from a dramatic viewpoint, however difficult it is to imagine any tragic interest in the story apart from the death of Rhesus.

Accius clearly did not derive all the matter of *Nyctegresia* from *Rhesus*, and it is not safe to say that he used it at all. His plot seems to have kept closely to the Homeric form of the narrative, and may have been directly based on it. If however he had a Greek tragedy as model, according to the normal Roman practice, it was probably not ours but some other one since lost. Welcker's idea that Accius was translating the lost *Rhesus* of Euripides cannot be entertained, because survival at this date of a *Rhesus* of Euripides other than ours is incompatible with the evidence of the Arguments and scholia.[3] Moreover, we do not know that Rhesus figured in Accius' play any more than in the *Doloneia*.

Rhesus then may not have been the only Greek tragedy based on the Homeric *Doloneia*: this is for us the only possible significance of Accius' fragments. But if such another tragedy did exist, we have no other knowledge of it.[4] It is always possible that Accius based his plot directly on Homer. We do not know whether the Roman tragic poets ever worked in this way, but may note that Accius wrote another play based on an episode of the *Iliad*, the *Epinausimache*, for which no Greek original is known.

The scholia

The publication of the Alexandrian edition of Euripides' works was followed by a period of active study of the texts, during which many scholars in both Alexandria and

---

[1] Vater, *op. cit.*   [2] *Die römische Tragödie*, pp. 364 ff.

[3] Welcker, 'Der Rhesos', *Zeitschr. für Altertumswiss.* LXXVI (1834), 629 ff.

[4] We know of no other play, tragedy or comedy, based on the episode except the *Dolon* of Eubulus.

Pergamum produced commentaries. Vestiges of their scholarship are preserved in the surviving scholia. *Rhesus* is one of the nine plays of Euripides for which scholia are extant, and it is to these that we must turn as a possible source of further external evidence about its authenticity, and especially for the views of the grammarians on this question.

The majority of the scholia contain nothing of relevance for us: they are paraphrases or glosses, concerned purely with the elucidation of the text. Besides these however there are notes which contain scholarly discussion of various points, including matters of mythological or antiquarian interest, passages of which the interpretation is disputed and peculiarities of usage. These notes sometimes cite the views of particular scholars, and censure of the poet for ignorance or carelessness may be either expressed or implied.

In several places the commentators have drawn attention to deviations from the traditional version of the myth, and in particular to differences of detail from the Homeric *Doloneia*; most of these are noted with disapproval. To this class belong the scholia on the following lines:

5. The night is divided into five watches, instead of three as in Homer.

165. It is ridiculous to suggest that Dolon might ask for Hector's princely power.

210. Dolon's four-footed walk is incredible.

239. The horses of Achilles are made feminine, although masculine in Homer.

393. The father of Rhesus is Strymon, and not Eioneus as in Homer. (This difference is noted without censure.)

502. The reference to the theft of the Palladium is an anachronism.

508. Dionysodorus in his *Errors in the Tragedians* points out that the Thymbraean altar, which is five stades from the city, is wrongly said here to be near the gates.

Another anachronism, besides that of 502, is criticized at 251. Other things to which exception is taken include the use of certain words (260, 427, 430, 716), an abnormal form (41), an unusual quantity (494), a careless self-contradiction (356), and an alleged error in astronomy (528).

Several of these critical notes are referred to a symbol χ, by which their author appears to have marked in his text passages on which he intended to comment. Specific reference to this *nota* is made at *vv.* 41, 239, 716. In addition, it may be inferred from the form of the scholia on *vv.* 5 and 427 that they too were originally attached to a χ. The scholia on 342, 356 and 502 may also have been written to explain such a symbol against the text, but there is nothing in their form to confirm this.

On the basis of this evidence Wilamowitz concluded that all the adverse criticism in the scholia to *Rhesus* was derived from a single commentary, which formed part of an '*editio* κεχιασμένη' of the play, and he further argued that this commentary was written with the main object of proving that *Rhesus* was not the work of Euripides.[1]

There is no substantiation for this view; for nowhere in the scholia is the authenticity of *Rhesus* called into question either openly or implicitly. Wilamowitz's case is founded principally on his own interpretation of schol. 41, for which the manuscript reading is τὸ χ ὅτι συνθέτως ἀναγιγνώσκεται καὶ ὅτι οὐκ ἔστιν Εὐριπίδου ὁ στίχος. The scholiast's text of the line was evidently πυραίθει στρατὸς 'Αργόλας and his particular objection is to the compound πυραίθει, the reading of all our manuscripts except O, which has πῦρ' αἴθει. For this Hartung's πύρ' αἴθει has been generally accepted. The difficulty lies in the additional comment that the line is not Euripidean. This is not a verse that can easily be deleted by itself: it is in strophic response and is syntactically in-

---

[1] *De Rhesi Scholiis*, Greifswald, 1877 (= *Kl. Schr.* I, 1–16); the view is re-iterated in *Einl.* p. 155. His arguments are opposed by Porter, *Hermathena*, XVII (1913), 366–8.

separable from what follows. Did the commentator wish to reject only one line or the whole passage? Wilamowitz's solution was to delete the words ὁ στίχος as the ignorant addition of a Byzantine scribe and to suppose that the original note was simply καὶ ὅτι οὐκ ἔστιν Εὐριπίδου, with which was to be understood ἡ τραγῳδία. In this emended form the scholium was then taken as evidence that the purpose of the symbol χ was to draw attention to places in the text of the play where signs of its spuriousness were detected.

So doubtful an emendation provides a poor foundation for Wilamowitz's case, and indeed his treatment of the scholium is quite unjustified. If anything in the note is an addition, it is more likely that all the second part (καὶ ὅτι...ὁ στίχος) has been supplied by a later scribe, who misunderstanding the purport of the symbol χ took it as implying that the verse was spurious. Another quite plausible suggestion is that this scholium as a whole was originally written for v. 824, where the manuscripts again have the form πυραί-θειν.[1] Here after πυραίθειν are added the words 'Αργείων στρατόν (στρατόν del. L, om. P), which are metrically superfluous and were rightly deleted by Kirchhoff as a later addition. It is quite possible that a grammarian observed that these words were not Euripidean and appended a note to this effect. If so, this could later have been transferred by error to v. 41 along with the note on πυραίθειν, which is relevant in both places.

In the absence of any other hint of suspicion in the scholia, it is impossible to accept Wilamowitz's theory, based on an emended version of a single scholium, of a commentary intended to prove *Rhesus* spurious. Nor can we accept his identification of the critics of the scholia with the critics of the Argument.[2] All we are told about the opinions of the latter is that they found in the play a Sophoclean quality.

---

[1] Schrader, *De notatione critica a vet. gramm. in poet. scaen. adhibita* (Bonn, 1864), p. 29.　　　　[2] *De Rhesi scholiis*, p. 12.

There is not a trace of this view in the scholia; for Sophocles is mentioned only in schol. 105, and there in order to contrast the sentiment with that of a Sophoclean line. The two lines do have some resemblance to each other in diction, but this is not stressed in the note.

In actual fact, if the scholia to *Rhesus* are compared with those to other plays of Euripides, it will be found that they are in no way obviously different in character, and certainly not in respect of this cavilling tendency. It is a remarkable feature of the Euripidean scholia, one not shared by those for other poets, that they are pervaded throughout by a current of hostile criticism.[1] This is for other plays of precisely the same kind as it is in *Rhesus*.

For example, divergences from tradition in mythology, with which the poet of *Rhesus* is reproached, at *vv.* 5, 210, 239 and elsewhere, are often criticized in the scholia to other plays.[2] Particularly notable is the tendency to point out minor differences of detail from Homer. In schol. *Hec.* 3 Euripides' fondness for innovation in genealogy is observed: examples of this were noted by the scholiasts at *Rh.* 342 and 393; with which may also be compared schol. *Andr.* 28, schol. *Or.* 176.

Schol. *Hec.* 3 also complains that Euripides sometimes contradicts himself. Our poet was criticized on this score at *v.* 356. Of a like kind is schol. *Tro.* 1107, where Euripides is censured for saying something inconsistent with an earlier passage in the same play.

Anachronism, censured at *Rh.* 251 and 502, is another tendency for which Euripides was notorious: the scholiasts comment upon it at *Hipp.* 231, 953, *Med.* 233, *Andr.* 734 and *Hec.* 254.

---

[1] Gudeman, *RE*, s.v. Scholia, 665; Haigh, *Tragic Drama of the Greeks*, p. 319; Schwartz, *Scholia in Euripidem*, pp. 404 f.

[2] E.g., Schol. *Hec.* 241, 421, 1279; *Or.* 176, 257, 1004; *Andr.* 107, 224, 616; *Tro.* 448. With the phrasing of Schol. *Rh.* 210 (ἀπίθανον) cf. Schol. *Hec.* 241, *Or.* 176. On the use of χ to mark a divergence from Homer see Schrader, *op. cit.* pp. 17 ff.

The loose or inaccurate use of words, to which exception is taken at *Rh.* 260, 427, 430 and 716, is also criticized in Euripides, for example at *Hec.* 99, *Or.* 562 and *Med.* 665.

Thus it appears that the faults against which objections are raised in the *Rhesus* scholia are generally faults of a kind for which Euripides himself was notorious among the ancient grammarians. And this tendency of the scholiasts to disparage the work of Euripides is one which is not matched in the scholia to other poets.[1] It looks then very much as if the scholiasts were treating *Rhesus* simply as another work of Euripides.

Also characteristic of the Euripidean scholia in general is the occasional defence of the poet against criticisms of this kind. In the scholia to *Rhesus* this was taken by Wilamowitz as evidence of the work of a vindicator defending the play's authenticity against the challenge of the earlier commentator.[2]

Nor is there anything especially remarkable about the use of the symbol χ in the *Rhesus* scholia. This sign was in common use among the ancient grammarians for drawing attention to passages in the text requiring comment. Examples of its use remain in the scholia to the tragedians and Aristophanes, as well as in those to Homer and Pindar.[3] References to such a *nota* are scattered throughout the scholia to Euripides. The points thus designated for comment are of various kinds; adverse criticism is often, but not always, involved.

There is therefore no reason for supposing that the scholia to *Rhesus* are of a special character. If the critical tendency seems to be more strongly marked in them than in the scholia to other plays of Euripides, it is rather because the scholia to *Rhesus* are otherwise less extensive than because the points of censure are more numerous.[4]

No trace is to be found in the scholia of a doubt about the

---

[1] The scholia to Sophocles, however, do contain a few examples of the use of χ noting a point to be censured: Schrader, *op. cit.* pp. 27 f.

[2] Wilamowitz, *Einl.*; Schwartz, *op. cit.* p. 405.

[3] Examples in Schrader, *op. cit.* It is found also in the text of Alcman, *Partheneion.* [4] Cf. Schwartz's lists, *op. cit.* pp. 404 f.

authenticity of *Rhesus*. On the other hand, there are a few pieces of positive evidence that it was regarded, by some at least, as the work of Euripides. There are several places in the scholia where the author is explicitly and unequivocally referred to as Euripides. These are schol. 5, 251, 508 and 528. In addition, this is implicit in schol. 430, where *Orestes* is quoted as a work of the same poet. Besides these, schol. 41, if accepted at its face value, also implies that the play as a whole is Euripidean.

It is fortunate that in some of these notes scholars are mentioned by name. At 5 and 528 views of Crates are quoted, and in both places he names Euripides as author. In the latter scholium, as we saw earlier, Crates accounts for a supposed error in astronomy on the grounds that Euripides was young when he produced *Rhesus*. This statement leaves no room for doubt that he held the play to be genuine. The same note goes on to point out that it is Crates who is at fault in his interpretation of the passage and to quote, in the scholar's own words, an alternative explanation by Parmeniscus, who also refers without qualification to Euripides as poet. This cannot be dismissed as merely a loose and conventional use of the name of the author to whom the work was commonly attributed. The point at issue involves a criticism brought against the author, and one does not either attack or defend by name someone whom one does not hold responsible.

It is significant that Crates and Parmeniscus are found to be in agreement about the authorship of *Rhesus*. They were contemporary grammarians of the second century B.C., important members of the rival schools of Pergamum and Alexandria respectively.[1] It is known that in many matters they were opposed to each other: Parmeniscus, in fact, was the author of a work Πρὸς Κράτητα.[2] If the question of the

---

[1] *RE*, xi, 1634 ff.; xviii, 1570–2. Breithaupt, *De Parmenisco Grammatico* (Στοιχεῖα iv, Berlin, 1915).

[2] Schol. A *Il.* Θ 513. Breithaupt, *op. cit.* pp. 2 ff.

authenticity of *Rhesus* had been a point of controversy between the two schools, some sign of it would have been likely to appear here. It may be added that the authority of Crates was considerable at Pergamum, so that his views would probably have been influential with his successors there. We may thus be less inclined to suppose that the authenticity of *Rhesus* was suspected at Pergamum.

Among the Alexandrians we have, besides Parmeniscus, Dionysodorus, whose work *Errors in the Tragedians* is quoted verbatim in schol. 508. Here he refers to the poet as Euripides, and again the fact that he is passing censure makes it improbable that the attribution is merely conventional. From the fact that Parmeniscus and Dionysodorus both believed *Rhesus* to be Euripidean it is not unnatural to infer that this was also the view of Aristarchus, whose pupils they both were. Aristarchus himself is named once in the scholia to *Rhesus*, at *v.* 540, where his interpretation of the passage is recorded but no indication is given of his opinion about its authenticity. If, however, his opinion can be assumed to coincide with that of his pupils, it would mean that at Alexandria too the most important scholars in the field of tragedy in the period after Aristophanes accepted *Rhesus* as authentic. The only other important Alexandrian commentator on tragedy at this period was Callistratus.[1] His name does not appear in the scholia to *Rhesus*, and its absence might perhaps be taken as indicating that he did not hold any revolutionary views about the play. The learned scholia are excerpted from the commentaries of the Alexandrian and Pergamene scholars. When most scholars at this period seem to have regarded *Rhesus* as genuine, some trace of a dissentient opinion on so important a question is likely to have been preserved, if it had been held by a contemporary scholar of standing.

The silence of the scholia to *Rhesus* on the question of its

[1] Named in Schol. *Or.* 314, 434, 1038. Cf. Barthold, *De scholiorum in E. veterum fontibus*, p. 9.

authenticity allows us to infer further that such later scholars as had part in their compilation agreed with the attribution to Euripides. For they would scarcely have concealed their opinions, if they had disagreed with their Alexandrian predecessors on so vital a point. Most important of these later scholars is Didymus (first century B.C.), to whose labour we probably owe in great measure the preservation of learned matter from the commentaries of the Alexandrian and Pergamene scholars.[1] Those of our scholia which cite the views of earlier scholars, with or without further comment, may well go back to his hand. Whatever our opinion of Didymus' ability as an original scholar, and it has perhaps too often been underrated, he was capable of expressing an opinion on his own account. If he had shared the suspicion that *Rhesus* was spurious, we should certainly have expected to find a trace of this view in the scholia.

The selection

The scholia do not necessarily reflect the views of scholars later than Didymus. If there were any who then doubted the authenticity of *Rhesus*, theirs would not be a judgement of any great significance, because their knowledge could hardly have been greater than that of the Alexandrians. But it does not seem that the play can have been widely suspected in this later period. For we owe its preservation to the fact that it was included in a select edition of ten plays of Euripides, which was made perhaps in the second century A.D.[2] However this selection came to be made, and whatever the grounds on which the plays were chosen, it seems unlikely that a work commonly adjudged spurious would have been included. It is more likely that later scholars accepted without question the ascription of *Rhesus* to Euripides. As

[1] Cf. Schol. *Med. subscr.*; Schwartz, *op. cit.* p. 382; Wilamowitz, *Einl.* pp. 157 ff.; *RE*, s.v. Scholia; Barthold, *op. cit.*

[2] Wilamowitz, *Einl.* p. 174. The inclusion of *Bacchae* among the select plays is disputed: cf. Dodds, *Bacchae*, 2nd ed. pp. li f.

we have seen, some late authors who quote our play refer to it as the work of Euripides;[1] if any thought otherwise, we hear nothing of them.

SUMMARY

The external evidence for the authorship of *Rhesus* does not by itself enable us to reach a certain conclusion. With the exception of the one statement in the Argument that some unnamed persons suspected it to be spurious, there is no indication of doubt of its authenticity at any period. Nor does the historical information about *Rhesus* that can be extracted from our sources give us any reason to suppose that our play might not be the work of Euripides. We have not however been able to reconstruct the history of *Rhesus* in detail, and we do not know enough to be able to say certainly that the extant *Rhesus* is not spurious.

The significant facts that we have been able to determine may now be assembled in chronological order.

(1) Euripides produced a *Rhesus*, in all probability his own work, at a date when he could still be called νέος. This is most naturally taken to mean a date before 440.

(2) There is no mention of a *Rhesus* in any fifth-century source, nor can we tell whether our play was known then. Possible reminiscences in Aristophanes are not certain enough to be acceptable as evidence.

(3) Aristotle recorded a *Rhesus* of Euripides in his *Didascaliae*. He may have added an express indication that he regarded it as genuine, but this is uncertain. We cannot be quite sure that Aristotle was acquainted with any *Rhesus* which he could identify with the work of Euripides whose title he found in the records. It cannot however be doubted that our *Rhesus* was in existence in his lifetime, and unless it then lay in obscurity, which appears unlikely, he probably took it to be the work of Euripides. This inference is supported by the facts which follow.

---

[1] See above, p. 2 n. 1.

(4) Dicaearchus, a pupil of Aristotle, writing about 300, knew our *Rhesus* and accepted it, apparently without question, as the work of Euripides. It is highly probable that the text of the play which he accepted had an iambic prologue beginning νῦν εὐσέληνον φέγγος ἡ διφρήλατος, and there is nothing to prevent our supposing that he regarded this as an original part of the play. It is likely that there was already in existence a second iambic prologue, which was later current in some copies of the play and was then believed to be the work of actors. The existence of variant versions of the opening may be taken as evidence that our *Rhesus* was produced on the stage during the fourth century.

(5) Aristophanes of Byzantium (*c.* 257–180), the Alexandrian editor of Euripides, published our *Rhesus* in his collected edition of the poet's works. He seems not to have doubted its authenticity. The text which he published lacked an iambic prologue, beginning like ours with the entry of the Chorus. Copies of the play may well have reached him in this form. Of the two iambic prologues he probably did not possess the first, but it is possible that he knew and rejected the second.

(6) After the publication of the Alexandrian edition *Rhesus* was studied by leading scholars of Tragedy at both Alexandria and Pergamum. We know for certain from the scholia that Parmeniscus and Dionysodorus of the former school, and Crates of the latter, believed it to be by Euripides; all three wrote as if the authorship of the play was not questioned. Since Parmeniscus and Dionysodorus were both pupils of Aristarchus, we may be confident that he too thought the play genuine.

(7) The scholia to *Rhesus* contain no hint that its authenticity was suspected. Since they derive material from the Alexandrian and Pergamene commentators who followed Aristophanes, it appears improbable that any of these can have treated the play as spurious. The same is true of their successors, particularly those who had a part in the compila-

tion of our scholia from the old commentaries. Didymus was almost certainly one of these, and we may be sure that he too accepted *Rhesus* as genuine. The scholia show further that the ancient grammarians approached *Rhesus* with the same censorious attitude that they generally adopted towards Euripides. As in the scholia to the other plays, a later critic sometimes defends the poet.

(8) The inclusion of *Rhesus* in a select edition of ten plays of Euripides, which was made probably during the second century A.D., leaves little doubt that it was then regarded as authentic. We have no reason to suppose that it was subsequently suspected until modern times.

The evidence thus does not rule out the possibility that *Rhesus* is a spurious work written after the time of Euripides. But belief that it is spurious cannot easily be reconciled with the known facts, unless the date of its composition is put quite early in the fourth century. It certainly could not be later than the middle of the century. Naturally it also remains possible for the play to be spurious but contemporary with Euripides.

A close investigation of the external evidence concerning *Rhesus* has not yielded any indication that its authenticity was doubted at all in antiquity except by the anonymous critics whose opinion is cited in the Argument. Our information is far from complete, but if this suspicion had been at all widely held among the ancient grammarians, we might have expected some other signs of it. This is especially true of the period of scholarship that followed the edition of Euripides by Aristophanes of Byzantium; for our scholia, which draw upon the commentaries of this time, would have been likely to preserve some trace of a view which was certainly then an unorthodox one.

Where then do these anonymous critics fit into our picture? With our knowledge so deficient as it is, we can hardly guess with any confidence. But there was less reason for a suspicion of this kind to arise after *Rhesus* had been accepted as authentic by scholars of such respected authority as Aristophanes and his successors. It therefore seems unlikely that the ἔνιοι are late. Nor does it seem probable that the suspicion arose very early. In the fourth century, at least before the time of Aristotle, there was little concern about such matters, and our evidence suggests that Aristotle himself and, in the next generation, Dicaearchus were in no doubt; not that we can eliminate this period on such slight evidence. If we are to look for a likely period for these critics, the most attractive is the earlier era of Alexandrian scholarship. It is in this period that we might expect questions of authorship to be reviewed by those who had the task of collecting and classifying the material of the Alexandrian library. They had to determine the genuineness of the works that had been acquired, and discussion of such matters appears to have been included in the Πίνακες of Callimachus, the comprehensive catalogue of the library's contents.[1] From this source, or less probably from the corresponding Πίνακες of the Pergamene library, our Argument might have derived both the record of the suspicion and its refutation. But this is only a guess. The ἔνιοι of the Argument must remain anonymous.

---

[1] See above, pp. 10 f.

CHAPTER II

THE PLOT AND CHARACTERS

In the previous chapter the external sources of evidence bearing upon the authorship of *Rhesus* were reviewed, and it was seen that these, while yielding no support for the ancient suspicion that the work was spurious, were nevertheless insufficient to prove its genuineness beyond doubt. Further evidence has to be sought internally by examining the text of the play and comparing it closely in the various departments of its composition with the other works of Euripides. It is indeed principally upon internal evidence that the case against the authenticity of *Rhesus* has been founded in modern times, and the arguments that have been accumulated touch all aspects of the poet's art.

In investigating this part of the evidence our attention must be directed primarily towards the case which scholars have built up on internal grounds against the authenticity of the play. At the same time it is not enough to limit the scope of our inquiry to an evaluation of the arguments of previous scholars. Although a proper consideration of these arguments will in itself involve a detailed treatment of many aspects of the play's composition, there may be other sources of internal evidence which have not hitherto received due attention. The aim therefore in the following chapters is not only to assess the significance of arguments brought forward previously, but also to seek for other possible sources of evidence relevant to the question of authorship.

The internal evidence is divisible into two broad categories, comprising respectively the dramatic and the poetic sides of the play's composition. The latter category embraces such matters as the poet's vocabulary and style, his choice and treatment of metre and the formal structure of the various parts of the play. It is in these things that we should expect to find the clearest marks of individuality, which might provide us with solid grounds for or against accepting the play as the work of Euripides. This part of the evidence will be reserved for consideration in later chapters. Meanwhile, in this chapter and the next, we shall consider *Rhesus* as a piece of dramatic art.

Here we are concerned with the actual substance of the plot and the poet's handling of his material, his portrayal of the characters, his competence in matters of stagecraft and his treatment of theatrical conventions. Within this field the opponents of the authenticity of *Rhesus* have always sought strong support for their case. At least one present-day critic, it appears, although prepared to concede that in matters of diction, metre and style no decisive case has been made out against Euripidean authorship, would still argue against authenticity on dramaturgical grounds.[1] Some arguments have been concerned with specific matters of dramatic technique, while other criticisms have been directed against the substance and the composition of the plot. The significance of the former can usually be assessed by comparison with other works of Euripides. Criticisms of the latter type, however, inasmuch as they are generally aesthetic in character, are less easily evaluated, and, even if they seem to be valid, carry less weight, since a dramatist does not necessarily maintain a consistent quality in all his works. Nevertheless, it is necessary to consider such arguments on their merits, both because they have been so prominent in the controversy and because their cumulative importance may not be negligible.

Our first task will be to review the matter of the plot and particularly to consider its relation to the Homeric version of

[1] A. Lesky, *Gnomon*, XXIII (1951), 141–4; cf. D. W. Lucas, *CR*, n.s. 1 (1951), 20, and G. Björck, *Arctos*, n.s. 1 (1954), 16–18. H. Strohm, *Hermes*, LXXXVII (1959), 257–74, defends the dramatist against the charge of incompetence in his art, but none the less finds in the dramatic technique evidence against authenticity.

the myth, which will enable us to form some assessment of the originality and skill of the dramatist. We shall then be in a better position to evaluate specific charges of incompetence in the construction of the plot and presentation of the characters.

THE SOURCES OF THE PLOT

Rhesus is the only extant Attic tragedy, if we exclude *Cyclops*, whose plot we possess also in its epic version. The drama is based on the *Doloneia* in the tenth book of the *Iliad*, and numerous close resemblances of detail make it clear that the author has made direct use of this source. This gives us a unique opportunity of studying his methods and judging the skill with which he has adapted the episode for presentation in the theatre.

Of other sources that the dramatist might have used we have little knowledge. We learn, however, from the Homeric scholia that the legend of the death of Rhesus was treated by Pindar. The following summary of his version appears in schol. A *Il.* K 435 (Pindar, fr. 277 Bowra):[1]

Ῥῆσος γένει μὲν ἦν Θρᾷξ, υἱὸς δὲ Στρυμόνος τοῦ αὐτόθι ποταμοῦ καὶ Εὐτέρπης μιᾶς τῶν Μουσῶν. διάφορος δὲ τῶν καθ' αὑτὸν γενόμενος ἐν πολεμικοῖς ἔργοις ἐπῆλθε τοῖς Ἕλλησιν, ὅπως Τρωσὶ συμμαχήσῃ, καὶ μίαν ἡμέραν συμβαλὼν πολλοὺς τῶν Ἑλλήνων ἀπέκτεινεν· δείσασα δὲ Ἥρα περὶ τῶν Ἑλλήνων Ἀθηνᾶν ἐπὶ τὴν τούτου διαφθορὰν πέμπει· κατελθοῦσα δὲ ἡ θεὸς Ὀδυσσέα τε καὶ Διομήδη ἐπὶ τὴν κατασκοπὴν ἐποίησε προελθεῖν· ἐπιστάντες δὲ ἐκεῖνοι κοιμωμένῳ Ῥήσῳ αὐτόν τε καὶ τοὺς ἑταίρους αὐτοῦ κτείνουσιν, ὡς ἱστορεῖ Πίνδαρος.

Some features of the story as told here, which are not to be found in the *Iliad*, are shared by the drama:

(i) The parentage of Rhesus. In the play he is son of the River Strymon and a Muse, who is unnamed (*Rh.* 917 ff. *et*

---

[1] I have assumed that Pindar's authority is cited for the whole of this account including the genealogical details; he is indeed likely to have referred to the parentage of Rhesus.

passim). Homer makes him son of Eioneus (K 435), but does not mention his mother.[1]

(ii) διάφορος δὲ τῶν καθ᾽ αὐτὸν γενόμενος ἐν πολεμικοῖς ἔργοις—Homer makes no reference to the past exploits of Rhesus. In *Rhesus* some details of his previous successes in war are introduced (426 ff.). It appears that these may not be entirely the dramatist's own invention but that some such details may have appeared in earlier versions.

(iii) In the Pindaric account Hera, in alarm for the safety of the Greeks, dispatches Athena to destroy Rhesus. The author of the second iambic prologue to *Rhesus*, of which our Argument quotes a short passage, has made use of this idea, although there is no mention of the specific danger of Rhesus in the passage preserved. The Argument states that this prologue was deemed spurious; it will however be argued below (pp. 105 ff.) that *Rhesus* originally possessed an iambic prologue, which may well have been conceived on similar lines.

The ways in which Pindar's version seems to have differed from *Rhesus* are also to be observed:

(i) Rhesus was present at Troy for a whole day before his death and during that time engaged in battle with conspicuous success.

(ii) Athena's part was not the same as in either Homer or *Rhesus*. She intervened at an earlier stage of the action to inspire Odysseus and Diomedes to the κατασκοπή, which seems to have been for the special purpose of killing Rhesus. The dramatist was not alone in assigning to Athena a more prominent role than she has in the epic.

(iii) No mention is made of Dolon in the summary, and he was probably omitted altogether by Pindar. He would have been unnecessary to this version of the legend.

---

[1] Eioneus is identified with the river-god Strymon by the mythographer Conon, fr. 4 Jacoby: Στρυμόνος τοῦ Θρᾳκῶν βασιλεύσαντος...οὗ καὶ ὁ πάλαι Ἡιονεὺς ποταμὸς ἐπώνυμος. J. Rempe, *De Rheso Thracum heroe* (1927), pp. 7 ff., is inclined to accept Conon's authority, but it has been rejected by others, including Leaf, *JHS*, xxxv (1915), 1 n.

These differences of treatment were appropriate to the more concentrated style of lyric narrative. It is significant that Pindar evidently made Rhesus the central figure of his myth. The renown of the Thracian hero may have been more widely celebrated than some would have us suppose. There is one other allusion to Rhesus in our remains of early poetry: his death at Troy is related by Hipponax (fr. 42 Bergk), with no new feature except that the hero is there described as Αἰνειῶν πάλμυς.

The dramatist appears to know nothing of a feature which occurs in later versions of the myth, a prophecy that, if the horses of Rhesus were once to graze on the Trojan plain and drink of the waters of Scamander, then their master would be invincible.[1] There is no allusion to this in *Rhesus*, although the germ of the idea is perhaps to be found in Athena's remarks at 600 ff.

The plot of *Rhesus* adheres rather more closely than the Pindaric version to the epic original, but adaptation to drama has made necessary some important changes. The scene of the play is laid throughout in the Trojan camp and therewith the main interest is shifted from the Greek side to the Trojan. Although only a few scenes correspond to events actually narrated in detail in the *Doloneia*, many others are developed from hints supplied by the epic version.[2] The adaptation will now be considered scene by scene.

(i) *Vv.* 1–51 (Parodos). *The Trojan guards, who form the Chorus, alarmed by fires and noise in the Greek camp, rouse Hector from his sleep. There is excited dialogue between Hector and the Chorus.*

All the action of *vv.* 1–148 of *Rhesus* is represented by only three lines of *Iliad* K (299–301), in which we are told simply that Hector did not allow the Trojan chiefs to sleep but called them together into council. The dramatist is therefore

[1] Schol. *Il.* K 435; Eustathius, *Il.* 817, 26; Vergil, *Aen.* 1, 469 ff. and Servius *ad loc.*; Roscher, *Myth. Lex.* s.v. Rhesos.
[2] The relationship between *Rhesus* and *Iliad* K is discussed by Richards, *CQ,* x (1916), 192 ff.; cf. Maykowska, *Eos,* xxvi (1923), 52 ff.

inventing in this scene and has constructed the action along the lines of the activity in the Greek camp which is depicted in full detail in the first half of K. He has transferred to the Greek camp the fires and din which in K (11 ff.) belong to the Trojans and provoke alarm in Agamemnon. The discussion among the Chorus and their dialogue with Hector owe something to the epic poet's description of the activity among the Greek chiefs: a few verbal resemblances prove that the author has this in mind (e.g. K 55: *Rh.* 25; K 68: *Rh.* 28–9; K 80: *Rh.* 7). Hector's questions to the Chorus (*Rh.* 11 ff.) match those of Nestor to Agamemnon (K 82–4). The idea of sending men to wake the other chiefs (*Rh.* 28 f.) comes from K (e.g. 108–10, also 299–300).

(ii) *Vv. 52–84. Hector regrets that nightfall has cut short his victorious advance and contemplates renewing action forthwith.*

Here the dramatist has gone back to the preceding action in the *Iliad*. Hector's speech is modelled after the harangue which in Θ (497–541) he delivers to the Trojans at the end of the day's fighting. From this source are derived the fear that the Achaeans may attempt flight (510 f.: *Rh.* 52–5, 68–9), the confident expectation that victory is all but won (498 f.: *Rh.* 56–8) and that only the coming of night has saved the Achaeans (500 f.: *Rh.* 59–62), and the intention of inflicting slaughter on the enemy as they board their ships (512–15: *Rh.* 72–3). Not to be found in this speech is the idea that Hector was eager to prolong the battle into the night and was dissuaded only by his seers (*Rh.* 63–7), but Hector's impatient attitude towards prophets is matched by his contempt for omens at M 237–40. The suggestion that Hector might contemplate an attack by night is made in K (101) by Agamemnon, and it is probably thence that the dramatist derived the idea.

The short dialogue between Hector and the Chorus (76–84), which leads up to the entrance of Aeneas, appears to be the poet's own invention, but the sentiment expressed in *v.* 84 may have been inspired by M 243.

(iii) *Vv.* 85–148. *Aeneas counsels Hector against a night-attack and advises sending a spy instead.*

The introduction of Aeneas is the poet's own device, although there is the suggestion of a discussion between Trojan leaders in K 300. Aeneas is far from superfluous, as has been suggested.[1] Although in K the idea of sending out a spy comes from Hector himself, in the play he is too much affected by the commotion and it is dramatically right that another character should be introduced to provide a calming influence and produce the rational plan. The dramatist has again copied the pattern of Homer's scene in the Greek camp, for there it is Menelaus who advises the distraught Agamemnon to calm himself and to discover the enemy plans by means of a spy (K 37 ff.).

The conception of Aeneas as a prudent and cautious counsellor is taken from the *Iliad* (e.g. E 166–238). But the Aeneas of the present scene is based primarily upon the Homeric Polydamas, with clear reminiscence of two passages:

(*a*) M 60 ff. Polydamas advises Hector against using chariots to attack the Achaean wall. In this speech are the arguments which provide the substance of Aeneas' advice to Hector in *Rh.* 109–15: the difficulty of crossing the trenches in chariots, the obstacle presented by the σκόλοπες, the impossibility of returning across the trenches in the event of a counter-attack or of ever getting safely back to the city. The reference to the menace of Achilles (119–22) is added by the dramatist.

(*b*) N 726 ff. The introductory *sententia* of Aeneas' speech (105–8) comes from these other words of advice which Polydamas gives to Hector, especially *vv.* 729–33:

> ἀλλ' οὔ πως ἅμα πάντα δυνήσεαι αὐτὸς ἑλέσθαι·
> ἄλλῳ μὲν γὰρ ἔδωκε θεὸς πολεμήια ἔργα,
> . . . .
> ἄλλῳ δ' ἐν στήθεσσι τιθεῖ νόον εὐρύοπα Ζεὺς
> ἐσθλόν . . . .

[1] E.g. by Menzer, *De Rheso Tragoedia* (Berlin, 1867), p. 15.

In both these places, it may be noted, Hector, as here in *Rhesus*, accepts the advice quietly and with good grace.

(iv) *Vv. 149–223. Dolon volunteers to go as a spy to the Greek ships. The subject of a reward is discussed on his initiative, and having secured the promise of the horses of Achilles, he describes his plans, then departs.*

The events of this scene are treated in the *Doloneia* itself. The dramatist has expanded the material, making one or two notable changes. Some use has also been made of the closely parallel scene in the Greek camp, in which Diomedes and Odysseus volunteer (K 203 ff.).

Hector's appeal (*Rh.* 149–53) is briefer than it is in K 303–12) but is expressed in similar terms. The reluctance of his hearers to volunteer, expressed in K by the Homeric formula οἱ δ᾽ ἄρα πάντες ἀκὴν ἐγένοντο σιωπῇ (313), is conveyed in the drama by repetition of the appeal a second and a third time (151, 152). Dolon volunteers (154–7) in much the same terms as in K 319 f. There has, however, been some change in the matter of the reward. In K Hector himself, as part of his first appeal, offers the reward of the best horses in the possession of the Greeks (305 f.); it only remains for Dolon to stipulate that these should be the horses of Achilles (322–3) and to extract an oath from Hector (321, 329 ff.). In *Rhesus* Dolon himself brings up the subject of reward (161 f.) and is allowed to name his own (165). Hector makes several offers before Dolon reveals his desire for the horses of Achilles. All this discussion is added by the playwright, apparently from his own imagination. But one or two details about Dolon, which he thereby brings in, his wealth (170) and the distinction of his father (159), are derived from the epic (315, 378–81); and in describing the horses of Achilles (185–8) the dramatist clearly has in mind the passages in the *Iliad* where Homer refers to them (Π 149–51, Ψ 277 f.). Hector's own desire for the same horses (184) is the poet's own idea, a fine dramatic stroke by which we obtain a glimpse of Hector's generous nature.

67

In Dolon's disguise (208 ff.) there has again been a striking departure from the Homeric version (K 334 f.), where Dolon simply throws the wolf-skin about his shoulders as a cloak and wears on his head a fur cap. The use of the wolf-skin as a complete disguise is not, however, the dramatist's innovation. A cup signed by Euphronius as maker bears a representation, which has been attributed to the Panaetius painter, of Dolon's interception by Odysseus and Diomedes.[1] The Trojan spy is seen wearing as a costume a close-fitting wolf-skin, complete with tail, which reaches from his neck to his wrists and ankles. The essential idea of disguise is thus already present in this scene, probably painted not later than about 480 and certainly earlier than any likely date of our play. The dress is not identical in every detail. Dolon in the painting simply wears on his head a helmet instead of the χάσμα θηρός of the play (209), but the latter could reasonably be assumed to be an original part of the disguise-motive. At all events this form of headdress was familiar in Euripides' day in the conventional garb of Heracles (cf. *Heracles* 465). Nor does the four-footed walk (*Rh.* 211) appear on the vase, where Dolon's hands and feet are bare, but it too is likely to have been an original part of the disguise-motive. The dramatist is therefore not to be ridiculed for this idea, which was already current in his day.

(v) *Vv. 264–526. A messenger reports the approach of Rhesus, and describes in rich detail the Thracian king and his army. The hero himself appears, justifies his late arrival in debate with Hector, and expresses his confidence of routing the Achaeans at the first attack.*

An important change has been made by the dramatist in dispatching Dolon before anything is known of the approach of Rhesus. As a consequence, Dolon can no longer betray the information of the Thracian's presence and, as will be seen below, another means of doing this has to be contrived. The motives for this change, for which the dramatist has been

---

[1] J. D. Beazley, *Attic Red-figure Vase-painters* (1942), p. 215; its relation to *Rhesus* is treated by J. A. K. Thomson, *CR*, xxv (1911), 238 f.

severely criticized, will be considered later in discussing the management of the plot.

These scenes which present Rhesus are all added by the dramatist. In K 435–41 there is a brief description of Rhesus by Dolon, but he is not mentioned again except in the scene of his slaying (474, 494). The vivid narrative in which the messenger describes the approach of Rhesus' army and the amazement caused by its appearance is presumably the poet's own invention, although he incorporates into his description the few details which Homer gives. Features derived from the epic include the whiteness of Rhesus' horses and his god-like appearance (*Rh.* 301, 304). The latter idea is developed in the following choral ode, where Rhesus is equated with Zeus (355–9), and recurs in *v.* 385, where the Chorus call him Ares.

For the subject-matter of the debate and the following dialogue between Hector and Rhesus the poet seems to have drawn chiefly on his own imagination. A possible source outside the *Iliad* for the principal idea of the debate will be mentioned below (p. 80). The depiction of Rhesus' character will also be reserved for later discussion. Here, however, it may be noted that a possible source for his contempt of the enemy and his confidence in his own might is to be found in *Iliad* M in the person of Asius, another ally of the Trojans, likewise famed for his horses (M 95–7, 110 ff., esp. 164 ff.). But, whereas Homer treats Asius with apparent contempt, calling him νήπιος, there is no justification for the view, which some critics have taken, that our poet means Rhesus to be regarded as a braggart or a fool. This question will be considered below, where other possible sources for the poet's conception of Rhesus will be mentioned.

One detail derived from Homer is the placing of Rhesus and his army apart from the rest of the Trojans and their allies (*Rh.* 520: K 434). This is essential to the plot.

(vi) *Vv. 527–64. The guards, who form the Chorus, depart to call the relief watch.*

The list of allies responsible for the watch (540 ff.) includes names from among the allies whom Dolon betrays to Odysseus in K (428 ff.). But in K the allies sleep without a guard and the Trojans alone keep watch (416 ff.).

The choice of the Trojan guards as Chorus and the handling of the idea, which have been much censured, will be discussed below (p. 94).

(vii) *Vv. 565–674. Odysseus and Diomedes, who have learnt from Dolon the location of Hector's tent, arrive to find it empty. Athena appears and informs them of the presence of Rhesus. While the two Greeks go off to kill him, the goddess encounters Paris. She then warns the two heroes that it is time to escape.*

This scene is based on events that are treated in some detail in K, whose narrative relates the interception of Dolon by the Greek spies and their intrusion into the Thracian camp. Little is said in *Rhesus* about Dolon's encounter with the enemy and his death, which have taken place off stage. These events are mentioned in passing allusions in the dialogue between Odysseus and Diomedes (573, 575, 591 ff.). Hence we learn that Dolon has been slain after revealing the Trojan password and the location of Hector's bed. The betrayal of Hector's position is in K (414–16), but the password, already mentioned at 521, is an innovation on the part of the dramatist. No more is said here of Dolon, but by a clever device of the poet Odysseus has σκυλεύματα (592 f.) stripped from the dead Trojan. From a later passage (783 f.: see below, pp. 76 f.) it seems quite possible that Odysseus, the master of disguise, is actually wearing Dolon's wolf-skin costume which has been so elaborately described earlier. By this visible token Dolon's fate is confirmed for the audience without need for a detailed description. The spoils are mentioned in the epic, but there they are left as a dedication to Athena at the scene of the murder (K 458 ff.).

The information about the arrival and station of Rhesus forms in K the climax of Dolon's betrayal, but in *Rhesus*, as a result of the new disposition of events, cannot come from him.

To convey this essential information Athena is used instead. The inspiration for her epiphany is taken from the Homeric version, in which she watches over the Greek spies in their expedition and finally appears beside Diomedes (K 274–98, 366, 461–4, 497, 507–11). In the drama the goddess's part has been expanded to make her a closer and more obvious participant in the actual slaying of Rhesus. In her encounter with Paris she demonstrates before the eyes of the audience her support for the enterprise: this interlude is invented by the dramatist for technical reasons, which will be examined below (pp. 125 f.).

The events of this scene thus correspond in their general outline to those of Homer's narrative, but in the detail of its treatment the adaptation is free. Nevertheless, the dialogue is, in several places, closely dependent on the original. The following are some obvious reminiscences:

(a) *Rh.* 608–9:

> Οδ. δέσποιν' 'Αθάνα, φθέγματος γὰρ ᾐσθόμην
> τοῦ σοῦ συνήθη γῆρυν . . . .

K 512 (Athena appears beside Diomedes):

> ὁ δὲ ξυνέηκε θεᾶς ὄπα φωνησάσης.

(b) *Rh.* 609–10:

> Οδ. . . . ἐν πόνοισι γὰρ
> παροῦσ' ἀμύνεις τοῖς ἐμοῖς ἀεί ποτε.

K 278–9 (Odysseus prays to Athena):

> . . . ἥ τέ μοι αἰεὶ
> ἐν πάντεσσι πόνοισι παρίστασαι.

(c) *Rh.* 611–12:

> Οδ. τὸν ἄνδρα δ' ἡμῖν ποῦ κατηύνασται φράσον·
> πόθεν τέτακται βαρβάρου στρατεύματος;

K 463–4 (Odysseus prays to Athena):

> . . . ἀλλὰ καὶ αὖτις
> πέμψον ἐπὶ Θρῃκῶν ἀνδρῶν ἵππους τε καὶ εὐνάς.

(d) *Rh.* 613–14 (cf. 520): The position of the Thracians is as in K 434.

(e) *Rh.* 616–17:

πέλας δὲ πῶλοι Θρηκίων ἐξ ἁρμάτων
λευκαὶ δέδενται, διαπρεπεῖς ἐν εὐφρόνῃ.

K 474–5:

'Ρῆσος δ' ἐν μέσῳ εὗδε, παρ' αὐτῷ δ' ὠκέες ἵπποι
ἐξ ἐπιδιφριάδος πυμάτης ἱμᾶσι δέδεντο.

(*f*) *Rh.* 616–21: Athena's description of the horses of Rhesus follows the lines of Dolon's in K 436 ff., which has already served as the model for the Messenger's description (303 ff.).

(*g*) *Rh.* 622–6, in which Odysseus and Diomedes discuss the division of their task, are expanded from K 480 f.:

. . . ἀλλὰ λύ' ἵππους·
ἠὲ σύ γ' ἄνδρας ἔναιρε, μελήσουσιν δ' ἐμοὶ ἵπποι.

(*h*) *Rh.* 668–74: Athena warns the two heroes to cease from slaughter and to escape without delay back to the ships, because the enemy have got wind of their presence. K 503–11: Diomedes would go on killing but Athena warns him to make his escape, before some other god rouses the Trojans.

(viii) *Vv. 675–727. Odysseus and Diomedes are intercepted by the Chorus, but Odysseus effects their escape by using the password and pretending to be Rhesus. After their departure the Chorus continue to wonder who the intruder may have been.*

The whole scene is added by the dramatist. In K the two spies escape without encountering any Trojans. But the motive for the scene comes from K 523–5:

Τρώων δὲ κλαγγή τε καὶ ἄσπετος ὦρτο κυδοιμὸς
θυνόντων ἄμυδις· θηεῦντο δὲ μέρμερα ἔργα,
ὅσσ' ἄνδρες ῥέξαντες ἔβαν κοίλας ἐπὶ νῆας.

In *Rhesus*, however, the Trojans do not come to the actual scene of the crime.

A note is perhaps needed here on the interpretation of the brief dialogue in trochaic tetrameters between Odysseus and the Chorus, about which there has been some uncertainty. This is one of the few passages in the play where the action is not altogether clear from the text. For this textual corruption does not appear to be responsible. The metrically unsound readings of codd. in 683 can be satisfactorily emended by a simple change of word-order to read εἰδέναι σ' οὐ χρή. In 685 we may read

Οδ. ἴστω. θάρσει.   Χο. πέλας ἴθι. παῖε πᾶς.

The confusion in some manuscripts has been caused by uncertainty about the metre (see below, p. 294) and does not affect the sense.

The real difficulty is caused by 686: why is the name of Rhesus mentioned, when the Chorus is unaware that he is dead and Odysseus would not wish to reveal the fact? Grégoire,[1] finding the name offensive, sought to eliminate it by reading

μὴ σὺ δείρῃς ὃν κατέκτας, ἀλλὰ τὸν κτενοῦντά σε

and assigning the line to Odysseus, an emendation which, although ingenious, is far from probable.

The situation must first be understood, and there is admittedly some obscurity for the reader. Odysseus and Diomedes have been intercepted by the Chorus and are both pursued on to the stage (681), having presumably abandoned the horses of Rhesus, to which we may suppose them to return later. A marginal note in V says Ὀδυσσεὺς ὑποκρίνεται εἶναι Τρωικός, and so Porter (*Rhesus*, 2nd ed. p. xiv) interprets the scene. The idea is on the right lines, but it is more satisfactory to suppose that Odysseus, who is probably carrying spoils stripped from Rhesus, actually pretends, as Musgrave suggested, to be the Thracian king. This deception, however, does not at once occur to him: at first (684–5) he tries to bluster his way out of trouble. Then comes the obscure line. The whole of 686 is assigned by codd. to HMIX., but most editors transfer the first half—ἦ σὺ δὴ 'Ρῆσον κατέκτας;—to Odysseus. This seems to create, rather

[1] In *Mélanges Navarre* (1935), pp. 231 ff. Cf. Wilamowitz, *Hermes*, XLIV (1909), 451 f.; Porter, *Rhesus* (2nd ed.), p. xiv.

than solve, difficulty. Why should Odysseus suddenly refer to the slaying of Rhesus, which it is in his interests to conceal? It is better to follow codd., which are here unanimous in their division of speakers. And since the two halves of the line are clearly spoken by different persons, we may give them to the two halves of the Chorus.

A possible interpretation, I would suggest, is to suppose that Odysseus is struck down by one of the blows which accompany the παῖε πᾶς of 685. Then members of the Chorus, approaching closer in the dark, recognize the arms he bears as those of Rhesus and so cry out to the one who has felled Odysseus: 'Have you killed Rhesus?' To which the other semi-chorus, rushing forward in turn, replies: 'No, but one who was going to kill you.' Odysseus then, recovering, tries to check the assailants with his ἴσχε πᾶς τις, which they refuse to heed (οὐ μὲν οὖν). He thereupon taking advantage, with characteristic quickness of wit, of the fact that he has been recognized as Rhesus by the other semi-chorus, pretends to be the Thracian. The rest of the scene is straightforward. Odysseus states the password and the Chorus, who have earlier heard Hector tell the password to Rhesus, naturally accept it now as confirmation of his identity. Odysseus proceeds to mislead the Chorus: his τῆδέ πη κατείδομεν sets them searching the immediate vicinity, while he and Diomedes make their escape.

(ix) *Vv. 728–881. The wounded Charioteer of Rhesus describes the slaying of his master and accuses Hector of the deed. Hector denies the charge.*

The anonymous Charioteer is substituted by the dramatist for Hippocoon, the Thracian counsellor and cousin of Rhesus, who in K (518 ff.) is awakened by Apollo to witness the slaughter in the Thracian camp.

> ὁ δ' ἐξ ὕπνου ἀνορούσας,
> ὡς ἴδε χῶρον ἐρῆμον, ὅθ' ἕστασαν ὠκέες ἵπποι,
> ἄνδρας τ' ἀσπαίροντας ἐν ἀργαλέῃσι φονῇσιν,
> ᾤμωξέν τ' ἄρ' ἔπειτα φίλον τ' ὀνόμηνεν ἑταῖρον.   (519–22)

This last line has suggested the cries of distress which the Charioteer utters as he enters, lamenting his own misfortune and that of Rhesus (728–35, 749 ff.). Then, after a brief reflection on the shame of so inglorious a death (756–61), which is the dramatist's own, the Charioteer gives an account of the murder of Rhesus, which derives much of its matter from the narrative of K 471 ff.

Vv. 763–9: The description of the Thracian encampment follows closely K 471–5, incorporating from K 421 the fact that they have posted no guards. The dramatist places rather greater emphasis on the carelessness of the Thracians.

Vv. 770–9: The idea that the Charioteer, while feeding his horses, sees the intruders and warns them off, is invented by the dramatist, a vivid touch by which he gives the Charioteer a greater personal part in the events that he narrates.

Vv. 780–6: The nightmare which in K (497 f.) visits Rhesus, in the form of a vision of Diomedes, is here transferred to the Charioteer and given a new form with rich detail of the poet's own invention:

> καί μοι καθ' ὕπνον δόξα τις παρίσταται·
> ἵππους γὰρ ἃς ἔθρεψα κἀδιφρηλάτουν
> Ῥήσῳ παρεστώς, εἶδον, ὡς ὄναρ δοκῶν,
> λύκους ἐπεμβεβῶτας ἑδραίαν ῥάχιν·
> θείνοντε δ' οὐρᾷ πωλικῆς ῥινοῦ τρίχα
> ἤλαυνον, αἱ δ' ἔρρεγκον ἐξ ἀντηρίδων
> θυμὸν πνέουσαι κἀνεχαίτιζον φόβῳ.

The immediate translation of the dream into reality was regarded by Geffcken as untragic, and indeed there is perhaps no parallel for it in the other dreams of extant tragedy.[1] But it is in fact a feature taken over from the epic poem, where Athena sends Rhesus a momentary vision of his murderer at the instant of his death. The way in which the dramatist has adapted this motive gives proof of his skill,

---

[1] Geffcken, 'Der Rhesos', *Hermes*, LXXI (1936), 407. Descriptions of dreams in tragedy: Aeschylus, *Pers.* 176 ff., *PV* 645 ff., *Ch.* 521 ff., *Eu.* 116 ff.; Sophocles, *El.* 417 ff.; Euripides, *Hec.* 68 ff., *IT* 42 ff.

because it allows his messenger to give a vivid account of things that took place while he was asleep: how much more effective than to have him say, 'I went to sleep and awoke to find the horses gone'. Surely this needs no parallel elsewhere in tragedy.

The dream is thus intended, like its epic counterpart, to be a close reflection of actuality. Why then does the poet introduce the wolves into his description? Wolves are of course marauders, and in Greek literature animal-symbolism is a common feature of dreams and visions;[1] so that perhaps it is enough to say that the poet added this detail because he wanted something to mark this description as a dream. It is, however, inevitable that any mention of wolves in this play should remind us of Dolon's wolf-skin disguise, and this, I feel, may be intentional. This passage is perhaps an indication that Odysseus, to whom the task of stealing the horses has been assigned (624), has actually donned the wolf-skin disguise which he has stripped from Dolon's body (592). The significance of this detail would at once be understood by the audience, if they had already seen Odysseus clad in the wolf-skin. Perhaps then he is wearing it in the earlier scene (565–626), when he first enters with Diomedes, and in referring at 592 f. to the σκυλεύματα points to the costume that he is actually wearing. If this is so and Odysseus has assumed the disguise of Dolon, there is a remarkable resemblance to the later scene of his escape (682 ff.), where he evidently uses the spoils taken from the dead Rhesus in order to pass himself off as the Thracian king.

I do not think it is a necessary objection to this view that there is no explicit indication of Odysseus' costume in the text. Ancient drama was not composed primarily for a reading public, and did not need to describe what was visible to the audience. References to the dress of characters are in fact rare in Greek tragedy.[2]

---

[1] Cf. Euripides, *Hec.* 90; Aeschylus, *Ag.* 1258 f.
[2] Pickard-Cambridge, *Dramatic Festivals of Athens*, pp. 223–5.

The elaborate use of disguise by Odysseus, in two separate scenes of the play if the above interpretation is right, would be the poet's own innovation in the present story. But such masquerade was a traditional part of the trickery practised by Odysseus, the αἰμυλώτατον κρότημα. Indeed we have twice in this play, both before and after Odysseus' appearance on stage (498 ff., 710 ff.), detailed description of an earlier occasion when he entered Troy in a false στολή. These passages gain additional point if Odysseus uses disguise again in this play.

The suggested interpretation of the reference to wolves in *v.* 783 must remain conjectural, but this question will not materially affect our appreciation of the dramatist's skill in refashioning the dream-motive from Homer as an element in the Charioteer's narrative.

There are a few further points of coincidence with the *Doloneia* in the Charioteer's speech. *Rh.* 789, κλύω δ᾽ ἐπάρας κρᾶτα μυχθισμὸν νεκρῶν, represents K 521, quoted above, and the στόνος ἀεικής of K 483. The idea for κρουνὸς αἵματος in *Rh.* 790–1 comes from K 484, ἐρυθαίνετο δ᾽ αἵματι γαῖα. The phrasing of *Rh.* 794:

παίει παραστὰς νεῖραν ἐς πλευρὰν ξίφει

is modelled after K 489:

ἄορι πλήξειε παραστάς.

The following scene, comprising Hector's castigation of the Chorus for negligence (808–32) and the charge of complicity brought against Hector by the Charioteer (833–76), has no counterpart in the *Doloneia* and owes nothing to it even in detail.

(x) *Vv. 882 982. The Muse appears in order to forbid the burial of her son Rhesus and to proclaim future divine honours for him. She enlightens the Trojans about the events that have passed during the night.*

This whole scene is an addition to the Homeric story, in which there is no special interest in Rhesus and not even a

77

word is said about the disposal of his body. For most of the matter of the Muse's speech we do not know whether the author had any source other than his own imagination. But, as we have seen above, the genealogy which makes Rhesus son of Strymon and a Muse, although foreign to Homer, appears to have been already known to Pindar. It is therefore possible that the account of the manner of the hero's birth (915 ff.), if not invented by the dramatist himself to explain the genealogy, is derived from a source earlier than Euripides. As for the prophetic utterances concerning the future of Rhesus, they are obviously based on some known existing institution. The introduction of the Muse as *deus ex machina* will be discussed further in the next chapter, where it will be argued that the matter and presentation of her speech are consistent with the dramatic practice of Euripides.

(xi) *Vv. 983–96. With the coming of day the Trojans prepare for a renewed attack.*

This conclusion, which some critics have needlessly supposed to point to a following play,[1] merely represents the renewal of battle which in the *Iliad* itself (Λ 56 ff.) takes place with the coming of daylight. The lines have been criticized as destroying the tragic effect of the last scene, but after the mother's lament any expression of grief by those less intimately affected is superfluous. The criticism is in any case not necessarily justified. Others have thought that the spectacle of the weary Trojans again equipping themselves for battle makes a highly effective ending, which quietly reinforces the pathos of the drama.[2] The lines, besides, fulfil a necessary technical function. When the Muse departs, Hector and the Trojans are left standing on the scene and some means has to be contrived of removing them. The ending of *Hecuba*, as Buchwald has pointed out,[3] is similar in character.

---

[1] E.g. Morstadt, *Beitrag zur Kritik der dem Euripides zugeschriebenen Tragödie Rhesos* (Heidelberg, 1827), p. 58.

[2] E.g. Murray, *Rhesus* (transl.), pp. 66 f.   [3] *Studien zur Chronologie*, p. 53.

From the foregoing survey it is obvious that the poet of *Rhesus* is heavily indebted to Homer, from whom he has derived, besides the general outline of his plot, the pattern for many individual scenes and numerous details of expression. But there are some scenes which have no counterpart in the epic poem, notably those which introduce Rhesus and the final epiphany of the Muse. In these parts, although it has occasionally been possible to suggest a source for certain details, we usually cannot tell whether the material already belonged to the legend of Rhesus in the poet's day or was invented by him. It may, however, be worth while to consider some other possible sources, particularly since certain scholars have used the non-Homeric elements in the plot to support theories about the dating of the drama.

Some elements in the plot of *Rhesus*, for which the *Doloneia* is not the source, especially matter relating to the hero himself, may have been taken over by the dramatist from legends of other heroes who likewise came as allies to Troy and there met an untimely death. The Trojan Cycle introduced several such heroes, notably Sarpedon in the *Iliad*, Eurypylus in the *Little Iliad*, Memnon in the *Aethiopis*, and Cycnus in the *Cypria*. The legends of these famous warriors, which were of course familiar to fifth-century Athenians in their epic versions, provided material for the tragedians. Among the lost works of Aeschylus and Sophocles were tragedies dealing with the deaths of each of these heroes.[1] The *Kares* of Aeschylus, the action of which was set in Lycia, probably had as its chief incident the bringing of the news of Sarpedon's death to his mother Europe. Memnon's story was the subject of the *Memnon* and *Psychostasia* of Aeschylus and the *Aethiopes* of Sophocles; the fate of Eurypylus at Troy was the subject of the play of Sophocles that bears his name, a few details of

---

[1] For fragments of the plays mentioned here and discussion of their plots see Nauck, *TGF*² (1889); Aeschylus, ed. H. Weir Smyth, Loeb Library, vol. II, 2nd ed., with Appendix by H. Lloyd-Jones (1957); *Die Fragmente des Aischylos*, ed. Mette (1959); Sophocles, *Fragments*, ed. Pearson (1917). For *Eurypylus* see also D. L. Page, *Greek Literary Papyri* (1950), pp. 16 ff.

which are known from papyrus fragments; Cycnus was the hero of an unknown play of Aeschylus[1] and of the *Poimenes* of Sophocles. Although our knowledge of these plays is meagre, a similarity in content to *Rhesus* can sometimes be detected, and other coincidences with the plot of our play are found in the myths of these heroes as known from other sources. *Rhesus* need not necessarily be later than every one of these plays, but its author would have been well acquainted with the sources from which their plots are derived. The following are some common features, not in the *Doloneia*, shared by *Rhesus* with these other legends or with tragedies based on them:

(*a*) Reluctance of the mother to let her son go to war (*Rh.* 900): an essential element in the myth of Eurypylus, which seems certainly to have been present in Sophocles' version; perhaps to be inferred for Aeschylus' *Kares* from fr. 99 N.[2] (for text see Lloyd-Jones, *op. cit.* pp. 599 ff.).

(*b*) Delay in the hero's arrival and the use of gifts as an inducement (*Rh.* 321 ff., 396–403): Eurypylus myth.

(*c*) Inconsolable grief of the mother at the loss of her son (Muse in *Rhesus*): Astyoche in Sophocles, *Eurypylus*, frr. 210–11; Eos for Memnon, probably in Aeschylus, *Psychostasia*, cf. Ovid, *Metam.* XIII, 576 ff.; in Aeschylus, *Kares* fr. 99 Europe expresses apprehension for her absent son, and lamentation doubtless followed upon the news of his death: but in *Il.* Π 431 ff. it is Sarpedon's father, Zeus, who expresses grief that his son is fated to die. Another model for this scene lay in the grief of Thetis for Achilles, with which the Muse is made to compare her own (974 f.). Aeschylus had presented the lamenting Thetis on the tragic stage, and a surviving fragment (fr. 350 N. = 284 Mette), in which she complains of Apollo's perfidy, suggests that here may have been a source of inspiration for the Muse's accusation of Athena.

(*d*) Divine intervention to rescue the body of the hero (*Rh.* 962 ff.): Memnon in Aeschylus, *Psychostasia*; Sarpedon

[1] Ar. *Ra.* 963; Nauck, *TGF*[2], p. 39.

in *Il.* Π 666–75 and perhaps in *Kares* (Weir Smyth, Loeb, vol. II, p. 415); perhaps Sophocles, *Eurypylus*.

(*e*) Return of the hero's body to his native land (*Rh.* 970–3): myth of Memnon, Sarpedon in *Il.* Π 673–5; Sophocles, *Eurypylus*, fr. 212.

Such are the coincidences between these legends that it is also possible that similar details were in the fifth century already attached to the Rhesus myth itself.

These resemblances to legends which formed the plots of fifth-century tragedies might seem to support the view that *Rhesus* is an imitation of the works of the great tragedians. Wilamowitz, in fact, who was the first to notice similarities to *Rhesus* in the fragments of the *Poimenes*, concluded that our play was a fourth-century imitation of that work.[1] He supported his argument by pointing to a resemblance between the Shepherd's speech in *Rhesus* and some fragments of the *Poimenes* (frr. 502 ff.) in which a goatherd speaks as messenger; and he also found a vaunting tone in one or two fragments reminiscent of Rhesus' boasts (see further below, p. 99). In these, however, there is nothing more than a general likeness of situation and nothing to establish that the poet of *Rhesus* had this play of Sophocles in mind. The existence of tragedies about Sarpedon, Cycnus, Memnon and Eurypylus simply proves that the legends of these heroes were popular in the fifth century. If the plot of *Rhesus* has elements in common with the plots of these plays, it can as well on these grounds belong to the same period as be a later imitation.

The above analysis of the plot and its sources makes way for the consideration of certain particular topics which are relevant to the question of the authorship and date of *Rhesus*.

---

[1] *De Rhesi Scholiis* (1877), p. 12; cf. *Einleitung in die gr. Trag.* p. 41 n. 81; *Hermes*, LXI (1926), 284.

Rhesus and Sitalces

This is a convenient point at which to mention the theory, put forward by Goossens and supported by Grégoire and Sneller,[1] that the motive for the scene between Rhesus and Hector is to be found in the relations between Athens and Thrace in the period from 428 and 424 and that Rhesus represents the Thracian prince Sitalces, at that time the temporizing ally of Athens. Now, as we have seen, this is one of the few scenes whose matter cannot be traced to a definite source. Goossens's hypothesis was an attempt to explain the poet's reason for the addition of this element to the drama, but it is hardly acceptable. There is no need to deal with the matter in detail here, since most of its points were success-fully refuted by Sinko (*Ant. Class.* III (1934), 233 ff., 411 ff.). The following arguments against the theory are cogent. First, although the plots of tragedy may sometimes have a particular relevance for a contemporary audience, a con-vincing case has yet to be made for the existence of elaborate political allegory of this kind in any tragedy.[2] Secondly, the resemblances between Rhesus and Sitalces, as he is depicted by Thucydides, are to a great extent in details which would commonly be associated with Thracians. Thirdly, if Euri-pidean authorship is accepted, stylistic evidence cannot easily be made to support a date in the period which suits this theory (i.e. 428–4). Finally, it may now be added that a leading motive of the debate between Rhesus and Hector, which is an important element in the parallel between Rhesus and Sitalces, namely, the delay in arrival in spite of repeated requests and the sending of gifts as inducement, is present also in the story of Eurypylus, from which the dramatist

---

[1] Goossens, *Ant. Class.* I (1932), 93 ff.; Grégoire, *Ant. Class.* II (1933), 91 ff.; Sneller, *De Rheso Tragoedia*, ch. VII.

[2] For proposed allegorical interpretation of Euripidean tragedies see esp. E. Delebecque, *E. et la guerre du Péloponnèse* (Paris, 1951). Sound arguments against such interpretation are put forward by G. Zuntz, 'Contemporary Politics in the Plays of E.', in *Acta Congressus Madvigiani*, I (1958), 155–62.

could have derived it. In general, the subject-matter of the debate is such as might have suggested itself to any poet for a discussion concerning a Thracian prince.

Military detail

From the above survey of the sources of the plot it does not appear that there is anything in its actual matter that could not belong to the fifth century. In particular, we can dispose of the argument that the tactical detail of the drama is proper to the fourth century. This was the contention of Geffcken, who supported his case by reference to passages in Aeneas Tacticus and Xenophon.[1] But the mention of similar military procedure by these writers, in particular their mention of passwords, night manœuvres and stratagems, is by no means proof that such things were unfamiliar in Greek warfare before the fourth century. The fact is that, with one or two exceptions, all the details of tactics and camp-life referred to by Geffcken are taken over from the *Iliad*. One exception is the treatment of Dolon's stratagem, but we have seen that the motive of disguise is older than the drama. The details of which the poet is himself the author are the password and part of the description of the Thracian army, including the use of the term πελταστής. The use of passwords is no innovation of the fourth century, and we may compare, for example, Herodotus IX, 98. As for πελταστής, its use in reference to Thracian troops would not be surprising at any date; for, although the word itself first occurs in Thucydides (II, 29), the πέλτη is named as an article of Thracian equipment by Herodotus (VII, 75; see below, p. 157).

Relation to Homer

Analysis of the relation between our play and the *Doloneia* has proved that it is far from being a straightforward dramatization of the epic. Although the framework of the plot and

---

[1] Geffcken, *op. cit.* p. 400.

6-2

much of the detail of its treatment are derived from Homer, there is abundant evidence that the author is an artist of skill and originality. Even in his borrowing he displays considerable ingenuity: in fashioning the opening scenes, for example, he has ranged widely, drawing material from the first half of the *Doloneia* and from other parts of the *Iliad*. Several scenes have been expanded into dramatic form from events that are treated only briefly in the epic; others, notably those in which Rhesus appears and the concluding scenes of the play, are entirely his own. Not all these alterations and additions have escaped censure, especially in their relation to the plot, and the main criticisms will be considered below. But reference may be made here to a few particular examples of the poet's powers of invention and dramatic ability. The vivid narrative speeches of the Shepherd and the Charioteer, which incorporate some matter from Homer but owe their form to the dramatist, are of acknowledged brilliance, and these two characters are themselves skilfully drawn. A fine dramatic sense is shown in the choice of the Muse as *deus ex machina* and of the Charioteer to perform the function of messenger. Finally, there is no little subtlety in the way in which the wolf-skin disguise and the password are used as connecting links between scenes.

Nevertheless, in spite of these many changes and other original elements, it is remarkable with what closeness the drama in many places follows its epic source. There is a heavy debt to Homer in the matter of some scenes, extending often to the very words and sentiments of the speeches. For some critics this kind of imitation has been in itself evidence of deficient inventive capacity, and hence an argument against attribution of the work to Euripides.[1]

We should, however, be cautious of supposing that so close an adaptation is unworthy of a great dramatist. Sophocles himself had a reputation for faithful adherence to the epic

[1] Hermann, *De Rheso Tragoedia*, p. 284; cf. A. Lesky, *Die tragische Dichtung der Hellenen* (1956), pp. 218 f.

sources from which his plots were derived. In the words of the anonymous Σοφοκλέους Βίος (§ 20):

τὸ πᾶν μὲν οὖν Ὁμηρικῶς ὠνόμαζε· τούς τε γὰρ μύθους φέρει κατ' ἴχνος τοῦ ποιητοῦ, καὶ τὴν Ὀδύσσειαν δ' ἐν πολλοῖς δράμασιν ἀπογράφεται. παρετυμολογεῖ δὲ καθ' Ὅμηρον καὶ τοὔνομα τοῦ Ὀδυσσέως·

> ὀρθῶς δ' Ὀδυσσεύς εἰμ' ἐπώνυμος κακοῖς·
> πολλοὶ γὰρ ὠδύσαντο δυσσεβεῖς ἐμοί.

ἠθοποεῖ τε καὶ ποικίλλει καὶ τοῖς ἐπινοήμασι τεχνικῶς χρῆται, Ὁμηρικὴν ἐκματτόμενος χάριν.

This description of Sophocles' methods implies an imitation of Homer which extends to thought and expression. Unfortunately his extant works give us no opportunity to find first-hand evidence of this. It would, however, be a mistake to suppose that close adherence to an epic source was not characteristic of fifth-century tragedy. In the success of Sophocles there is perhaps evidence that faithful reproduction of the epic legends found public favour.

On the other hand, Euripides' own reputation was rather for innovation in mythology. Perhaps then so close an imitation of Homer as is found in *Rhesus*, while it might be expected of Sophocles, is not to be associated with Euripides. It has indeed been suggested that this was in the minds of those ancient critics who found in *Rhesus* Σοφόκλειος χαρακτήρ. But there is no reason why Euripides should always have observed the same policy in the treatment of his sources. If Sophocles had established the principle of close adherence to the original, it was open to Euripides to follow him, even if he did so only once.

It so happens that *Cyclops* is the only other extant work of Euripides, or of any of the tragedians, whose epic source we possess. This play cannot fairly be compared in respect of the closeness of its adaptation. As a satyr-play it necessarily treats the myth with more freedom and in a spirit of burlesque; in particular, there have been many changes in order to accommodate Silenus and the chorus of satyrs. Nevertheless, even here Euripides is faithful to the main outlines of the plot, and quite often in points of detail *Cyclops* comes as close to the original as does *Rhesus*.[1] In this respect we may note especially the first passage of dialogue between Odysseus and the Cyclops (*Cycl.* 275 ff.: ι 252 ff.), the description of the preparations for the blinding (*Cycl.* 455 ff.: ι 319 ff.), Odysseus' concealment of his identity and the play on the name Οὖτις (*Cycl.* 548–50: ι 355, 369; *Cycl.* 672: ι 407; *Cycl.* 692 ff.: ι 503 ff.). In these and other places the material of the drama is drawn directly from Homer, and there is several times a verbal resemblance. The manner of the adaptation is sufficiently like that of *Rhesus* for both to be by the same hand, but it is not likely that more could be proved by pressing the comparison further.

THE STRUCTURE AND MANAGEMENT
OF THE PLOT

Consideration must now be given to certain miscellaneous criticisms of the construction and management of the plot. It is impossible to account for all the minor points of censure and it would be superfluous to deal with criticisms that have already been satisfactorily discounted by others. I propose here to treat only the more significant arguments of the critics, the general purport of which is that the plot lacks unity, is episodic in structure and develops a series of minor issues which are of no consequence. Weakness in the structure of the plot cannot, unless the faults are of a grave kind, be a decisive argument against Euripidean authorship. Not a few of his plays have been criticized for deficiencies in this respect, notably *Andromache*, *Hecuba*, *Heracles* and *Phoenissae*, and it must be allowed that in some cases at least the censure

---

[1] A similarity of technique between *Rhesus* and *Cyclops* in the adaptation of the epic material was pointed out by H. Steiger, *E., seine Dichtung und seine Persönlichkeit*, p. 92 n. 1.

is deserved.[1] This argument has nevertheless been prominent in the controversy about *Rhesus* and is still one of the mainstays of the case against its authenticity.[2] It is therefore desirable to establish how far the charge is justified.

The Dolon-episode

Among the criticisms of the plot-construction one main group is directed against the treatment of the Dolon-episode and its relation to the rest of the plot. The plot, it is claimed, is lacking in unity.[3] It falls into two parts, the first being concerned with the expedition of Dolon, the second, which does not begin until *v.* 264, with the arrival and fate of Rhesus. Between these two parts there is only a tenuous connection. To this cleavage in the plot the author himself is held to have contributed by his placing of Dolon's departure before the arrival of Rhesus and the consequent reduction of Dolon's importance in the action. Further, it is argued that, in view of the small significance of Dolon in the drama, the discussion of his reward and his disguise at such length is both inopportune and irrelevant. Conversely, why, when interest in Dolon has been aroused, is so little said in the sequel of the fate of his expedition?

In reply to these arguments several observations may be made. In the first place, it is in accordance with the author's conception of the drama that Dolon should not play so large a part as he does in the *Doloneia*. In the play divine responsibility for the death of the hero is emphasized. The guilt is shared by Athena and by the two Greek spies, who are the instruments of her will. The feelings of the audience are directed against the Greeks, especially against Odysseus

[1] See, c.g., P. Decharme, *E. et l'esprit de son théâtre*, pp. 324 ff.; G. M. A. Grube, *The Drama of E.* pp. 80 ff.

[2] Among more recent critics see Pearson, *CR*, xxxv (1921), 59; Wilamowitz, *Hermes*, LXI (1926), 287; Geffcken, *op. cit.* p. 406; Pohlenz, *Gr. Trag.*[2] (1954), p. 472; Lesky, *op. cit.* p. 144; Björck, *op. cit.* p. 17.

[3] Beck, *Diatribe*, p. 261; Menzer, *De Rheso*, pp. 13 ff.; Pearson, *op. cit.*; Pohlenz, *op. cit.*; Lesky, *op. cit.*; Björck, *op. cit.*; Harsh, *Handbook of Classical Drama* (Stanford, 1944), p. 251.

(e.g. 710–21, 893–4, 906–9), while the Trojans and their allies are sympathetically treated. This effect would be weakened by emphasizing the complicity of Dolon. This may well have been one reason for the alteration in the sequence of events.

But why is Dolon introduced at all, since he is by no means indispensable? A sufficient answer would be that he is an essential element in the story, too closely associated with Rhesus to be omitted.[1] Further, since the poet wishes to set the stage for his drama by means of a preliminary scene in the Trojan camp, the sending out of Dolon is an obvious choice. He is, moreover, given a significant, if small, function in the plot. He is made to betray two pieces of information to the enemy spies, the location of Hector's bed and the Trojan password. The former, which is derived from the epic, is useful dramatically: it serves to bring the two Greeks by a natural means to the actual scene of the drama, making way for the scene in which Athena appears and directs them to the camp of Rhesus. The password, an addition by the dramatist, also has its importance in the sequel, for it is used by Odysseus in effecting his escape, and the escape-scene itself is by no means superfluous (see below, p. 93).

The fact that Dolon himself is relevant does not necessarily justify the length at which his reward is discussed and his disguise described. There is, however, good reason for dwelling on the disguise, since, as we have seen, Odysseus is wearing it—or, if not, at least carrying it—when he first enters (see *vv.* 592 f.). It is essential that the audience should recognize the wolf-skin when it appears.[2] The talk about Dolon's reward is not strictly relevant, but besides illustrating the characters of Dolon and Hector, it serves effectively to heighten the impression of the Trojans' confidence, building

---

[1] So Maykowska in *Eos*, XXVI (1923), 52 ff.

[2] We may leave out of account Murray's idea that Dolon crosses the stage in his disguise at the end of the first stasimon (*Rhesus* transl. pp. 16, 58; cf. Porter, *Rhesus*[2], p. xii). Such a silent movement across the stage would be without parallel, and there is nothing in the text to warrant the assumption; *vv.* 201–3 indicate rather that Dolon is not to appear again.

up to the catastrophe. The emphasis on the horses of Achilles is not lacking in ironical significance.

It is a mistaken view that the dramatist, having created interest in Dolon's expedition, ought to let us know more of his fate. Greek tragedy does not as a rule take any further interest in minor characters after they have served their purpose. All we need to know is that Dolon has been slain after betraying the password, and this we are told briefly but effectively in the dialogue between Odysseus and Diomedes. The appearance of the wolf-skin in their possession confirms his fate without the need of detailed description. An extended reference to the fate of Dolon, who is after all only a subordinate character, would be undesirable at any later point in the drama; for anywhere else than in the Muse's speech it would interrupt the action, and there it might distract sympathy from Rhesus himself.

Dolon is therefore not irrelevant to the plot and the space devoted to him is not disproportionate. It is, however, not to be denied that all the first part of the play appears to be leading up to his expedition, so that with his departure and the sudden arrival of Rhesus there is an abrupt change of interest. The awkwardness of this transition could have been avoided if the poet had contrived by means of a prologue to give the audience foreknowledge of the coming of Rhesus. If, as will be argued below (pp. 101 ff.), the play originally had a prologue, it would certainly have established interest in Rhesus himself from the very start and have made it possible for the proper significance of the events preceding his arrival to be appreciated.

The Rhesus scenes

There is rather more justice in the allegation that the scenes of debate and dialogue between Rhesus and Hector are of no consequence to the plot.[1] The subject of the debate, Hector's charge of procrastination and Rhesus' defence of his goodwill,

---

[1] Cf. Pearson, *op. cit.*; Lesky, *op. cit.*

is by no means vitally significant; for Hector has already consented, at the end of the previous scene (340 f.), to receive Rhesus as an ally, and it is on this decision that the hero's fate might be said to hinge. Moreover, the charge of procrastination has been somewhat abruptly introduced in the last lines of the preceding scene (319 ff.). The debate is followed by dialogue, in which Rhesus boasts of his intention of routing the enemy and discusses his part in the next day's fighting, and this is likewise without consequence. Attempts to discover some relation between this dialogue and the subsequent fate of Rhesus have not succeeded. There is nothing to support Vater's opinion that Rhesus by his boasting is guilty of ὕβρις, for which his death is a punishment.[1] Subsequent events are in no way dependent on Rhesus' boasts and, if Rhesus could in some small way be held to have contributed to his own death by his lack of caution, the dramatist places no great emphasis on this aspect of the catastrophe.

The action of the plot is, in fact, not advanced at all by these scenes, but their dramatic purpose is clear: it is to present Rhesus himself. The poet of the *Doloneia* has given us a story of adventure, in which the assassins have the central role and Rhesus is of interest only as their sleeping victim. The dramatist, having chosen to build a tragedy round the death of Rhesus, is obliged to contrive a means of presenting him to the audience in a part of some magnitude. The Messenger's narrative, the debate between Hector and Rhesus and their dialogue are all devoted to this end. These scenes are given a central position in the play, and the stature of Rhesus is enhanced by thus delaying his first appearance.

It should be added that the poet's purpose in these scenes is not to give us a full portrait of Rhesus. The definition of the hero's character is limited to a few clearly marked traits which are significant for the action. The poet's main pre-

---

[1] *Vind.* II, §§ xxxix ff.; echoed by Paley, *Euripides*, I, p. 7; opposed by Menzer, *op. cit.* pp. 2–6, and others.

occupation in these scenes is, in fact, with the development of the tragedy itself. He has to establish Rhesus as the central figure in the action of the drama. The audience must feel the full impact of the catastrophe when it comes, and to be able to do so it needs to have seen for itself something of the splendour, might and warlike spirit of the hero. These are the qualities which are prominent in the portrayal of Rhesus.

For this purpose the theme of the debate is well chosen. It is important that we should be assured of Rhesus' loyal devotion to his ally, a loyalty which in fact brings him to his death, as Hector afterwards acknowledges (957). The debate further provides an opportunity for Rhesus to describe his past campaigns, thereby justifying his military renown. Having heard evidence of his prowess and of the strength of his armament we must take his threats seriously and feel that he is genuinely able to crown the efforts of the Trojans with victory. More will be said below about the spirit of Rhesus' boasting (pp. 96–8).

If the issue of the debate is of no consequence to the plot, this is by no means unique in Euripidean drama. In *Alcestis*, for example, the quarrel between Admetus and Pheres has no significant influence upon the future course of the action; it serves rather to bring into sharper focus the immediate dramatic situation caused by the death of Alcestis, and especially to show its significance for Admetus. In this way we are prepared for the *peripeteia* to be brought about by the recovery of Alcestis from Death. Similarly in *Rhesus* the rhetorical presentation, by making clear what the addition of Rhesus' forces means to Hector and the Trojans, helps to bring the dramatic situation into perspective, and thus leads up to the *peripeteia* caused by his death.

So far then as its dramatic function is concerned, the scene of debate between Hector and Rhesus is quite in keeping with Euripidean methods. It has however been suggested that in the composition of these speeches the characteristic qualities of Euripidean rhetoric are lacking. Geffcken, for instance, complained that there was here no trace of the celebrated Euripidean δισσὸς λόγος, no higher issue, that the arguments were confined to the immediate situation, with both accusation and defence on purely practical grounds.[1] There is some truth in this, in so far as there is a notable lack here of the gnomic philosophy with which Euripidean rhetorical speeches are often adorned. But ought we to regard this as an essential ingredient of his rhetorical style? These commonplace sentiments were part of a poet's stock-in-trade, which might be used according as they were appropriate to the speaker or the situation. We must remember that the dramatist's intention in this scene is to display Rhesus as a man of action. He chooses to do this by means of a debate on the question of Rhesus' loyalty, a subject which can best be argued by an appeal to actual deeds. Philosophizing and sophistry would be both inappropriate to the speakers and damaging to the dramatist's purpose. He shows himself conscious of this when he makes each speaker open with the prefatory remark that his words will be straightforward and blunt (394 f., 422 f.).

When these concessions have been made to the special needs of the situation, there does not appear to be so striking a difference from the normal manner of Euripides. In fact, the parties in his debates tend to argue mainly, as here, from the particular facts of the case.[2] And the speeches in *Rhesus*, although succinctly and bluntly expressed, are by no means artless. In the balance between accusation and defence, in the orderly disposition of the arguments, and in the force and clarity with which they are presented, there is evidence of a rhetorical skill not unworthy of Euripides.[3]

---

[1] Geffcken, *op. cit.* p. 406. To Murray (*op. cit.* p. 59), on the other hand, the scene read 'like a rather crude and early form of the celebrated psychological controversies of Euripides'; cf. Pearson, *op. cit.*

[2] Cf. e.g. *Alc.* 629–705; *Med.* 465–575; *Hcld.* 134–231.

[3] The rhetorical style generally is like that of Euripides without offering any especially remarkable parallels. With 399 οὐ γάρ τι λέξεις ὡς... cf. *Alc.* 658 οὐ μὴν ἐρεῖς γέ μ' ὡς..., and with 438 οὐχ ὡς σὺ κομπεῖς... cf. *Or.* 571 ὡς οὐ κομπεῖς, *Med.* 555 οὐχ, ἦ σὺ κνίζῃ,..., *Ba.* 686 οὐχ ὡς σὺ φῄς.... For other stylistic resemblances see pp. 244–5.

The part of Athena

In making Athena the divine helper of the Greek spies the dramatist, as we have seen, has followed his Homeric model, but he has expanded her role by making her convey the essential information concerning the presence and position of Rhesus. While such divine intervention is normal in epic, it has been held to be out of place in tragedy, and the poet has been charged with mismanagement in introducing the goddess in the middle of the play in order to direct the course of the action.[1] This is often regarded as a violation of the conventions of fifth-century tragedy and hence as evidence against Euripidean authorship. The question will be discussed in the next chapter. At this stage we may note, first, that the germ of the idea is in Homer, and secondly, that the poet's treatment of Athena's role accords with his intention of stressing the divine share in the responsibility for the death of Rhesus.

Miscellaneous additions

The dramatist has made a few other additions to the story of the *Doloneia*, which might, if considered purely in relation to the development of the plot, be considered irrelevant. There is however usually an obvious dramatic motive for these. The reason for the brief appearance of Aeneas has already been discussed (p. 66); the introduction of Paris will be considered below (p. 125). Another incident added by the poet is the interception of Odysseus by the Trojan guards. The motive for including this scene is not simply a predilection for vivid action and spectacle: on dramatic grounds it is important that the audience should know for certain that the Greek spies have escaped and will not appear again; this can only be ensured by actually representing their escape on the stage.

Finally, it has been held that the poet has introduced a

---

[1] E.g. by Pearson, *op. cit.*; Wilamowitz, *op. cit.*; Pohlenz, *op. cit.* (cf. p. 87 n. 2).

superfluous and pointless addition in making the Charioteer accuse Hector of responsibility for the murder of Rhesus (833 ff.).[1] So far as the plot is concerned we could easily dispense with this addition, since nothing is said about the charge in the sequel; it can however be justified on technical grounds, as will be shown in the next chapter.

The Chorus

One task confronting the dramatist in adapting the epic legend for presentation in the Attic theatre was to find a suitable role for the Chorus. In his choice of the Trojan guards as Chorus the poet of *Rhesus* has often been censured.[2] The burden of the criticism is that it is unrealistic for the guards to remain so long absent from their stations, that it is neither proper that all the guards should come to warn Hector, nor that they should all retire to call their relief.

We must remember of course that the action is set, not within a regular fortified camp, but in a temporary bivouac in the open field. Perhaps even so some awkwardness remains, but it is excessively fastidious to regard it as a serious mark of incompetence in the dramatist. In Greek tragedy the presence or the movements of the Chorus are quite often, in terms of strict realism, a cause of embarrassment. A certain lack of realism was readily accepted within the dramatic conventions.

The choice of the guards as Chorus has obvious merits, since they can be active participants in the drama. In particular, provided that we are not too much concerned about strict military propriety, the motive for the entrance of the Chorus at the beginning of the play is admirably contrived, and their later removal from the scene of action is also managed on a natural pretext. In fact, the very movements

[1] Björck, *Arctos*, n.s. 1 (1954), 16–18, and earlier critics.
[2] Beck, *op. cit.* pp. 265 f.; Patin, *Euripide*, p. 331; Wilamowitz, *Hermes*, LXI (1926), 286; Grube, *op. cit.* p. 440 n. 1. The dramatist is defended by Maykowska, *Eos*, XXVI (1923), 53 f.

of the Chorus to which exception has been taken are essential to the plot, since the guards must necessarily be absent from their posts while the Greek spies enter the Trojan camp.

We have already had cause to notice the play's lack of exposition. Here again the poet's design might have been made clearer if a prologue had preceded. In a prologue spoken by a god it could have been explained that the confusion among the guards was divinely inspired in order to assist the enterprise of the Greek spies. By introducing Athena, for example, at the beginning of the play the poet could have supplied all the preliminary information needed to knit the plot together, and at the same time he would have been able to link the prologue to the succeeding action by having the goddess disturb the Trojan guards.

In this section we have been concerned with certain specific allegations of mismanagement in the construction of the plot. Against most of these charges it has been possible to defend the dramatist. The points which we have severally treated add up to the common criticism that the play consists of a series of episodes loosely strung together without any real unity.[1] It has been shown that this criticism is by no means altogether justified. The plot can indeed be termed episodic, inasmuch as certain of its incidents—the arrival of Rhesus, the entry of the Greek spies, the epiphany of Athena—do not arise out of the immediately preceding action. These incidents however are all subordinated to the main theme, which is the tragic death of Rhesus. If the relevance of each incident is not at once clearly perceptible, it is very largely because the play lacks a formal exposition of its theme at the beginning. In this respect there is a very striking difference from the normal practice of Euripides. If there were a prologue, which announced the subject of the drama and foreshadowed some of the coming events, it would be possible to avoid the abruptness with which the various episodes of the drama

[1] Geffcken, *op. cit.*; Lesky, *op. cit.*; Björck, *op. cit.*

succeed one another. In the next chapter we shall see other reasons for believing it probable that our play originally possessed such a prologue.

CHARACTERIZATION

At this point a few remarks must be added about the characterization in *Rhesus*. We cannot here examine this aspect of the dramatist's art in any detail. To do so would hardly be profitable for our present purpose, unless we were also to undertake a general study of the treatment of character by Euripides. Here it must suffice to consider a few specific arguments against the authenticity of *Rhesus* which have to do with characterization. In particular, the criticism has to be considered that Rhesus, the hero of the play, is a ludicrous figure. He has, in fact, often been compared to the *miles gloriosus* of comedy.[1] The same charge is also, but less frequently, brought against Dolon and even Hector.[2] The implication of this criticism is pursued further by Pohlenz: arguing that the literary type of the boastful soldier, which he sees depicted in both Rhesus and Hector, originated with the growth of mercenary service in the fourth century, he concludes that the character-drawing of *Rhesus* yields evidence for its late date.

The argument is ill founded. In the first place, the charge of vanity and boastfulness levelled at these characters is exaggerated. Rhesus is not intended by the poet to appear as a vaunting ἀλαζών. If such an impression of him has been formed, it could be by the fault of the poet; it might, however, also be that the hero's behaviour has been judged by standards

---

[1] E.g. by Valckenaer, *Diatribe*, p. 104; Albert, *De Rheso Tragoedia*, p. 12; Wilamowitz, *op. cit.* p. 288; Pohlenz, *op. cit.* p. 473; Grube, *op. cit.* p. 444. Cf. Murray, *op. cit.* p. ix; Paley, *Euripides*, I, pp. 5 ff.; Steiger, E., *seine Dichtung und seine Persönlichkeit*, pp. 90 f.; Fabbri, *Riv. fil.* XLVIII (1920), 194.

[2] Against Dolon by Wilamowitz, *op. cit.*; Pohlenz, *op. cit.*; Grube, *op. cit.*; against Hector by Beck, *op. cit.* p. 263; Albert, *op. cit.*; Pohlenz, *op. cit.*; cf. Fabbri, *op. cit.* Wilamowitz and Grube consider that Hector is sympathetically treated in contrast with Rhesus.

of propriety accepted by a different age. The element of
boasting in Rhesus' speeches is in fact much slighter than it is
commonly represented. There is nothing in his reply to
Hector's accusations that is not appropriate to a straightforward and fair defence. His claim that one day will suffice
for him to rout the enemy has been thought boastful and
absurd. This is indeed a bold assertion, but not an idle one, as
is proved by Athena's estimate of the danger he constitutes to
the Greeks (600–4). It should also be noted that in the
Pindaric version (see above, p. 62) Rhesus slays many
Greeks in a single day's combat: this was evidently part of
the tradition. In his willingness to fight alone against the
enemy or to be stationed opposite Achilles (488–91) there is
no vanity, but rather a courageous spirit and a justifiable
confidence in his own might. The only part of Rhesus' schemes
to which Hector takes exception is his proposal to carry the
war into Greece (471 ff.). This promise is intended to be
audacious, but by no means frivolous. It must be remembered
that Hector has represented the victory at Troy as almost won,
so that Rhesus, to guarantee his good faith and demonstrate
his prowess, is required to propose some further enterprise.
Extravagant as the idea may seem to us, an Athenian audience
of the middle of the fifth century would hardly have laughed
at a threat of barbarian invasion, nor would they have thought
lightly of the might of Thracian hordes, while memories
remained alive of the destruction of their colony at Ennea
Hodoi in 465.

No more true is the belief that Rhesus is supposed by his
presumption to display ὕβρις which contributes to his doom.[1]
If this were the intention, he would not speak σὺν Ἀδραστείᾳ,
and some expression of disapproval or note of warning from
the Chorus would be expected. As it is, the poet has not
provided any hint that Rhesus is likely to provoke divine
displeasure. The genuineness of the hero's exploits is, in fact,
not to be doubted, and his threats are likewise to be accepted

[1] Vater, *Vind.* ii, §§xxv, xxxix ff.; cf. Paley, *op. cit.*; Harsh, *op. cit.*

at their face value. The qualities displayed by Rhesus are courage and a thirst for action, which the audience is meant to admire, combined with a heedless confidence, which may provoke their apprehension but not their censure. This is very different from the vain and bombastic arrogance of the comic *miles*.[1]

Hector is even less deserving of this title. It is true that he displays an impetuous confidence in the opening scenes, but it is a confidence based upon trust in divine favour and justified by recent success (*Rh.* 52 ff., esp. 56–64, 100–4). All this aspect of Hector's character is taken straight from the *Iliad*, where several of Hector's speeches show the same confidence in divine support (e.g. Θ 173 ff., 185 ff., 497 ff.; M 231 ff.; N 824 ff.). His restless energy and eagerness for action are derived from the same source (Θ 497 ff., K 299 f.).

Dolon, too, is close to his epic counterpart. Vanity and arrogance are in him appropriate traits. In the play these qualities appear chiefly in the demand for a reward which is still in the hands of the enemy, and in his promise to slay Diomedes or Odysseus. The former is suggested by the epic original, and the latter is an ironical point added by the dramatist. On the whole Dolon's shortcomings are more lightly treated than in Homer. As we have seen, his act of treachery is not stressed, and his spirit in volunteering is praised without reserve by the Chorus. Because we do not witness Dolon's cowardice, it would be irrelevant for the dramatist to dwell upon it; indeed he is a minor character, and we are not expected to spare him much thought once he has left the stage. Dolon is less of a *miles gloriosus* than in Homer.

We should hesitate to assert that a character appropriate to epic was inappropriate in fifth-century tragedy. It would anyway have been difficult to alter the essential character of Hector or Dolon without making fundamental changes in the myth.

---

[1] For qualities of the comic *miles* see Ribbeck, *Alazon*, pp. 28 ff.

With Rhesus the dramatist apparently had a freer hand. Such pomp, finery and magniloquence, although, as we have seen, not comic, are not very familiar to us in extant Greek tragedy. A delight in barbarian richness appears in the *Persae*, and for martial pomp and splendid trappings we may compare the Messenger's descriptions in the *Septem* (especially 375 ff.), but such display tends in these plays to be associated with ὕβρις. And so, in representing like qualities in a hero who is intended to win our approval, the poet of *Rhesus* has been thought to offend against fifth-century taste.

But if extant tragedy has no hero like Rhesus, there is some evidence that he belongs to a type not unknown in fifth-century tragedy. Attention has already been drawn (above, pp. 79 ff.) to similar legends about other Trojan allies, whose fates were made the subject of tragedies in the fifth century. There is a hint of the way in which Aeschylus depicted his Cycnus and his Memnon in Euripides' words in the *Frogs* (962-3):

οὐδ' ἐξέπληττον αὐτούς
Κύκνους ποιῶν καὶ Μέμνονας κωδωνοφαλαροπώλους.

The epithet at once calls to mind the Messenger's description of Rhesus (301-8) and suggests that Aeschylus may have shown the way to our poet in the portrayal of martial qualities.[1] Sophocles' treatment of Cycnus in the *Poimenes* may have been in similar spirit, if we may judge from a fragment (501 P.):

καὶ μὴ† ὑβρίζων αὐτίκ' ἐκ βάθρων ἕλω
ῥυτῆρι κρούων γλουτὸν ὑπτίου ποδός.

These taunts, which, we are told, are spoken by Cycnus himself, surely exceed in extravagance anything uttered by Rhesus. Wilamowitz,[2] who first drew attention to resemblances between *Rhesus* and the *Poimenes*, observed this similarity in the portrayal of the barbarian heroes, but, with some perversity, regarded it as evidence for the hand of a

[1] There was also Achilles in the famous Aeschylean trilogy (cf. fr. 286 Loeb²).
[2] See above, p. 81.

7-2

fourth-century imitator reverting to the Sophoclean style. But surely, if Sophocles could make his hero impetuous and magniloquent, there was no reason why Euripides should not do likewise.

Evidence that Euripides too may have introduced characters of this type is provided by Aristophanes. Lamachus in the *Acharnians* is obviously a caricature of a tragic figure, presumably of a type familiar to Aristophanes' audience. The way in which he is presented suggests a burlesque of the kind of tragic hero of which we have just seen examples: he is splendidly adorned, fearful of aspect, blustering and imperious (566 ὦ βλέπων ἀστραπάς, 567 ὦ γοργολόφα, 574 τίς Γοργόν' ἐξήγειρεν ἐκ τοῦ σάγματος; κτλ.). Further, it appears that the parody is of a character in the *Telephus* of Euripides; for this play is certainly parodied in the scene in which Dicaeopolis, wearing the costume of the beggar Telephus, is opposed to Lamachus. Lamachus, in this scene (566 ff.) at least, presumably represents an Achaean general from Euripides' play, either Agamemnon or Achilles.[1] Allowing for some comic exaggeration, the pomposity and the glorious trappings of the martial hero must have had some counterpart in the *Telephus*. It may be added that *Telephus*, produced in 438, was an early work of Euripides: possibly a taste for colour and spectacle, inherited from his predecessors, was a quality of Euripides' earlier period.

If we have not more tragic heroes like Rhesus in our extant plays, this appears to be accidental. At all events there is no cause for attributing our play to the fourth century on the grounds that he resembles a comic *miles gloriosus*. Not only is the comparison inexact, but we have in Lamachus a fifth-century comic *miles*; and Lamachus is himself a caricature of a tragic hero.

---

[1] On the relation of *Acharnians* to *Telephus* see Starkie's edition, pp. 248 ff. (and note on *vv.* 566 ff.), and E. W. Handley and J. Rea, *The Telephus of Euripides*, Univ. of London Inst. Class. Stud. Bull. Supp. 5 (1957), esp. pp. 22–4.

CHAPTER III

DRAMATIC TECHNIQUE

Our survey of the dramatic art of *Rhesus* has so far been confined to matters of plot-construction and characterization, and in these departments the arguments against Euripidean authorship are principally aesthetic. More important for the question of the play's authenticity is the technical side of its composition, to which we must now turn. Here we have to examine the formal structure of the play, the conventions observed in the handling of the actors and Chorus, and other aspects of stagecraft. An exhaustive study of the dramatic technique of *Rhesus* cannot be attempted here, nor would it be rewarding for our purposes; we may confine our attention to various particular matters in which the poet has been judged to deviate from the normal technique of Euripides or to fall short of his standards of execution. These will be treated in the order in which they appear in the play.

ABSENCE OF AN IAMBIC PROLOGUE

Rhesus in its present state has no iambic prologue, but opens with anapaests delivered by the Chorus as they hurriedly enter in search of Hector. After ten verses Hector responds, and a brief anapaestic dialogue leads on to a lyric strophe and antistrophe by the Chorus, which are separated from one another by a further short anapaestic speech of Hector. There is thus no formal prologos; the play begins with the parodos. This is quite unlike the normal practice of Euripides, whose plays ordinarily open with an iambic monologue, to which there may be added a passage of dialogue, and sometimes an actor's lyric, before the parodos, the prologue as a whole supplying the preliminary information needed for an understanding of the action of the play.

An anapaestic opening is known for only two plays of Euripides, *Iphigenia in Aulis* and the lost *Andromeda*. The opening of *Rhesus* is sometimes compared with these, but there is in fact no similarity.

The prologue of *Iphigenia in Aulis* is clearly divided from the following parodos. As we have it, it consists of three parts: a passage of dialogue in anapaests between Agamemnon and his old Servant (1–48), a monologue in iambic trimeters by Agamemnon (49–114) and another passage of anapaestic dialogue (115–63). There are, however, internal grounds for believing that it has suffered interpolation.[1] Different opinions have been held about its original form, but these have usually started from the hypothesis that the anapaests and the iambics belong to two originally separate prologues, and that an attempt to combine the one with the other has resulted in the mutilation of both. Some have concluded that the iambics are the work of Euripides and the anapaests of later origin;[2] on the other hand, it has recently been argued that the anapaests are authentic and the iambics spurious.[3] Even if the latter view were correct, the opening would not be comparable in form to that of *Rhesus*; for whereas *Rhesus* begins with the entry of the Chorus and lacks any formal exposition of its theme, the anapaestic dialogue between Agamemnon and his Servant is distinct from the parodos and does provide some, though not all, of the exposition which the drama requires.

It is however by no means certain that acceptance of the anapaests as authentic must mean the rejection of the iambics. It has been asserted that the two are incompatible, but if we except the final passage of the iambics (106–14), which bears

---

[1] For the evidence see D. L. Page, *Actors' Interpolations in Greek Tragedy* (1934), pp. 131–40.

[2] See England's edition of *IA*, pp. xxiii–xxv; this conclusion was also favoured by Murray (O.C.T., *app. crit.*) and Page (*op. cit.* p. 140).

[3] E. Fraenkel, 'Ein Motiv aus Euripides in einer Szene der Neuen Komödie', in *Studi U. E. Paoli* (1955), pp. 293–304; cf. M. Imhof, *Bemerkungen zu den Prologen der soph. u. eur. Tragödien* (1957), pp. 104–6.

marks of interpolation, this argument no longer stands.[1] In the rest of the iambics there is nothing at variance with the anapaests, nor is there any duplication of matter; on the contrary, the iambic monologue adds much information which is relevant and even essential to the explanation of the plot.[2] There is, further, no substantial case on linguistic or stylistic grounds against the authenticity of either the opening anapaests or the iambic monologue as far as v. 105.[3] The second passage of anapaests contains perhaps rather more peculiarities, but the question how far it may have suffered interpolation is not vitally important here.

It appears possible then, when due allowance has been made for some interpolations, to accept as original the traditional form of the prologue to *Iphigenia in Aulis*. If this be so, then the common Euripidean iambic monologue is not lacking even here, but is merely postponed until after an introductory passage of dialogue.[4] In this case the prologue of *Iphigenia in Aulis* is even less a parallel for the opening of *Rhesus*.

Our evidence for the prologue of *Andromeda* comes mainly from Aristophanes' parody of it in the *Thesmophoriazusae* (1015 ff.) and the scholia thereon.[5] We can assert little with confidence about its form, but have no grounds for rejecting

---

[1] Fraenkel's specific arguments (*op. cit.* pp. 298–300) are nearly all directed against *vv.* 106–14. His low estimate of the style of the iambic passage has by no means been shared by all other scholars (cf. England, *op. cit.*). The resemblance of 73 f. to *Tro.* 987 ff. is not necessarily evidence of interpolation (cf. Page, *op. cit.* p. 127), and the complaint that this description is inappropriate here seems excessively fastidious.

[2] E.g. the terms of Tyndareus' oath, the assembly at Aulis, the prophecy of Calchas, the conspiracy and the sending of the first letter—all essential background information of the kind usually included in a Euripidean prologue. (We need besides the names of the conspirators; 106–7 are not Euripidean but may be a mutilated version of the original.) Fraenkel (p. 302) recognizes that the two anapaestic passages cannot be joined to make a complete prologue, and supposes that some lines have been lost between 48 and 115; but the contents he proposes for this hypothetical lacuna would still leave gaps in the exposition.

[3] Page, *op. cit.* pp. 131–40; add Fraenkel's arguments (cf. n. 1 above).

[4] Menander's use of the postponed prologue is compared by M. Andrewes, *CQ*, XVIII (1924), 8 f.; cf. W. H. Friedrich, *Hermes*, LXX (1935), 92.

[5] See *TGF²*, pp. 392 ff., and also Schm.-St. III, 1, 517 f.

the scholiast's statement that the play opened with the anapaestic lines beginning ὦ νὺξ ἱερά.[1] It further appears that these lines were part of a monody sung by Andromeda.[2] Apart from this we learn only that Euripides introduced the nymph Echo in the prologue, but we cannot say what her role was.[3] It is possible that here too the formal exposition of the situation was given in an iambic monologue occupying a postponed position after the opening monody; if so, it might appropriately have been spoken by Andromeda herself. Alternatively, it is possible that the monody itself supplied the necessary exposition. Even so there would have been little formal resemblance to the opening of *Rhesus*, for Andromeda's monody seems to have preceded the entry of the Chorus and to have been quite separate from the parodos.

We cannot be sure that Euripides ever dispensed altogether with the explanatory iambic monologue. Certainly there is no parallel in his works for an anapaestic opening by the Chorus like that of *Rhesus*. Indeed it is unique in Greek tragedy, for it is not to be compared with the long and stately anapaestic systems with which the *Persae* and *Supplices* of Aeschylus begin.

It is not, however, certain that *Rhesus* originally began as it does now. In the Argument to the play there is mention of two different iambic prologues which existed in antiquity. There is, as we have already seen (pp. 35 ff.), no reason to doubt that both of these were written for our own *Rhesus* and not for another play. The Argument records the opinion that one of these iambic prologues, of which it quotes eleven lines, was not by Euripides, who is tacitly accepted to be the author of the play, but was the work of actors. On the other prologue, of which only one line is given, it passes no judgement. As we have seen, Dicaearchus knew this prologue and prob-

---

[1] Fr. 114 = Ar. *Thesm.* 1065–8 (Schol. *ad loc.*: τοῦ προλόγου τῆς Ἀνδρομέδας εἰσβολή). Attempts to discount this evidence have not been convincing: see, e.g., W. Nestle, *Die Struktur des Eingangs in der attischen Tragödie* (1930), pp. 130–3.

[2] Cf. *Thesm.* 1077; Lucian, *de conscr. hist.* 1, 2, 2.

[3] Fr. 118 (from which it appears that she remained unseen).

ably accepted it as genuine, but it may not have reached Alexandria. Our evidence provides no reason against supposing that it belonged to the original text of the play.

The external evidence is not sufficient by itself to enable us to decide whether *Rhesus* originally possessed an iambic prologue. If, however, the question is considered in relation to the internal structure of the play, there appear to be several reasons for suspecting that a prologue has been lost. These may now be enumerated.

(*a*) In the first place, *Rhesus* lacks the exposition of the dramatic situation which is normally to be found at the beginning of any Greek tragedy. The critics have not failed to remark this deficiency.[1] We are plunged straight into the midst of lively and rather confused action without first being told either where the scene is laid or what mythological episode is being dramatized. Admittedly it is not difficult to gather many of the essential details from the opening scenes. It is clear at once that it is night, that guards are seeking the place where Hector is sleeping and that therefore the scene must be set in the Trojan camp. The reason for the guards' commotion emerges, though somewhat confusedly, from the following dialogue. Then from Hector's speech we learn that this is the night following a great Trojan victory. But there is nothing in all this to establish precisely the episode that is being presented. It is only at *v.* 125 that the proposal to send a spy is mentioned, from which the audience may begin to guess that they are witnessing the events of the *Doloneia*. The name of Dolon is first mentioned at *v.* 159. As for Rhesus, however, until his name is mentioned at *v.* 280, we have no means of knowing that he is to appear at all, let alone that he is to be the central figure of the play.

It is not to be argued that the audience would have known from the title of the play what events were taking place.

---

[1] Wilamowitz, *Hermes*, LXI (1926), 288: 'Hier fehlt die Exposition ganz'; Geffcken, *Hermes*, LXXI (1936), 396; Albert, *De Rheso*, p. 14; cf. Grube, *The Drama of E.* p. 439.

Admittedly Rhesus, so far as we know, was celebrated only for his death. But even assuming that the titles of plays were publicly known beforehand, it was not the habit of the ancient dramatists to expect the audience to infer the subject in this way. We may likewise discount any suggestion that the plot of this play would have been well enough known to a contemporary audience from the *Iliad*. Most Attic tragedies had plots which were already familiar in epic poetry; yet they never dispense with preliminary information, by which the audience may know which version of the myth is being presented and the point in the story at which the drama begins. Furthermore, *Rhesus*, although in many respects remarkably close to its source, is by no means a straightforward dramatization of the *Doloneia*: besides other changes, there is a significant alteration in the sequence of events. An audience acquainted with the *Doloneia* might well assume, if not otherwise informed, that when Dolon is sent out, Rhesus is already in the Trojan camp.

No other extant tragedy lacks a formal exposition in its opening scene of the circumstances of the action. Even the *Persae* and *Supplices* of Aeschylus, although they have no iambic prologue, yet contain a clear explanation of the situation in the opening anapaests of the Chorus.

(*b*) It cannot be said that *Rhesus* has no need of preliminary exposition. In addition to the divergence from its source just mentioned, the plot contains, of necessity, several events which occur without forewarning, it being impossible that any of the characters should know about them in advance. These include the arrival of Rhesus, the coming of the Greek spies to the Trojan camp and the intervention of Athena. In the present state of the play each of these events comes as a surprise; as a result the structure of the plot appears somewhat disjointed, and the connection between its episodes, for example between the departure of Dolon and the arrival of Rhesus, is not immediately clear. Moreover, without knowledge of what is to follow it is not possible to appreciate fully the significance of some scenes, especially those in which Rhesus appears.[1]

Since all the characters must be ignorant of what is to happen, forewarning of these events could only be given by means of a prologue to be spoken by a god. In similar circumstances Euripides has recourse to this device in several plays. Sometimes, notably in *Alcestis* and *Hecuba*, he uses the prologue to forewarn the audience of events which would otherwise come by surprise, and thus to give coherence to the plot.[2] Although elsewhere he admits unexpected events, for example the arrival of Aegeus in *Medea*, it is a different matter to leave the audience for more than a quarter of the play in ignorance of the coming of the chief character. We should not expect this of Euripides or of any other dramatist.

(c) The present form of the opening of *Rhesus*, as we have seen, does not resemble that of any other tragedy we know. On the other hand, if we suppose that an iambic prologue preceded, the opening passage of *Rhesus* as it stands can be regarded simply as the parodos, and as such it belongs to a type not uncommon in extant tragedy.[3] A similar kind of epirrhematic structure, in which anapaests alternate with lyric strophes, is to be found in the parodoi of Aeschylus' *Prometheus Vinctus*, Euripides' *Alcestis* and *Medea*, Sophocles' *Philoctetes* and *Oedipus Coloneus*. Of all these perhaps the parodos of *Alcestis* approaches most closely in form and style to our opening passage of *Rhesus*. It is different in so far as no actor participates, also in having a second strophe and antistrophe without intervening anapaests. But the ana-

---

[1] The lack of cohesion between the Dolon-episode and what follows has often been criticized: see esp. Menzer, *De Rheso Tragoedia*, p. 13; Pohlenz, *Die griechische Tragödie*, 2nd ed. p. 472; also Beck, *Diatribe*, p. 261; Morstadt, *Beitrag zur Kritik der Tragödie Rhesos*, p. 47; Albert, *op. cit.* p. 14; Pearson, *CR*, xxxv (1921), 59. For a defence see Vater, *Vind.* II, §§xxii, xxviii; Maykowska, *Eos*, xxvi (1923), 52 ff. See also above, pp. 87–9.

[2] On *Alc.* see below, p. 109; in *Hec.* 47 ff. the ghost of Polydorus foretells the finding of his own body, which takes place at 658 ff.

[3] On epirrhematic parodoi in Euripides see Decharme, *E. et l'esprit de son théâtre*, pp. 328 f.

paestic parts, with their rapid exchange of dialogue between the members of the Chorus, are highly reminiscent of *Rhesus*; and the manner of the Chorus' actual entrance is similar in both plays.

(*d*) The fact that *Rhesus* is so short supports the view that a prologue has been lost.[1]

As we have it, *Rhesus* with 996 lines is the shortest extant tragedy. But it is not very much shorter than most of the plays of Aeschylus: the *Eumenides* is longer by only 50 lines; the *Persae*, the *Seven against Thebes* (as it stands),[2] the *Supplices* and the *Choephori* each by about 80 lines; and *Prometheus Vinctus* by 100 lines. Two works of Euripides are comparably short. *Heraclidae* is shortest with 1055 lines, of which the prologue contains 72; it has commonly been regarded as incomplete, but this is by no means certain.[3] Otherwise the shortest is *Alcestis* with 1176 lines (prologue: 76 lines).

The length of the iambic prologue varies considerably in Euripides' plays, and so also does its proportion to the total length of the play. Even with a prologue, unless it were disproportionately long, *Rhesus* would probably still be shorter than any extant play of Euripides. But suppose it once had a prologue of 70 lines, a reasonable length in proportion to the size of the play: it would then be appreciably closer in length to the shorter works of Euripides, and would be commensurate with six of the seven plays of Aeschylus.

(*e*) It is by no means unlikely that an iambic prologue to *Rhesus* should have perished with no obvious internal evidence of its loss.

Among the plays of Euripides there are some in which the

---

[1] Sneller, *De Rheso Tragoedia* (1949), p. 37. We need not, however, suppose with Norwood (*Essays on Euripidean Drama*, pp. 32 ff.) that certain limits of length were imposed on the tragedians by the conditions of competitive performance. Although *Rhesus* is a little shorter than any other play of Euripides, this is not in itself a reason for doubting its authenticity.

[2] On the authenticity of the end of the *Seven against Thebes* see now H. Lloyd-Jones, *CQ*, IX (1959), 80–115.

[3] A strong case against the view that the play is mutilated is put forward by G. Zuntz, *CQ*, XLI (1947), 46–52.

prologue, or a portion of it, is not integral to the drama and could be removed without leaving any trace. Examples are *Alcestis* (monologue of Apollo and the dialogue that follows), *Hippolytus* (monologue of Aphrodite), *Hecuba* (monologue of Polydorus' ghost), *Troades* (monologue of Poseidon and dialogue between him and Athena), *Ion* (monologue of Hermes). In these plays a god, or supernatural being, is introduced at the beginning to give the audience information relevant to the drama, which could not be communicated to them by means of any of the characters in the play itself. Since the god's appearance is unknown to other persons in the drama, there can be no reference to the prologue later in the play. Further, the information which the prologue supplies is, except perhaps in *Ion*, by no means so indispensable that an audience could not follow the action of the play reasonably well without it.

In this respect *Alcestis* provides a relevant illustration. The prologue informs us of the circumstances of the action: that Apollo has saved Admetus from Death, because the Fates have agreed to accept another in his place; that his wife Alcestis is alone willing to die for him, and that this is the day on which it is fated she should die. This much the audience could have gathered from the dialogue of the parodos and the following scene with the Servant (e.g. 77–85, 105, 112 ff., 147, 155). Besides this, however, the prologue gives forewarning of events later in the play, the coming of Heracles and his rescue of Alcestis from the hands of Death. It is by no means essential for the audience to know in advance that this is going to happen, but the knowledge allows them to appreciate the full significance of the action from the very beginning and also prepares for the otherwise unpredictable turn in the plot provided by the abrupt arrival of Heracles.

The circumstances in *Rhesus* are essentially similar. There are, as we have seen, surprise events in the plot, of which warning could not be given except by means of a prologue.

An audience could comprehend the plot without advance knowledge of these events. Nevertheless it is certainly desirable that they should have previous warning of the arrival of Rhesus, and hardly less desirable that they should expect the coming of the Greek spies.

If there was once a prologue, it must clearly have been spoken by a god, since no human character in the play could have performed the functions required of the prologue.[1] Hartung's theory of an opening scene set in the Greek camp, corresponding to the early part of the *Doloneia*, is not worthy of consideration;[2] for apart from the fact that a change of scene before the parodos would be unique and difficult to manage, it is hard to see how such a prologue could have provided the necessary exposition.

For a prologue spoken by a divinity there is ample precedent in Euripides, as there is also for one in the form of dialogue between two gods. Either form could quite well be associated with our *Rhesus*.

One possible form which the prologue might have taken is suggested by the second fragment preserved in the hypothesis and there assigned to actors. These eleven lines clearly were part of a dialogue between Hera and Athena, our fragment being only a small portion of the whole prologue. The likely content of the rest may be guessed. Hera probably warned Athena of the impending arrival of Rhesus and, in accordance with the version of the myth attributed to Pindar, dispatched her to effect his destruction. Then Athena herself before departing may have outlined her scheme for using Odysseus and Diomedes as her agents.

All the necessary preliminary information could have been conveyed in this way; alternatively, of course, though less dramatically, it could have been given by means of a mono-

---

[1] Menzer's argument (*op. cit.* pp. 45 ff.) that no character in the drama could have spoken the prologue does not hold, as Sneller (*op. cit.* p. 39) points out, for Athena; but none of the human characters could have provided the necessary exposition.

[2] *Eur. restitutus*, pp. 11 ff. See above, p. 46.

logue delivered by either Athena or Hera. There is no reason to object to the introduction of a third goddess into the drama, as Menzer does, simply because no other play of Euripides contains three goddesses; nor is there any need to argue against the appearance of Athena in a prologue, on the grounds that in other plays the divinities who speak prologues do not appear again later in the play.[1] We have no reason to suppose that the Greek tragedians were bound by artificial restrictions of this kind.

It is likely enough therefore that *Rhesus* originally had a prologue of similar form to the one to which our second fragment belonged, even if this prologue itself was spurious. Whether the ancient authority is right about the authorship of this prologue we are not in a position to judge. Certainly in the eleven lines that are quoted there is little enough to hinder us from associating them with our play, whether we hold that its author was Euripides or another poet. Although scholars have differed widely in their views about their quality,[2] they contain nothing which could not have been written by Euripides. Of the vocabulary προήκειν occurs nowhere else in tragedy and is first found in Thucydides; στροβέω is not found in Euripides, but is used by Aeschylus. The phrasing of the first line is like that of *Alc.* 1136 (ὦ τοῦ μεγίστου Ζηνὸς εὐγενὲς τέκνον), and the phrase πρόρριζον ἐκτετριμμένην in the last line is reminiscent of *Hipp.* 684 (πρόρριζον ἐκτρίψειεν). Apart from these resemblances the diction is quite ordinary and has nothing to mark it as especially characteristic of Euripides. The metrical style is

[1] Menzer, *op. cit.* p. 49; the latter argument belongs to Kamerbeek, *Mnemosyne*, III (1950), 347 ff.

[2] Valckenaer, *Diatribe*, pp. 92 f.: 'ista naturae congrua simplex oratio... ne Sophocle quidem est indigna'; with this judgement Beck, *op. cit.* p. 262 n., and Morstadt, *op. cit.* p. 73, agreed, but of the three only Morstadt held that the prologue resembled the rest of the play in diction and versification. Those who have subscribed to the view of the hypothesis that the prologue is pedestrian include Hermann, *De Rheso Tragoedia*, p. 271; Vater, *op. cit.* II, §lx; Welcker, *Die griechischen Tragödien*, p. 1105; Porter, *Rhesus of Euripides*, 2nd ed., p. xxxviii; Sneller, *op. cit.* p. 35.

conservative, like that of *Rhesus* itself: there are two resolutions, but both are caused by proper names.[1] If there is to be
any objection to these lines, it is that their expression is in
some places colourless and wooden. This is not altogether like
the ordinary style of the play itself, although there is at times
to be observed in *Rhesus* a certain baldness of expression (see
below, pp. 228 ff.). But the prologues of Euripides do at times
tend to become pedestrian.

If this prologue was a forgery, it was, to judge by this
fragment, a competent work by one well versed in Euripidean
diction. But it is difficult to judge from a few lines, and we
should hesitate to challenge the ancient verdict, which was
based on more complete evidence than we now possess.

Of the other prologue, of which only one line survives, even
less can be said. The line contains two rare words, which are,
however, compounds of a kind common in tragedy. There is
nothing to be said for Morstadt's argument that the line is at
variance with *v.* 534 of the play.[2] The right interpretation of
the latter verse is perhaps uncertain; at all events we can
hardly judge whether it agrees with our fragment of prologue
when this is itself not a complete sentence.

The view that *Rhesus* originally possessed an iambic
prologue, now lost, is strongly supported by the general
tendency of the evidence, both internal and external. If a
prologue has been lost, it will explain the lack of exposition,
for which there is certainly no parallel in extant tragedy, and

[1] The only notable metrical point is in *v.* 7, where the resolved syllable
Κύπριν violates two of the ten laws established by Zieliński in respect of resolution in iambic trimeter in Euripides' earliest works (before 425) (*Tragodumenon
Libri Tres* (1925), pp. 133 ff.; see below, pp. 267 ff.), namely (i) that both
syllables of a resolved long must be short by nature and not merely by 'weak
position'; (ii) that resolution is admitted only in words of three or more
syllables. The former law is broken once in *Rhesus* itself and a few times in the
early works of Euripides, notably twice in this name (in the genitive) in
Hippolytus; to the latter there are no exceptions in *Rhesus* and few in Euripides'
earliest period. In view of the licence admitted with proper names this one
metrical anomaly need not prevent us either from assigning these lines to
Euripides at any date or from associating them with *Rhesus*, which Zieliński has
shown to conform closely to Euripides' earliest metrical style.

[2] Morstadt, *op. cit.* pp. 72 f.

it may also have some relevance to various other objections which have been raised against the structure and management of the drama. The most important of these points have been discussed here.

THE ENTRANCE OF DOLON

It is uncertain when Dolon makes his appearance on the stage. Hector's appeal for a volunteer (149) is addressed to Τρώων οἳ πάρεισιν ἐν λόγῳ (ἐν λόχῳ LP). It is not clear to whom these words refer. At 154 the challenge is suddenly answered by Dolon, of whom nothing has previously been heard. Is Dolon already present on the stage when Hector makes his appeal and, if so, when and how has he entered? The explanations commonly proposed for this difficulty would involve departure from the normal technique of the tragedians.

Vater, reading λόχῳ in 149, believed that the Chorus was thus designated, and therefore that Dolon is brought in at the beginning of the play with the Chorus and speaks his part as a παραχορήγημα.[1] This supposition involves a mistaken interpretation of the use of the term παραχορήγημα. The extra performer occasionally so denoted by ancient commentators was not drawn from the Chorus but was provided by the χορηγός to supplement the normal number of actors;[2] we have no evidence that the members of the Chorus were ever called upon to play even minor speaking parts, let alone assume a major acting role. Further, it would be an extraordinary procedure to have Dolon present from the beginning among the Chorus, presumably in addition to the normal number, and to have him singled out only after 150 lines have elapsed.

Another solution is to suppose that there is present on the stage with Hector a λόχος of Trojan warriors, who are in

---

[1] *Vind.* II, §liv; cf. Morstadt, *op. cit.* p. 8 n. 1.
[2] Pickard-Cambridge, *Dramatic Festivals of Athens*, pp. 138 f.

attendance upon him.[1] These must be presumed to have entered earlier, either along with Hector himself, in answer to the summons of the watch, or with Aeneas, remaining when he departs (at 148). But again it would be irregular to have Dolon brought on as one of an anonymous body of this kind, to remain unidentified for so long after his entrance. A character might remain silent for some time after entering, but it is a different matter for his identity to remain concealed.[2] Although the dramatic circumstances might justify such a procedure here, it is not possible to find a parallel.

If this is thought to be a breach of dramatic convention, another explanation is possible and certainly no less likely. It may be that Dolon enters only after Hector has issued his proclamation, being supposed to have heard it from somewhere off stage. The conventions of Greek tragedy allowed that words spoken by an actor should be audible off stage when so required. Sometimes, for example, a character enters in answer to a summons from someone on the stage (e.g. *Hcld.* 646, *El.* 751, *Hel.* 437, *Ph.* 301, 1072, *Ba.* 172, 918); sometimes, without being summoned, a character appears, having overheard from within proceedings on stage (Sophocles, *OT* 634; Euripides, *Hcld.* 474). In the present passage the circumstances of the dramatic situation are to be taken into account. The scene is set in the Trojan camp, the stage itself representing the area immediately about Hector's bed. We are to imagine that the rest of the Trojan host is encamped all round in the immediate vicinity. That the events taking place on stage can be heard elsewhere in the camp is shown by the fact that both Aeneas and Paris enter after hearing the commotion about Hector's bed.

---

[1] So Menzer, *op. cit.* p. 44; Maykowska, *op. cit.* p. 47; Porter *ad loc.* From *v.* 26 it is rather to be inferred that Hector's λόχος is not close at hand, although he is evidently attended by some φίλοι.

[2] Clytemnestra's first entrance in Aeschylus' *Agam.* is therefore not parallel (see Denniston–Page on *vv.* 83 ff.); nor are the delayed first speeches of other persons in Attic tragedy, e.g. Prometheus in Aeschylus' *PV* and Adrastus in Euripides' *Su.*

We may therefore read οἳ πάρεισιν ἐν λόγῳ. Hector may address himself, for the sake of appearances, to the Chorus or to a band of Trojans on the stage, but his words may be taken to mean 'those who are within hearing of my words'. It is notable that his appeal is at first greeted by silence (as in Homer, K 313) and has to be repeated twice (151 and 152). Dolon would therefore have plenty of time to appear and to come forward before speaking.

The phrase recurs in Ar. *Av.* 30 ὤνδρες οἱ παρόντες ἐν λόγῳ, where in accordance with comic convention it is to be taken as designating the audience. For the way in which the phrase is used in *Rhesus* we may compare Sophocles, *Ichneutae* fr. 314 P., *vv.* 34–5, where Apollo says:

ὡς εἴτε ποι]μὴν εἴτ' ἀγρωστή[ρων τις ἢ
μαριλοκαυ]τῶν ἐν λόγῳ παρ[ίσταται.

Pearson translates: 'is at hand to hear my words'. Apollo is alone on stage and his words are addressed to all within hearing. Silenus and the Chorus enter in response, having heard the proclamation from a distance. Apollo, being a god, is audible far and wide. But this need not prevent our attaching to the phrase ἐν λόγῳ a similar significance in *Rhesus*, since Hector's words are required to be heard only in the near vicinity. It is even possible that Dolon enters from a tent represented by the stage building.

SILENCE OF HECTOR, 195–263

Hector does not speak during these lines, which include a short dialogue between Dolon and the Chorus (201–23) and a stasimon (224–63). There is nothing to indicate whether he simply stands inactive on the stage throughout this interval, or retires and then re-enters at the end of the lyric, his entry coinciding with the arrival of the Messenger.

Similarly, during the other stasimon (342–87) it is uncertain whether Hector remains on the stage.

For Wilamowitz this uncertainty was evidence of a clumsiness of technique which he deemed to be uncharacteristic of Euripides or of old tragedy.[1] A very different opinion has been expressed by W. Kranz, who, assuming that Hector does remain on stage during both the choral odes, sees in this one of several archaic features in the composition of the play.[2] Neither view is justified. In the first place, the presence of an actor on the stage during a choral ode is not by any means a peculiar characteristic of 'archaic' tragedy; there are instances in the works of all three tragedians. In Sophocles and Euripides the phenomenon is not confined to a few earlier plays, as Sneller supposes, but occurs in the great majority of their extant works.[3] Sometimes there is a realistic dramatic motive for the character's presence during the ode; he may, for example, be represented as a suppliant at an altar, as having fainted, as resting or as being asleep.[4] It is also quite common for a character who remains on the stage, with or without a special motive, to be addressed by the Chorus during their ode.[5] But quite often no attempt at all is made to overcome the awkwardness of having a character stand idle on the stage while an ode is sung.[6] This was clearly an accepted convention of fifth-century tragedy, in which the dramatist was not expected to preserve a realistic appearance.

---

[1] *Hermes*, LXI (1926), 287. [2] *Stasimon*, pp. 263 ff.

[3] Sneller, *op. cit.* p. 55. Examples occur in all extant plays of Euripides except *Ion* and *El.*, and perhaps *IT, Ba.* and *IA* (on which see below), and in all extant plays of Sophocles; see the following notes. I have not considered Aeschylus. Cf. A. Spitzbarth, *Untersuchungen zur Spieltechnik der eur. Trag.* pp. 51 ff., 75 f.

[4] Especially in Euripides, e.g. *Hcld.* 353 ff., 608 ff., *Hipp.* 525 ff., *Andr.* 117 ff., 274 ff., *Hec.* 444 ff., *Su.* 42 ff., 598 ff., *HF* 107 ff., *Hel.* 1107 ff., *Or.* 316 ff.

[5] Nearly all the Sophoclean instances are of this kind (*Ant.* 944 ff., *Tr.* 94 ff., *OT* 1086 ff., *El.* 472 ff., 1058 ff., *OC* 668 ff., 1044 ff.) and many in Euripides, especially in the earlier plays (*Alc.* 962 ff., *Med.* 410 ff., 627 ff., 824 ff., 976 ff., *Hcld.* 353 ff., 608 ff., 892 ff., *Andr.* 117 ff., 274 ff., *Su.* 42 ff., *HF* 107 ff., *Or.* 316 ff.).

[6] Certain examples include Sophocles, *Aj.* 1185 ff. (but Tecmessa is here represented by a κωφὸν πρόσωπον), *Ant.* 582 ff., *OC* 1211 ff.; Euripides, *Hcld.* 748 ff., *Hipp.* 1268 ff., *Hec.* 905 ff., *Tro.* 511 ff., 799 ff., 1060 ff., *Ph.* 784 ff.

Hector, however, is silent not only while a stasimon is being sung but also during a short passage of dialogue which immediately precedes. In this the poet might appear to be imposing a strain on the convention. But there is a parallel case in *Hcld.* 720–83, where Alcmene is silent during the dialogue between Iolaus and the Servant (720–47) and during the following stasimon (748–83). She is evidently present on stage all the time, for she has no pretext for retiring, and is addressed immediately at the end of the lyric passage by the Servant, who has just returned.

There are some other examples in Euripides of the long silence of a character who is present on the stage, notably Lycus (252–331) and Amphitryon (1214–1404) in *Heracles*, Creon (1356–1584) in *Phoenissae*, Adrastus (381–513, 513–734) in *Supplices*. In this last example the silence is dramatically justified, since Adrastus is a suppliant, and when, at 513, he does venture to speak, he is promptly silenced by Theseus. But in the other examples cited there is no motive for the silence.

Alternatively, Hector may withdraw at 195, perhaps to a tent (although the stage building is nowhere else needed for the action), returning after the stasimon. It need not be taken as a sign of inferior workmanship that there is no explicit reference to his movements. It is not true that Euripides always makes clear the entrances and exits of his characters. An ambiguity similar to the present one exists in some places in his works, of which the following are worth comparing:

(*a*) *Ba.* 370. In view of the outspoken censure of Pentheus which the Chorus expresses in the stasimon, it would seem more fitting that he should not be present during its delivery, and we might also infer from the closing lines of Tiresias' speech that he is already absent then. There is however nothing to indicate that he withdraws at the end of his speech (357) or at any subsequent point. If he does depart, he makes a prompt re-entry at the end of the ode, when he is addressed immediately by the newly arrived Servant. There is again no certain indication of Pentheus' departure at the end of the following scene (518), but here the subsequent action proves that he does retire.

(*b*) *IT* 391. It is possible, as some editors suppose, that Iphigenia retires into the temple, returning at the end of the ode. If this is so, it is not indicated by the poet.

(*c*) *IA* 542. There is no indication that Agamemnon leaves the stage before the stasimon, but it seems probable that he does, since he is apparently not on the stage at the beginning of the following scene (607 ff.). At least Clytemnestra and Iphigenia do not acknowledge his presence until 630, so that he might naturally be supposed to enter at this point. Here however the obscurity may well be due to interpolation at the beginning of the scene.

In[1] *Rhesus* it appears rather more probable that Hector remains on the stage during both stasima. At the end of each he is addressed immediately by a newly arrived character. If he has not been on the scene all the time, he is required to make a timely return. This would be no more realistic than to allow him to remain present throughout.[1]

Μετάστασις καὶ ἐπιπάροδος χοροῦ (564–674)

The departure and return of the Chorus in the course of the action must be included in a list of the unusual technical features of *Rhesus*, but should not of itself give cause for doubting the play's authenticity. It is indeed a comparatively rare phenomenon in Attic tragedy, but is known in five other plays, including three of Euripides. These are Aeschylus' *Eumenides* (231–44), Sophocles' *Ajax* (814–66), Euripides' *Alcestis* (746–861), *Helen* (385–515) and *Phaethon* (fr. 781 N.[2], 13–61). It therefore appears to have been

---

[1] Patin (*Euripide* (Paris, 1894), p. 335) felt that there would be some impropriety if the Chorus' unrestrained praise of Rhesus were uttered in Hector's presence; but the Chorus has already declared its feelings about Rhesus, and Hector has accepted him as an ally.

accepted from a period earlier than Euripides as an occasional device permissible when the handling of the plot required it.[1]

In both the *Eumenides* and *Ajax* the exit of the Chorus is associated with a change of scene. The Chorus justifies its departure by the pretext of pursuit (*Eumenides*) or search (*Ajax*). Both orchestra and stage are momentarily empty, then an actor enters and in monologue lets the audience realize that the scene has changed. The return of the Chorus follows.

In the three Euripidean examples the motive is different. The Chorus are removed, not in order to change the scene, which remains the same, but because their presence would be awkward for dramatic reasons. In *Alcestis* and *Helen* a scene takes place during the absence of the Chorus, of which it is essential that they should remain ignorant. The Chorus of *Alcestis* must not know of Heracles' promise to rescue Alcestis. In *Helen* Menelaus must reveal his identity to the audience but, for the sake of the subsequent recognition-scene, it is necessary that the Chorus as well as Helen should be unaware of it. In *Phaethon* the circumstances are only slightly different: here the Chorus share the knowledge of Phaethon's death, which Clymene wishes to keep secret from Merops. They must therefore be absent when he enters.

In *Rhesus* the motive behind the removal of the Chorus is again a dramatic one. The poet wishes to introduce the Greek spies on the stage and the absence of the Trojan guards must first be contrived. The way in which this device is used in *Rhesus* is thus quite consistent with the technique of Euripides in the three other places where it occurs. It is a somewhat bolder expedient than the brief μετάστασις of the Chorus necessary to a change of scene, which was employed by Aeschylus and Sophocles. We cannot, of course, say that the removal of the Chorus when their presence is dramatically undesirable is a peculiarly Euripidean licence. But we can

---

[1] On *epiparodos* in Euripides: Decharme, *op. cit.* 426–8; cf. Dale on *Alc.* 743. The *epiparodos* in *Phaethon* is discussed by Wilamowitz, *Hermes*, XVIII (1883), 408f.

say that *Rhesus* in this respect is fully in keeping with the practice of Euripides.

It may be added that the device is handled very adroitly by the poet of *Rhesus*. He provides a natural pretext for the departure of the Chorus by making them go to summon the relief watch. This purpose, however, is not carried out. It is the same body of guards which, having fallen in with the intruders, returns in pursuit of them.

THE EPIPHANY OF ATHENA, 595 FF.

The opponents of authenticity have not failed to observe the singular features of the scene in which Athena appears and guides Odysseus and Diomedes to the Thracian encampment, then protects them by practising deceit upon Paris. Arguments against Euripidean authorship have been found here on both technical and aesthetic grounds. From the point of view of dramatic technique the critics have taken exception to the employment of divine machinery in the middle of the play in order to direct the course of the action. This is very different from the introduction of a deity to speak the prologue or epilogue, and it has been held to be altogether contrary to the practice of the fifth-century tragedians.[1] The epiphany has also been criticized from an aesthetic standpoint. Gods, it is argued with the support of Aristotle, should be introduced only at the beginning or the end of the drama and should deal only with things which lie outside the action; the plot itself should not be advanced by means of an external divine agency. And so Athena has been condemned as a 'mischievous stage-puppet'.[2]

It must be allowed that technically the sudden intervention of Athena is a contrivance of a quite unusual kind for Attic tragedy. There is, however, certainly one comparable

---

[1] Among earlier scholars see, e.g., Beck, *op. cit.* pp. 269 ff.; Morstadt, *op. cit.* p. 48; Menzer, *op. cit.* p. 17; more recently Pearson, *CR*, xxxv (1921), 59; cf. Grube, *The Drama of E.* p. 439.

[2] Pearson, *CR*, xxxv (1921), 59; cf. Aristotle, *Poetics* xv.

instance in the extant works of Euripides, namely, the epiphany of Iris and Lyssa in *Heracles*.[1] The sudden appearance aloft of these two divinities, in the middle of the action (817), is no less startling than the similar entry of Athena in *Rhesus*, and it is in no less degree a use of divine machinery to forward the action of the plot. Moreover, the epiphany is equally a concrete one; for, although Iris and Lyssa do not engage in dialogue with humans, they are represented as actually visible to the members of the Chorus, who are thrown into consternation by the sudden apparition. Doubtless sophisticated minds in Euripides' day might have accepted Lyssa as a personified abstraction, a symbolical way of representing Heracles' fit of insanity, but Euripides by making her visible to other human beings has excluded this interpretation. We are bound to accept Lyssa literally as she is presented, as the agent of Hera, and to understand that we are witnessing a manifestation of the might of an Olympian deity.

Heracles is not the only play which has divine characters elsewhere than in the prologue and exodos. It is also relevant to mention here the *Eumenides* and the *Bacchae*. It is true that the part played by gods in these plays is much more fundamental to the action and therefore scarcely comparable to the sudden and capricious intervention of Athena in *Rhesus*. Nevertheless, they may cause us to ask where an Athenian audience of the fifth century would have begun to feel surprised or shocked at the sight of gods in converse with humans on the tragic stage. Some evidence concerning certain lost tragedies must also be taken into account. Plato objected to an Aeschylean scene, probably in the *Semele*, a play belonging to a Dionysiac trilogy, in which Hera appeared to the Chorus, consisting of servants of Semele, in the disguise of a priestess.[2] In the *Xantriae* of the same poet Lyssa was introduced, as a speaking character, in order to

---

[1] On this scene see Wilamowitz, *Herakles*, pp. 121–4.
[2] Fr. 168 (Pl. *Rep.* II, 381 D); attributed to *Semele* by K. Latte, *Philologus*, XCVII (1948), 47 ff.; cf. Lloyd-Jones, *Aeschylus* (Loeb, 2nd ed. 1957), II, 567 f.

produce frenzy among the followers of Dionysus;[1] and in the celebrated weighing-scene of his *Psychostasia* Zeus appeared presiding over the scales, while Thetis and Eos pleaded for the lives of their sons engaged in combat with one another.[2] We are told that this scene was enacted on the θεολογεῖον, and the play therefore apparently included besides human action which took place on the stage itself. It seems too that the play did not end with the weighing-scene, for in a later scene, after Achilles had slain Memnon, Eos bore aloft her son's corpse to ask of Zeus immortality for him.[3] This play thus appears to have depicted, in parallel fashion, conflicts on both the human and the divine planes, making liberal use of elaborate stage machinery.

It is clear then that the fifth-century tragedians did sometimes introduce gods in visible form in the body of the drama and show them directly influencing the course of human affairs. There is no clear line of distinction on technical grounds between the Athena-scene of *Rhesus* and these other examples of divine participation in the action of Attic tragedy. The latter by their very diversity ought to warn us against trying to lay down definite rules for the use of divine machinery in tragedy.

One or two detailed points of technique in the handling of the epiphany need to be considered. In the first place, we need not take it as evidence against an early date for the play that the θεολογεῖον is used in this scene and again for the Muse's appearance. Wilamowitz was mistaken in his view that this device was an invention of the 420's; for Pollux in defining the term cites as an example of its use the title-scene of the *Psychostasia* of Aeschylus, and as confirmation of this we have the further information that in this play Eos, bearing the body of Memnon, was raised aloft by means of

---

[1] Photius, *Lex.* p. 326, 22 ἐπιθειάζουσα ταῖς βάκχαις (Aesch. fr. 169).
[2] Plut. *Mor.* 17A; Nauck, *TGF²*, p. 88. Use of θεολογεῖον: Pollux, IV, 130; Pickard-Cambridge, *op. cit.* p. 46.
[3] Pollux, *op. cit.*

the γέρανος in order to beg Zeus to grant him immortality.[1]
There is no doubt that the mechanical devices of the tragic
stage were highly developed before the time of Euripides.

Wilamowitz also objected to the management of the epiphany, whereby Athena, although visible to the audience, is
supposed to be invisible to the actors on the stage.[2] But the
situation in this respect is less complicated than in the
prologue of *Ajax*, where Athena is not seen by Odysseus (15)
but is visible to Ajax (91), while the audience is asked to
imagine besides that the goddess has made Odysseus invisible
to Ajax (83–5). All this of course we readily accept as the
product of Athena's divine powers, but there is nevertheless
a heavier demand on our imaginations than in *Rhesus*,
especially as Athena in *Ajax* is evidently on the stage itself
and not above the level of the other actors on the θεολογεῖον.
The use of the θεολογεῖον, as Wilamowitz himself has pointed
out, simplifies the representation of divine invisibility.[3]

So much for the technical aspect of the scene. On the
aesthetic side one's verdict will be a matter of private taste,
but many will agree with Patin's opinion that the divine
intervention is natural and probable in the particular mythological context and in a plot which follows the *Iliad* closely.[4]
As we have already seen, the poet has derived from his epic
source the idea of introducing Athena at this point. In the
Doloneia she is protectress of the two Greek heroes in their
enterprise, sending them an omen as they set out (272 ff.),
actively helping in the subsequent events (366, 482, 507, 516),
and finally coming, invisible, to the side of Diomedes to warn
him to make good his escape (507 ff.). It is from this
momentary apparition that the dramatist has derived the
idea of introducing Athena, but, as we saw, he has altered
and expanded her role to accommodate it to his changes in
the plot. By making her convey to the Greek spies the

---

[1] Wilamowitz, *Herakles*, pp. 148 f.; cf. *Hermes*, LXI (1926), 287, and Schm.–St.
III, 705 n. 10. Pollux, *op. cit.*
[2] *Hermes*, LXI (1926), 287.   [3] *Herakles*, p. 149.   [4] Patin, *op. cit.* p. 341.

information about Rhesus, which can no longer be given by Dolon, he has succeeded in creating for her an essential function in the drama.

The poet would be open to censure for so using divine intervention to forward his plot, if his intention had been to keep the conflict of the tragedy entirely on the human plane. The Muse's speech at the end of the play makes it clear that this is not his purpose, that for him the human responsibility is overshadowed by the divine. The sufferings of men are to be traced back to the caprice of the gods; the human figures of the drama become little more than puppets subservient to the divine will. One is reminded of Euripides' treatment of his theme in *Hippolytus*. There the significance of the action as the result of conflict between divine wills is brought out in the prologue and epilogue, spoken by Aphrodite and Artemis respectively. In *Rhesus* the idea of divine responsibility is prominent in the closing scene. If however, as has been argued above, *Rhesus* originally had also a prologue spoken by a deity, this might have foreshadowed, among other things, divine participation in the subsequent events, and might have prepared the way for the appearance of Athena later in the play. Such a prologue would do much to soften the abruptness of Athena's entrance and allow us to appreciate the true meaning of her epiphany.

Some critics have been offended by the trick which Athena plays on Paris, regarding it as unbecoming to a goddess and inappropriate to tragedy.[1] But the behaviour of Athena is in keeping with her traditional character as it was known from Homer, and it is unlikely that an Athenian audience would have felt it to be out of harmony with its present context. Whether such divine conduct is proper for fifth-century tragedy is another question, which is best answered by referring again to the scene in the *Semele* of Aeschylus in which Hera appeared in disguise, and especially to the prologue of *Ajax*, where Athena is represented as practising deception

[1] E.g. Valckenaer, *op. cit.* p. 106; Menzer, *op. cit.* p. 17; Pearson, *op. cit.*

and as having visited Ajax with madness to punish a personal slight. The Sophoclean Athena may strike us as a more awe-inspiring figure than her counterpart in *Rhesus*, but this need not blind us to the fact that both poets are satisfied to depict her attributes and conduct essentially as they are in epic.[1] Nor does the treatment of the gods in certain Euripidean tragedies, for example *Hippolytus*, *Troades* and *Ion*, give us reason to expect from him a nobler conception of divine morality than we find in Homer.

THE INTRODUCTION OF PARIS, 642–64

The brief interlude in which Paris encounters Athena, besides being censured for its bad taste, has also been criticized as dramatically superfluous. Wilamowitz went so far as to say that Paris is introduced solely for the sake of the trick played on him.[2]

It is certainly unlike the customary technique of Euripides to introduce a character, especially so celebrated a figure of mythology as Paris, for so brief an appearance and in a part which, it must be admitted, is of no real consequence to the plot. The poet's purpose, however, is obvious enough and has been recognized by all but the most obstinate critics.

Paris is brought in principally as a means of filling the interval required for the murder of Rhesus off stage. According to the normal practice of Greek tragedy such an interval would be filled by the Chorus, either with an ode or in dialogue with an actor. Here, in the necessary absence of the Chorus, the poet has been obliged to contrive some other way of filling up time. In the introduction of Paris he has devised an admirable expedient. The main dramatic purpose is effectively served. At the same time a moment of suspense

---

[1] Some verbal resemblances between the Athena-scene in *Rhesus* and the prologue of *Ajax* were pointed out by Nock, *CR*, XLIV (1930), 173. These do not necessarily indicate imitation of the one by the other, but are a natural consequence of the general similarity of presentation.

[2] *Hermes*, LXI (1926), 287; cf. Morstadt, *op. cit.* p. 48; Norwood, *Greek Tragedy* (London, 1948), p. 293.

is added to sustain the level of excitement during the absence of the two Greeks. There is besides an opportunity to reveal Athena in action as the protectress of the Greek heroes, and thus to provide a visible demonstration of the divine control of events, which it is the dramatist's purpose to emphasize. That one of the Trojans should have been disturbed is natural enough. Paris is for several reasons an ideal choice: he is so well known that he needs no formal introduction; his traditional character fits him for this role and prepares the way for the particular trick that Athena plays on him; finally, it is in accordance with tradition that the goddess should practise her wiles upon one of the heroes rather than upon a mere servant. Needless to say, Aeneas, the calm and prudent counsellor, was out of the question for this purpose.

It is true that Paris makes an unusually fleeting appearance. But are we to say that Euripides would not have done something of this kind in similar circumstances? We have little opportunity to see how Euripides deals with such a situation. The Chorus is rarely absent from the scene and, when it is, it is not usually necessary to find an expedient for filling in time. In *Phaethon* however there is a small interval from the time when Clymene, together with the Chorus, enters the palace bearing the burning body of Phaethon before the fire takes hold within. This has to be filled in by action on stage and Euripides resorts to a device no less bold than that adopted in *Rhesus*. With Merops he brings on a subsidiary chorus of bridesmaids, who occupy the time with a wedding-hymn (fr. 781, 32 ff.). Although the introduction of a second chorus is known in other plays, its use in combination with a μετά-στασις χοροῦ illustrates the boldness with which Euripides handles technical difficulties.

THE FOURTH ACTOR, 642 FF.

From time to time it has been asserted that for the scene between Athena and Paris a fourth actor is needed, and this has been put forward as further evidence against the authenticity of the play. Although this view is discounted by most recent scholars, it was upheld by Wilamowitz and, following him, by Geffcken.[1] The question must therefore be examined.

If the scene is to be performed by three actors, the actor who plays Odysseus must also take the role of Paris. This appears to be possible. The scene is so managed that Odysseus may leave the stage at 626. In the following line Athena notices the approach of Paris, but he is, of course, still off stage and supposed to be not yet within the range of human vision, as Diomedes' question (630) makes clear. He does not actually enter until 642, the interval being filled in by dialogue between Athena and Diomedes, who goes off at 637, and a few lines of monologue by Athena. There is thus a space of sixteen lines for the change, and it looks very much as though Odysseus' exit is contrived earlier than that of Diomedes in order that he may have time to assume the mask and costume of Paris.

A slightly quicker change is required for the actor's return to the part of Odysseus. Paris can leave at 665 (the next two lines being spoken in his direction after he has actually left the stage). Odysseus presumably returns with the Chorus at 674, although his presence is not indicated until 677 (τοῦτον αὐδῶ). The change must therefore be made within nine iambic lines. In production however there would be room here for slight delay, which is indeed suggested in 673. A little confusion in the entrance of the Chorus would add to the delay.

Such swift changes of role are not common in Greek tragedy. I have not found anything comparable in Aeschylus or Sophocles. In Euripides however there are one or two possible instances of similarly quick change:

(i) *Alc.* 741–6. If the play is to be performed by only two

---

[1] Wilamowitz, *Einl.* p. 41 n.; Geffcken, *op. cit.* p. 396. Earlier exponents of this view include Menzer, *op. cit.* pp. 41 f., and Rolfe, *Harv. Stud. Cl. Phil.* IV (1893), 96. It is rejected by Vater (see below); Haigh, *Tragic Drama of the Greeks* (Oxford, 1896), p. 284; Porter, *Hermathena*, XVII (1913), 379; Sneller, *op. cit.* pp. 59 f., and others.

actors, he who plays Admetus must change during these six anapaestic verses to the part of the Servant. But time would be occupied here in the departure of the Chorus from the orchestra, no doubt in a slow procession.

(ii) *Med.* 204–13. Again if the play is to be performed by two actors, there is need of a quick change of role in the course of these ten lines of lyric. The actor playing the Trophos leaves the stage at 203 and must return at 214 as Medea. But the interval is filled by the Chorus with a song, which could be prolonged in performance.

(iii) *Ph.* 88–100. The Paedagogus addresses Antigone, who has not yet entered. He looks to see that all is clear before beckoning her on. The scholiast's note on 93 explains this as a device of Euripides in order that the protagonist, who speaks the prologue as Iocasta (exit 87), may reappear in the person of Antigone (enter 101). The explanation is doubtful, since Antigone and Iocasta are on the stage together later in the play (1270–82). The roles can be otherwise distributed without need for dividing any part between two actors or for any quick change. Perhaps actors altered the distribution, so that the protagonist might take Iocasta's prologue speech. The scholiast's note nevertheless indicates that twelve lines were thought sufficient to enable an actor to make the changes required for appearing as another character.

The change in *Phoenissae* would probably need to be quicker than in *Rhesus* or the other plays, for these involve movement or song of the Chorus, which would give scope for delay in the actual production. In *Rhesus* no great transformation would be needed. With a change of mask and different helmet and shield, Paris could become Odysseus in a matter of seconds.

I discard altogether the possibility that Athena does not appear at all but, as she is invisible to the other characters, speaks from behind the scenes.[1] Although quite commonly in Greek tragedy cries and short utterances are heard from

[1] Vater, *Vind.* II, §lvi n.

within, nowhere is a part of such magnitude spoken in this way. There would probably be considerable difficulty in making the voice audible. Further, the opportunity for spectacle offered by the appearance of Athena was not to be so tamely thrown away.

THE INTERCEPTION OF ODYSSEUS
BY THE CHORUS, 675–91

Although the point has not been adduced against the authenticity of the play, this short scene is technically of an unusual kind. Extant Greek tragedy contains only a handful of instances of physical contact between an actor and the Chorus, and it is still rarer for such an encounter to involve physical violence.[1] There appear to be only two comparable examples: the attempted seizure of the Danaids by the Egyptian herald and his attendants in the *Supplices* of Aeschylus (836–910), and the efforts of the Chorus in Sophocles' *Oedipus Coloneus* to prevent the arrest of Antigone (829 ff.), in the course of which they apparently lay hands upon Creon (856–7).[2] These two parallels, one belonging to a date before Euripides' first production and the other to a date near his last, make it reasonably certain that such treatment of the Chorus was admissible within the conventions of the tragic stage throughout his career.

It is perhaps worth observing here, with due caution, that the *Telephus* of Euripides, produced in 438, may have included a scene of a similar kind. One of the recently published papyrus fragments of that play shows the Chorus engaged in a search for Telephus, and it is possible that this was followed by a pursuit and encounter, just as in the *Acharnians*, which

---

[1] Haigh, *Attic Theatre*[3] (1907), p. 169, cites eight other instances of physical contact between actor and Chorus in tragedy; these include four in Euripides, of which one is doubtful (*Hel.* 1627 ff.) and another fairly certainly interpolated (*IA* 598 ff.). Some cases of supplication are perhaps to be added, e.g. *Med.* 853, *Supp.* 277, *Phoen.* 293, *IT* 1068 ff. (see Pickard-Cambridge, *op. cit.* p. 57).

[2] Add Euripides, *Hel.* 1627 ff., if the Chorus is the speaker; but there is a serious objection to this attribution (see Murray, O.C.T. *ad loc.*).

contains extensive parody of *Telephus*, the Chorus seeks and discovers Dicaeopolis (204–40), and finally comes to blows with him (280 ff.).[1] We have noticed already (p. 2) a verbal resemblance between the latter passage (280–3) and the passage of *Rhesus* under discussion; parody of *Rhesus* could not be established, but parody of *Telephus* is another possibility which cannot be excluded.

We might also compare the pursuit of Orestes by the Furies (*Eumenides*, 254 ff.), although this scene does not involve an actual physical encounter.

TWO-ACTOR THEORY:
EXIT OF THE CHARIOTEER, 878

Vater's theory that the play could be performed with only two actors is quite untenable.[2] In the first place, a space of seven lines or less (878–85) barely suffices for the change of character from the Charioteer to the Muse, especially as this would involve a complete change of costume and preparation for entry by machine. Further, the theory depends on the fantastic notion that Dolon's part is taken by a person from the Chorus, which, as we have already seen, would be quite without parallel. Vater would also have both Athena and Paris played by παραχορηγήματα, although the part of Paris could be played by the same actor as Odysseus. As we have already seen, the Athena-scene requires three actors, and it is a desperate resort to assign one or more of the parts to a παραχορήγημα. Vater's theory in fact rests upon an erroneous interpretation of the meaning of this term (see above, p. 113), and is plainly unworkable.

---

[1] See fr. 1 of the Oxyrhynchus papyrus text published by E. W. Handley and J. Rea, *The Telephus of Euripides*, Univ. of London Institute of Classical Studies, Bull. Supp. 5 (1957), pp. 1–3. The place of the fragment in the tragedy is discussed by Handley *ibid.* pp. 35 f. We cannot say whether the Chorus left the orchestra and returned, but the use of anapaestic dimeters at least suggests movement. The search in *Telephus* is further parodied by Aristophanes in *Thesm.* 598 ff., 655 ff., but the parody there does not extend to the discovery.

[2] II, § liii.

Vater was led to his conclusion that the play was intended to be performed by only two actors because he was unable otherwise to explain the poet's motive in making the Charioteer depart before the entry of the Muse. Why, after falsely accusing Hector of the murder of Rhesus, is the Charioteer removed forthwith instead of being kept on the stage to hear Hector exonerated from his charge by the Muse? In this matter Hagenbach too censured the poet for bad management.[1] There is however a sufficient dramatic reason for the removal of the Charioteer. It would indeed be un-realistic to keep a sorely wounded man on the scene for a long time, though this consideration would not be sufficiently important to risk marring the drama by taking him off pre-maturely. A more cogent reason for his removal is that in the following scene it is highly undesirable that the sympathy of the audience should in any way be distracted from the Muse. If the Charioteer remained present in his state of distress, the attention of the audience would almost inevitably be divided.

Too much importance should not be attached to the Charioteer or to his accusation. Suspicion of Hector is no-where suggested in the Charioteer's early speeches (see 739 f.), but occurs later (835) as a symptom of his delirious state of mind and in his incoherent final speech seems already to have passed from his mind. Clearly the charge is not taken seriously by anyone present, for the Chorus displays no reaction. This being so, the audience, who are in possession of the truth, need pay no heed to it. The Charioteer himself, finely drawn as he is, is nevertheless only a minor character and it is consistent with the practice of Euripides that there should be little interest in his fate after his main function has been performed. Certainly no one is to worry about him or his opinions after he leaves the stage. The important thing for the drama is that Hector and the Chorus should not be left in error about the events that have just taken place. The

---

[1] *De Rheso Tragoedia*, p. 25; more recently A. Lesky, *Gnomon*, XXIII (1951), 144.

Charioteer's accusation serves to illustrate the general state of ignorance and doubt, which it is left for the Muse to resolve, and its dramatic function is thus to prepare for the following scene.[1]

DEUS EX MACHINA: THE MUSE, 885 FF.

The drama is brought to a conclusion by the appearance of the Muse as *dea ex machina*. This is, of course, a thoroughly Euripidean device. Nevertheless, its use in *Rhesus* has sometimes been adduced as evidence against the view that the play is an early work of that poet.[2] The argument is ill-founded. The *deus ex machina* is used as early as *Hippolytus* (428). Only three of the extant plays are of earlier date. Of these *Alcestis* simply has no place for a *deus* in addition to Heracles; *Medea*, if it has no *deus ex machina*, at least has its dénouement effected by means of a spectacular μηχανή, and Medea herself is made to perform the prophetic function for which Euripides elsewhere uses a god; in *Heraclidae*, since Eurystheus is not to be rescued from the sentence of death, there is hardly scope for divine intervention, but Euripides ingeniously makes the doomed Eurystheus recall a prophetic oracle of Apollo.[3] The evidence is therefore far from proving that the *deus ex machina* was an invention of Euripides at a comparatively late date in his career, unlikely to have been used before the 420's. As for the placing of the goddess on the θεολογεῖον, we have already seen that there is no ground for the opinion that this device was a late invention, for it was used by Aeschylus.

The inspiration for the present scene may even have come from Aeschylus. In the *Psychostasia*, to which reference has already been made, there was a scene in which, by means of

---

[1] See now Strohm, *Hermes*, LXXXVII (1959), 262.

[2] Pearson, *CR*, XXXV (1921), 58; cf. Porter, *op. cit.* p. 1; Grégoire, *Ant. Class.* II (1933), 110.

[3] It is here assumed that nothing is missing at the end of the play (see p. 108 n. 3 above).

the γέρανος, Eos was raised aloft bearing the corpse of her son Memnon, in order to beg Zeus to grant him immortality.[1] A machine of this kind is evidently used in *Rhesus* (887 f.), and the general circumstances of the scene bear a strong resemblance to those of the scene in the *Psychostasia*. It seems that our poet may be consciously imitating Aeschylus, and, if this is not certain, we can at least say that this Aeschylean precedent would allow the present scene to be placed at any date in Euripides' career.

Even if the motive comes from Aeschylus, the manner of the divine epiphany is fully Euripidean. The goddess appears suddenly in motion above the heads of the company, her entry being greeted by cries of alarm from the Chorus:

> ἔα ἔα. ὢ ὤ.
> τίς ὑπὲρ κεφαλῆς θεός, ὦ βασιλεῦ,
> τὸν νεόκμητον νεκρὸν ἐν χειροῖν
> φοράδην πέμπει;
>   ταρβῶ λεύσσων τόδε πῆμα.

This is quite similar to the reaction of the Chorus in *Andromache*, when Thetis suddenly appears floating through the air (1226 ff.):

> ἰὼ ἰώ.
> τί κεκίνηται; τίνος αἰσθάνομαι
> θείου; κοῦραι, λεύσσετ' ἀθρήσατε·
> δαίμων ὅδε τις λευκὴν αἰθέρα
> πορθμευόμενος τῶν ἱπποβότων
> Φθίας πεδίων ἐπιβαίνει.

Compare also *Ion* 1549 ff.; *El.* 1233 ff.; *HF* 815 ff. In other plays the entry of the god is unheralded.

The use made of the *deus ex machina* in *Rhesus* conforms well to the dramatic practice of Euripides. Geffcken is very far from right in saying that the Muse is introduced solely to explain a cult and not, after the Euripidean manner, to

---

[1] See above, p. 122; resemblances between *Rhesus* and the *Psychostasia* were discussed by Buchwald, *Studien zur Chronologie* (Königsberg, 1939), p. 52.

clear up the situation.[1] This is to miss the significance of her speech. The Muse performs two main functions, both of which are commonly associated with Euripidean *dei ex machina*. One of these functions is essential to the drama, the other is concerned with matters lying outside it.

Within the drama the Muse is needed to reveal to Hector and the Trojans the true account of the events which have just taken place. This is done, not in the interests of the audience, who already know the truth, but solely for the benefit of the persons in the drama. To leave them in a state of ignorance or doubt would be contrary to the practice of Greek tragedy. The Charioteer's accusation of Hector, although not in itself of any account, does serve as a forceful expression of the fact that, despite the accurate surmises of the Chorus (692–721), no one is certain of the truth. And, since the facts can be revealed in no other way, the introduction of a divinity is indispensable.

This use of the *deus ex machina* to enlighten the characters of the drama is quite Euripidean. It is to be noted particularly in *Hippolytus* and *Ion*. In these plays, as in *Rhesus*, the chief persons of the drama are ignorant or doubtful of the facts of the situation, which cannot be made known to them otherwise than by divine agency.

The second function of the Muse, which is external to the drama, is to reveal the future destiny of Rhesus, particularly to identify the Rhesus of the tragedy with the Rhesus whose cult was known in Thrace, perhaps thereby giving the drama a special significance for a contemporary audience.[2] From this function is contrived the motive for the Muse's epiphany, for she enters to forestall the burial of Rhesus, which Hector has just ordered (879–81). The fate of Rhesus is not mentioned in the Muse's first speech, but Hector brings her to the subject by offering to accord Rhesus full burial honours. She thereupon ordains that Rhesus shall be returned to his native Thrace, there to dwell in a cave as ἀνθρωποδαίμων. This

---

[1] Geffcken, *op. cit.* p. 405.   [2] See further below, pp. 360–1.

prophecy is made with such detail and such certainty that it must relate to circumstances which were actually in existence when the play was written.

An aetiological interest of this kind is a regular ingredient of the speeches of Euripidean *dei ex machina*.[1] There is always a prophecy in which the events of the drama are connected with some existing rite or institution. For the prophecy of divine or heroic honours we may compare *Hipp.* 1423 ff. and *Andr.* 1253 ff.

In addition to these main functions, which are to be paralleled in the *dei ex machina* of Euripides, the Muse has another, subsidiary purpose in *Rhesus*. The introduction of the mother of the dead hero grieving for the loss of her son adds a measure of pathos, proper to the tragedy but which could not otherwise be given effective expression. The choice of the Muse as goddess is therefore a singularly happy one, since, at the same time as performing the dramatic purpose for which she is required, she evokes appropriate feelings of pity and indignation in the audience. It is worth noting that Euripides in a similar way sometimes chooses as his *deus* one who is closely related to the hero of the play, e.g. Thetis in *Andromache*, the Dioscuri in *Electra* and *Helen*. The ties of kinship provide a pretext for the divine intervention and help to save this type of ending from frigidity. *Rhesus* in this respect is certainly not the least successful of the plays in which a *deus ex machina* is used.

NIGHT-ACTION

Almost the whole of the action of *Rhesus* takes place by night. Although at 527 ff. the Chorus greets the approach of dawn, the subsequent action is still in darkness (see, e.g., 737), and it is only at the very end of the play that daylight appears (985). In the ancient theatre there was of course no artificial means of contriving darkness, plays being presented in the

[1] Schm.–St. III, 705 n. 7.

open air and in broad daylight; the audience is therefore required to imagine throughout that the action is taking place in the dark. It is a remarkable feature and one which some have found difficult to associate with a tragic poet of the fifth century. Wilamowitz, for example, included this in his list of the unusual features of *Rhesus*, from which he argued against its authenticity, and Norwood suggested that it might give grounds for supposing *Rhesus* to be the work of 'one of the ἀναγνωστικοί of the fourth century'.[1]

We know of no other tragedy whose action passes entirely in darkness. Quite commonly, however, the events represented in the prologue are supposed to take place early in the morning before dawn, there being some reference to the fact that it is dark or a later reference to the appearance of the dawn. The prologues to Aeschylus' *Agamemnon*, Sophocles' *Antigone*, Euripides' *Hecuba*, *Ion* (the speech of Hermes), *Electra* and *Iphigenia in Aulis* are of this kind, and those of Sophocles' *Ajax*, Euripides' *Alcestis* and *Troades* may well be imagined to take place before daylight. But *Rhesus* is the only extant tragedy in which the action after the prologue takes place in darkness.

Of plays now lost *Andromeda* and *Phaethon* certainly began in darkness. In the latter the Chorus welcomes the dawn in the parodos, but it may be supposed to remain dark for rather longer, since with the rising of the sun is associated the catastrophe of the play.[2]

It was thus clearly within the range of ancient dramatic convention to require the audience to imagine darkness, as well as the changing light of dawn. Is there any reason why the illusion should not, if required, be sustained for the whole play? It is not surprising that *Rhesus* is unique in this respect. There were few plots whose action needed to be confined to the night. It is known, however, that the plot of the *Lacaenae*

---

[1] Wilamowitz, *Hermes*, LXI (1926), 287; Norwood, *op. cit.* p. 293 n. 4 (despite this remark Norwood was inclined to accept *Rhesus* as genuine); cf. Sneller, *op. cit.* pp. 56 f.

[2] Wilamowitz, *Hermes*, XVIII (1883), 396 ff.

of Sophocles was concerned with the theft of the Palladium, which like the *Doloneia* was a nocturnal episode.[1]

In *Rhesus* the fact that it is night is vital to the action and must not be forgotten. But the dramatist is careful not to place too heavy a burden on the imagination of his audience. Special care is taken at the beginning, by means of frequent allusion, to stress that it is night, and there are constant reminders of the fact in the course of the play, especially when it is dramatically important.[2] After 825 there is no further mention of darkness, so that at the end we are quite prepared to accept that it is now day.

In this chapter an examination has been made of several alleged peculiarities and weaknesses of dramatic technique in *Rhesus*, in which arguments have been found against its authenticity. Investigation has proved the majority of these arguments to be groundless. Some derive from a mistaken or improbable interpretation of the scenic arrangements, and are removed by adopting a different and more likely view: these include the notion that a fourth actor is required, or that Dolon enters some time before his presence is noticed. In respect of other points, in which *Rhesus* has been supposed to diverge from Euripidean technique, it has been shown that similar phenomena occur in his works: among these are the silence of Hector, the epiparodos, the divine epiphany in the middle of the action. Furthermore, the use of the *deus ex machina* and the θεολογεῖον are not criteria against assigning the play to an early date in Euripides' career. If the brevity of Paris' appearance is exceptional, then so are the circumstances which occasion it, and it is the sort of expedient we might expect of Euripides in such a situation. Exceptional too is the fact that the entire action takes place by night, but

[1] A. C. Pearson, *The Fragments of Sophocles*, II, 34 ff. The action of the Φρουροί of Ion may also have taken place by night.

[2] At *vv.* 5, 13, 17, 19, 21, 42, 53, 55, 59, 64, 69, 87, 89, 92, 95, 111, 139, 146, 223, 226, 285, 289, 331, 518, 527 ff., 570, 571, 587, 600, 615, 617, 678, 691, 697, 727, 736 and 825. Note the use of such compounds as νυκτηγορέω, νυκτηγορία.

to imagine darkness was within the powers of a fifth-century audience, as single scenes of other plays prove. These miscellaneous matters of technique do not have, either individually or cumulatively, any significance for the question of authorship.

The only feature of the technique of *Rhesus* that is decidedly abnormal for Euripides is the absence of an iambic prologue and any kind of formal exposition. The evidence, however, both external and internal, gives strong cause for believing that the play originally possessed an iambic prologue, which has been lost.

APPENDIX

The two messenger-scenes of *Rhesus* have hitherto provided little material for the case against its authenticity. Indeed, even critics who deny that Euripides wrote the play have acknowledged that the narrative speeches of the Shepherd and the Charioteer are very much in his manner. Nevertheless, in a recent study of the play ('Beobachtungen zum *Rhesos*', *Hermes*, LXXXVII (1959), 257–74), H. Strohm has found here differences from the form and technique of Euripidean messenger-speeches, which he regards as evidence that they are the work of a different poet. His points must be examined briefly.

In the Shepherd's scene Strohm alleges two principal divergences from Euripidean technique:

(i) Euripidean messengers narrate events that are already complete and irrevocable, but this speech describes activity that is still in progress and lacks finality.

(ii) After his speech the messenger takes part in the pleas which the Chorus addresses to Hector.

But there are exceptions to (i) in Euripides, as Strohm himself admits, especially *Ba*. 660 ff. (cf. also *Alc*. 152–207); and Sophocles does not observe this 'rule' (cf. *Aj*. 719 ff.). As for (ii), the attribution of speeches in the dialogue following the Shepherd's narrative is in some doubt; but if the messenger does take further part, this has parallels in *Su.* 752 ff. and *Hel.* 700 ff., where the messenger's role is much more extensive. Moreover, Euripidean messengers often tender advice to their superiors (*Med.* 1121–3, *Hipp.* 1263 f., *IT* 336 ff., 1411 ff., *Ph.* 1259 ff., *Or.* 953, *Ba.* 769 ff., and, if genuine, *IA* 435 ff.).

In the treatment of the Charioteer's scene Strohm finds the following differences from Euripidean practice:

(i) The Charioteer is too closely involved in the events he narrates, and his speech becomes polemical.

(ii) There is no parallel for a messenger who brings not explanation, but confusion.

(iii) The way in which the messenger is introduced is unusual; in particular, there is no question from the Chorus to provide a motive for his narrative, so that he speaks, as it were, into the void.

In reply to (i) it may be pointed out that the Charioteer's accusation of Hector is quite separate from his narrative, being introduced only at the end of it (803), so that it does not affect its objectivity. It is misleading to say that this messenger brings only confusion. He conveys quite clearly the essential news of Rhesus' death and the manner of its accomplishment. He is as reliable an eye-witness as the circumstances permit; only a deity can reveal the whole truth. It is certainly curious that the Charioteer does not state his identity in reply to the Chorus' inquiry, and does not specifically acknowledge their presence; but, although not directly addressed, they provide an audience for his narrative and prevent its being a soliloquy. The poet's purpose is evidently to have the Charioteer deliver his narrative before introducing the charge of Trojan treachery.

The differences from Euripidean technique which Strohm finds in *Rhesus* are of an unimportant kind and are traceable to the special dramatic requirements of the particular situation. It may be broadly true that in his handling of conventional dramatic forms, such as the messenger's speech,

Euripides tends to adopt a stereotyped technique. But this does not allow us to define the rules governing his art in terms of his actual practice in the plays which we happen to possess. In fact, each play will be found to present some unique formal features. The dramatist does not work to set rules, but adapts his technique to the needs of his dramatic material.

CHAPTER IV

VOCABULARY AND SYNTAX

So far our examination of the internal evidence relating to the authorship of *Rhesus* has been confined to questions of dramaturgy. We may now turn to consider the evidence to be derived from the author's poetic art. In this category the main constituents are vocabulary, style and versification; it is also relevant to consider some characteristics of the play's formal structure, especially in the lyric parts.

It is appropriate to begin this part of our study with an analysis of the vocabulary of *Rhesus*, since it is in the poet's choice of words that we should expect any difference from the style of Euripides to be most readily discernible. It has to be determined whether in respect of vocabulary the poet of *Rhesus* conforms to the normal usage of Euripides. This might appear to be a relatively easy question to decide; for we possess eighteen plays of Euripides of which the authorship is undisputed, as well as fragments of his other works amounting to over three thousand lines, and can thus claim a reasonable acquaintance with his style and vocabulary. But while it is easy enough to observe resemblances and differences between *Rhesus* and the other works of Euripides, it is by no means so easy to assess their significance. It is as well to notice at the outset the factors which hinder a clear interpretation of the evidence, and the caution which must therefore be observed in drawing conclusions from it.

In the first place we cannot claim to know the whole vocabulary of Euripides. We possess altogether, including the fragments, rather less than a quarter of his total output. Although this is sufficient to enable us to determine many characteristic qualities of his diction and to observe a preference for certain words, we are obviously not justified in claiming that a particular word is not Euripidean simply because it does not happen to be found in his extant works.

Secondly, our limited knowledge of Attic tragedy apart from Euripides makes it extremely difficult to find a standard against which to measure the importance of similarities and differences that we may note between *Rhesus* and other works of Euripides. The only other tragedians of whom we have any detailed knowledge are Aeschylus and Sophocles, and we possess only a small fraction of their work. We cannot claim a thorough knowledge of the vocabulary of either of these poets, nor can we always decide which words are to be thought especially characteristic of one poet and which belong to a common stock of tragic language.

Thirdly, it is essential to take notice of both sides of the evidence: to determine on the one hand what proportion of the vocabulary is to our knowledge foreign to Euripides, on the other hand whether the vocabulary shows any characteristic marks of the Euripidean style. Concentration on the one side to the exclusion of the other could produce a distorted impression.

Fourthly, in considering the evidence of vocabulary it is unsafe to base any conclusions on selected material. It is only by exhaustive analysis that reliable results are likely to be achieved. Further, the significance of any such analysis we may make of the vocabulary of *Rhesus* is only to be determined by comparison of a parallel and equally complete analysis of the vocabulary of other works of Euripides.

Finally, comparative analysis of this kind inevitably involves the reduction of evidence to a statistical form. In assessing the value of such evidence it is important not to attach too much significance to the figures alone, especially when these are based on a total knowledge which is so incomplete. We must always consider the quality of the particular words on which the statistics are based.

These observations have been made here with particular reference to the study of the evidence of vocabulary, but most of them are also relevant to other aspects of the investigation into the internal evidence. They are to be kept in mind at all stages of the present inquiry.

Many scholars in the past have attempted to derive evidence from the vocabulary of *Rhesus* for the question of its authorship, but the majority of them have failed to observe these precautions. Too often conclusions have been based upon an arbitrary selection of evidence. Valckenaer contended that *Rhesus* contained more peculiarities of diction than all the other works of Euripides together, but in proof of this claim he was content to cite only a few chosen examples. Later critics, notably Hermann and Hagenbach, accumulated larger collections of words and phrases, which were adduced as evidence of a grandiose style foreign to Euripides and of imitation of all three tragedians. There was however still no attempt to prove the case by a detailed study of the vocabulary. Only two previous examinations of the vocabulary of *Rhesus* have made a significant contribution to our question, and these alone deserve serious attention. They are the studies of J. C. Rolfe (1893) and L. Eysert (1891–3) (see the Bibliography below, p. 363). These two scholars alone have undertaken a thorough analysis and have not merely used a random collection of evidence to support a preconceived opinion. The treatment of the evidence to be presented here, although substantially a fresh one, to some extent follows the lines laid down by Rolfe and Eysert, and it will therefore be useful to review briefly their methods and results.

Rolfe sought to make a comprehensive collection of the rarer vocabulary of *Rhesus*, which he classified in lists of ἅπαξ λεγόμενα, ἅπαξ τραγῳδούμενα and of words shared by *Rhesus* with only one of the three tragedians. He collected besides words shared by *Rhesus* with two of the three tragedians, except that he omitted to compile a list of words found otherwise in Sophocles and Euripides, but not in Aeschylus. As a result of this omission there was a lack of balance in his presentation of the evidence, and he was led to the conclusion, which a fuller inquiry would have shown to be unsound, that the poet of *Rhesus* displays a marked tendency to imitate Aeschylus. An equally important fault in Rolfe's method was his failure to test the significance of his statistics for *Rhesus* by making a corresponding analysis of other works of Euripides.

The work of Eysert is of much greater importance. It is divided into two parts, the first dealing with the rarer words and phrases of *Rhesus*, the second with peculiarly or characteristically Euripidean elements in its vocabulary. With the latter, which is the only treatment of that aspect of the evidence, I shall deal more fully below. The main conclusions of the first part of Eysert's investigation were the following:

(*a*) ἅπαξ λεγόμενα. Eysert determines the total number of such words for each of the plays of Euripides, and also the frequency of their occurrence (per 100 verses). His total for *Rhesus* is 28, and this is found to be exceeded in five plays, *Phoenissae* (40), *Ion* (36), *Iphigenia in Tauris* (32), *Iphigenia in Aulis* (32), *Bacchae* (31), and equalled in *Heracles*. On the other hand, according to Eysert's figures the percentage frequency of 2·81 for *Rhesus* exceeds that of any other play except *Cyclops* (3·1). But the corresponding figures for *Iphigenia in Tauris* (2·34), *Phoenissae* (2·27), *Bacchae* (2·23), *Ion* (2·22) are so close that little importance can be attached to the position of *Rhesus* in this table.

(*b*) *Voces Euripideae* κατ' ἐξοχήν. Eysert lists 74 words which are found in Euripides more than once but in no other Greek author: of these eight occur in *Rhesus* (see my list VIII below and the comments there).

(*c*) ἅπαξ τραγῳδούμενα. From this classification Eysert excludes words found in verse before Euripides, unique forms and senses of words which are not themselves unique in tragedy, and adverbs when the corresponding adjective occurs in tragedy. With these omissions he arrives at a total of 54 ἅπαξ τραγῳδούμενα for *Rhesus* (5·42 %). An analysis of *Bacchae* produces 103 such words (7·40%).

(d) *Imitation of Homer.* Eysert lists 55 words and forms from *Rhesus* which are found in Homer but are uncommon in Attic. Only six of these are not found elsewhere in Attic tragedy. By comparison he finds 12 Homeric expressions peculiar in Attic to *Phoenissae* and 14 peculiar to *Cyclops.*

(e) *Borrowings.* Eysert considers lists made by Hagenbach of words and phrases in *Rhesus* supposedly reminiscent of Aeschylus and Sophocles. Of the words in Hagenbach's collection only six are found to be otherwise peculiar in tragedy to Aeschylus and 14 otherwise peculiar to Sophocles. (Compare my lists III and IV below.)

Nothing of value has been added to Eysert's results by subsequent writers. The opponents of authenticity have for the most part been content with the repetition of a few acknowledged rarities, while others, including Sneller, have taken the results of Eysert as a basis for further discussion. Only Pearson (*CR*, xxxv, 1921) attempted to break new ground by comparing the frequency with which certain neutral words, prepositions, pronouns, particles, etc., occur in *Rhesus* and in an equivalent number of lines of *Alcestis.* In several instances, for example in the occurrence of the words ἄν, ὅς, ἐγώ, γε, ἔτι, ἐκεῖνος, δή and δῆτα, he discovered a quite wide divergence between the two plays. But in order to determine whether this had any significance it would be necessary to carry out a similar analysis for several other plays of Euripides. There would not at first sight appear to be any reason for expecting such words to occur with constant frequency. In fact they do not, as is proved, for example, by a count of the occurrences of ἐκεῖνος in various plays of Euripides, as they are listed in the *Concordance.* This word occurs as follows: in *Rhesus* twice, in *Alcestis* 14 times, *Medea* 9, *Hippolytus* 6, *Andromache* 17, *Heracles* 4, *Orestes* 19, *Bacchae* 9. *Rhesus* indeed has the smallest number, but even allowing for differences of length there is no approach to constancy among the other plays, and we may add that two of the four instances in *Heracles* are within the last twenty lines of the play. This random example seems to be sufficient to discredit this type of evidence, and it certainly does not encourage the pursuit of further inquiry along these lines.[1]

In the first part of the present survey the method adopted by Rolfe is followed and a collection made of all that part of the vocabulary of *Rhesus* which is not found in all three tragedians. Rolfe's failure to include a list of words occurring in Sophocles and Euripides, but not in Aeschylus, has been rectified, and his lists of words in the various other classes have been substantially amended. In order to determine the value of the statistical data thus obtained a parallel analysis has been made of the vocabulary of three plays of Euripides, chosen from different periods of his career, *Medea* (produced in 431), *Troades* (415) and *Bacchae* (406). This evidence should enable us to answer two important questions:

(i) Whether the vocabulary of *Rhesus* stands in the same relation to the vocabulary of Euripides as does that of other single works of Euripides;

(ii) Whether there is any substance in the allegations of deliberate imitation of one or more of the three tragedians.

The analysis of *Rhesus* and the other three plays leads to the comparative table opposite.[2]

These statistics cover for each play all words which are not otherwise common to all three tragedians, and thus enable us to study the relation between the vocabulary of each play and the vocabulary of each of the tragedians, and to compare one play with another in this respect. It is clear that the statistics expressed in percentage form offer a more reliable basis for

---

[1] Further proof of the unreliability of this type of evidence is provided by Sneller, *De Rheso Tragoedia*, pp. 70 f.

[2] In preparing the evidence presented in this table and throughout this chapter the following authorities have been used: for Euripides, Allen and Italie, *A Concordance to Euripides* (1954); for Aeschylus, G. Italie, *Index Aeschyleus* (1955); for Sophocles, F. Ellendt, *Lexicon Sophocleum* (1867–72), and A. Nauck, *Tragicae Dictionis Index* (1892), supplemented by Index 1 to *Oxyrhynchus Papyri*, vol. IX and by perusal of other fragments published later than Nauck. Some doubtful occurrences of words have not been counted. The new tragic fragments in *Oxyrhynchus Papyri*, vol. XXVII, are not taken into account (but see p. 150 n.).

A. Numerical totals	Rhesus	Medea	Troades	Bacchae
ἅπαξ λεγόμενα	27	7	27	29
⌠ἅπαξ τραγῳδούμενα	68	38	60	119
⌡Incl. first occurrence*	39	21	33	75
Found elsewhere in Tragedy:				
In A. only	23	28	15	24
In S. only	20	13	14	24
A. S. only	21	14	10	13
A. E. only	84	88	102	106
S. E. only	86	126	120	141
⌠E. only	89	102	139	190
⎱Incl. first occurrence				
⌡ in E.	33	27	41	71
Not found in A.	290	286	360	503
Not found in S.	291	263	343	468
Not found elsewhere				
in E.	159	100	126	209

B. Frequency per 100 verses†	Rhesus (996 vv.)	Medea (1419)	Troades (1332)	Bacchae (1392)
ἅπαξ λεγόμενα	2·7	0·5	2·0	2·1
ἅπαξ τραγῳδούμενα	6·8	2·7	4·5	8·7
A. only	2·3	2·0	1·1	1·7
S. only	2·0	0·9	1·05	1·7
A. S. only	2·1	1·0	0·75	0·9
A. E. only	8·4	6·2	7·7	7·6
S. E. only	8·6	8·9	9·0	10·1
E. only	8·9	7·2	10·4	13·7
Not found in A.	29·0	20·2	27·0	36·1
Not found in S.	29·1	18·5	25·7	33·6
Not found elsewhere				
in E.	15·9	7·0	9·5	15·0

* These totals include words otherwise first occurring in Thucydides or in Aristophanes, unless in a play certainly earlier than the first occurrence in Euripides. For the sake of comparison the date of *Rhesus* is here taken as earlier than 425.

† These percentages are based on the figures of the preceding table, i.e. on the number of words in each class and not on the number of separate occurrences. In calculating the frequency with which the words of each class occur one ought strictly to take account of repetitions, but it would not in any instance significantly affect the figures.

10-2

comparison than the absolute totals, but it is nevertheless useful to have in mind at any time the actual number of words involved. For example, although *Rhesus* yields here the highest percentage of ἅπαξ λεγόμενα, it has no more words in this class than *Troades* and two fewer than *Bacchae*.

Some salient features of the percentage table are to be noted. It is remarkable that *Bacchae* tends to yield higher figures than *Troades*, and *Troades* higher than *Medea*. The plays occupy this order in all but two of the sets of figures. The chief exception is in the figures for words found otherwise in Aeschylus alone of the tragedians, *Medea* having here a higher percentage than either of the other works.

It would not however be safe to infer from these figures that the number of rare words used by Euripides increased progressively as he got older. Indeed it would be surprising to find anything like a steady rate of increase in the number of words in any one of the classes considered here, let alone in all or several of them. We may in part at least attribute the pattern of the figures to chance. One reason for the high totals yielded by *Bacchae* is to be found in its subject-matter. The low figures for *Medea* are perhaps partly due to the fact that it has a lower proportion of lyric verses than the other two plays; for in Euripides uncommon words certainly occur with markedly greater frequency in the lyric parts.[1]

Thus these statistics do not provide a criterion for dating, and we should not expect to be able to use them to fix even approximately the date of another work of Euripides relative to the three plays examined.

This point is relevant, since it is immediately apparent that

---

[1] For the plays under consideration J. Smereka, *Stud. Eurip.* 1, 46, gives the total numbers of lines of spoken dialogue and lyric (including anapaests) respectively as follows: *Rh.* 688, 308 (2·23:1); *Med.* 1051, 368 (2·86:1); *Tro.* 824, 508 (1·62:1); *Ba.* 969, 423 (2·29:1). The greater frequency of rare words in the lyric parts is shown by Smereka's figures (*ibid.* p. 239) for ἅπαξ λεγόμενα for all plays of Euripides. (He includes in this class all words occurring only in Euripides, including those used by him in more than one play.) These occur as follows: 380 in 21,850 lines of dialogue, or 1 in 57·5 lines; 321 in 7,909 lines of lyric, or 1 in 31 lines.

while the order of the other three plays remains the same for nearly all the sets of figures, *Rhesus* has no fixed position in relation to this tendency. Its percentage is sometimes the highest of all, sometimes the lowest and sometimes it lies between the extremes.

But nowhere do we find that *Rhesus* yields a figure of a vastly different order from the corresponding ones for the other plays. Although its percentage total is in several instances at one extreme or the other, it is regularly found that one or the other of the three Euripidean plays stands fairly close to it. Thus *Rhesus* has 2·7 ἅπαξ λεγόμενα in every 100 verses, but this is not far in excess of *Bacchae* with 2·1. Eysert's calculations already mentioned (p. 144) show that in fact there are other plays of Euripides even closer to it. Similarly, the frequency of words not otherwise occurring in Euripides is in *Rhesus* 15·9 per 100 verses, but *Bacchae* again approximates closely to this figure with 15·0. The biggest difference from the other plays is seen in the frequency of words found otherwise only in Aeschylus and Sophocles of the tragedians; but here the total number of words for each play is very small.

Thus the statistical material does not appear to contain any significant evidence against the authenticity of *Rhesus*. The figures do not reveal any remarkable divergence from the normal Euripidean vocabulary. If one or two particular points still seem worthy of note, we should be cautious in interpreting their significance. An inference drawn from one set of figures may be contradicted by another set, for example:

(i) *Rhesus* has a higher percentage than the other plays examined of words which otherwise occur in tragedy in Aeschylus only, in Aeschylus and Sophocles only, or in Aeschylus and Euripides only. This might lead to the inference, which was in fact made by Rolfe, that the poet was striving consciously to imitate Aeschylean diction. But at the same time *Rhesus* has a higher percentage of words *not* found in Aeschylus than either *Medea* or *Troades*..

(ii) *Rhesus* has the highest percentage of words not occurring elsewhere in Euripides. Although it only slightly exceeds *Bacchae* in this respect, the fact might be taken as an additional point against its authenticity. But against this figure must be balanced the fact that *Rhesus* does not fall short of the other plays in the frequency of words which otherwise occur in Euripides alone of the tragedians.

These two examples illustrate the danger of attaching too much importance to isolated pieces of statistical evidence. It is only the overall picture presented by the statistics that needs to be taken into account, and this contains no apparent evidence against the authenticity of *Rhesus*.

Enough has been said of the statistics. We may now proceed to examine the vocabulary of *Rhesus* in each of the classes for which totals have been given above.

1. ἅπαξ λεγόμενα (TOTAL 27)

909	ἀριστότοκος	215	δίβαμος[1]	304	ἐξαυγής
327	ἐπίμομφος (act.)			515	θοιναυτήριον
260	κακόγαμβρος	349	καλλιγέφυρος	817	καρανιστής
964	καρποποιός	33	κερόδετος	534	μηνάς
552	νυκτίβρομος	363	οἰνοπλάνητος	965	ὀφειλέτις
361	πανημερεύω	716	πολυπινής	361	προπότης
273	προσαύλειος	296	προὔξερευνητής		
712	ῥακόδυτος	134	ταχυβάτης	5	τετράμοιρος
3	τευχοφόρος	9	φυλλόστρωτος	921	χρυσόβωλος
340	χρυσοτευχής	716	ψαφαρόχροος		

I have included ἐπίμομφος used in an active sense, which Eysert classified as ἅπαξ τραγῳδούμενον. The word is used in a passive sense by Aeschylus, *Ag.* 553 (cf. *Ch.* 831), but the active sense which appears here is unique. Porter (on *Rh.* 327) compares ἐπίφθονος, which is active in Aeschylus, *Ag.* 135, passive in *Ag.* 931 and in *Rh.* 334.

Eysert's total of 28 ἅπαξ λεγόμενα in *Rhesus* is made up by two words which may now be excluded from this category:

---

[1] δίβαμος occurs in a new fragment of Euripides, *P. Oxy.* 2461, 1, 15.

(i) 417 ἄησις. This word is now read in Euripides, *Phaeth.* 288 Volmer (= fr. 781, 46), and is cited by Photius ed. Reitzenstein (1907), s.v., as occurring in Euripides, *Alcmaeon.* It is therefore recorded below in my list VIII.

(ii) 737 ἀμβλώψ. In Photius ed. Reitz. this word is cited from Euripides, *Thyestes* (ἀμβλῶπας αὐγὰς ὀμμάτων ἔχεις σέθεν), Ion Trag., Sophocles (= fr. 1001) and Plato Com. It is accordingly placed in list VII.

The fact that these two words are now known to have been used by Euripides provides an apt illustration of the extreme uncertainty of rare words as evidence for the question of authorship. Formerly part of the evidence against authenticity, these two words are now a not insignificant addition to the evidence for the opposite case.

The remaining ἅπαξ λεγόμενα are, for the most part, unimportant. Some words barely qualify for inclusion, e.g.:

ἀριστότοκος	H. *Il.* XVIII, 54 has δυσαριστοτόκεια.
καρανιστής	A. *Eu.* 186 has καρανιστήρ in the same sense.
ὀφειλέτις	S. *Aj.* 590 has masc. ὀφειλέτης in the same construction (ὁ. εἶναι + infin.).
προὐξερευνητής	E. *Ph.* 92 has προὐξερευνάω, which is found also in Aeneas Tacticus.
θοινατήριον	Cited by Hesych. in the form θοινητήριον. θοινατήρ occurs in A. *Ag.* 1502, θοινάτωρ in E. *Ion* 1206, 1219. Cf. εὐνατήριον (A. *Pers.* 160, S. *Tr.* 918, E. *Or.* 590), νυμφευτήριον (ἅπ. λεγ. in E. *Tr.* 252).

A little more curious is μηνάς = μήνη, which is itself rare in tragedy, occurring only at Aeschylus, *PV* 797 and Euripides, fr. 1009. Similar pairs, both being found in tragedy, are Μαιάς = Μαῖα, πελειάς = πέλεια. Compare also οἰνάς (Ion Eleg.) = οἴνη (Hes., Euripides).

The rest are simply formed compounds, of which δίβαμος is perhaps the most striking. Compounds in -βάμων are more frequent, but we may compare παλίμβαμος (Pi. *P.* IX, 18), χορταιόβαμος = χορταιοβάμων (Trag. adesp. 601).

τευχοφόρος occurs in anapaests; at 267 in ia. trim. the

form is τευχεσφόρος, which is found also in Aeschylus, *Ch.* 627 (lyr.), Euripides, *Su.* 654.

Of the others several, e.g. καλλιγέφυρος, ῥακόδυτος, τετράμοιρος, φυλλόστρωτος, χρυσόβωλος, are appropriate to the particular context in which they occur and it is hardly surprising if they do not occur again. It may be added that Euripides is especially fond of compounds in καλλι- (Smereka I, 136), including many of his own coinage which do not recur (*ibid.* p. 163), χρυσο-, and with numeral prefixes. The list of ἅπαξ λεγόμενα for all plays of Euripides contains a very high proportion of compound adjectives.[1]

If *Rhesus* has a slightly higher proportion of ἅπαξ λεγόμενα than other plays of Euripides, the quality of the words is such as to render this fact quite unimportant.

II. WORDS OCCURRING AGAIN OUTSIDE TRAGEDY, BUT NOT FOUND ELSEWHERE IN TRAGEDY (ἅπαξ τραγῳδούμενα) (68)[2]

(a) In Homer (14)

514	ἀναπείρω	Hdt., Ar., etc.
348	ἀσπαστός	Hdt.
232	δέμω	Hdt., Pl., Theoc., A.R.
525	δέχθαι (form)	
100	ἐπιθρῴσκω	(θρῴσκω A., S., E.)
97	εὔσελμος	Cj. for εὔσημος in E. *IT* 1383 (uncertain).
804	ἡνίοχος	Sappho, Pi.
740	κοῖτος	Hes.
881	λεωφόρος	Prose; diff. sense in Anacreon, *P. Oxy.* 2321, i, 13.
629	μέμβλωκα	Callim.
509	μέρμερος	Hes., Pl., later.
797	πρηνής	Hes., Hp., later prose.

[1] The ἅπαξ λεγόμενα for all plays of Euripides are collected by L. Eysert, *Rh. im Lichte des eur. Sprachgebrauches* (1891), I, 10 ff.; also by Smereka, *op. cit.* pp. 154 ff. (see p. 148 n. 1).

[2] In this and the following lists there is recorded for each word a representative, though not necessarily complete, collection of other authors in whose works it occurs.

683	σήμερον	Pi., Comedy (cf. E. fr. 698 = Ar. *Ach.* 440–1).
744	τολυπεύω = *accomplish*	Cf. ἐκτολυπεύω Hes., A. *Ag.* 1032.

(b) *In verse before Euripides* (3)

358	ἐλευθέριος	Epithet of Zeus, Pi. *Ol.* XII, 1.
382	πολίαρχος	Pi.
701	σπορός	Pi., Hdt. and prose.

(c) *In fifth-century prose or Old Comedy* (24)

761	ἀβούλως	Hdt., Antiphon, Pherecr.; ἄβουλος S., E.
588	ἀκινδύνως	Antiphon, Th.; ἀκίνδυνος E.
814	ἄπληκτος	Eupolis, Pl.
25	ἀφυπνίζω	Cratinus, Pherecr., Plu.
234	διόπτης	Ar. *Ach.* 435; Dio Cass. διοπτήρ *Il.* K 562.
604	εἰσδρομή	Th. once; Josephus
139	ἐκκλησία	Hdt., Th., prose and Comedy
322	ἐξώστης	Hdt., Hp., Aeschin.; ἐξωθέω S., E., cf. esp. *Cy.* 279.
195	ἐπινοέω	Hdt., prose.
942	ἐπιχράομαι	Hdt., Th., Pl. (w. personal obj.; w. inanimate obj., as here, otherwise later).
553	κατακούω	Hdt., Th., Ar. *Ra.*, Pl., etc.
318	κατάντης	Ar. *Ra.*, Hp., X., Arist.
446	κυβεύω	Cratinus, Ar.
550	μελοποιός	Ar. *Ra.*, Pl., later; here only adj.
789	μυχθισμός	Hp., and late.
136 *et passim*	ναύσταθμον	Th. only; in later prose ναύσταθμος.
830	παράκαιρος	Epicharmus, Men.; παρακαίριος Hes.
311	πελταστής	Th., Lys., X., inscr.
6	προκάθημαι	Hdt., Th., X., later prose.
210	πρόσθιος	Adj. of *forefeet*, Hdt. and prose, Ar.
503	πτωχικός	Ar. *Ach.* (? from E. *Telephus*), Pl., later prose.
64	ῥύμη	Th., Ar., Hp., X.
613	συναθροίζω	Ar. *Lys.*; 4th-c. prose.

364 ὑποδέξιος   Hdt. (ἐπιδέξιος, conjectured here, is also ἅπ. τραγ., occurring in H., Comedy).

(d) In fourth century (11)

177, ? 466 ἀποινάομαι   Act., *lex ap.* Demos.; med. here only.

401, 936 γερουσία   = *embassy* here only (cf. πρεσβεία); = *council* of elders, esp. that at Sparta, D. and later (cf. γερωχία Ar. *Lys.* 980).

176 γεωργέω   Ar. *Eccl.*; 4th-c. prose.

492 ἐντάσσω   = ἀντιτάσσω here only; but verb used by X., military writers.

496 εὐδοξέω   X., D.; but E. has εὐδοξία, εὔδοξος, ἀδοξέω.

205, 512 κλωπικός   Pl. *Crat.* 408 A only; κλώψ is found in tragedy in E. only (list VIII (c) below).

923 μελῳδία   Pl. and later; μελῳδός E.

233 ναυκλήριον   D., Plu., later; ναύκληρος A., S., E.; ναυκληρία S., E.

19 νυκτηγορία   Arist., Libanius; νυκτηγορέω (*Rh.* 89) found in A. (list III below).

166, 821 πολίοχος   πολιάοχος, πολιοῦχος as cult-title in Pi., A., Hdt., Ar., etc.; this form found in inscriptions (*RE*, s.v. Poliochos) and as proper name (Athenaeus).

523 προταινί   προτηνί in Boeot. inscr. from 4th–3rd B.C.

(e) Later than fourth century B.C. (16)

500 ἀηδονίς   Callim., Theoc., *A.P.*

971 ἀνθρωποδαίμων   Procopius (*c.* 6th c. A.D.); cf. βροτοδαίμων· ἡμίθεος Hesych.

900 ἀπομέμφομαι   Josephus, Plu.

288 αὐτόρριζος   Diod. Sic. (diff. sense).

75 γαπονέω   Philo (γεωπονέω); for γα- in comp. in Trag. cf. γαπόνος E., γαμόρος A., γάπεδον A., γαπετής E.

374 δίβολος   *A.P.*, inscr.; διβολία Ar.

811 ἐξαπωθέω   Late; with form ἐξαπώσατε cf. ἀπῶσε S. fr. 479 codd.

192	εὐσπλαγχνία	Late papyri; adj. εὐσπλαγχνος A. in *P. Oxy.* 2246, 34, and in lit. sense Hp.; other -σπλαγχνος comp. in trag. in present metaph. sense are ἀ- S. *Aj.* 472; θρασύ- E. *Hipp.* 424, A. *Pr.* 730; κακο- A. *Sept.* 737; μεγαλό- E. *Med.* 109.
317	εὐσταθέω	Plu.; εὐσταθής H.
441	κρυσταλλόπηκτος	Late; but κρυσταλλοπήξ A.
887	νεόκμητος	Nicander; νεόκμητος LP preferable here to νεόδμητος Haun., which is found in *Med.* 623.
307	πρόσδετος	A. *Pl.* (1st c. A.D.).
489	συνεμπίμπρημι	Nic. Dam. (1st c. B.C.), Str.
353	ὑδροειδής	Late.
730	ὑφίζω	Dio Cass., later.
414	χωστός	Plb.; πολύχωστος A., τυμβόχωστος S.

I have not followed Eysert in omitting altogether words already used by Homer or by poets before Euripides. These words may be of some interest, although of very much less significance for the present question than words which are not otherwise found until after the fifth century. I have therefore classed the words of my list in groups according to their occurrence elsewhere.

Of words included by Eysert in his corresponding list I have omitted the following:

ἄγρυπνος	List III.
αἶθος	Codd. at E. *Su.* 208, possibly to be retained there. List VIII.
δύομαι	Quite common in tragedy in the active.
καράτομος	List VII.
μῖμος	List III.
πυρσά, τά	List VIII. The noun πυρσός occurs in sg. three times in E. The heteroclite pl. is found here only; cf. τὰ σύνδεσμα, which occurs in E. only (3 times).
τείνομαι εἴς τι	Not an especially unusual sense; see LSJ τείνω I, 4, here passive.
φαναῖος	A title: used by the 5th-c. tragedian Achaeus, fr. 35, of Apollo, with uncertain significance; see Cook, *Zeus*, I, 7 n. 6.

I also omit λύκειος (208), although it otherwise appears in tragedy only as an epithet of Apollo.

My list, however, includes several words omitted by Eysert, apart from those found in verse before Euripides: these are ἀβούλως, διόπτης, ἐκκλησία, ἐντάσσω, ἐπινοέω, νεόκμητος and ἀπομέμφομαι. We may now consider the words in the various groups.

Words found in Homer

I have included the forms δέχθαι and μεμβλωκώς, which are unique in tragedy, although the words to which they belong are common. Euripides often introduces Homeric forms (Smereka, pp. 54 ff.; Eysert, p. 22). Others which occur in *Rhesus* are found again in plays of Euripides (e.g. καπφθιμένου, κέλσαι, ἤλυθον). There is no particular significance in the fact that these two are unique. The words of this list do not point to an extensive imitation of Homeric vocabulary. *Rhesus* takes little from Homer that is not known to have been current poetic usage. Of the 14 words in this group more than half appear in other authors earlier than Euripides. In this respect the findings of Eysert (pp. 22 ff.), based on a slightly different presentation of the evidence, coincide with mine. He lists 55 words in *Rhesus* which are found in Homer but are not common in Attic; of these only six (ἀμπείρας, δέχθαι, ἐπιθρώσκω, μέμβλωκα, μέρμερος and τολυπεύω) are not found elsewhere in tragedy. With this is to be compared a total of 12 such words in *Phoenissae* and 14 in *Cyclops*.

Some verbal reminiscence of Homer is not at all surprising in a play of this subject. One or two of these words, notably μέρμερος and ἐπιθρώσκω, are taken over from the *Doloneia* (cf. 234, διόπτης < διοπτήρ Κ 562).

Words found in verse before Euripides

None of these three words needs comment.

Words found in fifth-century prose or Old Comedy

The majority of these words are in common use in Attic and give no grounds for suspicion that the play is not by Euripides. They include, however, two against which particular objections have been raised:

(i) ναύσταθμον. Sinko, deeming this word to be prosaic, declared that Euripides would not have used it several times as it is used in *Rhesus*, and he was supported in this point by Geffcken.[1] Objection to the word on these grounds is unjustified. In fact, ναύσταθμον occurs elsewhere only in Thucydides (III, 6; VI, 49; ναύσταθμος is found in post-classical prose), and this does not allow us to brand it as prosaic; σταθμός itself is common in poetry (H., Hes., tragedians).

(ii) πελταστής. Wecklein, followed by Rolfe and Geffcken, adduced this word as evidence of post-Euripidean authorship on the grounds that peltasts were not familiar to the Athenians until after the fifth century.[2] But, although the introduction of πελτασταί into a Greek army is commonly attributed to Iphicrates in the early fourth century, the name might be properly applied to Thracian troops at any date, and so used would have been fully understood by an Athenian audience of the fifth century. The πέλτη is named as a standard piece of Thracian equipment in Hdt. VII, 75, as well as by Euripides in several places, and Thracian πελτασταί are referred to without explanation in Thuc. II, 29.

Words not otherwise found until the fourth century or later

These are the only words among the ἅπαξ τραγῳδούμενα which can fairly be considered as potential evidence for assigning *Rhesus* to a date later than the fifth century. They

---

[1] Sinko, *Ant. Class.* III (1934), 423; Geffcken, *Hermes*, LXXI (1936), 399.

[2] Wecklein in *Berl. Phil. Woch.* (1891), coll. 1613 f.; Rolfe in *Harv. Stud. C.P.* IV (1893), 82, 96; Geffcken, *op. cit.* p. 400. Porter, *Hermathena* (1913), p. 377, opposes Wecklein on this point.

are, however, not impressive either in number or, for the most part, in quality.

Among those recurring first in the fourth century there are several that are closely related to words found in fifth-century tragedy, e.g. εὐδοξία, κλωπικός, μελῳδία, ναυκλήριον, νυκτηγορία, πολίοχος. In addition, ἀποινάομαι and γεωργέω are straightforward derivatives from words in common use in the fifth century. There is nothing remarkable about the use of any of these words with the possible exception of ναυκλήριον. If we take ναυκλήρια in *Rh.* 233 as precisely equivalent to ναύσταθμα in 244 (so Murray, followed by Porter, LSJ), the sense is indeed unique. It is however possible to take it as meaning simply *ships*, parallel to the examples cited by LSJ, s.v. 1 (ναυκλήριον = *property of a* ναύκληρος). We may compare Euripides' use of ναυκληρία = *ship* in *Hel.* 1519; elsewhere he has it in the sense of *voyage*.

The remaining words of this group (*d*) are in unusual senses:

(i) γερουσία. In both occurrences in *Rhesus* (not only in 936, as LSJ) it is equivalent to πρεσβεία (*embassy*), an unparalleled use. In its usual sense of *a council of elders* (esp. the Spartan) the Attic form γερουσία first occurs in Demosthenes (οἱ γέροντες Hdt., γερωχία Ar. *Lys.* 980, γεροντία X. *Const. Lac.* 10: see *RE*, s.v. Gerontes). The use of the word in a sense other than its specialized one is at least as likely to be early as late.

(ii) ἐντάσσω. The sense in *Rhesus* (= ἀντιτάσσω) is not that which occurs in the fourth century. Parallels to this sense of the prefix ἐν- are found in fifth-century writers: Porter compares ἐνστάτης in Sophocles, *Aj.* 104; note also ἐνίστημι in Th. VIII, 69 (LSJ, s.v. B IV).

(iii) προταινί. Parmeniscus (schol. *ad v.* 523) states that this is a Boeotian word, and his claim is supported by the occurrence of the form προτηνί in Boeotian inscriptions as early as the fourth to third centuries B.C. (*IG*, VII, 1739, 14;

2406, 6, *BCH*, 21, 554, 2). On the replacement of αι by η in Boeotian, a change which took place early in the fourth century, see Buck, *Gk. Dial.* §26, Page, *Corinna*, p. 59, and on προτηνί Buck, §126, 1, Bechtel, *Gr. Dial.* 1, 309 f., Boisacq, *Dict. Étym. de la langue grecque*, s.v., Schwyzer, *Gr. Gramm.* 1, 612², 619, 3; II, 507⁸.

In the inscriptions cited above προτηνί is always used adverbially and in a temporal sense (= πρότερον); the present prepositional use in a local sense (= πρό) is unique. But a comparable variety of use is found in other words of the same or like significance, e.g. πάροιθε, πάρος, πρόσθεν, πρόπαρ (the last itself a rare word found twice in Aeschylus, twice in Euripides).

The occurrence of προταινί and of another alleged Boeotism in *Rhesus* has been adduced by Wilamowitz and others as an argument against its authenticity. We shall return to this question later (pp. 176 f.).

Of the words which are not otherwise found until after the fourth century the great majority are, like the ἅπαξ λεγόμενα, compound verbs and adjectives remarkable in neither form nor sense. Such words are so characteristic of the diction of fifth-century tragedy that no special significance attaches to their otherwise rare occurrence. The only word in this group to have been cited as evidence against authenticity is ἀνθρωποδαίμων. In its formation this word belongs to the relatively uncommon class of copulative compound (see Schwyzer, *Gr. Gramm.* 1, 453 f.): this type is more frequent in later Greek, but the Aeschylean ἰατρόμαντις provides a parallel in fifth-century tragedy. No date can be assigned to the closely related βροτοδαίμων, which Hesychius attests in a sense similar to that of ἀνθρωποδαίμων in *Rhesus*. Wecklein alleged that the word involved an idea impossible to associate with a Greek of Euripides' day.[1] But before denying to

---

[1] Wecklein, *op. cit.* For a full discussion of the Thracian cult of Rhesus see J. Rempe, *De Rheso Thracum heroe* (1927); P. Perdrizet, *Cultes et mythes du Pangée* (1910).

Euripides the passage dealing with Rhesus' future estate one should compare *Alc.* 995 ff., where the Chorus predicts that Alcestis will after death be worshipped at her tomb as a δαίμων. If in fact a novel idea is involved in *Rhesus*, allowance must be made for the fact that the poet is representing a Thracian belief and not a Greek one. Acquaintance with Thracian religious institutions is not to be denied to an Athenian poet of the mid-fifth century, whether before or after the foundation of Amphipolis. There seems indeed to be no good reason for preferring to associate ἀνθρωποδαίμων, or the passage in which it occurs, with a date later than the fifth century.

III. WORDS FOUND IN AESCHYLUS, BUT NOT IN SOPHOCLES OR EURIPIDES (23)

29	ἀγός	*Su.* 248, 905	H., Pi.
3, 825	ἄγρυπνος	*PV* 358	Hp., Pl., Arist., *A.P.*
697	ἀδείμαντος	*Pers.* 162; advb. *Ch.* 771	Pi.
184	ἀντεράω	*Ag.* 544 (diff. sense)	Plu. (sense as in *Rh.*).
826	βρίζω	*Ag.* 275, *Ch.* 897, *Eu.* 280	H.
117	γέφυρα	*Pers.* 726	H., etc.
247	δυσήλιος	*Eu.* 396	Plu.
724, 805	δυσοίζω	*Ag.* 1316	Hesych. (δυσοίζει · δυσχεραίνει, ὑπονοεῖ · Λάκωνες).
881	ἐκτροπή	*PV* 913	Th., prose.
553	ἰά	*Pers.* 937	Orac. *ap.* Hdt.
117	ἱππηλάτης	*Pers.* 126 (adj.)	H. (as epithet).
828	κότος	23 times	H.
817	μάραγνα	*Ch.* 375	Pl. Com., Pollux.
256	μῖμος	*Fr.* 57	D., prose (various senses).
31	μόναρχος	*PV* 324	Thgn., Ar., Th., etc.
794	νεῖρα (cj.)	*Ag.* 1479 (dub.)	(Cf. Fraenkel on *Ag.* 1479.)
89	νυκτηγορέω	*Sept.* 29	No other.
202	πρεπόντως	*Ag.* 687	Pi., Th., Pl.

405	προπίνω	Fr. 131 (cf. *P. Oxy.*	D., later.
	(= *betray*)	2163, 1)	
785	ῥέγκω	*Eu.* 53	Ar. *Nu.*, Eupolis.
250, 994	συμμαχία	*Ag.* 213	Pi., Hdt., Th., etc.
58	σύρδην	*Pers.* 54	Late (2nd c. A.D.).
158	φιλόπτολις	*Sept.* 176	Pi., etc.

We have already seen that the number of words in this category (23) does not show any significant divergence from the corresponding total for *Medea* (28) or *Bacchae* (24). A glance at the words themselves clearly confirms that there is no evidence here of a greater leaning towards the vocabulary of Aeschylus than we should expect in Euripides. Of these 23 words 11 are known, apart from their occurrence in Aeschylus, either in Homer or in other verse before Euripides, and so cannot be adduced as proof that the poet of *Rhesus* is imitating Aeschylus. There are in fact only eight words here which do not otherwise occur before the end of the fifth century. Since most of these are found only once in Aeschylus, we are hardly justified in regarding them as evidence for imitation of his diction. The vocabulary of Euripides is rich in words first found in Aeschylus, and *Rhesus* seems to have no more than its due share of such words.[1]

Our poet's supposed predilection for rare and high-flown vocabulary is not much in evidence here: only δυσοίζω, ἰά and σύρδην could possibly be so called.

Two words of the list are used in *Rhesus* in a sense that calls for comment:

μῖμος = *imitation*: this may be the sense in A. fr. 57 too, although it is usually taken there as personal. The word recurs in the fourth century, when it is found meaning either *actor* or *thing acted* (see LSJ).

ἀντεράω = *love in return* A., *rival in love* Rh. The former sense is found also in Xenophon and later; the latter in Plutarch, but ἀντεραστής = *a rival in love* occurs at Ar. *Eq.* 733.

[1] A fairly comprehensive collection of words in Euripides which previously occur only in Aeschylus is given by H. Burkhardt, *Die Archaismen des E.* (1906), pp. 62 ff.

It may be noted that Euripides quite often uses Aeschylean words in a different sense.[1]

IV. WORDS FOUND IN SOPHOCLES, BUT NOT IN AESCHYLUS OR EURIPIDES (20)

503, 715	ἀγύρτης	*OT* 388	Lysippus (O. Com.); 4th c.
426	ἀγχιτέρμων	Fr. 384	Theodectes (4th c. tragedian), X.
435	δασμός	*OT* 36, *OC* 635	H., *h.H.*; Th., X., Isoc.
925, 951	δεννάζω	*Aj.* 243, *Ant.* 759	Thgn.
781	διφρηλατέω	*Aj.* 845	Late prose; but διφρηλάτης A. and E.
524	ἐγερτί	*Ant.* 413	Heraclitus
560	εἰσπαίω	*OT* 1252	Xenarchus (4th c.), Josephus; cj. in E. *Or.* 1315.
715	ἐπαιτέω	3 times	H.
771	ἑωθινός	Fr. 502	Hdt., Ar., Pl., etc.
447	καταρκέω	Fr. 86	Hdt., late.
518	κατανλίζομαι	*Ph.* 30	Hipponax (dub.), X., Plu.
499	κρότημα	Fr. 913	No other.
384	κωδωνόκροτος	Fr. 859	No other.
896	ὀλοφύρομαι	*El.* 148	H., Hdt., Th.
283	πεδιάς	*Ant.* 420, *Tr.* 1058	Pi., Hdt.
187, 624	πωλοδαμνέω	*Aj.* 549	X., later.
215	σύγκειμαι	*Aj.* 1309	Hdt., prose.
740	ὑπασπίδιος	*Aj.* 1408	ὑπασπίδια adv. H.; adj. Asius
711	ὕπαφρος	Frr. 236, 312	Hp.
463	ὑπομένω	*OT* 1323	H., Hdt., Th.

The words of this class, as was seen above, occur with slightly greater frequency than in *Bacchae* and markedly greater frequency than in *Medea* or *Troades*. But their total number is still small and the majority are of little significance. Of the 20 words five are found in Homer, a further three or four in other verse before Euripides, four more in fifth-century

[1] A list is given by Burkhardt, *op. cit.* § 27, pp. 79–82.

prose and one in Old Comedy. Only six are not otherwise attested until after the fifth century, including two, κρότημα and κωδωνόκροτος, found outside *Rhesus* only in Sophocles. Even if to these two are added ἀγχιτέρμων, πωλοδαμνέω and ὕπαφρος, there is still not enough to support the argument of Wilamowitz that the poet was an imitator of Sophocles.[1]

There are more rare words here than in the previous list, but they include several compounds of a quite normal type. The most striking, perhaps, is ὕπαφρος, but its sense (ὁ μὴ φανερός, schol. *v.* 711) is a well attested one (see Pearson on Sophocles, fr. 236).

V. WORDS FOUND IN AESCHYLUS AND SOPHOCLES, BUT NOT IN EURIPIDES (21)

122	αἴθων	A. *Sept.* 448; S. *Aj.* 147, 1088	H., Pi., Bacchyl., etc.
444	αἰχμάζω	A. *Pers.* 756; S. *Aj.* 97, *Tr.* 355	H.
456	ἄμαχος	A. 4 times; S. *Ant.* 800	Pi., Hdt., X.
312	ἄτρακτος (= *arrow*)	A. fr. 139; S. *Ph.* 290	In this sense, Th. iv, 40.
112	αὐλών (= *trench*)	A. fr. 419; S. fr. 549, *Tr.* 100	In this sense, Hdt., X.
419	δεξιόομαι	A. *Ag.* 826; S. *El.* 976	h.H.; 4th c.
105	εὔβουλος	A. *Ch.* 696 (adv.); S. *OC* 947	Thgn., Pi., Bacchyl., etc.
30	ἔφορος	A. *Pers.* 25; S. *OC* 145	Pl., late.
814	κακανδρία	A. in *P. Oxy.* 2163, 4; S. *Aj.* 1014	No other.
308	κώδων	A. *Sept.* 386, 399; S. *Aj* .17 (fem.)	Th., prose.
720	πανδίκως	A. 5 times; S. 3 times	No other (πάνδικος A., S. once each, not E.).
437	πεζός	A. 6 times; S. fr. 16	H., etc.
303	πλάστιγξ	A. *Ch.* 289; S. fr. 576	*trag. adesp.* 179; *lyr. adesp.*; Ar.

---

[1] *De Rhesi Scholiis* (1877), p. 12; reiterated in *Einl. in die gr. Trag.* p. 41 n. 81, and in *Hermes*, LXI (1926), 284.

390	πρόσημαι	A. 5 times; S. *OT* 15	No other.
249	σαλεύω	A. *PV* 1081; S. *OT* 23, *El.* 1074	4th c., later; σάλος, ἀσάλευτος E.
172	συναινέω	A. twice; S. 4 times	Hdt., X., Pl.
456, 703	ὕπατος	A. 5 times; S. *Ant.* 1331	H., Pi., etc.
217	φηλήτης	A. *Ch.* 1001; S. fr. 933, *Ichn.* fr. 314, *v.* 332	*h.H.*
55, 128	φρυκτωρία	A. *Ag.* 33, 490; S. fr. 379	Ar., Th.
920	φυτάλμιος	A. *Ag.* 327; S. fr. 957, *OC* 151	Plu.
118	χνόη	A. *Sept.* 153, 371; S. *El.* 717	Parmenides.

This list is appreciably longer than the corresponding one for *Medea*, *Troades* or *Bacchae*. But an inspection of the words that it contains shows that this fact is of little significance and is largely attributable to chance. Many of these words are part of the common stock of poetic vocabulary; the use of these in *Rhesus* does not imply a leaning towards the manner of Aeschylus or Sophocles rather than Euripides. Nor is the use of ordinary prose words, such as αὐλών and συναινέω, of any importance. The words which might be said to belong particularly to tragic diction are πανδίκως, πρόσημαι, σαλεύω, φυτάλμιος; it must be purely a matter of chance that these are not found elsewhere in Euripides.

VI. WORDS FOUND IN AESCHYLUS AND EURIPIDES, NOT IN SOPHOCLES (84)

		Aeschylus	Euripides	
948	ἀγκάλη	4	30	Hdt.
480	ἄδην	2	2	H., Hdt., Achaeus.
306	αἰγίς	3	4	H.
284	ἀκριβῶς	1	2	Hdt. (ἀκριβής E. 5 times, not A. or S.).
647	ἀμνημονέω	1	3	Th., prose.
222	ἀναίμακτος	1	1	Pythag.
792	ἀνάσσω	2	5	H., Pi.

		Aeschylus	Euripides	
143	ἀπαίρω	1	11	Hdt., prose.
860, 978	ἀπο-κτείνω	1	45	H., etc.
467	ἀπουσία	2	3	Achaeus, Th.
124	ἀρείφατος	2	1	H.
499	ἀρκούντως	1	1	Hp., Th.
537	ἀστήρ	1	12	H., Hes., Sappho, Pi.
873	αὐθέντης	2	8	Hdt., prose.
944	αὐτανέψιος	2	2	Plato.
668	αὐτέω	7	11	H.
452	αὐχέω	8	19	Hdt., *Batr.*
719	βάζω	4	1	H., Hes., Pi.
333, 412	βοη-δρομέω	1	6	Plu. (A. in *P. Oxy.* 2256, 72, 6).
730	βόλος	1	3	Orac. *ap.* Hdt.
908	γέννα	11	14	Pi.
7	γοργωπός	1	4	*A.P.* (1st c. B.C.); γοργῶπις S., poss. E.
353	δινέω	2	2	H., Sappho.
928	δίνη	3	14	H., Hes., etc.
741	δίοπος	2	1	Hp., late.
212	δυσεύρετος	1	1	Late.
472	ἐκπέρθω	3	3	H.
334	ἐπίφθονος	4	9	Hdt., prose.
278	ἐρημόω	4	7	Pi., Hdt., Th.
435	ἔτειος	1	1	Pi.
422	εὐθύς (adj.)	2	2	Tyrt., Pi.
510	εὔψυχος	1	2	Th.
303	ζυγηφόρος	1	1	No other (ζυγοφόρος E. *HF*, Plu.).
290	ἠχή	1	10	H., Hes.
678, 687, 784	θείνω	8	9	H., lyr.
669	θηκτός	1	5	Later verse.
57	θοίνη	2	10	Hes. *Sc.*, Thgn., Bacchyl.
492	θοῦρος	3	1	H.
235	θυμέλη	1	7	Pratinas (see Denniston on E. *El.* 713).
895	ἰάλεμος	1	6	Men., Theoc.
643	καθεύδω	3	2	H., Thgn.

		Aeschylus	Euripides	
388	καταπνέω	1	1	Old Com.
134 et pass.	κατόπτης	2	1	h.H., Hdt.
385	κελαδέω	1	8	Sappho, Pi., Bacchyl.
154	κίνδυνος	4	18	Thgn., Pi., Hdt.
618	κύκνος	1	9	H., etc.
485	λαιός	1	9	Poet. (Tyrt., etc.), later prose.
411	λακτίζω	4	3	H., Pi.
287, 921	λέπας	2	8	Simon., Th.
759, 803	λυπρός	3	24	H., Hdt.
962	μελάγχιμος	5	1	X. (also in interpolated line at E. Ph. 372).
871	μονόω	1	6	H., Hdt.
913	μυριάς	1	3	Simon., Hdt.
549	παιδολέτωρ	1	1	No other.
22	πάνοπλος	1	4	Tyrt.
832	παραιτέομαι	2	4	Pi., Hdt., Th.
180	πασσαλεύω	4	1	No other.
254, 763	πεδο-στιβής	2	4	No other.
557	πελάθω	1	1	Ar. (paratragic).
430	πελανός	6	10	Plato.
575	πετεινός	1	1	H. πετεεινός, Thgn. (πετηνός in A.).
929	πηγαῖος	1	3	Hp., Plato.
334	πλέκω	3	6	H., Pi., Hdt.
226	πομπή	4	7	H., Pi., Hdt.
646	πρευμενής	8	6	No other.
696	προσεικάζω	4	2	4th-c. prose.
972	προφήτης	4	3	Pi., Bacchyl.
122	πυργόω	1	11	H., orac. ap. Hdt., Ar.
170	σπανίζω	3	14	Pi., Hdt., Th.
263	στρατεία	2	5	Hdt.
276	στρατηλατέω	2	11	Hdt.
6 et pass.	στρατιά	6	5	Pi., Hdt., Th.
495	συναίρομαι	1	1	H. (συναείρω), Sappho (συναέρρω), Th.
59	συνέχω	1	5	H., etc.
267	τευχεσφόρος	1	1	No other.

		Aeschylus	Euripides	
836, 847, 849	τιτρώσκω	1	7	H., etc.
77, 656, 737	τορῶς	13	1	Emped. (τορός A. 6, not S. or E.).
40	τρανῶς	2	1	Plu. (τρανής once in S.).
751, 796	τραῦμα	2	12	Hdt., prose.
79	ὕποπτος	1	7	Antiphon, Th.
932	φιλαίματος	1	1	Anacreon.
5 et pass.	φυλακή	2	9	H., Hdt.
27	ψάλιον	2	2	Ar., 4th c.
363	ψαλμός	1	2	Pi., Phryn. Trag., later.

The words of this list, since they occur in Euripides, are clearly not to be considered as evidence against the authenticity of *Rhesus*, and so there is no need to study them in detail. Indeed the majority belong to Homer or to other verse before tragedy, so that little significance attaches to the fact that they are not extant in Sophocles. A few, however, are to be noted which *Rhesus* shares with Aeschylus and Euripides, but which are otherwise found only later or not at all: these include ἀναίμακτος, δυσεύρετος, ζυγηφόρος, θηκτός, ἰάλεμος, παιδολέτωρ, πασσαλεύω, πεδοστιβής, πελανός, πρευμενής and τευχεσφόρος. Some of these may fairly be regarded as Aeschylean coinages taken over by Euripides. There is thus an Aeschylean element in the vocabulary of *Rhesus* which it shares with other plays of Euripides. It is therefore the less significant that *Rhesus* contains a few Aeschylean words that do not recur in Euripides (list III).

We should not look too closely for positive evidence of authenticity in a list of words that are not peculiar to Euripides in tragedy. But in this collection there are to be observed several words which are favourites of Euripides and which certainly help to impart a Euripidean flavour to the diction of *Rhesus*. Such are, for example, ἀγκάλη, ἀποκτείνω, βοηδρομέω, δίνη, ἠχή, θοίνη, θυμέλη, ἰάλεμος, κελαδέω, λέπας, λυπρός, πυργόω. We shall return to this aspect of the evidence later.

VII. WORDS FOUND IN SOPHOCLES AND EURIPIDES, BUT NOT IN AESCHYLUS (86)

		Sophocles	Euripides	
534	αἴγλη	4	4	H., Pi., Bacchyl.
851	αἰτιάομαι	2	6	H., etc. (ἐπαιτιάο-μαι A.).
250	ἄλκιμος	4	11	H., etc. (A. fr. 99. 18?)
283	ἀμαξιτός	2	1	H., Pi., Thgn., Hdt.
737	ἀμβλώψ	1	1	Ion Trag., Pl. Com. (v. Phot. Reitz. 89, 18).
516	ἀνάκτορον	1	14	Hdt.
786	ἀναχαιτίζω	1	2	H., later.
136	ἀντίπρῳρα	1	1	Hdt.
901	ἄντομαι	2	8	H., poet.
118, 236, 373, 567	ἄντυξ	2	6	H.
943	ἀπόρρητος	1	3	Hdt.
334	ἀπωθέω	11	22	H., Hdt., etc.
27	ἁρμόζω	8	11	H., etc. A. in compounds.
793	αὐγάζω	1	3	H.; Hes.
98	ἀφορμάω	2	4	H., etc.
718	βασιλίς	2	5	Pl., later.
294, 549, 609	γῆρυς	3	6	H., Hdt.
418	δέμνιον	2	16	H., Pi., *Gyges* frag.
208	δορά	4	4	Thgn., Hdt.
69	δραπέτης	2	3	Hdt.
815	ἐγγελάω	3	5	Later.
878	ἐγκαλέω	3	1	Th., prose.
869	ἐνθνήσκω	1	2	Lys. (dub.).
45, 226	ἐν-νύχιος	4	3	H.
570	ἐντυγχάνω	4	5	Pi., Hdt., Th.

		Sophocles	Euripides	
922	ἐξασκέω	1	2	4th c.
189	ἐπαίρω	5	22	H., Alcaeus, Sappho.
448	ἐπεισπίπτω	1	3	Hdt.
151	εὐεργέτης	3	4	Pi., Hdt.
509	θάσσω	1	22	θαάσσω H.; θάσσω Alcaeus, Ar.
15, 45	θόρυβος	2	7	Pi.
740	ἰαύω	1	2	H.
416	ἵππειος	2	6	H., Pi.
202	καθάπτομαι	2	1	H., Hes., Hdt.
210, 767	καθαρμόζω	1	3	Inscr., Philo.
500	καθυβρίζω	5	8	Hdt.
586	καράτομος	1	2	καρατόμος cj. in A. *Ag.* 1091.
611, 614	κατευνάζω	3	1	H.
654	κειμήλιον	1	3	H.
669, 826	κοιμίζω	2	5	Alexn. poet.
281	κουφίζω	3	8	Hes.
790	κρουνός	1	1	H., Pi.
714	κρύφιος	2	6	Hes., Pi.
308	κτυπέω	3	13	H.
325	κυνηγέτης	1	4	Pi.
510	λάθρα	9	32	H.
716	λάτρις	3	17	Thgn.
293	λεηλατέω	1	1	Hdt., prose.
326	λεία	5	2	Pi., Hdt., etc.
516	λῃστής	5	5	Hdt., prose.
981	λογίζομαι	4	13	Hdt., prose.
131	μετατίθημι	1	2	H., Hdt.
33	νευρά	1	1	H.
477	νομός	1	2	H., etc.
842	ξενία	1	2	H., Pi., Hdt.
760	ὄγκος	5	7	Emped., Parm.
146, 673	ὁλκός	1	2	Hdt.
784	οὐρά	1	1	H., Hes.
509	παλαίω	1	3	H., Hes., Pi.
773	περιπολέω	1	2	4th c.
270, 552	ποίμνιον	4	3	Hdt.
384	πόρπαξ	1	3	Bacchyl.

		Sophocles	Euripides	
183, 371	προ-βάλλω	4	3	H.
107, 162, 266	πρόσκειμαι	9	13	Hdt., prose.
145	προσμείγνυμι	2	2	Pi., Hdt.
78	πρόφασις	2	8	H., Pi., Thgn., Hdt.
90, 713	πυκάζω	1	4	H., Hes., Sappho.
784	ῥινός	1	2	H.
501	σηκός	1	5	H., Hes., Hdt.
202	σκευή	1	4	Hdt., prose.
620	σκῦλον	2	11	Th.
382	σκύμνος	1	7	H.
245	σπάνις	2	4	Hdt., Th. (σπανία less likely *v.l.* in *Rh.*).
958	συνήδομαι	1	3	Hdt.
521, 572, 684, 763	σύνθημα	2	1	Hdt., Th.
525	σῶς	3	7	H., Hdt.
254	σφαγεύς	1	3	4th c.
950	τροχηλάτης	1	1	No other.
924	τυφλόω	1	4	Pi., Hdt. ἐκτυφλόω A.
111	ὑπερβαίνω	3	9	H.
53	ὑπηρετέω	7	4	Hdt.
49	ὑποπτεύω	1	2	Hdt.
834	ὑφαιρέω	1	1	H., Pi.
888	φοράδην	1	1	4th c.
382	χρυσόδετος	2	1	Alcaeus, Hdt.
565	ψόφος	6	5	*h.H.*, Sappho.

Three words which would otherwise have been included in this category, ἀγρώστης, φαεννός and φυτεύω, are read in the Aeschylean fragments published in *Oxyrhynchus Papyri*, vol. xx, and are therefore omitted. The words δορά, καθαρμόζω and κυνηγέτης come into this list on account of their occurrence in *Ichneutae*, which also contains four of the six Sophoclean examples of ψόφος.

The words of this list are again of no special significance for the question of authorship. It is a remarkably ordinary collection. The greater number occur before tragedy in

Homer or the lyric poets, many more occur in Herodotus or are common in prose. It must therefore be purely accidental that many of them are not also extant in Aeschylus.

It is notable that there are several words here, as in list VI, which but for the chance of a single occurrence in Euripides might have provided material for the opponents of authenticity. This is further proof of the danger of arguing from a partial view of the evidence.

VIII. WORDS FOUND IN EURIPIDES, BUT NOT IN AESCHYLUS OR SOPHOCLES (89)

(a) In Homer (23)

244	ἄγαμαι	4 times	Hes.
752, 761	ἀκλεῶς	*Or.* 786 (ἀκλεής 3 times)	Hdt.
374	ἄκων (= *dart*)	*Ph.* 1402	Pi.
775	ἀναχωρέω	*IT* 265, *Ph.* 730	Hdt.
356	βαλιός	3	In H. only Βαλίος, name of horse.
515	γύψ	*An.* 275, *Tr.* 600	
376	δάπεδον	12	Pi., Hdt., Ar., etc.
43	διιπετής	3	Hes.
372	δόχμιος	3	Ap. Rhod.
101	ἐπίκειμαι	*Su.* 716	Thgn., Hdt.
937, 956	ἐπικουρέω	*IA* 1452	Once H., Th., Ar.
291	θάμβος	*Hec.* 179	Simon., Pi.
68	θυοσκόος	*Ba.* 224	
933	κορύσσω	*An.* 279, *IA* 1073	Hes., Pi.
877	λάζυμαι	8 (also 7 times in compounds)	λάζομαι H.; this form in *h.H.*, Hp., Ar.
85	πάμπαν	*Med.* 1091, fr. 196	Sappho, Pi., Hdt.
43, 97	πυρσός	3 (all sg.)	πυρσά n.pl. here only, but cf. τὰ σύνδεσμα (E., 3 times), τὰ σταθμά (S., E.).
73	ῥαίνω	Fr. 384, 2; *IA* 1516, 1589	Pi., *trag. adesp.* (*IA* 1516 is probably, 1589 certainly spurious).

668	ῥώννυμι	Hcld. 636	ῥώομαι H.; ἐρρωμέναι prob. Pi. (Parth. 1, 3 Snell); ἐρρωμένως A. PV 65, 76.
116	σκόλοψ	4	Hdt.
618	στίλβω	3	h.H., Bacchyl.
979	φαρέτρα	HF 969	Pi.
771	χόρτος	3	Hes., Pi., Hdt.

(b) In verse before Euripides (18)

419, 438	ἄμυ- στις	Cy. 417	Anacr.; freq. comedy.
895	αὐθιγενής	Fr. 472, 5	Bacchyl.; Hdt.
617	διαπρεπής	Or. 1483, Su. 841 [IA 1588]	Pi., Democr.
529	ἑπταπόρος	Or. 1005, IA 7	h.H.
760	εὐδοξία	5	Simon., Pi.
882	εὐτυχία	15	Pi., Hdt.
927	εὔυδρος	IT 398	Simon., Pi., Hdt.
904	κοινωνία	5	Pi., Th., Ar.
363	κύλιξ	5	Sappho, Alcaeus, Phocyl., Pi., Bacchyl.
196	μακάριος	40	Pi., Ar., 4th c.
42 et pass.	ὄρφνη	6	Thgn., Pi.
7	πῆχυς	3	Alcaeus; Hdt.
548	πολύχορδος	Med. 196	Simon.; Pl., Theoc.
639	σαθρός	3	Pi., Hdt., Hp.
891 etc.	σύγ- γονος subst.	70 (mostly as subst.)	Pi.; as adj. also A., S.
36	τρομερός	7	Sappho., Hp., Ar. (pass. sense Rh. and late).
943	φαναί	Ion 550	Hes. (sg.).
209	χάσμα	7	Hes.; Hdt.

(c) In Herodotus or other fifth-century prose before Euripides (15)

783	ἑδραῖος	An. 266	Hp., Pl., Plu.
97	ἐκκαίω	Cy. 633, 657	Hdt., Ar., Pl.
872	ἐξιάομαι	El. 1024	Hdt., Pl.
362	θίασος	15	Hdt., Ar., later.
144	καραδοκέω	8	Hdt., trag. adesp. 16.

172

125 etc. κατά- σκοπος	4		Hdt., Th., Ar., 4th c.
645, 678, 709, 777 κλώψ	3		Hdt., X., Aen. Tact.
849 μειзόνως	*Hec.* 1121		Hdt. (μεз-); prose.
437 ὅρισμα	4		Hdt. (οὔρ-); *trag. adesp.* 560.
980 παιδοποιός	*An.* 4, *Ph.* 338		Hdt., Josephus.
305, 371, 410, 487 πέλτη	4		Hdt., Ar.
211, 255 τετ- ράπους	*Hec.* 1058		Hdt., Th., Ar.
675 τρίβων (= *peritus*)	4		Hdt., Ar.
2 ὑπασπιστής	*Ph.* 1213		Hdt., X. (-τήρ A. *Su.* 182).
506 φρουρός	*Hel.* 1673, *Ion* 22		5th- and 4th-c. inscrr., Th., etc.

(d) *Not found before Euripides* (33) [1]

417 ἄησις	2 (see p. 151)		
990 αἶθος	*Su.* 208 (codd., dub.)		
754 αἰνιγμός	*Ph.* 1353		Ar. *Ra.*; 4th c. (αἴνιγμα A., S.).
785 ἀντηρίς	*Fr.* 1111 (dub.)		Th., X., later.
356 διφρεύω	4		Archestratus (4th c. B.C.).
791 δυσθνήσκω	*El.* 843		Cj. in A. *Ag.* 819; no other.
532 ἔγρομαι	*Fr.* 773, 29		Dub. in Sopater (4th c. B.C.); Callim.
441 ἐπιзαρέω	*Ph.* 45		Arcadian acc. to Eust.
768 ἐφεδρεύω	*Or.* 1627, *El.* 55		Th., Hp., 4th c.
370, 439 зά- χρυσος	*Alc.* 495, *IT* 1111		Libanius.
586 καρατομέω	*Alc.* 1118		Lycophron (κάρατομος, see list VII).
625 κομψός	5		Freq. in comedy.
351, 393 με- λῳδός adj.	4		As subst., Pl.
48 ναυσιπόρος	*IA* 172		ναυσίπορος (pass.) X., Arist.
520 νυχεύω	*El.* 181, *Hyps.* 9, 13		Nicander.

[1] To these now add δίβαμος: see note on p. 150.

713	ξιφήρης	8	Later prose.
434	ὁμηρεύω	Ba. 297	Aeschines, Antiphanes.
282	ὀργάς	3	X., D.
927	παρθενεία	3	E. only; παρθενία Sappho, Pi., A., E.
372	πεδαίρω	3	E. only in Attic; μετ- D., etc.
858	πλημμελής	Hel. 1085, Med. 306	Democr., Pl., Arist.
62, 465	πολυφόνος	HF 420	No other.
442	πόρπαμα	El. 820, HF 959	Inscr. (380/79 B.C.).
936	πρέσβευμα	Su. 173	Plu.
593	σκύλευμα	6	Th.
391	συγκατασκάπτω	Or. 735, Ph. 884	Andocides.
960	συμπυρόω	Cy. 808, Su. 1071	No other.
226	τοξήρης	3	No other.
651	ὑμνοποιός	Su. 180	No other.
970	ὑπάργυρος	Cy. 294	X., Pl.
440	φύσημα	4	Ar. Ra., X., Pl.
262	χιλιόναυς	3	Strabo.
305	χρυσοκόλλητος	Ph. 2	Antiphanes (χρυσόκολλος S., E.).

With this list we have come to words which are evidence for the authenticity of *Rhesus* rather than against it. The only possible exceptions are words which are used in a different sense in *Rhesus* from that found elsewhere in Euripides. These are only three in number:

36 τρομερός in a passive significance (τρομερᾷ μάστιγι). The passive use is otherwise late (LSJ), but there is a good parallel in φοβερός, for which both the active and passive senses are common. 783 ἑδραῖος used in a unique sense in the phrase ἑδραία ῥάχις = 'horse's back on which the rider sits'; but cf. the use of ἕδρα itself in this sense (LSJ, s.v. I, 4). 785 ἀντηρίδες = apparently μυκτῆρες. This, if the right reading, is remarkable, but in the absence of a parallel from any date we cannot say that Euripides is less likely to have written it than another poet.

Of the other words in the list those that occur before Euripides are not especially interesting for our purposes.

They include, however, a few that are sufficiently common in Euripides to make it worth noting that they appear in him alone of the tragedians: such are (from groups (*a*), (*b*) and (*c*)) δάπεδον, λάζυμαι, εὐτυχία, μακάριος and καραδοκέω. The remainder are not without a cumulative significance.

Much more important are the words which appear for the first time in Euripides. Such words, as we have seen, are more numerous in *Rhesus* than in *Medea*, and as frequent as in *Troades*. Even here, however, it is not safe to single out particular words as especially striking. The fact that βοη-δρομέω, which formerly belonged to this class, is now found in a papyrus fragment of Aeschylus (see list vi above) provides an illustration of the danger of treating any vocabulary as the exclusive property of Euripides among the tragedians. On the other hand, a number of these words together must carry an appreciable weight. The impression made by the list as a whole is enhanced by the fact that all but a few of the words are quite rare.

Another of Eysert's results is relevant here.[1] His research included a collection of *Voces Euripideae* κατ' ἐξοχήν, that is, words found in no other classical author but occurring more than once in Euripides. His list of 74 words in this class contains eight which occur in *Rhesus*: ἐπιζαρέω, ζάχρυσος, ναυσιπόρος, πεδαίρω, πολίοχος, πολυφόνος, συμπυρόω, τοξήρης. Of these we may remove πολίοχος, since its two occurrences are both in *Rhesus*, but ὑμνοποιός might be added to the list. I have not verified the accuracy of Eysert's complete list, but minor variations would not alter the fact that *Rhesus* has a significant share in this peculiarly Euripidean vocabulary.

The occurrence of such words as appear in my list viii (*d*) is always attributable to imitation of Euripides, but these particular words are of such a kind that we should have to imagine an imitator very intimately acquainted with all the words of the poet. Alternatively, it might perhaps be claimed

---

[1] Eysert, *Rhesus im Lichte des euripideischen Sprachgebrauches*, part i, 15.

that the words are not too numerous to be attributed entirely to coincidence; for the fact that we do not know these words in other tragedians may simply be due to the deficiencies of our knowledge. This is without doubt to some extent true. But although it is probable that some at least of these words were used by other writers before Euripides, this does not destroy their cumulative weight as evidence for Εὐριπίδειος χαρακτήρ in the vocabulary of *Rhesus*. Before dismissing the whole list on such grounds, it will be profitable to consider further evidence for the participation of *Rhesus* in the characteristic vocabulary of Euripides. This aspect of the evidence of vocabulary has been most fully treated by Eysert in the second part of his dissertation. The results of his investigation will be considered below.

Before leaving the study of the rarer elements in the vocabulary of *Rhesus* there are several miscellaneous peculiarities of form, sense and grammatical construction which should be noticed. These may be taken under several headings.

Boeotisms

In the view of Wilamowitz a major argument against the authenticity of *Rhesus* was to be found in its admission of two alleged Boeotisms.[1] This argument has subsequently been reiterated by Morel and Geffcken, the former going so far as to advance on these grounds the theory that the author was an unknown Boeotian.[2]

The supposed Boeotisms are the word προταινί (523) and the adjectival use of μυριάς (913). The former was discussed above (pp. 158 f.), where it was seen that the evidence of

---

[1] See esp. *Gr. Verskunst*, pp. 585 ff. It is true that no other specifically Boeotian word is forthcoming in Euripides, but he does now and then admit forms of other non-Attic dialects (esp. Dorisms and Aeolisms): see Smereka, *op. cit.* pp. 47 ff.; Sneller, *op. cit.* pp. 78 f.; Hoffmann–Debrunner, *Gesch. d. gr. Sprache*, I (1953), 109 ff. Curiosities include ἐπιχαρέω at *Rh.* 441 and *Ph.* 45 (Arcadian?), and the unique ἔροτις at *El.* 625 (see Denniston, *ad loc.*).

[2] Morel in *Bursians Jahresb.* 259, p. 61; Geffcken, *op. cit.* p. 396.

inscriptions clearly supports the claim of Parmeniscus (*ap.* schol.) that this word is Boeotian. Its occurrence outside *Rhesus* is in fact confined to that dialect. The commonly accepted derivation (see the authorities cited above, p. 159) is from πρὸ ται-νί (*sc.* ἀμέραι), and a corresponding adjectival form is attested by Hesychius (προταίνιον· πρὸ μικροῦ, παλαιόν). With this we may compare the adjective ποταίνιος, *new, fresh,* to which corresponds the adverb ποταινί (cited by Zonaras). The etymology of ποταίνιος is uncertain, but there is some support for the derivation parallel to that of προταινί, that is, from ποτὶ ταινί (so Bechtel, *loc. cit.*). Now the adjective ποταίνιος is found in Doric, and is not uncommon in Attic tragedy, occurring in both Aeschylus and Sophocles, a fact which may make it easier for us to accept the form προταινί as a possible one for fifth-century Attic tragedy.

The other alleged Boeotism rests on a very weak foundation. The adjectival use of μυριάς was held by Wilamowitz to be Boeotian on the strength of its occurrence in Corinna, *Pap. Berol.* I, 34: ἐ]μ μου[ρι]άδεσσι λάυς. But the dialect of Corinna is not, as Wilamowitz supposed, the Boeotian vernacular: it is an artificial literary dialect using Boeotian spelling but displaying many features foreign to Boeotian.[1] We are therefore not justified in taking this lone example as evidence for Boeotian usage. Moreover, there is some reason for doubting the adjectival use in *Rhesus*. The sense (cf. *Hel.* 692, *Tro.* 369) requires that μυριάδας be taken with ἀνδρῶν rather than with πόλεις. Either then we have here, as Vater suggested (*ad loc.*), an irregular construction of κενόω with two accusatives (cf. the construction of ἐρημόω in Pi. *Py.* 3, 97) or we must suspect corruption from μυριάδων or μυριάδος.

---

[1] So Maas, *RE*, s.v. Korinna. For an analysis and discussion of Corinna's dialect see also Page, *op. cit.* pp. 46 ff., 65 f.

Unusual forms

Many of these have been included in the lists of vocabulary already given. They include μηνάς (list I), δέχθαι (II (*a*): Homeric), πυρσά (VIII (*a*)). The form ἐξαπώσατε (811, see list II (*f*)) is Homeric, but there is a possible parallel in Sophocles, fr. 479, where ἀπῶσε is given by Eustathius. In 245, where the text is corrupt, σπάνις (list VII) seems preferable to the otherwise late form σπανία.

Another unusual form is the plural δόρη (274) for δόρατα. Björck in asserting that this form occurs nowhere else in tragedy overlooked Aeschylus, fr. 74, 5.[1] Further, although δόρυ is extremely common in tragedy, its plural is of comparatively rare occurrence, δόρατα being found only twice in Euripides. We need not then be troubled about δόρη, which is found besides in the fifth-century comic poet Theopompus, fr. 25, while the dat. sg. δόρει is fairly common in tragedy.

The vocative ἄνα (828) is very rare in tragedy, being otherwise found only in Sophocles, *OC* 1485 and perhaps Euripides, *Ba.* 554. There is a further oddity in the fact that in *Rhesus* it is addressed to Hector, whereas elsewhere in Greek the form is found only in addresses to gods; but the general rarity of ἄνα makes this peculiarity less remarkable.

Other unusual forms do not lack Euripidean parallels. The epic aorist forms ἤλυθον, etc., which appear three times in *Rhesus* (50, 263, 660), are not found in Aeschylus and only once in Sophocles (*Aj.* 234 anap.), but are quite common in Euripides, occurring nine times in lyric, once in tr. tetram. (*IA* 1349) and twice in ia. trim. An instance in Neophron fr. 1 (ia. trim.) is also to be noted.

There may be some small cumulative significance in the fact that the following forms are shared especially with Euripides:

372 (lyr.) πεδαίρω Euripides has πεδαίρω 3 times (incl. once in lyr.), μεταίρω once; the word does not occur elsewhere in

[1] *Eranos*, LV (1957), 12.

tragedy, but Aeschylus has πεδάρσιος and other πεδα- compounds.

378 (lyr.) κατφθίμενον Apocope in this word is paralleled in Euripides at *Su.* 984, *El.* 1299 (both anap.), not in Aeschylus or Sophocles, but all three tragedians have it in κατθανεῖν. Euripides has apocope besides in several other compounds of ἀνα- and κατα- (cf. Burkhardt, *Die Archaismen des E.* pp. 34 f.).

257 (lyr.) Μενέλαν Euripides alone of the tragedians has this Doric form of the name: gen. Μενέλα *Andr.* 487, *Tr.* 1100; dat. Μενέλᾳ *ibid.* 212. Burkhardt, *op. cit.* p. 30.

462 (lyr.) Ἀχιλεύς This epic form, found 7 times in Euripides, is not met in Aeschylus or Sophocles, in whom however the name is of less frequent occurrence.

708 (lyr.) Ὀδυσσῆ The acc. sg. ending in -ῆ is paralleled in Euripides at *Alc.* 25 (ἱερῆ), *El.* 439 lyr. (Ἀχιλῆ), fr. 781, 24 lyr. (βασιλῆ). As Dale (on *Alc.* 25) points out, the difference from Attic -εα pronounced with crasis may be only one of orthography.

393 μητέρος Euripides alone of the tragedians has this form in dialogue (9 times). In lyric ματέρος appears once in Aeschylus, not at all in Sophocles, and 16 times in Euripides. Burkhardt, *op. cit.* pp. 30 f.

Unusual senses

The few words which merit inclusion under this heading have already been mentioned in the earlier lists, namely: ἐπίμομφος active (list 1), γερουσία = πρεσβεία (II (*d*)), ἐντάσσω = ἀντιτάσσω (II (*d*)), ναυκλήριον (II (*d*)), μῖμος (III), ἀντεράω (III), τρομερός passive (VIII (*b*)), ἑδραῖος (VIII (*c*)), ἀντηρίδες = μυκτῆρες (VIII (*d*)). Of these the last is certainly the most remarkable, but in the absence of a parallel from any date it can as easily be attributed to Euripides as to any other poet. Nor do any of the others point to a date later than the fifth century. This collection is no larger than we might expect to find in any work of Euripides.

Syntax: peculiarities observed by Rolfe

The syntax of *Rhesus* in general conforms closely to the usage of Euripides and the other fifth-century tragedians, and has not been a fruitful source of evidence against its authenticity. Rolfe in his review of the question assembled a miscellaneous collection of syntactical points which he thought might possibly be relevant.[1] Some of these appeared to him to weigh in favour of Euripidean authorship, others against it. It has however been shown by both Pearson and Sneller that they are for the most part of little account as evidence.[2] They need therefore be reviewed here only briefly.

Nothing is proved by the occurrence twice in *Rhesus* of πρίν with the indicative, which occurs five times in the other works of Euripides, and once each in Aeschylus and Sophocles: it is not an especially unusual construction (K.–G. II, 453 f.).

The fact that μετά with the genitive occurs only once in *Rhesus* is equally insignificant: the *Concordance* cites only 97 examples altogether in Euripides, and *Hecuba* too has only one. In such circumstances it is not right to base conclusions on statistical evidence, for the number of occurrences in a particular play may easily be affected by chance factors. The same objection may fairly be brought against Tachan's evidence, which Rolfe cites, on the frequency of the use of the final infinitive.

Rolfe records, besides, the observation of Harmsen that Euripides rarely places a possessive genitive after a preposition and that *Rhesus* with eight examples of this departs from the Euripidean practice. When, however, it is seen that six of the eight instances are in the same phrase ναῦς ἐπ᾽ Ἀργείων, this point loses any significance it might have had. Harmsen's other point, that anastrophe of the preposition is much rarer in *Rhesus* (three examples) than in any other play of Euripides (*Alcestis* with eight being next), is likewise unimportant, and one need hardly pause to inquire why the phrases of the ναῦς ἐπ᾽ Ἀργείων class are here excluded. Statistical evidence is of little value in dealing with phenomena which are generally of rare occurrence.

---

[1] Rolfe, *op. cit.* pp. 94 f.

[2] Pearson, *CR*, xxxv (1929), 55; Sneller, *op. cit.* pp. 68 f.

Finally, Rolfe points to the use in *v.* 115 (for which Schaefer's reading μὴ οὐ μόλῃς πόλιν is the most probable) of μὴ οὐ with the subjunctive in an independent sentence expressing apprehension that something may not happen, a construction first found after Homer in Euripides, at *Tro.* 982. But this coincidence is not so remarkable as Rolfe believed, the corresponding positive form with μή being found in Aeschylus as well as Euripides. (See Goodwin, *M. and T.*[2], 1929, §264 and Fraenkel on Aeschylus, *Ag.* 134.)

Alleged epic usages

The following points of syntax were listed by Pearson as Homeric usages which are contrary to the normal practice of Attic tragedians:[1]

(*a*) 865 χρόνον used alone adverbially = *aliquamdiu*. Pearson compares 3 295. But this use of χρόνον is found also in Herodotus (LSJ). It is parallel to the use of χρόνῳ alone adverbially, which is very common in tragedy. It is doubtful if this usage would be felt to be specifically Homeric.

(*b*) 42 ἀνά with temporal force. But in πᾶσαν ἀν' ὄρφναν the preposition is surely local rather than temporal in sense, conveying the idea of fires scattered through the darkness. Cf. Thuc. III, 22, ἀνὰ τὸ σκοτεινόν.

(*c*) 4 δέξαιτο jussive optative. This has indeed an epic flavour. It is rare in Attic (Ar. *Vesp.* 1431 and Pl. *Rep.* II, 362 D both being proverbial), but is found in Aeschylus, *PV* 1047, 1049, 1051.

(*d*) 469 ἐπεὶ ἄν. It is ἐπεὶ δ' ἄν and not ἐπειδάν that is wanted here, but the former can hardly be called Homeric on the strength of a single occurrence at Z 412. Probability favours ἐπεὶ δ' ἄν also at *Sept.* 734, but it is generally rare.

(*e*) 972 ὥστε (*as*) with a finite verb, if this is the correct reading, is not so rare in tragedy as to be strongly felt as an epicism. It is used by Euripides at *Ba.* 1066, where Dodds cites further examples in tragedy at Aeschylus, fr. 39, Sophocles, *Tr.* 112, 699 and fr. 474 P.

(*f*) 720 ὄλοιτο = εἴθ' ὤλετο. This is an epic usage, but in a stereotyped phrase. *Hipp.* 407 affords at least a rough parallel.

(*g*) 864 δέδοικα μὴ κατακτάνῃ: the subjunctive after a verb of

---

[1] Pearson, *op. cit.* pp. 56–7.

fearing in relation to a past event. It is easy to alter the text to κατέκτανεν or κατέκτονεν, but there is no reason for supposing that it is corrupt. The parallel of *Il.* K 538, cited by Porter, ἀλλ' αἰνῶς δείδοικα κατὰ φρένα μή τι πάθωσιν, suggests that the Homeric construction is here being imitated. But for this parallel the interpretation 'lest he may slay' would be possible, since Hector does not know that Odysseus has already encountered Dolon.

To Pearson's list may be added

268 ἀγγέλλειν ποίμνας. Porter notes that ἀγγέλλω with a *concrete* object is Homeric. The distinction of usage, however, is so fine that the epic colour is felt lightly, if at all; compare the construction of Sophocles, *OT* 955.

Undoubtedly a slight Homeric flavour is felt in some of these usages, but few are without parallel in tragedy or entirely foreign to Attic. In view of the subject of the play, some Homeric influence was to be expected, but in fact it does not exceed the limits that we might expect in any Attic tragedy of the fifth century.

Unusual constructions

In addition to the foregoing syntactical points there are a very few other constructions that are sufficiently uncommon to deserve notice here.

(*a*) 46 νέαν ἐφιέμενοι βάξιν. For the accusative there is a parallel in Sophocles, *OT* 766, τί τοῦτ' ἐφίεσαι; On the use of the accusative with verbs of this class see K.-G. I, 352 A. 10.

(*b*) 387 καταπνεῖ σε. If codd. are right, καταπνεῖν with the accusative occurs also in *Med.* 837: Page, *ad loc.*, notes that καταπνεῖν nowhere certainly governs a genitive.

(*c*) 677 τοῦτον αὐδῶ: *I mean him.* Cf. *Hipp.* 352, Ἱππόλυτον αὐδᾷς;

(*d*) 595 λείπειν intransitive is not elsewhere found in the sense of *depart*, although the same construction, λείπειν ἐκ, is not very far from this sense in Euripides, *HF* 133 and Sophocles, *El.* 514. Cf. also Thuc. v, 41, ἀπολιπόντες ἐκ τῶν Συρακουσῶν.

The few syntactical peculiarities that have been considered contribute little to the case against Euripidean authorship.

There are indeed a few usages which are without an exact parallel in Euripides, but such would be the case with any play. None of these points is of such a kind as to suggest that *Rhesus* is other than a work of the fifth century.

EURIPIDEAN ELEMENTS IN THE VOCABULARY OF 'RHESUS'

The foregoing analysis of the vocabulary of *Rhesus* has been confined to the rarer words, specifically those that do not appear in the extant works of all three tragedians. The principal aim has been to determine what proportion of the vocabulary of *Rhesus* is strange to Euripides. Of words shared by *Rhesus* with Euripides only those that are not common to both the other tragedians have come under consideration, but there has already been some indication of a leaning by our poet towards the favoured vocabulary of Euripides. This aspect of the evidence deserves fuller treatment. We do in fact find in *Rhesus*, besides the words already considered, many others which, while not belonging exclusively to Euripides among the tragedians, are nevertheless strongly characteristic of his diction and which help to impart a Euripidean flavour to the style. These words must also have some value as evidence. An exhaustive analysis of the remaining vocabulary of *Rhesus* is not here called for, since a large proportion of the words are necessarily in such common use that they have no significance for the present inquiry. But if the play be the work of Euripides, the vocabulary ought to bear the stamp of his personal taste; for even within the range of everyday usage, any writer will show a preference, largely unconscious, for certain words.

The only study of the vocabulary of *Rhesus* from this point of view has been made by Eysert.[1] His method was to collect from the total vocabulary of Euripides all the words that he

---

[1] Eysert, *op. cit.* part II (1893).

uses with a remarkable frequency; these he included in lists of *voces Euripideae* in two classes:

(*a*) *Voces absolutae*, i.e. words which are more common in Euripides than in any other writer, whether in tragedy or elsewhere; (*b*) *voces relativae*, i.e. words in common use in Attic prose, which in tragedy are used with much greater frequency by Euripides than by Aeschylus and Sophocles. The frequency with which these words occur in *Rhesus* and in other works of Euripides was then compared.

The composition of both lists is inevitably to some extent dependent upon the subjective judgement of the compiler. Eysert has, however, been thorough in his research and has shown a sound discretion. His results may therefore be accepted as reliable, and it will suffice here to quote the relevant parts of his findings, offering where necessary some minor amendments of detail.

(*a*) *Voces absolutae*

There is no need to set out the full list of 132 words compiled by Eysert from the complete vocabulary of Euripides. The list includes 48 words which occur in *Rhesus*, and these are the following. (Eysert's figures for the number of occurrences of each word in the three tragedians have been checked and, where necessary, revised to include occurrences in fragments published since his day.[1] The totals for Euripides are here given exclusive of *Rhesus*, and if a word appears more than once in *Rhesus*, the number of occurrences there is indicated in brackets.)

	Euripides	Aeschylus	Sophocles
ἀγκάλη	30	4	—
ἄμιλλα	21	2	3
ἀνάκτορον	14	—	1
ἀπαίρω	11	1	—
ἄπαις (2)	38	4	2
βρόχος	30	2	1
γῆρυς (3)	6	—	3

[1] See p. 146 n. 2 above.

	Euripides	Aeschylus	Sophocles
Γοργώ	19	3	1
δάπεδον	12	—	—
δυσδαίμων	20	5	4
ἐπαίρω	22	—	5
εὐτυχία	16	—	—
θάσσω	22	—	1
θίασος	15	—	—
ἰάλεμος	6	1	—
καραδοκέω	8	—	—
κατάσκοπος (9)	4	—	—
κελαδέω	8	1	—
κρυπτός (2)	21	2	2
λαιός	9	1	—
λάτρις	17	—	3
λέκτρον	c. 100	5	5
λέχος	c. 125	6	15
λυπρός	24	3	—
μακάριος	40	—	—
μέλεος	77	9	13
ξιφήρης	8	—	—
ὄρφνη (7)	6	—	—
πάτρα	50	3	8
πλάτη	30	2	4
πορθμεύω	12	1	1
ποτάμιος (2)	12	1	1
προθυμία	25	1	4
πυργόω	11	1	—
ῥοή	30	2	1
σκαιός (2)	22	1	3
σκάφος	27	4	2
σπανίζω	14	3	—
στρατηλατέω	11	2	—
στρατηλάτης (4)	33	1	5
σύγγονος (4)	70	3	2
συνάπτω	58	5	3
σφάγιον	29	3	2
φάσγανον	44	1	4
φαῦλος (2)	24	1	2
φόνιος	53	5	3
φροῦδος (4)	35	1	13
χορεύω	22	3	5

Of these words γῆρυς and κατάσκοπος have little significance for our purposes. Only one Sophoclean use of the
former word was known to Eysert, and κατάσκοπος owes its
place in his list primarily to its repeated occurrence in *Rhesus*
itself, his totals for Euripides being reckoned inclusive of
Rhesus. A similar objection might be raised to other words in
Eysert's full list of *voces absolutae*, which occur predominantly
in a single play: e.g. βάκχη (36 of 45 occurrences in *Bacchae*),
θίασος (10 of 16 occurrences in *Bacchae*), θύρσος (20 of 22
occurrences in *Bacchae*), μαινάς (19 of 26 occurrences in
Bacchae), προθνήσκω (8 of 9 occurrences in *Alcestis*). Such
words might better have been omitted from Eysert's collection, but they are not very numerous, and their removal
would not alter the overall impression made by the list.

The important point is that the words of Eysert's collection
of *voces absolutae* are as well represented in *Rhesus* as in most
other plays of Euripides, and better than in some. Of the 132
words the following numbers occur in each play (Eysert's
figures): *Phoenissae* 86, *Troades* 85, *Heracles* 79, *Orestes* 79,
Iphigenia in Tauris 79, *Iphigenia in Aulis* 77, *Ion* 74, *Helen* 72,
Electra 71, *Bacchae* 69, *Andromache* 68, *Medea* 57, *Suppliants*
56, *Hecuba* 53, *Hippolytus* 50, *Rhesus* 48, *Alcestis* 44, *Heraclidae*
44, *Cyclops* 37. If the differences in length of the plays are
taken into account, it will be seen that the words occur in
no smaller proportion in *Rhesus* than in most other plays.

The significance of the above list of 48 words, about half
of which have appeared in one of my own lists, is cumulative. There is no one word among them that could safely
be called the peculiar property of Euripides and the great
majority do, in fact, appear in either one or both of the other
tragedians. Together, however, they prove convincingly that
the poet of *Rhesus* was well acquainted with the characteristic
vocabulary of Euripides. Furthermore he uses this vocabulary with a natural fluency that bears no trace of conscious
imitation.

(b) Voces relativae

Under this heading Eysert has compiled a list of words occurring in Euripides, which are in quite common general use, but which are used by Euripides with markedly greater frequency than by Aeschylus and Sophocles. Eysert's criterion for inclusion of a word is that it should be three times as frequent in Euripides as in Aeschylus and Sophocles combined (whereas the proportion of surviving work of Euripides to that of Aeschylus and Sophocles combined is about 3:2), and further that it should be found a minimum of six times in Euripides (*Rhesus* again included). Of words which fall within these limits Eysert has excluded many whose occurrence he deems to be a matter of accident, attributable, for example, to the subject-matter of surviving plays. He also excludes some words belonging generally to prose, while retaining others common in prose, which are, however, especially favoured by Euripides. The limits of his collection are thus rather vaguely defined. Nevertheless it has been compiled with sufficient care and discrimination to merit consideration as a body of typically Euripidean vocabulary.

The full list of *voces relativae* compiled by Eysert contains 452 words. Among the 97 that occur in *Rhesus* πνέω, which Eysert mistakenly records as not found in Aeschylus, is wrongly included. The 96 that remain are as follows. (Eysert's totals have been revised as in the preceding list. The number of occurrences in Euripides is given exclusive of *Rhesus*, and multiple occurrence in *Rhesus* is indicated in brackets.)

	Euripides	Aeschylus	Sophocles
ἄγαλμα	53	9	3
αἰθέριος	10	2	1
αἴθω (4)	5	1	2
ἀκλεής (2)	4	—	—
ἀκριβής	7	1	—
ἄλκιμος	11	—	4
ἀναΐσσω	5	2	—

	Euripides	Aeschylus	Sophocles
ἀναρπάζω	15	1	2
ἄντομαι	8	—	2
ἀοιδός	13	1	2
ἀπαιτέω	12	1	1
ἀποκτείνω (2)	45	1	—
ἀριστεύς	7	1	1
αὐθέντης	8	2	—
βασιλίς	5	—	2
βλέφαρον (2)	30	2	1
βοηδρομέω (2)	6	1	—
δαίς	32	4	4
δειμαίνω (2)	14	3	4
δέμνιον	16	—	2
δέσποινα	c. 65	5	11
δεσπότης (6)	c. 125	18	20
διαφέρω (2)	20	1	2
δινεύω	4⎱		
δινέω	2⎰	2	—
δίνη	14	3	—
δόρυ (21)	c. 160	37	28
δυστυχής	c. 70	5	7
ἐκτρέφω	19	2	5
ἔννυχος (3)	4	1	1
ἐπίκουρος	13	1	2
ἔραμαι	16	2	2
ἔρις (2)	48	9	7
εὐπρεπής	13	3	1
εὐτυχέω (8)	c. 100	12	15
εὐτυχής	c. 60	6	10
ἤλυθον (3)	12	—	1
ἠχή	10	1	—
θηκτός	5	1	—
θοίνη	10	2	—
θόρυβος (2)	7	—	2
θυμέλη	7	1	—
ἴχνος (2)	29	5	4
καρτερέω (2)	9	1	2
κασίγνητος	55	4	12
καταθνήσκω (2)	c. 110	8	8
κατασκάπτω	7	1	2
κατόπτης (5)	1	2	—

	Euripides	Aeschylus	Sophocles
κίνδυνος	18	4	—
κλῖμαξ	13	1	1
κλώψ (4)	3	—	—
κοιμίζω (2)	5	—	2
κοινωνία	5	—	—
κοίρανος	16	1	2
κομψός	5	—	—
κρύφιος	6	—	2
κτυπέω	13	—	3
λάθρα	32	—	9
λέπας (2)	8	2	—
λογίζομαι	13	—	4
λόγχη (5)	42	3	9
μεθίστημι	31	3	5
μονόω	7	1	—
μυρίος (4)	66	4	10
ναός	53	1	6
οἰκέω (2)	92	10	11
ὁπλίζω (4)	16	1	2
ὄχημα (3)	13	3	2
ὄχλος (2)	55	7	3
πέλτη (4)	4	—	—
πέπλος (2)	c. 100	18	6
πίμπρημι	13	2	2
πολέμιος (22)	80	11	6
πρόθυμος	33	1	2
πρόφασις	8	—	1
πυκάζω (2)	4	—	1
πωλικός (4)	6	1	1
πῶλος (meton.)	5	1	—
σηκός	5	—	1
σκύλευμα	6	—	—
σκῦλον	11	—	2
σκύμνος	7	—	1
σπουδή	30	3	6
στρατεία	5	2	—
στρατεύω	8	1	1
συνέχω	5	1	—
σφαγή (3)	47	7	7
σῶς	7	—	3
τιτρώσκω (3)	7	1	—

	Euripides	Aeschylus	Sophocles
τρίβων	4	—	—
τύραννος	88	8	2
ὕποπτος	7	1	—
ὑφίστημι (3)	17	3	1
φαεννός	10	1	2
φονεύω (2)	31	1	6
φυλακή (9)	9	2	—
χάσμα	7	—	—

This list too might be shortened by removing a number of words whose place there is due largely to the fact that they occur more than once in *Rhesus*, notably αἴθω, ἔννυχος, θόρυβος, κατόπτης, κλώψ and κοιμίζω. Others that might be discarded as unimportant, statistically at least, include ἀναΐσσω, βασιλίς, δινέω and σῶς. The remainder have a fair claim to a place in a list of typically Euripidean vocabulary.

Once again the significance of the words is to be assessed collectively. Where the total number of occurrences is small, as with many of these words, the disproportionately greater frequency in Euripides might in any single instance be attributed to chance. But where a large number of words all show a similar tendency, they have together a cumulative value as evidence. In addition, the present collection includes many words of more frequent occurrence, where the figures indicate more decisively the strong predilection of Euripides for their use. Among these it would be safe to include the following: ἀποκτείνω, βλέφαρον, δέσποινα, δεσπότης, δόρυ, δυστυχής, εὐτυχέω, εὐτυχής, ἴχνος, καταθνῄσκω, μυρίος, ναός, οἰκέω, ὄχλος, πέπλος, πολέμιος, πρόθυμος, σπουδή, φονεύω. These are nearly all words in quite common general use but not of such a kind that their occurrence is inevitable. Among the tragedians their predominance in Euripides is quite marked, and he habitually prefers them where often other means of expression are available. Their significance as a group is therefore hard to deny, and it is further to be noted that several of them occur twice or more often in *Rhesus*.

Eysert's *voces relativae* include a high proportion of words in quite common use in prose. His full list of 452 words in this class illustrates the well-known preference of Euripides for a less exalted vocabulary than that used by either Aeschylus or Sophocles, and his tendency to make repeated use of every-day words of no special colour. The above list of *voces relativae* occurring in *Rhesus* establishes clearly that its author shares this characteristic of the style of Euripides. It is, in fact, an important quality of the diction of *Rhesus*, which deserves to be emphasized in opposition to the more notorious fact that a few words and forms of a rare kind are admitted.

Eysert supplements this evidence with a further list of 39 words from *Rhesus*, not included in his previous classes, which are found in Euripides but not at all in Aeschylus or Sophocles, and another group of 27 such words which occur only once in the works of these two dramatists. These words have been entered in one or other of my own lists above and need not be enumerated again. They do nevertheless add a little to the total weight of evidence in the present class. Finally, Eysert adds a group of *phrases Euripideae*, which will be included with material to be considered in the next chapter.

The above analysis has not revealed in the composition of the vocabulary of *Rhesus* any feature abnormal for Euripides. Rare words are not present in a greater number than we should expect in his work; those that do appear are, in general, not remarkable in quality. The total number of words other-wise foreign to Euripides is, in proportion to the length of the play, not significantly greater than in other plays of his. On the other hand, it is quite clear that the ordinary vocabulary of *Rhesus* has much in common with that of Euripides. This is established by evidence which cannot easily be dismissed. Such resemblance might be attributed to conscious imitation, but the use of Euripidean vocabulary in *Rhesus* is too much an essential part of its style to be explained satisfactorily in this way. Alternatively, inasmuch as many of the Euripidean words are in common use outside tragedy (*voces relativae*), it could be supposed that *Rhesus* is the work of an unknown poet sharing the preference of Euripides for words in everyday use. This hypothesis, however, would not account for the occurrence of a number of words favoured by Euripides but uncommon elsewhere (*voces absolutae*). The presence of a quite substantial number of such words in *Rhesus* is a strong argument in favour of its authenticity.

CHAPTER V

STYLE

By a comparative analysis of the vocabulary used in *Rhesus* and in certain selected plays of Euripides we have established that our dramatist's choice of words is not to any remarkable degree different from that of Euripides, and indeed for the most part is strikingly similar. But important as this result is, the statistical evidence can have only a limited significance if it is not supplemented by a consideration of the manner in which words are used; for however much the vocabulary of *Rhesus* resembles that of Euripides, there may still exist notably different habits of style. In the present chapter we shall seek to discover whether the style of *Rhesus* yields any evidence for or against its authenticity.

It has in fact been held that the style of *Rhesus* differs from the habitual style of Euripides in several important respects, and to these alleged differences some scholars have attached considerable weight.[1] In spite of this there has not yet been a thorough treatment of the stylistic evidence. The opponents of authenticity have brought forward from time to time miscellaneous charges of divergence from the style of Euripides, often with meagre supporting evidence, and discussion of the play's style has been concentrated largely upon these points. Yet not even these matters have been as fully investigated as they might be, and few aspects of the style of *Rhesus* have been studied in any detail.[2]

---

[1] See especially Murray, *Rhesus* transl. p. viii, and Pearson, *CR*, xxxv (1921), 53–4; Valckenaer, *Diatribe*, p. 95; Beck, *Diatribe*, pp. 297 ff. *et passim*; Morstadt, *Beitrag zur Kritik*, p. 63; Hermann, *De Rheso Tragoedia*, p. 274; Hagenbach, *De Rheso Tragoedia*, p. 63.

[2] Sneller, *De Rheso Tragoedia*, pp. 67–82, has collected the principal arguments of earlier scholars on grounds of style, without adding significantly to them.

In examining the evidence of style our first task will be to review the arguments that previous scholars have found there against Euripidean authorship. But the study of these particular points will involve only a partial treatment of the style of *Rhesus*, and we ought, without attempting an exhaustive analysis, to pursue the inquiry far enough to determine on the one hand whether there exist other important differences from the style of Euripides which have not previously been observed, and on the other hand whether there are any resemblances to his style so striking as to provide positive evidence of the play's authenticity.

The fact that we possess eighteen other works of Euripides may make us feel reasonably confident that we know something of his ordinary style and that any significant divergence from it will not go undetected.[1] But in seeking positive resemblances of style between *Rhesus* and the other works of Euripides we are on less certain ground; for while it is easy to pick out similarities of style, it is for several reasons difficult to assess their importance. In the first place, the styles of the Attic tragedians obviously have much in common with one another. And even if *Rhesus* is found to share with Euripides some striking traits of style which do not belong to the other tragic poets, these may still not deserve to be regarded as distinctively Euripidean. Here again we are faced with our limited knowledge of Attic tragedy. Virtually our only evidence for tragic style other than that of Euripides is supplied by two poets whose styles are both marked by a high degree of individuality; it is not unlikely that other poets may have approached more closely to the manner of Euripides. For these reasons we must treat similarities of style between *Rhesus* and Euripides with some caution.

Finally, the possibility of imitation, which has had to be kept in mind at all stages of this inquiry, confronts us

---

[1] We are assisted by detailed studies of many aspects of Euripides' style: of particular importance are J. Smereka, *Studia Euripidea*, II (Lwów, 1937) and W. Breitenbach, *Untersuchungen zur Sprache der Euripideischen Lyrik* (Stuttgart, 1934); unfortunately Breitenbach omits *Rhesus* from his survey.

especially in dealing with evidence of style. The very resemblances of style to Euripides may betray the hand of the imitator. That some leading characteristics of Euripides' style were readily imitable is proved by the facility with which it is parodied by Aristophanes; and it appears not unlikely that some tragedians of the fourth century were quite strongly influenced by his manner. Individual points of likeness to Euripides can easily be attributed to imitation, but we ought not to be too anxious to explain them thus. The evidence that we collect here must be considered cumulatively. As the separate points of resemblance are multiplied, the likelihood of imitation may be reduced rather than increased. The deeper the similarities penetrate into the texture of the style, the less likely will it seem that they have been produced by an imitator.

The evidence of style will be presented in the following three classes: (1) The differences which have been alleged to exist between the style of *Rhesus* and the ordinary style of Euripides; (2) a comparison of various aspects of style in *Rhesus* and in Euripides; (3) some further miscellaneous resemblances of style between *Rhesus* and Euripides.

ALLEGED DIFFERENCES FROM THE STYLE OF EURIPIDES

The specific arguments on stylistic grounds against the authenticity of *Rhesus* are not very numerous. We need not here be concerned further with Hermann's charge that the play contains imitation of Homeric expression to an extent incompatible with the style of Euripides. This argument has not been maintained by recent opponents of authenticity, and since the whole question of our play's relation to its Homeric source has already been considered in some detail, little more needs to be said on this point.[1] It is not surprising that a play which takes its plot directly from Homer should

---

[1] See above, pp. 64 ff.

show the influence of his language and phraseology. We have no parallel except in *Cyclops* for the derivation of a plot directly from Homer, but this, although a freer adaptation, suffices to show that Euripides did not avoid verbal reminiscence of his source. It is further apparent that the tragic poets in general drew freely upon the common stock of Homeric vocabulary and expression, and for Euripides in particular this can be abundantly illustrated from any of his works. It is enough to refer here to the numerous reminiscences of Homeric phraseology collected by W. Breitenbach from the lyric parts alone.[1]

The remaining points of style on which authenticity is opposed may be considered in greater detail. They are the following: (i) The diction is marked by imitation of other tragedy; (ii) the expression is at times incongruously pretentious in a manner unlike that of Euripides; (iii) the poet shows a tendency to repeat his own words and phrases to excess; (iv) the gnomic element, so much a part of the Euripidean manner, is lacking; (v) there is a quality of terseness about the style, which contrasts with the usual fullness and flexibility of Euripides.

Imitation of other tragedy

The opponents of Euripidean authorship have made much of this argument. Resemblances of word and phrase to all three tragedians have been accumulated, first by Hermann, then by Hagenbach, whose material was more systematically analysed by Rolfe; among later scholars Pearson has treated this evidence again and has made a few additions to the material already collected.[2] That part of the charge of imita-

---

[1] Breitenbach, *op. cit.* pp. 268–88. For the use of Homeric epithets by the tragedians cf. L. Bergson, *L'Épithète ornementale dans Eschyle, Sophocle et Euripide* (Lund, 1956), pp. 73–126.

[2] Hermann, *op. cit.* pp. 289 ff.; Hagenbach, *op. cit.* pp. 27 ff.; Rolfe, *op. cit.* pp. 83 ff.; Pearson, *op. cit.* p. 56. On Hermann's case for imitation see Murray, *op. cit.* p. vi. An independent case for imitation of Sophocles was put forward by Wilamowitz, *De Rh. Schol.* (1877), p. 12 and *Hermes,* LXI (1926), 284 ff.

tion which relates to vocabulary has already been examined in the preceding chapter. A collection of rare words which *Rhesus* shares with Aeschylus and Sophocles was cited by critics as proof of imitation of those poets, but our analysis has established that other plays of Euripides have as many such words and that *Rhesus* does not differ significantly from these other works in the composition of its vocabulary.

Further evidence of imitation of the great tragedians by the poet of *Rhesus* has been found in certain specific resemblances to their phraseology. In this connection similarities of expression not only to Aeschylus and Sophocles but also to Euripides have been brought forward as evidence that the dramatist was an imitator of later date. Such was the conclusion of Hermann, for whom resemblances of diction between *Rhesus* and the late plays of Euripides were an indication that it was composed by a later poet. Hagenbach supported a similar argument with a larger collection of supposed reminiscences in *Rhesus* of every other extant tragedy. His evidence however was treated in a more sober fashion by Rolfe, who concluded that there was no convincing proof of servile imitation of any of the three tragedians. A rather different view was taken by Pearson. Selecting from Rolfe's collection of parallels to Euripidean diction a small number which he deemed to be striking, and adding to these a few more of like quality observed by himself, he concluded that if Euripides did not write *Rhesus*, then either he copied it or its poet copied him. But on the further grounds of supposed imitation in *Rhesus* of the vocabulary and phraseology of both Aeschylus and Sophocles, as well as that of Homer, Pearson gave his verdict in favour of the latter interpretation.[1]

Our investigation so far does not give us cause to feel confidence in Pearson's judgement. Indeed we have already seen that reminiscence of Homer, such as it is, does not count against Euripidean authorship; nor is *Rhesus* exceptional among the plays of Euripides in the relation of its vocabulary

---

[1] Pearson, *op. cit.*

to that of Aeschylus and Sophocles. All that remains then of Pearson's evidence for imitation of Aeschylus and Sophocles is in each case a handful of phrases, the importance of which has been differently assessed by Pearson himself and by other scholars, including Rolfe.[1]

Since the whole case that *Rhesus* is the work of an imitator of the great tragedians, a view that is still current, rests upon this evidence, it is desirable to examine it again in detail. Each possible instance of imitation must be considered separately in order to determine whether the resemblance is really significant or merely superficial. Resemblances to the phraseology of Euripides ought to be investigated in the same spirit as those to the other two tragedians. When unimportant coincidences have been eliminated, we shall be in a better position to assess the value of the remaining evidence.

The parallels of phraseology considered in the following pages are derived mainly from the collections made by Hagenbach, and revised and supplemented by Rolfe, Pearson and others. A reading of the remains of tragedy in quest of further material of this kind produced no worthwhile addition in the case of either Aeschylus or Sophocles, but one or two other resemblances to Euripidean diction have been thought worthy of inclusion.

In order to determine the value of these resemblances of expression as evidence we have to consider closely the quality of the words and phrases involved in each instance. Is the expression far enough removed from the ordinary to justify suspicion that the resemblance is other than accidental? When tested by this criterion the majority of the examples brought forward are discounted, and we are left with a more easily manageable quantity worth retaining with our other evidence for the final assessment.

Passages in *Rhesus* where imitation of Aeschylus or Sophocles has been alleged will be considered first. Here,

[1] Rolfe, *op. cit.* p. 97, Grégoire, *Ant. Class.* II (1933), 111 ff., and Sneller, *op. cit.* p. 68, discount their value as evidence for imitation.

although a few of the examples collected by previous scholars have been omitted as being too unimportant to quote, the majority have been retained, from which it will be possible to assess the general quality of evidence in this class.

(i) Resemblances to the diction of Aeschylus:

(a) 54 ἀρεῖσθαι φυγήν. 126 αἴρωνται φυγήν.
Pers. 481 αἴρονται φυγήν.

Although this phrase is not found elsewhere, Euripides has such comparable expressions as αἴρεσθαι πόλεμον (fr. 50), αἴρεσθαι κίνδυνον (*Hcld.* 504). There is no need to suspect conscious imitation.

(b) 162–3   παντὶ γὰρ προσκείμενον
κέρδος πρὸς ἔργῳ τὴν χάριν τίκτει διπλῆν.
Sept. 437   καὶ τῷδε κέρδει κέρδος ἄλλο τίκτεται.

This is so common a metaphor that the slight verbal resemblance may be considered fortuitous.

(c) 179–80 Εκ. καὶ μὴν λαφύρων γ' αὐτὸς αἱρήσῃ παρών.
Δο. θεοῖσιν αὐτὰ πασσάλευε πρὸς δόμοις.
Ag. 578–9 θεοῖς λάφυρα ταῦτα τοῖς καθ' Ἑλλάδα
δόμοις ἐπασσάλευσαν ἀρχαῖον γάνος.

Both πασσαλεύω and λάφυρα occur first in Aeschylus, but more than once, and both are found again in Euripides. The parallel might be more impressive if πασσαλεύειν were not the obvious action to take with λάφυρα. Nevertheless, there remains here a slight possibility of conscious reminiscence.

(d) 288 οἰκοῦμεν αὐτόρριζον ἑστίαν χθονός.
Su. 372 κρατύνεις βωμόν, ἑστίαν χθονός.

The phrase is quite commonplace.

(e) 306–8   Γοργὼν δ' ὡς ἐπ' αἰγίδος θεᾶς
χαλκῆ μετώποις ἱππικοῖσι πρόσδετος
πολλοῖσι σὺν κώδωσιν ἐκτύπει φόβον.
Sept. 385–6   ὑπ' ἀσπίδος δ' ἔσω
χαλκήλατοι κλάζουσι κώδωνες φόβον.

The resemblance here is certainly more striking, but the verbal coincidences are not very numerous and the elements of the description differ considerably in the two passages. Although conscious reminiscence is possible, there is not enough similarity to prove dependence of one on the other; the similar elements are obvious ones for describing a terrifying martial figure.

(*f*) 375   σὲ γὰρ οὔτις ὑποστάς.
   Pers. 87–8   δόκιμος δ' οὔτις ὑποστὰς
            μεγάλῳ ῥεύματι φωτῶν.

The resemblance is confined to the two words οὔτις ὑποστάς; identity in so ordinary an expression is of no account. It may also be observed that in *Pers.* ὑποστάς is followed by the dative, in *Rhesus* by the accusative, as in Euripides, *Cy.* 199–200 μυρίον δ' ὄχλον Φρυγῶν ὑπέστην.

(*g*)   430–1   ἔνθ' αἱματηρὸς πελανὸς ἐς γαῖαν Σκύθης
            ἠντλεῖτο λόγχῃ.
   Pers. 816–17   τόσος γὰρ ἔσται πελανὸς αἱματοσφαγὴς
            πρὸς γῇ Πλαταιῶν Δωρίδος λόγχης ὕπο.

But cf. Euripides, *Alc.* 851 πρὸς αἱματηρὸν πελανόν, a closer coincidence; the rest of the parallel amounts to nothing, λόγχη being common in tragedy.

(*h*)   514   πυλῶν ἐπ' ἐξόδοισιν ἀμπείρας ῥάχιν.
   Eu. 190   ὑπὸ ῥάχιν παγέντες.

Simply a coincidence of one word.

(*i*)   863   καί τί μου θράσσει φρένας.
   PV 628   σὰς δ' ὀκνῶ θράξαι φρένας.

The verb θράσσειν is found once in Euripides, but this is in the possibly spurious *Pirithous* (fr. 600).[1] It occurs however in Pindar, Sophocles and Old Comedy. Since φρένας is a natural object for it, there is no need to suppose imitation.

---

[1] The evidence on the authorship of *Pirithous* is reviewed by Page, *GLP*, pp. 120–1. The ancient suspicion that the play was spurious, which rests on unreliable authority, finds no supporting evidence in the surviving fragments, but too little remains for us to form a judgement.

Rolfe's list included, besides, 22: *Ag.* 1540; 934: *Su.* 15 (both unimportant coincidences of vocabulary); 168: *PV* 890 (a similar, but commonplace, sentiment, and there is no verbal resemblance). Pearson added 290: *Sept.* 80 (but cf. Euripides, *IT* 1437); 183, 446: *Sept.* 414 (but cf. Euripides, *Su.* 330).

The collection is a very small one, and although it includes one or two exact coincidences of phrase, these are of an insignificant kind. Among the nine parallels there are three to the *Persae* and two to the *Septem*, and some at least of these are attributable to similarity of subject-matter rather than to conscious reminiscence. In the whole collection only (*c*) and (*e*) look like possible cases of dependence, but even here chance is by no means excluded. If there is imitation of Aeschylus here, it is not on a scale sufficient to provoke doubt of the play's authenticity. It is well known that Euripides often echoes phrases of his predecessors, particularly Aeschylus. Collections of such reminiscences of Aeschylean expression in Euripides have been made by O. Krausse and others;[1] they are often far more striking than anything we find in *Rhesus.*

(ii) Resemblances to the diction of Sophocles:

(*a*) 55 σαίνει μ' ἔννυχος φρυκτωρία.
   Ant. 1214 παιδός με σαίνει φθόγγος.

The similarity is confined to the metaphorical use of σαίνειν, which recurs at Euripides, *Ion* 685.

(*b*) 201 ἐλθὼν δ' ἐς δόμους ἐφέστιος.
   Tr. 262 ἐλθόντ' ἐς δόμους ἐφέστιον.

But cf. Euripides, *Med.* 713 δέξαι δὲ χώρᾳ καὶ δόμοις ἐφέστιον. The two words are often combined (LSJ, s.v. ἐφέστιος).

(*c*) 249 σαλεύῃ πόλις.
   OT 22–3 πόλις...σαλεύει.

---

[1] O. Krausse, *De Euripide Aeschyli instauratore* (Diss. Jena, 1905). Cf. G. Italie, 'De Eur. Aeschyli imitatore', in *Mnemos.* III (1950), 177–82: Italie's collection of resemblances between *Alcestis* and *Eumenides*, although some are insignificant, proves that Krausse has not exhausted the evidence.

σαλεύειν is not found elsewhere in Euripides, but he has σάλος and ἀσάλευτος (*Ba.* 391, metaphorical). The image is a common one.

(*d*) 329 ἀρκοῦμεν οἱ σῴζοντες Ἴλιον πάλαι.
    Ant. 547 ἀρκέσω θνήσκουσ' ἐγώ.

But cf. A. *PV* 621 τοσοῦτον ἀρκῶ σοι σαφηνίσας μόνον.
    E. *Alc.* 383 ἀρκοῦμεν ἡμεῖς οἱ προθνήσκοντες σέθεν.

Of these the Euripidean passage provides the closest parallel.[1]

(*e*) 498–9 αἱμυλώτατον κρότημ' 'Οδυσσεύς.
    Aj. 388–9 (of Odysseus) τὸν αἱμυλώτατον, ἐχθρὸν ἄλημα.

Also fr. 913 τὸ πάνσοφον κρότημα, Λαέρτου γόνος.

But cf. besides

    E. fr. 715 (*Telephus*) οὗ τἄρ' 'Οδυσσεύς ἐστιν αἱμύλος μόνος.
and *Cy.* 104 (of Odysseus) οἶδ' ἄνδρα κρόταλον δριμύ, Σισύφου
                                   γένος.

These further parallels make it unnecessary to suppose that there is a particular debt here to Sophocles; it seems rather that the tragedians knew a common fund of opprobrious appellations for Odysseus.

(*f*) 715 βίον δ' ἐπαιτῶν.
    OC 1364 ἐπαιτῶ τὸν καθ' ἡμέραν βίον.

The fact that ἐπαιτεῖν is found nowhere else in Euripides is not enough to make this parallel significant; it is not common before the fifth century, but later usage shows that it normally had the sense *to beg as a mendicant*, with which βίον is a natural complement.

(*g*) 819 τὸ μηδὲν εἶναι. 82 ἐν τροπῇ δορός.
    Aj. 1275 ἤδη τὸ μηδὲν ὄντας ἐν τροπῇ δορός.

There are many instances of τὸ μηδὲν εἶναι in tragedy, including several in Euripides (*Hcld.* 167, *El.* 370, *Tr.* 613,

---

[1] In her note on *Alc.* 383 Dale states that the sense of ἀρκεῖν there is different from that in *Rhesus*. But in both places (as in *Ant.* 547) the speaker declines an offer to participate in his or her undertaking, and the sense of ἀρκοῦμεν in both is 'we are sufficient'. The distinctive feature shared by the *Rhesus* and *Alcestis* passages, and not by that in *Antigone*, is the use of the article, the effect of which is, as Dale puts it, to make the participle do duty twice over.

fr. 332, 8); ἐν τροπῇ δορός is a more striking phrase, but τροπή occurs in all three tragedians (cf. esp. Aeschylus, *Ag.* 1237 ἐν μάχης τροπῇ), and δόρυ is a favourite word of Euripides.

(*h*) 866   οὐκ οἶδα τοὺς σοὺς οὓς λέγεις Ὀδυσσέας.
    S. *El.* 1110   οὐκ οἶδα τὴν σὴν κλῆδον'.
    Aj. 792   οὐκ οἶδα τὴν σὴν πρᾶξιν.
    Fr. 165   οὐκ οἶδα τὴν σὴν πεῖραν.

This rhetorical formula, found thrice in Sophocles, has not so close a parallel in Euripides, but with the contemptuous tone of τοὺς σούς we may compare *Hcld.* 284, *Hipp.* 113. The sigmatism is also characteristic of the Euripidean style: cf. *Med.* 476 (and schol. thereon).

(*i*) 882–4   τί ποτ' εὐτυχίας ἐκ τῆς μεγάλης
        Τροίαν ἀνάγει πάλιν ἐς πένθη
        δαίμων ἄλλος, τί φυτεύων;
    Aj. 131–2   ὡς ἡμέρα κλίνει τε κἀνάγει πάλιν
        ἅπαντα τἀνθρώπεια.

The only resemblance is in a collocation of two common words which are naturally found together.

(*j*) 965–6   ὀφειλέτις δέ μοι
      τοὺς Ὀρφέως τιμῶσα φαίνεσθαι φίλους.
    Aj. 589–90   οὐ κάτοισθ' ἐγὼ θεοῖς
      ὡς οὐδὲν ἀρκεῖν εἴμ' ὀφειλέτης ἔτι;

Resemblance is confined to one uncommon word; this periphrasis for ὀφείλειν is not otherwise found, but there is no need to suppose that one poet is imitating the other.

This is a quite undistinguished collection. Cases where the same phrase is used also by Euripides cannot fairly be used as evidence for imitation of Sophocles; but even if these are allowed to remain, there is nothing here that cannot be attributed without the slightest qualm to chance. Indeed, in the majority of examples any other explanation is surely out of the question. The one or two places where the one poet may have had the other's phrase in mind do not constitute evidence of imitation. On the other hand, these resemblances of usage to one of the fifth-century tragedians could legitimately be regarded as supporting a fifth-century date for *Rhesus*.

We may now turn our attention to some resemblances in *Rhesus* to the phraseology of Euripides. Whereas for Aeschylus and Sophocles we have considered the majority of the parallels that have been collected by previous scholars, whatever their actual value, the resemblances that have been found to Euripides are so much more numerous that it would be tedious to reproduce the list in full. Rolfe recorded 80 supposed reminiscences of Euripidean diction in *Rhesus*, compared to his 14 for Sophocles and nine for Aeschylus.[1] Many of these however involve such commonplace forms of expression that their significance may be discounted. These have been excluded here, and only those are retained in which the language seems to have a distinctive quality.

The following collection includes the most important of Rolfe's parallels, together with a few added by Pearson and one or two that have not previously been observed. Some of the other Euripidean parallels noted by Rolfe and Pearson are not to be discarded altogether, but do not belong here, because the resemblance involved is not one of phraseology: these will be mentioned later with another class of evidence.

In considering the resemblances to the diction of Aeschylus and Sophocles we had simply to decide whether they were to be attributed to chance or to imitation; for it would not be seriously maintained that either of these poets wrote *Rhesus*. In the case of resemblances to Euripides there are three possibilities: they may be due to chance, to imitation or to identity of authorship. Since those which could readily be attributed to coincidence have been excluded here as far as possible, we are left to decide in most cases whether there is evidence of conscious reminiscence or of the hand of the same poet.

[1] See his lists IX, X, XI (*op. cit.* pp. 83–91).

(iii) Resemblances to the diction of Euripides:

(a) 7 ὄρθου κεφαλήν.
     Alc. 388 ὄρθου πρόσωπον.
     Hcld. 635 ὄρθωσον κάρα.
     Hipp. 198 ὀρθοῦτε κάρα.
     Ba. 933 ἀλλ' ὄρθου κάρα.

Although there is nothing particularly unusual about the expression here, it is nevertheless worth noting these several similar phrases in Euripides, especially as the combination of this verb with this object is not found in the other tragedians. The resemblance here to Euripides is interesting, because the phrase in *Rhesus* is apparently suggested by *Il.* K 80 ὀρθωθεὶς δ' ἄρ' ἐπ' ἀγκῶνος, κεφαλὴν ἐπαείρας, so that the hypothesis that our poet is here imitating Euripides is unnecessary.

(b) 80 πάντ' ἂν φοβηθεὶς ἴσθι, δειμαίνων τόδε.
     Hipp. 519 πάντ' ἂν φοβηθεὶς ἴσθι· δειμαίνεις δὲ τί;

In spite of the very striking similarity we should perhaps hesitate to attach too much significance to this one coincidence. It does sometimes happen that we find a whole verse or more of one dramatist repeated with little or no variation by another, e.g. Euripides, *Ion* 1488, Sophocles, *Ph.* 1290 (identical); Sophocles, *El.* 677, Euripides, *Hec.* 683; Sophocles, *Tr.* 416, Euripides, *Su.* 567; Aeschylus, *PV* 505, Euripides, fr. 364, 5; Aeschylus, fr. 36, Euripides, *Ph.* 1194 (cf. schol.); Aeschylus, *Sept.* 62, Euripides, *Med.* 523.

On the other hand Euripides sometimes repeats his own verses in this way, e.g. *Hipp.* 380, *IT* 491; *Hipp.* 80, *Ba.* 316; fr. 602 = *Med.* 693.[1] So close a resemblance certainly need not be a sign of imitation of one poet by another.

---

[1] The subject of repetitions in the work of the same or of different tragedians is discussed by M. Parry, *HSCP*, XLI (1930), 97–114; A. B. Cook, *CR*, XVI (1902), 151–3; D. L. Page, *Actors' Interpolations*, p. 127; P. W. Harsh, *Hermes*, LXXII (1937), 435 ff. The evidence that they present demonstrates clearly that the tragedians not seldom borrowed phrases or whole verses from one another, and were indifferent to the repetition of their own expressions. These facts are to be remembered in considering all the evidence now under review.

AUTHENTICITY OF 'RHESUS' OF EURIPIDES

ἴσθι with the nominative participle is common in the tragedians, but it is relevant to note its occurrence in an apparent parody of the Euripidean style at Ar. *Ach.* 456 and 460, where it carries as here a tone of irritation: cf. also *Hel.* 452.

(c) 122   αἴθων γὰρ ἀνὴρ καὶ πεπύργωται χερί.
 Or. 1568 Μενέλαον εἶπον, ὃς πεπύργωσαι θράσει.
 HF 238   σὺ μὲν λέγ᾽ ἡμᾶς οἷς πεπύργωσαι λόγοις.

In Aeschylus πυργόω occurs once only, *Pers.* 192 χἠ μὲν τῇδ᾽ ἐπυργοῦτο στολῇ, but the same metaphor is in *Su.* 98 ἐλπίδων ἀφ᾽ ὑψιπύργων. In Sophocles πυργόω is not found. In Euripides, besides the instances cited here, it is used in the metaphorical sense in the active at *Med.* 526, *Hcld.* 293, *HF* 475, *Su.* 998, *Tr.* 612, 844, fr. 286, 15, and in a literal sense at *Andr.* 1009, *Ba.* 172. The metaphorical sense occurs also in Bacchylides, 3, 13 πυργωθέντα πλοῦτον and Ar. *Pax* 749, *Ra.* 1004. It is then clearly a favourite word of Euripides, and sufficiently rare in other writers to make the present parallel of form and sense worth noting.

(d) 154-5 κίνδυνον...ῥίψας.
 Hcld. 148-9 κίνδυνον...ῥίπτοντες.
 Fr. 402   κίνδυνον μέγαν ῥίπτοντες.

There is no other example of ῥίπτω in this phrase; elsewhere we find κίνδυνον ἀναρρίπτω (LSJ, s.v. ἀναρρίπτω), with which cf. Aeschylus, *Sept.* 1028 ἐγώ σφε θάψω κἀνὰ κίνδυνον βαλῶ.

The expression is therefore distinctive.

(e) 164   ναί, καὶ δίκαια ταῦτα κοὐκ ἄλλως λέγω.
 271   σκαιοὶ βοτῆρές ἐσμεν, οὐκ ἄλλως λέγω.
 Hec. 302   σώζειν ἕτοιμός εἰμι κοὐκ ἄλλως λέγω.
 El. 1035 μῶρον μὲν οὖν γυναῖκες, οὐκ ἄλλως λέγω.
 Or. 709-10   δεῖ δέ μ᾽, οὐκ ἄλλως λέγω,
        σώζειν σε σοφίᾳ.
 Hel. 1105-6   ἡδίστη θεῶν
        πέφυκας ἀνθρώποισιν· οὐκ ἄλλως λέγω.

Cf. *El.* 226 μείνασ᾽ ἄκουσον, καὶ τάχ᾽ οὐκ ἄλλως ἐρεῖς.
Also A. *Sept.* 490 ἔφριξα δινήσαντος, οὐκ ἄλλως ἐρῶ.

206

The only other occurrence of the phrase οὐκ ἄλλως λέγω is in Ar. *Ra.* 1140, where it is spoken by Aeschylus to Euripides; cf. *Eccl.* 440 τίς δὲ τοῦτ' ἄλλως λέγει; (ἄλλως λέγειν = *to talk idly* in Pl. *Phd.* 115D is not relevant.)

In spite of one close parallel in Aeschylus the number of examples in Euripides is enough to stamp this tag as typically Euripidean. In addition, the similarity of form between 271 and *El.* 1035 is to be observed.

(*f*) 296 προὐξερευνητὰς ὁδοῦ.
   Ph. 92 προὐξερευνήσω στίβον.

The noun occurs nowhere else, the verb again only in Aen. Tact. 15, 5.

(*g*) 333 ὕστερον βοηδρομεῖν.
   412 ὕστερος βοηδρομεῖς.
   Ph. 1432 ὑστέρα βοηδρόμος.

Since βοηδρομεῖν now appears in a fragment of Aeschylus (*P. Oxy.* 2256, 72, 6), it can no longer be thought peculiarly Euripidean. It does however occur six times in Euripides (*Rhesus* excluded), and not again before Plutarch; βοηδρόμος is found five times in Euripides (including the above) and nowhere else. The present resemblance is therefore remarkable.

(*h*) 370–1 τὰν ζάχρυσον...πέλταν.
   Alc. 498 ζαχρύσου Θρηκίας πέλτης.

ζάχρυσος is found in tragedy here and at Euripides, *IT* 1111 only; it does not otherwise occur until late. πέλτη occurs in Euripides again at *Ba.* 783, frr. 369, 530, but is not otherwise common, the only other fifth-century occurrences being IIdt. vii, 75, 1 and Ar. *Lys.* 563. Its use is always in a Thracian context. Although πέλτη is thus the appropriate word here in *Rhesus*, the phrase as a whole nevertheless has a decidedly Euripidean flavour.

(*i*) 395 and 423 κοὐ διπλοῦς πέφυκ' ἀνήρ.
   Med. 294 χρὴ δ' οὔποθ' ὅστις ἀρτίφρων πέφυκ' ἀνήρ.
   Hcld. 2 ὁ μὲν δίκαιος τοῖς πέλας πέφυκ' ἀνήρ.

Hipp. 1031 (ὀλοίμην)...εἰ κακὸς πέφυκ' ἀνήρ.
Ibid. 1075 καὶ μαρτυρήσαιτ' εἰ κακὸς πέφυκ' ἀνήρ.
Ibid. 1191 Ζεῦ, μηκέτ' εἴην, εἰ κακὸς πέφυκ' ἀνήρ.
Or. 540 ἐγὼ δὲ τἄλλα μακάριος πέφυκ' ἀνήρ.
Fr. 325 (*Danae*) κρείσσων γὰρ οὗτις χρημάτων πέφυκ' ἀνήρ.
Fr. 425 (*Ixion*) ὅστις γὰρ ἀστῶν πλέον ἔχειν πέφυκ' ἀνήρ.

This parallel has not been included in the collections of previous scholars, but it is remarkable that the phrase πέφυκ' ἀνήρ is confined to Euripides, who uses it as a formula for the end of the trimeter, ἀνήρ being superfluous to the sense.[1] There is a further coincidence in the fact that we find here a half-line repeated in *Rhesus*, just as it is in the parallel expression in *Hippolytus*.[2]

(*j*) 529–30   ἑπτάποροι
          Πλειάδες αἰθέριαι· μέσα δ' αἰετὸς οὐρανοῦ ποτᾶται.
IA 7–8 Σείριος ἐγγὺς τῆς ἑπταπόρου
          Πλειάδος ᾆσσων ἔτι μεσσήρης.
Or. 1005 ἑπταπόρου τε δράμημα Πελειάδος.
Cf. fr. 779, 4 (*Phaethon*) ἵει δ' ἐφ' ἑπτὰ Πλειάδων ἔχων δρόμον.

The only important verbal coincidence is in the use of ἑπτάπορος as an epithet for the Pleiads. This adjective occurs before Euripides in *h.H* 8, 7 and is an obvious enough epithet to apply to the Pleiads. References to this constellation are frequent in Euripides: to the above add *Phaeth.* fr. 773, 22, *Ion* 1152 and *Hel.* 1489; it is also mentioned by Aeschylus at *Ag.* 826 and fr. 312. The latter Aeschylean passage is ignored by Porter in his statement that Euripides is the first extant author to speak of *seven* Pleiads.[3] Nevertheless the present

[1] In arguing that there is a lacuna after *Hcld.* 2, Zuntz (*The Political Plays of E.* p. 110) has mistaken the pleonastic use of ἀνήρ in this Euripidean formula; ὁ μέν is here the subject of πέφυκε and δίκαιος (ἀνήρ) predicative: 'One man is just towards his fellows.' That ἀνήρ does not belong to the subject is clear from the examples where the verb is in the first person. If in *Hcld.* 2–5 the antithesis as it stands appears trite, and its two members are of uneven size, this need not mean that something is missing. It is after all the second part of the antithesis that is to be illustrated in the following narrative, and the antithesis is merely a rhetorical device for giving this sentiment pointed expression.
[2] Repetitions of phrase in *Rhesus* are discussed below, pp. 218–25.
[3] Note on *vv.* 528 ff.; repeated by Macurdy, *AJP*, LXIV (1943), 409, and Sneller, *op. cit.* p. 80 n. 1.

parallel, even if of minor significance, deserves to be recorded.

We must also remember here that the anapaestic prologue to *IA* has itself often been supposed to be spurious. But reasons have already been offered for accepting it as genuine (see above, p. 102), and there is here the further parallel in *Orestes*, to which no doubt attaches.

At this point it is convenient to refer to the evidence presented by Porter of other resemblances between *Rhesus* and the anapaestic prologue of *IA*.[1] Although there are several points of coincidence, they are individually of slight significance. Perhaps most striking is the similarity of manner between *Rh.* 16 (θάρσει. –θαρσῶ) and *IA* 2–3 (στεῖχε. –στείχω and σπεύδεις; –σπεύδω), but the possibility that the text of *Rhesus* is corrupt at this point should make us treat this coincidence with some reserve.[2] The other resemblances are mainly in isolated words and phrases, the occurrence of which is attributable to a similarity of dramatic context. There is however some interest in the fact that a similar dramatic situation has called forth similar motives in both plays.

(*k*) 639 σαθροῖς λόγοισιν.
  Hec. 1190 τοὺς λόγους εἶναι σαθρούς.

This parallel is worthy of note because this metaphorical use of σαθρός is uncommon before Euripides, being found only in Pi. *N.* viii, 34 σαθρὸν κῦδος and Hdt. vi, 109, 5 (of *thought*) πρίν τι σαθρὸν ... ἐγγενέσθαι. The word is not found in either Aeschylus or Sophocles, but is used again in this sense by Euripides at *Su.* 1064 and *Ba.* 487. As a medical term σαθρός is found in Hippocrates; the metaphorical use becomes more common in the fourth century.

(*l*) 721 πρὶν ἐπὶ γᾶν Φρυγῶν ποδὸς ἴχνος βαλεῖν.
  IT 752 μήποτε κατ᾽ Ἄργος ζῶσ᾽ ἴχνος θείην ποδός.
  Ph. 105 (lyr.) ποδὸς ἴχνος ἐπαντέλλων.
  Tr. 3 κάλλιστον ἴχνος ἐξελίσσουσιν ποδός.

---

[1] *Rhesus of Euripides*, 2nd ed. (Cambridge, 1929), p. xliv.
[2] See below, pp. 290–1.

Fr. 530, 7 τὸ λαιὸν ἴχνος ἀνάρβυλοι ποδός.
HF 124 ὅτου λέλοιπε ποδὸς ἀμαυρὸν ἴχνος.
Ion 792–3 τῷ συνῆψ᾽ ἴχνος ποδὸς
πόσις ταλαίνης;

ἴχνος is a common word but Euripides is especially fond of it. He alone has this combination ἴχνος ποδός, which he uses in the manner of a formula (see Eysert, II, p. 37). With this use of βαλεῖν cf. also Euripides, El. 1344 ἴχνος βάλλουσ᾽ ἐπὶ σοί.

(m) 730 ἐς βόλον τις ἔρχεται.
Ba. 848 ἐς βόλον καθίσταται.
Alexandros fr. 43, 43 Snell ...] δεῦρ᾽, εἰς βόλον γὰρ ἂν πέσοι.

The application of the metaphor is the same in all three occurrences. No parallel exists to the phrase outside Euripides; βόλος = casting-net occurs elsewhere only in orac. ap. Hdt. I, 62, 4 and later authors (in Aeschylus, Pers. 424 and Euripides, El. 582 it means catch).

(n) 737 ἀμβλῶπες αὐγαὶ κοὔ σε γιγνώσκω τορῶς.
Thyestes, ap. Phot. ed. Reitz. 89, 16,
ἀμβλῶπας αὐγὰς ὀμμάτων ἔχεις σέθεν.

Before the appearance of the Photius fragment ἀμβλώψ was counted among the ἅπαξ λεγόμενα of Rhesus (cf. Aeschylus, Eu. 955 ἀμβλωπός). Photius cites it in this passage of Euripides, Thyestes, and attests it also in Sophocles, Ion Tragicus and Plato Comicus. It is an interesting addition to the collection of coincidences of phrase between Rhesus and Euripides.

With αὐγαὶ ὀμμάτων cf. Sophocles, Aj. 70, Euripides, HF 132, Ion 1072, Ph. 1564; also Hec. 1105 ὅσσων αὐγαί; but the use in Rhesus of αὐγαί alone = eyes is paralleled only at Andr. 1180.

(o) 742–4 οἷα πεπόνθαμεν, οἷά τις ἡμᾶς
δράσας ἀφανῆ φροῦδος, φανερὸν
Θρηξὶν πένθος τολυπεύσας.
Hipp. 1288–9 ψευδέσι μύθοις ἀλόχου πεισθεὶς
ἀφανῆ; φανερὰν δ᾽ ἔσχεθες ἄτην.

There is a resemblance worth noting in the correspondence of contrast between ἀφανής and φανερός, which is combined with a certain similarity in the arrangement of words.

(*p*) 751 πῶς ἂν ὀλοίμαν;

The same phrase occurs in similar anapaestic passages of lamentation at *Alc.* 864, *Med.* 97, *Su.* 796. Sneller (*op. cit.* p. 67) regards the coincidence as insignificant, but the fact that three examples are met in Euripides and none elsewhere warrants its inclusion.

(*q*) 796 βαθεῖαν ἄλοκα τραύματος.
    HF 164 δορὸς ταχεῖαν ἄλοκα.

ἄλοξ is sufficiently uncommon in tragedy for its use in this identical metaphor and closely parallel phrase to be striking. There is a comparable metaphorical use in Aeschylus, *Ch.* 25 ὄνυχος ἄλοκι νεοτόμῳ. *Sept.* 593 has βαθεῖαν ἄλοκα, but in a quite different application. The other instances of ἄλοξ in tragedy are Aeschylus, *Ag.* 1015 (literal sense), Sophocles, *OT* 1211 and Euripides, *Ph.* 18 (different metaphor).

Some minor resemblances of phrase to Euripides

To the above may be added a few small phrases which occur exclusively or preponderantly in Euripides:

116 δὶς τόσως: Euripides, *Med.* 1194, *El.* 1092 only, τόσως being confined to these places. Cf. δὶς τόσος *Rh.* 160, 281, 757 and six other times in Euripides (incl. twice *Medea*), but also Sophocles, *Aj.* 277, Homer and elsewhere.

421 κατ' ὄμμα: καὶ λέγω κατ' ὄμμα σόν. Cf. esp. Euripides, *El.* 910, ἅ γ' εἰπεῖν ἤθελον κατ' ὄμμα σόν. Also *Andr.* 1064 κατ' ὄμμ' ἐλθὼν μάχῃ, *ibid.* 1117 κατ' ὄμμα στάς, *Ba.* 469 νύκτωρ ἢ κατ' ὄμμα. In plural, *Or.* 288–9 εἰ κατ' ὄμματα | ἐξιστόρουν νιν. The phrase is not elsewhere found in this hostile sense. Cf. Sophocles, *Ant.* 760 (κατ' ὄμματ' αὐτίκα παρόντι) and *Tr.* 102.

452 μέγ' αὐχοῦντας: Cf. *Hcld.* 353 μέγ' αὐχεῖς, fr. 1007 αὐχοῦσιν μέγα, also *Andr.* 463 μηδὲν τόδ' αὔχει. Outside Euripides cf. Hdt. VII, 103 τοσοῦτον αὐχεῖν. αὐχέω does not occur in

Sophocles; it is common in Aeschylus (but not in this phrase) and Euripides.

855 τὸ πάμπαν: Fr. 196. Also without article, *Med.* 1091. Not at all in Aeschylus or Sophocles. Without article in Homer and Herodotus.

There are other resemblances in *Rhesus* to the style of Euripides which consist not so much in a distinctive quality of phrase as in the arrangement of words within the line or in grammatical construction. These will be considered later (pp. 243 ff.).

We have now examined in detail the evidence for resemblance in *Rhesus* to the diction of each of the three tragedians. It is apparent that the resemblances to Euripides not only exceed those to Aeschylus and Sophocles in quantity, as we might have expected in view of the greater bulk of his extant work, but also differ from them in quality. In the case of Sophocles there is not one similarity in which conscious reminiscence is more than a remote possibility. We have found a few phrases, as we earlier found a few words, which our poet might be thought to have derived directly from Aeschylus, but these are no more than might occur in any play of Euripides. The only substantial evidence of similar phraseology occurs in the case of Euripides. Here the resemblances that we have considered are of a much more distinctive character than for the other poets. The phrases are often not merely similar but identical, and the language has been seen to possess a typically Euripidean stamp. These resemblances are too many to be coincidental, and we have to decide whether they point to imitation or to identical authorship. The evidence is necessarily of ambiguous significance. The possibility of imitation cannot be ruled out altogether, but it would be imitation of an unusually penetrating kind by a poet intimately acquainted with Euripides' habits of expression. Further evidence will help us to determine whether this is a more likely hypothesis than that Euripides himself is the author of *Rhesus*.

Inflated expression

Since Scaliger first described the author of *Rhesus* as *poeta grandiloquentior* it has been a constant argument of the opponents of Euripidean authorship that the poet tends to an elevated and pretentious style of diction that is foreign to the manner of Euripides.[1] A striving after rare words and elaborate forms of phrase is alleged. The charge has already been examined so far as it concerns vocabulary: it was found that the number of rare words in *Rhesus* does not exceed a total that might be expected in a play of Euripides. It remains to consider here the validity of the assertion that the phraseology is pretentious and unlike that of Euripides.

Unfortunately, many of the critics who repeat this charge do not think it necessary to quote specific examples in support. We have to go back to some earlier works, notably that of Beck, to find detailed reference to phrases to which exception is taken. These are not remarkable either for their number or for their quality. The following is a full list of the passages cited by Beck with a few more from other sources:[2] a reading of the play suggests that it would be difficult to make significant additions to this collection.

8 λῦσον βλεφάρων γοργωπὸν ἕδραν.
Cf. 554–5 θέλγει δ' ὀμμάτων ἕδραν ὕπνος.

Here only the periphrastic use of ἕδρα is unusual, there being no parallel to the expressions βλεφάρων ἕδρα and ὀμμάτων ἕδρα. But ἕδρα is a favourite word of Euripides, and is used by him in a more common type of periphrasis at, e.g., *Tro.* 557 Περγάμων ἕδρας. In other respects the diction here is

---

[1] J. Scaliger, *Prolegomena ad Manilium*, pp. 6 ff. Cf. Beck, *op. cit.* pp. 297 ff.; Morstadt, *op. cit.* pp. 62 ff.; Hermann, *op. cit.* pp. 289 ff.; Welcker, *Die griechischen Tragödien* (Bonn, 1841), p. 1118; Menzer, *De Rheso Tragoedia*, p. 38; Hagenbach, *op. cit.* p. 27. Grégoire, *Ant. Class.* II (1933), 120, while believing *Rhesus* to be authentic, nevertheless felt that there was a difference of style in this respect. Geffcken, *Hermes*, LXXI (1936), 404 f., unsuccessfully seeks here an argument in support of his fourth-century dating of the play.

[2] Beck, *op. cit.*; Hagenbach, *op. cit.*; Menzer, *op. cit.*

thoroughly Euripidean: γοργωπός occurs in four other places in Euripides (cf. esp. *HF* 868 γοργωπούς κόρας); he also has γοργώψ three times (cf. esp. *HF* 131 γοργῶπες ὀμμάτων αὐγαί). Cf. also *El.* 740 χρυσωπὸν ἕδραν.

73   νῶτον χαραχθεὶς κλίμακας ῥάνῃ φόνῳ.

Again only one word is striking in the context: χαραχθείς is colourful, but there is nothing abnormal in its use here (cf. Pi. *P.* 1, 28). Euripides has the word twice in metaphorical uses (fr. 431, *Med.* 157).

111   νυκτὸς ἐν καταστάσει.

The phrase is not exactly paralleled, but the use of κατάστασις is comparable with *Med.* 1197 ὀμμάτων κατάστασις and *Hipp.* 1296 ἄκουε . . . σῶν κακῶν κατάστασιν. The sense ('in the still of the night') is neither obscure nor strained.

257 ff.   ἕλοι Μενέλαν,
           κτανὼν δ᾽ ᾽Αγαμεμνόνιον κρᾶτ᾽ ἐνέγκοι
           ῾Ελένᾳ κακόγαμβρον ἐς χέρας γόον.

Slightly awkward, but not difficult, is the compressed form of expression, in which it is necessary to understand ᾽Αγαμέμνονα as the object of κτανών from the phrase that follows. With the appositional κακόγαμβρον . . . γόον Porter rightly compares *Hipp.* 756 κακονυμφοτάτην ὄνασιν.

276   ἀνὴρ γὰρ ἀλκῆς μυρίας στρατηλατῶν.

The diction is straightforward; for the use of ἀλκή compare *Or.* 690.

278   ποίας πατρῴας γῆς ἐρημώσας πέδον;

Certainly not a specimen of non-Euripidean style: cf. *Andr.* 314 κεῖ μὴ τόδ᾽ ἐκλιποῦσ᾽ ἐρημώσεις πέδον.

283   πλαγχθεὶς πλατείας πεδιάδος θ᾽ ἁμαξιτοῦ.

Only the alliteration makes this at all striking. Alliteration as a quality of the style of *Rhesus* will be discussed below, pp. 241 f.

288 οἰκοῦμεν αὐτόρριζον ἑστίαν χθονός.

An elaborate periphrasis: the fact that αὐτόρριζος is rare, and unique in this sense, was noted earlier.

318 ἕρπει κατάντης συμφορὰ πρὸς τἀγαθά.

With this use of ἕρπειν, a favourite word of Euripides, cf. esp. *IT* 477. Although κατάντης is found only here in tragedy, we may compare the metaphorical use of προσάντης in *Med.* 381, *Or.* 790 and elsewhere; also comparable, as the opposite of the present metaphor, is *Alc.* 500 πρὸς αἶπος ἔρχεται (*sc.* ὁ ἐμὸς δαίμων).

322–3   ἡνίκ᾽ ἐξώστης Ἄρης
            ἔθραυε λαίφη τῆσδε γῆς μέγας πνέων.

A vivid metaphor but one belonging to a class common in Euripides, as indeed among all the tragedians. The vocabulary here is all Euripidean except ἐξώστης, with which cf. *Cyc.* 278–9 πνεύμασιν...ἐξωσθέντες.

360–5   ἆρά ποτ᾽ αὖθις ἀ παλαιὰ Τροία
            τοὺς προπότας παναμερεύ-
            σει θιάσους ἐρώτων
            ψαλμοῖσι καὶ κυλίκων οἰνοπλανή-
            τοις ὑποδεξίαις ἁμίλλαις;

This passage is indeed remarkable for its collocation of several rare and unique words: προπότης, πανημερεύω, οἰνοπλάνητος are all ἅπαξ λεγόμενα, and ὑποδέξιος is found nowhere else in tragedy.

This fact does not in itself tell against Euripidean authorship; for a similar accumulation of neologisms cf. *Ba.* 120–5, which contains four ἅπαξ λεγόμενα. In the present passage the unfamiliar words are compounds of the kind that abounds in the lyrics of tragedy.[1] There is an evident striving after originality of expression, but the manner is not foreign to Euripides' lyric style at any date (cf. e.g. *Alc.* 445 ff.).

[1] The richness of Euripides' lyric style in compounds of this type is demonstrated by Breitenbach, *op. cit.* pp. 53–114.

A comparable picture of the joys attendant upon peace is to be found in fr. 453 (*Cresphontes*).

370–3   τὰν ζάχρυσον προβαλοῦ
Πηλεΐδα κατ' ὄμμα πέλ-
ταν δοχμίαν πεδαίρων
σχιστὰν παρ' ἄντυγα.

There is nothing extravagant about the expression here. Parallels to ζάχρυσον πέλταν and κατ' ὄμμα have already been noted in Euripides; in addition, πεδαίρων is a form characteristic of Euripides' style and used only by him among Attic writers; δόχμιος, used elsewhere by Euripides, is appropriate here, as is σχιστάν as an epithet for ἄντυγα (see Porter's note).

425   λύπῃ πρὸς ἧπαρ δυσφορῶν ἐτειρόμην.

It is hard to see in what respect this could be regarded as an example of inflated style; there is no deviation from the normal diction of Euripides.

566   ψόφος στάζει δι' ὤτων.

For the metaphorical use of στάζω in reference to sound Porter compares Pi. *P.* iv, 136. The word is frequent in Euripides (cf. esp. *Hipp.* 525 f. Ἔρως, ὃ κατ' ὀμμάτων στάζεις πόθον).

783   λύκους ἐπεμβεβῶτας ἑδραίαν ῥάχιν.

ἑδραία ῥάχις is certainly an unusual periphrasis for ἕδρα = *horse's back on which the rider sits* (LSJ, s.v. ἕδρα 4), but Euripides is as likely as any other poet to have used such an expression.

785–6   ἔρρεγκον ἐξ ἀντηρίδων θυμὸν πνέουσαι.

ἀντηρίδες = μυκτῆρες, if the scholiast is right in so interpreting it, is perhaps the most curious usage in the play; alternatively, the word could refer to some part of the horse's equipment. In either case the expression is much less bombastic than Aeschylus, *Sept.* 461–4 and quite characteristic of the florid style sometimes found in Euripidean narrative speeches (cf. e.g. *Hipp.* 1223–6).

987 πληροῦν τ᾿ αὐχένας ξυνωρίδων.

A somewhat pretentious phrase; there is no exact parallel to this use of πληροῦν, but it is a verb frequently used by Euripides in a variety of contexts.

This collection includes all that is in the least degree out of the ordinary in the diction of *Rhesus*. Inspection shows that much of it is quite within the range of normal tragic diction, indeed fully in the manner of Euripides. Here and there we find a mannered phrase, involving the use of a word in a sense hard to parallel and occasionally a little strained. These few abnormalities of expression stand out the more conspicuously in a dialogue whose general impression is one of extreme simplicity and plainness.

There is nothing here to justify doubt in the authenticity of *Rhesus*. These few singular phrases are no more than one might expect to come across in any work of Euripides. In *Alcestis*, to take a single example, a play whose diction is likewise characterized generally by simplicity, one finds occasional indulgence in a highly coloured phrase, e.g. (in dialogue only):

177–8 παρθένεια...κορεύματα.
184 ὀφθαλμοτέγκτῳ δεύεται πλημμυρίδι.
494 ἄνδρας ἀρταμοῦσι λαιψηραῖς γνάθοις.
537 τόνδ᾿ ὑπορράπτεις λόγον.
757 πίνει μελαίνης μητρὸς εὔζωρον μέθυ.
797–8 τοῦ νῦν σκυθρωποῦ καὶ ξυνεστῶτος φρενῶν
μεθορμιεῖ σε πίτυλος ἐμπεσὼν σκύφου.
951–2 ξύλλογοι γυναικοπληθεῖς.

Is this very different from the kind of expression which in *Rhesus* is held to be unlike Euripides?

A tendency of Euripides to use pretentious phrases, which

217

are sometimes incongruous in their context, is parodied by Aristophanes (e.g. *Ach.* 449, 479).[1]

Repetition

A tendency to the monotonous repetition of words and phrases has often been remarked as characteristic of the style of *Rhesus*, and has been held up as a mark of inferior workmanship, by which is betrayed the hand of a poet less competent than Euripides.[2] It is justly observed that the words and phrases repeated are often quite colourless and unemphatic, so that their recurrent use contributes to a certain flatness of style.

As examples of simple verbal repetition Pearson cites especially κατόπτης, κατάσκοπος, κλῶπες, ὄρφνη, ναύσταθμα, κέλσαι, στείχειν, μολεῖν;[3] to these one might add several others, including δόρυ, στρατός, βαίνειν. The repeated use of certain words was noted earlier (pp. 184 ff.), where it was observed that this verbal repetition is in keeping with a tendency of Euripides to make heavy demands on a stock of favourite words, most of them common in Attic. *Rhesus* does not appear to offend more than other plays of Euripides in this respect. Of the words cited by Pearson some may arrest attention because they are not otherwise common in tragedy, but in *Rhesus* these are required by the subject. The poet could hardly avoid the repeated use of κατάσκοπος and κατόπτης without employing the most tedious kind of periphrasis. The repetition of ὄρφνη is justified on the

---

[1] Examples of pretentious expression in Euripides are cited by Schm.–St. III, 800 n. 5; Breitenbach, *op. cit.* pp. 199 ff.; Haigh, *Tragic Drama of the Greeks*, p. 258 n. 3.

[2] See especially Pearson, *CR*, xxxv (1921), 58; Porter, *op. cit.* pp. xlvii f.; also Morstadt, *op. cit.* p. 64, and Beck, *op. cit.* p. 297. Gruppe, *Ariadne* (Berlin, 1834), p. 291, considers some of the repetitions intentional, and, surprisingly, finds them Sophoclean in character; elsewhere (p. 335) he holds that the tendency to repetition may be the mark of a youthful poet. Ridgeway, *CQ*, xx (1926), 16, attributes the repetitions to a lack of revision. Sneller, *op. cit.* pp. 71–2, has relevant, but scarcely sufficient, evidence against Pearson's arguments.

[3] Pearson, *op. cit.*

grounds that the fact that it is dark is dramatically important and needs to be emphasized; likewise νύξ and εὐφρόνη each occur several times. The fact that στείχειν and μολεῖν (we may add βαίνειν) are much more frequent than in *Alcestis*, as Pearson observes, is surely attributable to the importance in the drama of movements to and fro. As a parallel to repetition of this kind one might compare the frequency of θνῇσκειν and its compounds in, for example, *Alcestis* or *Hippolytus*, of ξένος and θύειν in *Iphigenia in Tauris*, of ἱκέτης in *Heraclidae*, and of such words as θίασος, μαινάς, βάκχη, βάκχευμα, κτλ., in *Bacchae*. These are but a few random examples.[1] It is clear that frequent recurrence of certain everyday words is not foreign to the style of Euripides.

Another aspect of verbal repetition, which need not particularly concern us, although it appears in *Rhesus*, is an indifference to the use of the same word more than once within a brief space, notably at the ends of verses close to one another. In *Rhesus* there are several instances of this kind of repetition, but it is, in fact, generally common in Euripides and is not fastidiously avoided by any of the tragedians.[2] In *Rhesus* there are no strikingly harsh examples and the tendency is no more prominent than in other plays of Euripides.

We may safely leave the matter of repeated words and proceed to the more important question of repetition of phrase. The following is a fairly complete list of the instances in *Rhesus* of recurrence of similar collocations of words:

1   βᾶθι πρὸς εὐνὰς τὰς Ἑκτορέους.
         23–4   συμμάχων, Ἕκτορ, βᾶθι πρὸς εὐνάς.
Also   606   τὰς δ' Ἕκτορος εὐνάς.   631   πρὸς εὐνὰς Ἕκτορος.
         660   εὐνὰς . . . πρὸς Ἕκτορος.

---

[1] Others of the same kind in *Phoenissae* are cited by Sneller, *op. cit.* p. 72.

[2] *Rh.* 58, 60, 63; 87, 89; 102, 104; 165, 166; 178, 180; 331, 332; 473, 474; 492, 495; 519, 522; 612, 613; 653, 655; 786, 788; 810, 813; 834, 837; 840, 842; 973, 974. For evidence of Euripides' indifference to repetition of this sort see Page, *Actors' Interpolations*, p. 123. It is less frequent in Sophocles: for examples see the index to the Jebb–Pearson edition, s.v. Repetition.

13, 17, 691 ἐκ νυκτῶν.
18 φυλακὰς προλιπὼν κινεῖς στρατιάν.
37 φυλακὰς δὲ λιπὼν κινεῖς στρατιάν.
23 ὁπλίζου χέρα. 84 ὁπλίζειν χέρα. 99 ὁπλίζῃ χέρας.
41, 78, 824 πῦρ᾽ αἴθειν (cf. 95).
54, 126 αἴρεσθαι φυγήν.
57, 78, 127, 146 Ἀργείων στρατόν (στρατῷ).
60 εὐτυχοῦν δόρυ. 319 εὐτυχεῖ δόρυ.
62 πολυφόνῳ χερί. 465 πολυφόνου χειρός.
72 νεὼς θρῴσκων ἔπι. 100 κἀπιθρῴσκοντας νεῶν.
82, 116 ἐν τροπῇ.
125 κατάσκοπον δὲ πολεμίων. 140 πολεμίων κατάσκοπον.
129 ἐχθρῶν μηχανάς. 141 ἐχθρῶν μηχανήν.
150, 155 κατόπτης ναῦς ἐπ᾽ Ἀργείων μολεῖν.
221, 589 ναῦς ἐπ᾽ Ἀργείων μολεῖν.
203, 502 ναῦς ἐπ᾽ Ἀργείων.
160 δὶς τόσως. 281 δὶς τόσου. 757 δὶς τόσον.
164, 271 οὐκ ἄλλως λέγω.
169, 181 αἰτήσεις γέρας.
190 κάλλιστον οἴκοις κτῆμα. 620 κάλλιστον οἴκοις σκῦλον.
203 ἥσω . . . πόδα. 798 ἵεσαν πόδα.
279, 652 πατρὸς δὲ Στρυμόνος κικλήσκεται.
333 ὕστερον βοηδρομεῖν. 412 ὕστερος βοηδρομεῖς.
351 τᾶς μελῳδοῦ Μούσας.
393 παῖ τῆς μελῳδοῦ μητέρος Μουσῶν μιᾶς.
395, 423 κοὐ διπλοῦς πέφυκ᾽ ἀνήρ.
404 βάρβαρός τε βαρβάρους. 833 βάρβαρός τε βαρβάρου.
409, 491, 511 κατὰ στόμα.
438, 876 ὡς σὺ κομπεῖς.
543–5 οὐκοῦν Λυκίους πέμπτην φυλακὴν
βάντας ἐγείρειν
καιρὸς κλήρου κατὰ μοῖραν.
562–4 αὐδῶ Λυκίους πέμπτην φυλακὴν
βάντας ἐγείρειν
ἡμᾶς κλήρου κατὰ μοῖραν.
621, 797 ὄχημα πωλικόν.
750 μ᾽ ὀδύνη τείρει. 799 ὀδύνη με τείρει.
856 χρόνον μὲν ἤδη. 865 χρόνον γὰρ ἤδη.
937, 956 ἐλθεῖν κἀπικουρῆσαι.

In addition we find the same idea repeated in similar words
at 161:182; 216:233 ff.; 187:240 f.; 211:255 f.; 219 ff.:257 ff.;
343:454.

It is necessary to make clear the particular type of repetition that is in question. We are very little concerned here with a kind of repetition that is met in some other plays (e.g. in *Medea*), namely the recurrence of whole lines or groups of lines. In repetition of this kind one has often to reckon with the possibility of interpolation by a later hand.[1] This is a question that arises seldom, if at all, in *Rhesus*. Of the examples listed above only two (18:37 and 543–5:562–4) provoke any suspicion of this sort of textual corruption. These are the only places where a whole line or more is repeated in substantially identical form. Both instances are in anapaestic passages which contain other uncertainties of text;[2] nevertheless in neither case is the repetition certainly to be attributed to textual corruption.

The bulk of the examples of repetition listed above are of a different class. They are collocations of two or more words repeated with or without some variation. These closely similar expressions are separated sometimes by only a short interval, but often by a quite long one. The poet in repeating an earlier idea takes no pains to vary his expression but uses again the words that have served him on the previous occasion. It is here that the charges of inferior workmanship and 'sterile talent' arise.

This frequent repetition of phrases may offend the modern reader as a mark of uninspired and even careless writing. By the standards of the present day it is undoubtedly a serious fault of the style of *Rhesus*, and it has certainly been an important contributing cause to the adverse impression formed by many critics of the play. The question which we must consider, however, is not the artistic effect of these repetitions, but whether they can be associated with the work of Euripides.

Now it is a notorious fact that Euripides is much less at

---

[1] See Harsh, *Hermes*, LXXII (1937), 435–49: in this class he includes *Rh.* 37 f. (p. 437 n. 4, p. 449).
[2] See below, pp. 289 ff.

pains than either Aeschylus or Sophocles to avoid monotony of expression. In the words of Schmid: 'Eine gewisse Lässigkeit des Wortgebrauchs fällt auf, wenn Euripides ohne stilistischen Zweck ein tonloses Wort oder eine Phrase nach kurzem Zwischenraum wiederholt.'[1] Our present concern is especially with his repetition of phrases. Examples of this tendency could be taken from any play of Euripides, but for purposes of comparison with *Rhesus* we need to measure the extent to which his style is affected by such repetition. I have therefore taken two specimen plays from different periods, *Hippolytus* and *Bacchae*, and have collected the examples of repeated phrases to be found *within* each of these plays. The results are set out in the lists which follow.

(i) *Repetitions of phrase in 'Hippolytus'*

12	τῆσδε γῆς Τροჳηνίας.	29	τήνδε γῆν Τροჳηνίαν.
73	ἀκηράτου λειμῶνος.	76	ἀκήρατον λειμῶνα.
131	νοσερᾷ κοίτᾳ.	179	νοσερᾶς κοίτης.
135–7	τριτάταν . . . ἁμέραν.	275	τριταίαν . . . ἡμέραν.
155–6	ναυβάτας . . . ἀνήρ.	1221	ὥστε ναυβάτης ἀνήρ.
281	ἔκδημος . . . χθονός.	659	ἔκδημος χθονός.

415, 522 δέσποινα ποντία Κύπρι.

423 κλεινῶν 'Αθηνῶν.   760, 1094 κλεινὰς 'Αθήνας.

438 ὀργαὶ δ' ἐς σ' ἀπέσκηψαν θεᾶς.

1417 f. θεᾶς ἄτιμοι Κύπριδος ἐκ προθυμίας.
ὀργαὶ κατασκήψουσιν ἐς τὸ σὸν δέμας.

440 ἔρωτος οὕνεκα.   456 ἔρωτος εἵνεκα.

779 κρεμαστοῖς ἐν βρόχοις.   802 βρόχον κρεμαστόν.

846 οὐ τλητὸν οὐδὲ ῥητόν.   875 οὐ τλητὸν οὐδὲ λεκτόν.

898 ξένην ἐπ' αἶαν λυπρὸν ἀντλήσει βίον.

1049 ξένην ἐπ' αἶαν λυπρὸν ἀντλήσεις βίον.

1031, 1075, 1191 εἰ κακὸς πέφυκ' ἀνήρ.

1241 ὦ πατρὸς τάλαιν' ἀρά.

1378 ὦ πατρὸς ἐμοῦ δύστηνος ἀρά.

---

[1] Schm.–St. III, 795; some examples are cited there (n. 1). See also the works of Cook, Parry and Page cited in p. 205 n. 1 above.

(ii) *Repetitions of phrase in 'Bacchae'*

Refrains are omitted and certain other repetitions in the lyrics which are appropriate to the style of a hymn or prayer (e.g. 116, 165, 986).

118 ἀφ' ἱστῶν παρὰ κερκίδων τ'.
    1236 τὰς παρ' ἱστοῖς ἐκλιποῦσα κερκίδας.
186 γέρων γέροντι.   193 γέρων γέροντα.
227 πανδήμοισι . . . στέγαις.   444 πανδήμου στέγης.
231, 451 ἐν ἄρκυσιν.
243 ἐκεῖνος ἐν μηρῷ ποτ' ἐρράφθαι Διός.
    286 ὡς ἐνερράφη Διὸς μηρῷ.
    295 βροτοὶ ῥαφῆναί φασιν ἐν μηρῷ Διός.
244 ὃς ἐκπυροῦται λαμπάσιν κεραυνίαις.
    288 ἐκ πυρὸς κεραυνίου.
    594 κεραύνιον αἴθοπα λαμπάδα.
261 ὅπου βότρυος ἐν δαιτὶ γίγνεται γάνος.
    382 f. ὁπόταν βότρυος ἔλθῃ | γάνος ἐν δαιτὶ θεῶν.
272, 322 ὃν σὺ διαγελᾷς.
349, 602 ἄνω κάτω.   741, 753 ἄνω τε καὶ κάτω.
469 νύκτωρ ἢ κατ' ὄμμα.   485 νύκτωρ ἢ μεθ' ἡμέραν.
497 εἰρκταῖσί τ' ἔνδον.   549 ἐν εἰρκταῖς.
509 καθείρξατ' αὐτὸν φάτναις.
    618 πρὸς φάτναις . . . , οὗ καθεῖρξ' ἡμᾶς.
660, 961, 1043, 1202 (τῆσδε) Θηβαίας χθονός
    Cf. 1 τήνδε Θηβαίαν χθόνα.
749 Ἀσωποῦ ῥοαῖς.   1044 Ἀσωποῦ ῥοάς.
797, 1219 ἐν Κιθαιρῶνος πτυχαῖς.   62, 945 Κιθαιρῶνος πτυχάς.
836, 852 θῆλυν ἐνδῦναι στολήν (cf. 853 ἐνδύσεται).
956 μαινάδων κατάσκοπον.   981 κατάσκοπον μαινάδων.
1070 ἐλατίνων ὄζων.   1098 ὄζοισί τ' ἐλατίνοισιν.
1122 διαστρόφους κόρας.   1166 διαστρόφοις ὄσσοις.

Comparable is the repetition in a similar context of an unusual, and therefore striking, word: several words are thus repeated in *Bacchae*, sometimes close together, as διαμεθείς (627, 635), προνώπιος (639, 645); sometimes further apart, as οἰστρέω (32, 119), θεομαχέω (45, 325, 1255), παράκοπος (33, 1000).

It appears then that repetition of phrases is a common

enough phenomenon in both *Hippolytus* and *Bacchae*. Some of the instances are insignificant enough and might well pass unnoticed, but in other cases a quite distinctive phrase is repeated after only a few verses in a manner that betrays indifference to any inharmonious effect. In neither of these plays, however, is the repetition on the same scale as in *Rhesus*, especially if difference of length is taken into account. There would indeed seem to be no other play of Euripides which approaches *Rhesus* in this respect. The amount of repetition varies in different plays, but in the two considered it has perhaps slightly more than average prominence.[1] There is therefore an appreciable difference of degree between *Rhesus* and other plays of Euripides in the matter of repetition.

Is this difference of degree significant? Certainly we have discovered a prominent feature of the style of *Rhesus*, but it is one which belongs, if a little less noticeably, to other works of Euripides. The striking examples of repeated phrases in other plays of his prove that he was not highly sensitive in this respect, and give us reason to doubt that he would have been disturbed by the amount of repetition that appears in *Rhesus*.

A further point may be noticed, although of ambiguous significance. Several of the phrases repeated in *Rhesus* are used elsewhere by Euripides, some of them several times, as οὐκ ἄλλως λέγω, δὶς τόσως, πέφυκ' ἀνήρ (see above), others once or twice, as κατὰ στόμα, ὁπλίζειν χέρα, ὡς σὺ κομπεῖς (see *Concordance*), ναῦς ἐπ' Ἀργείων μολεῖν (*Tro.* 954, cf. *Andr.* 401). For others closely parallel phrases could be found, e.g. *Hec.* 18 εὐτύχει δορί, *Ph.* 1432 ὑστέρα βοηδρόμος, *IT* 31 βαρβάροισι βάρβαρος. One might say then that these were phrases which Euripides carried in his mind, so that it is not surprising that he should use them more than once within the same play. On the other hand one could see here again

---

[1] It is stated by Schm.–St. III, 795 n. 1, that the number of repetitions increases in the latest works of Euripides, with the exception of *Bacchae*. I have not, however, noticed this to be true of the kind of repetition we are considering.

evidence for the work of an imitator, who having picked up a few typically Euripidean turns of phrase proceeds to use them to excess. It is however dangerous to found any hypothesis on such isolated scraps of evidence.

Some of the repeated phrases in *Rhesus* involve proper names. This accords with a tendency of Euripides' style, to be observed in the plays considered above and elsewhere: in the case of recurring proper names he does not seek variety but is content to use an established phrase as a convenient formula. Here too the other tragedians seem to be more careful to avoid monotony.

Repetition is undoubtedly a marked feature of the style of *Rhesus*, but the fact that Euripides himself shows a strong tendency to carelessness in this respect makes this much less significant as evidence that the play is spurious. Insistence upon variety of expression is indeed much less characteristic of Greek poetry than it is of modern literature. To the taste of the present day such repetition as we have been discussing, both in *Rhesus* and the other two plays, may appear a serious defect of style, but it does not appear to have offended against the aesthetic standards of the time of Euripides. This being so, we ought not to be perturbed if this known characteristic of Euripides' style is a little more prominent in *Rhesus* than in any of his other works.

Deficiency of the gnomic element

Euripides is notoriously fond of introducing in the mouths of his characters philosophical reflections of a sententious kind. These gnomic utterances range in sentiment from traditional popular wisdom to the advanced and extravagant ideas of contemporary sophistic thought, and may be expressed in a few words or in several lines; but whatever their content or length, they are characterized by a pithy, pointed style that is familiar to all readers of Euripides. They occur in all the extant plays and by reason of their lasting appeal to anthologists bulk large among the surviving fragments of lost plays.

In *Rhesus* the gnomic element is not totally lacking, but such *sententiae* are much fewer than we are accustomed to expect in Euripides, and the majority of them are expressed very briefly.[1] Some of the early critics found in this deficiency a serious argument against authenticity, and although later scholars discounted its significance, it has been brought forward again by a few more recent opponents of Euripidean authorship.[2]

Those who would see here an important difference of style disregard the elementary fact that this kind of philosophizing is not an indispensable ingredient of the style of Euripides, but a purely incidental rhetorical embellishment, which is essentially separable from its context. The quantity of such gnomic philosophy is entirely at the discretion of the poet, and although it is characteristic of Euripides' style, the amount varies considerably from play to play, and within any play the distribution is irregular. In *Medea* the gnomic passages add up to over 150 verses, in *Hippolytus* to more than 200; but in *Alcestis* (1158 lines) the total is only 40 lines, and in *Iphigenia in Tauris* (1496 lines) it is 55.[3] Now the gnomic utterances in *Rhesus* add up to only 26 lines in a total of 996. This is an even smaller proportion than in either *Alcestis* or *Iphigenia in Tauris*, but for each of these plays the total includes one or two quite long pieces of philosophizing which are especially appropriate to their place in the drama.[4] In the latter half of *Iphigenia in Tauris*, which is marked by lively

[1] Gnomic passages in *Rhesus*: 69, 106–7, 132, 161–3, 176, 198, 206, 245 ff., 266, 317–18, 332, 333, 334, 482, 626, 758–60, 980–2.
[2] Especially by Pearson, *CR*, xxxv (1921), 53; Nestle, *Euripides*, p. 381 n. 28. Murray, *op. cit.* p. viii, also notes the lack of philosophy among the differences from the ordinary style of Euripides which lead to doubt of the play's authenticity. Among older scholars cf. Valckenaer, *op. cit.* p. 95; Beck, *op. cit.* pp. 283 f.; Hermann, *op. cit.* p. 274; Hagenbach, *op. cit.* p. 25. Vater, *op. cit.*, ch. v, §21; Albert, *op. cit.* p. 21, and Ridgeway, *CQ*, xx (1926), 15, are among those who deny the significance of this argument.
[3] The totals are approximate and include some pieces of philosophizing which perhaps ought not strictly to be called gnomic.
[4] The total for *Iphigenia in Tauris* includes one passage of 12 lines (380–91); in *Alcestis* some of the philosophizing comes from the drunken Heracles (782–6, 799–802).

226

dramatic action, the gnomic element is certainly no more prominent than in *Rhesus*.

The variation in quantity needs no special explanation, for the dramatist is obviously not bound to adhere to a fixed measure in such matters. There is however no doubt that for Euripides appropriateness to character and to the dramatic situation was important. His taste for philosophizing was not so great that it had to be indulged both in and out of season. Although there may be exceptions, the sententious speeches are usually given to suitable persons at suitable times. In *Rhesus* the nature of the plot and characters provided abundant reason for including only a small quantity of moralizing. In particular the debate, which in Euripides is often richly studded with gnomic reflections, is in *Rhesus* between two persons to whom such a style would be inappropriate.[1]

The thought of γνῶμαι tends to be commonplace, but it is to be observed that those in *Rhesus* are in both sentiment and expression quite in the manner of Euripides. The brevity with which most are expressed is not, as some critics have suggested, foreign to his style. The following comparisons may be made with Euripides in respect of either thought or expression or both: *Rh.* 106–7: *Ph.* 745; *Rh.* 206: *Ba.* 179; *Rh.* 332: frr. 254, 536, 554, *Tro.* 509 f.; *Rh.* 333: fr. 886 (= Ar. *Ra.* 1427); *Rh.* 334: *Alc.* 566 f.; *Rh.* 758–60:[2] fr. 734, *Cycl.* 201, *Hcld.* 533 f., *Tro.* 401 f.

The expectation of εὔκλεια as the reward of πόνος, a leading idea of the Dolon-scene, is a recurrent motive in Euripides, to be found in many fragments, notably those of *Archelaus*.[3]

In particular, the sentiment of *Rh.* 980–2 may be singled

---

[1] Both Hector and Rhesus are expressly characterized as men of plain speech (394 f., 422 f.). Debates rich in gnomic philosophy: e.g. *Med.* 465–575, *Hipp.* 373–481, *Andr.* 319 ff., 590 ff. Cf. also the lengthy moralizing of frr. 360, 362.

[2] Pearson, *op. cit.* p. 53 n. 2, contrasts the thought of these lines with *Tro.* 633; but the sentiments which a dramatist puts into the mouths of different characters in different situations need not be consistent.

[3] Frr. 236–40; cf. frr. 134, 364, 474 and the paraphrase of *Philoctetes* by Dio Chrysostom (*Orat.* 59; cf. *Orat.* 52, 11 f.: Nauck, *TGF*[2], pp. 613 ff.).

out as distinctively Euripidean: with it are to be compared especially *Med.* 1090 ff., *Alc.* 882 ff., and for the wording fr. 757.

Terseness of expression

The style of *Rhesus* is described by Murray as terse, in contrast with a fullness and flexibility which he regards as characteristic of the ordinary style of Euripides.[1] He thus sums up in a word a quality which is insistent in the style of *Rhesus* and may well impress the reader as unlike the familiar manner of Euripides. Throughout the play, in both lyric and dialogue, the tendency is towards rapidity and economy of expression, at times approaching baldness. This is in fact a much more fundamental quality of the style of *Rhesus* than the opposite tendency, discussed above, to a so-called high-flown diction, but has caused less uneasiness among critics. It has however been noticed from time to time,[2] and the difference of manner is real enough to deserve discussion.

Brevity of style is most strongly marked in two lyric passages, the parodos and the epiparodos (674 ff.). In both places it is explicable on dramatic grounds: the staccato manner of expression is appropriate to the rapid, breathless action of these two scenes. A good parallel to this manner in similar circumstances is to be found in the scene of the pursuit of Orestes in the *Eumenides* (254 ff.). But a lack of fullness in the expression is felt rather more widely in *Rhesus*, and is not always associated with hurried movement on the stage. A few observations may help to remove misgivings about this quality of the style. It is indeed not difficult to find examples

[1] Murray, *op. cit.*: 'The ordinary style of Euripides is full, flexible, lucid, antithetic, studiously simple in vocabulary and charged with philosophic reflection.' The style of *Rhesus*, on the other hand, he describes as 'comparatively terse, rich, romantic, not shrinking from rare words and strong colour and generally untinged by philosophy'. The other points at issue here have been dealt with already. In respect of *lucidity* I do not see that *Rhesus* differs at all from other works of Euripides.

[2] E.g. Beck, *op. cit.* p. 298; Morstadt, *op. cit.* p. 63; Hermann, *op. cit.* p. 274; Porter, *op. cit.* p. xlix, by way of illustration of the terseness of style, mentions the piling-up of interrogations.

of the same concentrated, terse style in other works of Euripides.

So far as the lyrics are concerned, brevity and simplicity of expression are decidedly characteristic of the earlier, as opposed to the later, style of Euripides. The closest parallel in manner to the lyrics of *Rhesus* is certainly to be found in those of *Alcestis* and *Heraclidae*;[1] the lyrics of *Medea* have something of the same quality but are on a rather more elaborate scale. The parodos of *Rhesus* resembles closely both in form and style that of *Alcestis*: the dramatic motive and mood are of course very different, but there is a similar exchange of question and answer in brief, clipped phrases, and little variation of manner accompanies the change from anapaests to lyric metre. Similarly, in the two stasima brevity and simplicity of phrase is the general rule, relieved now and then, as we saw earlier, by an uncommon turn of phrase or rich epithet: this is the manner of the lyrics of *Alcestis* (especially perhaps 435 ff., 568 ff.) and of *Heraclidae*. I do not wish here to pursue a comparison in detail, merely to point out places where the terseness of expression of the lyrics of *Rhesus* is matched in the lyrics of Euripides.[2]

In the iambic dialogue one is conscious of a brevity of style throughout *Rhesus*. This quality is less pronounced in some passages, for example the messengers' speeches, which have been commonly acknowledged as Euripidean in character, and in the final scene; elsewhere it is strongly marked, especially in scenes where there is rapidity of action or urgency of decision. The paucity of the gnomic type of philosophy contributes to the impression of concentration, but quite apart from this there is often found an extreme economy of words and a total absence of ornament. A few examples will suffice for illustration:

76–7 "Εκτορ, ταχύνεις πρὶν μαθεῖν τὸ δρώμενον·
ἄνδρες γὰρ εἰ φεύγουσιν οὐκ ἴσμεν τορῶς.

---

[1] Grube, *The Drama of E.* p. 445, makes the same comparison.
[2] The structure of the lyrics will be discussed below, pp. 336–44.

81   οὔπω πρὶν ἧψαν πολέμιοι τοσόνδε φῶς.
83   σὺ ταῦτ' ἔπραξας· καὶ τὰ λοιπὰ νῦν σκόπει.
90   Αἰνέα, πύκαζε τεύχεσιν δέμας σέθεν.
104   φεύγειν ἐᾶσαι πολλὰ δράσαντας κακά.
137-9 νικᾶτ', ἐπειδὴ πᾶσιν ἀνδάνει τάδε.
        στείχων δὲ κοίμα συμμάχους· τάχ' ἂν στρατὸς
        κινοῖτ' ἀκούσας νυκτέρους ἐκκλησίας.

(Cf. 215, 218, 223, 264 f., 328, 332, 335, 467 f., 599, 661 f., 665 f., 859–62, 952 f., 957, 961, 975, 985.)

The expression in these places is neither crude nor lacking in vigour, but it is unadorned, compressed and terse. Although Euripides is normally simple in vocabulary, one is accustomed to associate with him a fuller and less austere style. In most plays this highly condensed and severely plain style is only rarely found outside passages of stichomythia. In one play however, *Heraclidae*, compression and brevity are marked qualities of the expression.[1] Allowing for the fact that it has a much larger measure of the gnomic type of philosophy,[2] the general impression of the style of *Heraclidae* is not unlike that of *Rhesus*, as a comparison of the following passages of *Heraclidae* may serve to illustrate: 55–133, 250–87, 329–52, 630–701, 784–98, 975–80. In these passages the vocabulary consists largely of everyday words and the expression is highly concentrated, economical and generally lacking in poetic ornament. The qualities of style are essentially those found in *Rhesus*. *Heraclidae* resembles *Rhesus* in the urgent rapidity of its action: this has probably influenced the character of the style in both plays.

We have now reviewed the differences that have been said to exist between the style of *Rhesus* and the ordinary style of Euripides. Analysis of the evidence has disposed of the case

---

[1] Zuntz, *The Political Plays of E.* pp. 26 f., comments on the rapidity and concentration which mark both the action and the style of *Heraclidae*.

[2] But even the γνῶμαι of *Heraclidae* tend, like those of *Rhesus*, to be expressed succinctly: compare, e.g., *Hcld.* 476–7 with the similar but much more elaborate sentiment of *Med.* 214–18.

for imitation of the diction of Aeschylus and Sophocles, and nothing foreign to the style of Euripides has been found in certain supposedly bombastic forms of expression. The other alleged peculiarities of the style of *Rhesus* are real enough to account for an impression of dissimilarity, but comparison with the other works of Euripides shows that they are not altogether without parallel. In the frequency of repetition, in the paucity of gnomic philosophy and in its tendency to terseness of style *Rhesus* occupies an extreme position among the works of Euripides; but in none of these respects is it so far removed from some other plays as to justify doubt of its authenticity. The differences are simply in degree and not in the essential character of the style.

SOME QUALITIES OF THE STYLES OF 'RHESUS' AND EURIPIDES COMPARED

Does the above collection of points noted by various scholars account for all the important stylistic differences between *Rhesus* and the remaining work of Euripides? This question justifies a broader consideration of the style of *Rhesus* in some of its leading departments. Here all that needs to be established is simply whether or not the style of our drama conforms to the normal manner of Euripides. If here and there points of close resemblance are noticed, the limitations of our evidence may make it difficult for us to assess their significance.

Imagery

It is to be observed that the style of *Rhesus* is coloured only very lightly by simile and metaphor. This is in accordance with the manner of Euripides, who avoids the richer imagery of Aeschylus or Sophocles.[1] Developed similes of the Aeschylean type, rare in Euripides, are not to be found in *Rhesus*, whose few similes are so brief as almost to pass un-

[1] Schm.–St. III, 797 ff.; cf. *ibid.* II, 292 ff., 495 ff. Detailed analysis of imagery in Euripides by Smereka, *op. cit.* II, 76 ff.; for lyric parts only by Breitenbach, *op. cit.* pp. 133 ff.

noticed.[1] Metaphorical expression is mainly confined to single words and is often of such an everyday kind that it is doubtful if an image is consciously intended.[2] The few more elaborate metaphors are derived from sources from which Euripides commonly draws images, as indeed do other poets, notably: (a) navigation: 246–9, 322–3, 423; (b) hunting: 325–6, cf. 56–7; (c) dice: 154–5, 183, 446. The diction of one or two of these passages has already been considered; beyond this there is nothing especially to be noted about the way these metaphors are expressed.[3]

Among the metaphorical applications of single words a few are uncommon enough to retain some special poetic colour. Of these the majority are to be paralleled in tragedy and especially in Euripides. The following are matched in Euripides:

122 πεπύργωται χερί: see above, p. 206.
290 ῥέων στρατός: cf. Aeschylus, *Sept.* 80, *Pers.* 412, Euripides, fr. 146, *IT* 1437 (ῥεῦμα στρατοῦ).
318 ἕρπει κατάντης: see above, p. 215.
338 χάρις διώλετο: cf. Euripides, *Hcld.* 438, fr. 736.
353 κόλποι: cf. Euripides, *Hel.* 1145.
381 σκύμνος and 386 πῶλος, of humans: Eysert notes both these uses as characteristically Euripidean.[4] Outside *Rhesus* Euripides has σκύμνος seven times, and in five of these it is applied to humans; the only other occurrence in tragedy is in the original application at Sophocles, *Aj.* 987. Similarly, πῶλος is used of humans five times in Euripides outside *Rhesus*, but elsewhere in tragedy it is so used only at Aeschylus, *Ch.* 795, where it is part of an extended metaphor (so too in Anacreon, fr. 75, 1). These uses are not met in earlier poetry.

[1] *Rh.* 301, 304 (comparison), 306, 618. The first three are in the Messenger's speech, and this is where Euripides most often uses similes in dialogue (Schm.–St. III, 797 n. 3). All are in the Euripidean manner.
[2] Besides those quoted below the following verses contain metaphors, all of them of the everyday variety: 8, 55, 195, 281, 411, 412, 425 (cf. 750, 799), 450, 509, 596, 690, 744, 834, 884.
[3] On 246–9 see pp. 201 f.; on 322–3, p. 215; on 154–5, p. 206. With the phraseology of 423 (not the metaphor) cf. fr. 124, 3.
[4] *Rhesus im Lichte des euripideischen Sprachgebrauches*, II, 30.

566 στάӡει δι’ ὤτων: cf. Aeschylus, *Ag.* 179 f., Euripides, *Hipp.* 526. See above, p. 216.

674 σκηπτοῦ πολεμίων: cf. Euripides, *Andr.* 1046 and *Phoen.* 113.

796 βαθεῖαν ἄλοκα τραύματος: see above, p. 211.

875 οὐ γὰρ ἐς σὲ τείνεται γλῶσσα: the metaphor is found in Euripides in the intransitive use of the verb.

In addition, one or two metaphors not found in Euripides are paralleled in the other tragedians:

405 προπίνω, *betray*: cf. Aeschylus, fr. 131.

711 ὕπαφρον ὄμμ’ ἔχων: explained as follows by schol.: ὕπαφρος ὁ μὴ φανερός, ἐκ μεταφορᾶς τῶν ὑπ’ ἀφρὸν νηχομένων, ἢ τῶν ὑφάλων πετρῶν αἷς ἐπανθεῖ ἀφρός.

In this sense cf. Sophocles, frr. 236, 312.

This leaves without parallel

669 θηκτὰ κοιμίσαι ξίφη: κοιμίӡω is used in a variety of metaphorical applications; cf. Euripides, *Ph.* 184 μεγαλαγορίαν... κοιμίӡεις.

785 ἐξ ἀντηρίδων: see above, pp. 216 f.

It is clear that there is no evidence here of a divergence from the style of Euripides. The general simplicity of the imagery is fully in the Euripidean manner. The few unusual expressions are no more than one might expect to find in any play. In addition, one or two metaphorical usages have been noticed which seem especially characteristic of Euripides.

Periphrasis

A familiar and important characteristic of the style of Euripides is his addiction to a form of periphrasis which uses certain everyday words. For example, such simple verbal ideas as *go, come, stand* are constantly expressed by phrases involving the word πούς; similarly, χείρ is found in many phrases for a variety of manual actions.[1] Such phrases are of

[1] For examples see *Concordance*, s.vv. χείρ, πούς. Eysert (*op. cit.* pp. 36–9) dealt in some detail with this tendency of Euripides' style, with particular reference to the frequency of phrases involving πούς and δόρυ. See also Schm.–St. III, 800 n. 5, with references.

course to be found in the other tragedians, but Euripides' style is marked by a lack of restraint in their use. Here, as in other respects, he shows less regard for variety of expression than either Aeschylus or Sophocles. The monotonous recurrence of stereotyped phrases of this kind contributes significantly to the particular character of the Euripidean style.

In *Rhesus* the same type of periphrasis occurs with a frequency which matches the manner of Euripidean diction. Particularly noticeable is the fondness for phrases using words for certain parts of the body, especially πούς and χείρ, also ὄμμα. Combinations using πούς include σπουδῆ ποδός (85), ἵημι πόδα (203, 798), τίθημι πόδα (280, 571), ποδὸς ἴχνος βαλεῖν (721), ἀδειμάντῳ ποδί (697). Periphrases with χείρ, most of them for a simple noun or pronoun, occur at 286, 607, 635, 694, 762, 772, 792, 802, 873, 928, and with ὄμμα at 54, 371, 554, 825–6. In addition, there are various other phrases of a similar kind, e.g. with δόρυ and δέμας, which help to give the style a Euripidean stamp.[1]

Many of these expressions, it is true, could be paralleled individually in Aeschylus or Sophocles as well as in Euripides, but the tendency to this form of expression is much less marked in the other two tragedians. There are, besides, a number of periphrastic expressions in *Rhesus* which are otherwise known only in Euripides and seem especially characteristic of his diction. These include:

4   κληδόνα μύθων: cf. *Hel.* 1250 λόγων κληδόνα.
63   ἰέναι δόρυ: *Ph.* 1247.
495   συναίρεται δόρυ: cf. *Hcld.* 313, *Hel.* 1597, *Ph.* 434.
85   σπουδῇ ποδός: *Hec.* 216.
286   πολεμίας χερός: *Med.* 1322.
721   ποδὸς ἴχνος βαλεῖν: see above, pp. 209 f.

[1] Periphrasis of this type occurs in *Rhesus*, besides places already cited, at 4, 8, 43, 59, 63, 66, 82, 90, 95, 111, 112, 118, 132, 144, 145–6, 151, 213, 235, 278, 282, 287, 288, 331, 354, 376, 392, 398, 408, 417, 426, 432, 447, 459, 471, 490, 495, 553, 601, 608–9, 622, 700, 701, 709, 718, 735, 769, 784, 796, 850, 921, 934, 960, 962, 967, 969, 971, 985, 989, 992. On the use of δέμας in periphrasis see Burkhardt, *Die Archaismen des E.* p. 90.

Other similar phrases have a Euripidean stamp, although found in other poets too, e.g. 392 νεῶν σκάφη (cf. Aeschylus, *Pers.* 419; for Euripidean parallels see *Concordance*, s.v. σκάφος).

The phrases quoted are representative of the type of expression with which we have been dealing and which strongly affects the style of *Rhesus*. There is a tendency to indulge in this colourless kind of periphrasis, which imparts no originality to the expression. In this respect the style of Euripides is precisely similar and the styles of Aeschylus and Sophocles markedly different. Thus a quality fundamental to the style of Euripides is found deeply ingrained in the style of *Rhesus*.

Pleonastic dative

The strongly Euripidean flavour of the style of *Rhesus* is exemplified further in another characteristic, which is related to what we have just been discussing but does not properly fall under the heading of periphrasis. This is the fondness of the poet for supplementing the sense of a verb by a dative, usually instrumental, which is not strictly necessary to the sense. In the most frequent form of this mannerism a disyllabic dative is used to complete the iambic trimeter. Here the same favourite words of Euripides (and of the poet of *Rhesus*) are in evidence again: in *Rhesus* we find especially χερί and δορί so used, also ποδί, ξίφει, φρενί.[1] These words when used in this position very often occur alone, without a qualifying adjective, in which case they are attached pleonastically to a verb; less frequently they are combined with an epithet to make a periphrasis for a simple adjective or adverb. The following are the examples in *Rhesus*:

58 τῷδ' ἀναλῶσαι δορί.   62 τῇδε πολυφόνῳ χερί.
105 ὡς δρᾶσαι χερί.   122 πεπύργωται χερί.   214 ἐμβαίνω ποδί.

[1] For examples in Euripides see these words in the *Concordance*. Eysert, *op. cit.*, also treats this aspect of style.

222–3 οὐδ' ἀναιμάκτῳ χερὶ | ἥξω.
266 ἦ πόλλ' ἀγρώταις σκαιὰ πρόσκειται φρενί.
315 οὔθ' ὑποσταθεὶς δορί.   326 συγκαμὼν δορί.
407 τῆδ' ἔθηκ' ἐγὼ χερί.
451 μή τις ἀσπίδ' ἄρηται χερί.
452–3 τοὺς μέγ' αὐχοῦντας δορὶ | πέρσας Ἀχαιούς.
472 Ἑλλάδ' ἐκπέρσαι δορί.   478 πορθεῖν . . . δορί.
586 καρατομεῖν ξίφει.   772 ἀφθόνῳ μετρῶ χερί.
794 παίει . . . ἐς πλευρὰν ξίφει.

Instances of such a complementary dative, similarly placed, could be found in any play of any of the tragedians, but the tendency is strongly pronounced only in Euripides. His inclination to the use of such disyllabic datives (especially the words so used in *Rhesus*, also one or two others) at the end of the trimeter may be observed in any play. It is, however, also true that the habit is probably not so prominent in any other play of Euripides as it is in *Rhesus*. In *Phoenissae*, for example, a much longer play, I find only about a dozen such datives, in *Medea* or *Hecuba* 10, in *Electra* 7. There is here a difference of proportion, for which perhaps a partial explanation could be found in the subject-matter of our play: the emphasis on action, especially warlike action, offers scope for the use of the words χερί and δορί. But the difference of degree and the possible reasons for it are of minor importance. The significant point is that the tendency here displayed by *Rhesus* is familiar in the style of Euripides.

Rhetorical figures

Scholars who have analysed the style of Euripides have observed his fondness for certain rhetorical figures.[1] Notable among these are the doubling of words (anadiplosis), the repetition of a word at the head of successive clauses (anaphora) and the juxtaposition of different inflections of the same word (paregmenon). These devices are, in different degrees, common to the styles of all the tragedians, but a

[1] Schm.–St. III, 801 ff.; Smereka, *op. cit.* II, 152 ff.; Breitenbach, *op. cit.* pp. 214 ff.

brief survey will establish that both the extent and the manner of their employment in *Rhesus* are in full conformity with the practice of Euripides.

(a) Anadiplosis

This figure is used to only a limited extent by Aeschylus, but is freely employed by both Sophocles and Euripides, being generally commoner in lyric than in dialogue.[1] There is a marked increase of frequency in the lyrics of late plays of Euripides.

In *Rhesus* anadiplosis occurs in lyric at 250 (ἔστι), 346–7 (ἥκεις), 357 (ὤ), 357–8 (νῦν), 385 anap. (θεός), 535 (ἀώς), 675–6 (βάλε four times and θένε), 720 (ὄλοιτο), ? 821 (μέγα), 902–3 (φιλία); in dialogue at 396 (πάλαι), 579 (θρασύς).

It is thus found 10 or 11 times in lyric (four times unseparated, six or seven times separated), twice in dialogue (once unseparated, once separated).

That these totals fall within the limits for the use of this figure by Euripides is shown by comparison of the statistics compiled by Smereka and the lists of Breitenbach for the lyric parts.[2] In dialogue the number of occurrences per play ranges from 0 (*Cyclops*) to 8 (*Medea*), the frequency of occurrence having no relation to date.[3] In lyric the number of occurrences varies between 1 (*Heraclidae*) and 45 (*Orestes*); here the tendency is to increase in the later plays, a peak being reached in *Orestes* and *Phoenissae* (28 times), but the increase is irregular and the number of instances in the lyric parts of *Rhesus* is compatible with an early date among the works of Euripides (cf. *Alcestis*, which has 14).[4]

---

[1] Anadiplosis in Aeschylus: Schm.–St. II, 296, with references in n. 2; in Sophocles, *ibid.* p. 489 n. 7; in Euripides, *ibid.* III, 802 f. (see also the next note).

[2] Smereka, *op. cit.* II, 169; Breitenbach, *op. cit.* pp. 218 ff.: in general I have followed their figures, although my own calculations have sometimes yielded slightly different results. Minor variations do not affect the general picture.

[3] The figures quoted are those of Smereka, who gives (*op. cit.*) totals for the dialogue parts of all plays.

[4] The figures given here are based on the analysis of Breitenbach, *op. cit.* pp. 217–21.

A more notable point is that in lyric the separated kind of anadiplosis is generally commoner in the earlier works of Euripides, the proportion of the unseparated kind tending to increase greatly in later plays. The change corresponds to a difference in the use made of the device: whereas in the earlier plays the word repeated usually carries special emphasis, in Euripides' late style the device is often employed for its rhythmical or pathetic effects with little regard for the importance of the repeated word.[1] In this respect *Rhesus* associates itself with the works of the earlier group.

It is hardly possible to distinguish here individual traits of style, but of particular forms of anadiplosis occurring in *Rhesus* the following may be noted:

(i) 396 The pair of words stands unseparated at the beginning of the trimeter. The majority of examples of unseparated anadiplosis in the dialogue parts of Euripides occur in this position, but the form is not rightly thought to be peculiarly characteristic of Euripides:[2] cf. Aeschylus, *PV* 266, *Eu.* 140, Sophocles, *Tr.* 1144, Ar. *Av.* 921; also Sophocles, fr. 753.

(ii) 570 The repeated word is at the beginning and the end of the trimeter. This form is found several times in Euripides: *Alc.* 722, *Hcld.* 307, *Hipp.* 327, *Ba.* 963, fr. 414; cf. also *IT* 991–3, *IA* 1026. Note besides Sophocles, fr. 753:

βαρὺς βαρὺς ξύνοικος, ὦ ξένοι, βαρύς,

also Sophocles, fr. 210, 46.

(iii) 357–8 νῦν, ὦ πατρὶς ὦ Φρυγία,
ξὺν θεῷ νῦν σοι.

For anadiplosis of ὦ cf. Euripides, *Tro.* 601 ὦ πατρὶς ὦ μελέα,
Ibid. 1081 ὦ φίλος ὦ πόσι μοι,
Alc. 234 βόασον ὦ, στέναξον, ὦ Φεραία χθών,
also *Alc.* 460, *Cyc.* 52.

(iv) 346–7 ἥκεις, ὦ ποταμοῦ παῖ, | ἥκεις.
385 θεός, ὦ Τροία, θεός.
357–8: see (iii) above.
A word is repeated after an apostrophe.
Cf. *Andr.* 843 ἀπόδος, ὦ φίλα, 'πόδος.

---

[1] As, e.g., in *Or.* 1426 ff. The tendency is parodied by Ar. *Ra.* 1352–5.

[2] Breitenbach, *op. cit.* p. 215, who refers here to Fr. Marx (*Festschrift für Gomperz*, p. 130), is to be corrected in this point.

Hec. 693 δείν', ὦ τάλαινα, δεινὰ πάσχομεν κακά,
also *Alc.* 218, *Ph.* 818, *Cyc.* 510. Note also, however, an equally close parallel in Aeschylus, *PV* 577.

With 357–8, repetition after apostrophe together with anadiplosis of ὦ, cf. *Alc.* 460 f.

σὺ γάρ, ὦ μόνα, ὦ φίλα γυναικῶν, | σύ.

(v) 720 ὄλοιτ' ὄλοιτο.
So too *Ion* 704.

(vi) 675 βάλε βάλε βάλε βάλε.

Quadruple repetition is not paralleled in Euripides, but is found in Aeschylus, *Eu.* 130 λαβὲ λαβὲ λαβὲ λαβέ, likewise in a scene of pursuit, and in Sophocles, *fr.* 314 (*Ichneutae*), 94. The closest parallel to our passage is that of Ar. *Ach.* 280 ff.:

οὗτος αὐτός ἐστιν, οὗτος.
βάλλε βάλλε βάλλε βάλλε,
παῖε πᾶς τὸν μιαρόν.

The possibility that Aristophanes may here be parodying Euripides, if not *Rhesus* itself, has already been suggested (see above, pp. 2 f., 129 f.).

These few examples show at least that there are several points of similarity between *Rhesus* and the works of Euripides in the manner in which anadiplosis is employed.

(b) Anaphora

This figure is greatly favoured by both Sophocles and Euripides; in Aeschylus it is rather less common. In Euripides it is particularly common in the lyric parts, where it is not less marked in the earlier than in the later plays. Breitenbach gives a total of 136 occurrences in the lyrics of 18 plays and the fragments of Euripides.[1] This total includes only some of the numerous examples of pairs of interrogative clauses introduced by the same word, a very frequent form of anaphora in Euripides. If these are added, the total is considerably greater.

Rhesus has 15 instances of anaphora in lyric (eight times interrogatives), 16 in dialogue (three times interrogatives). This is again consistent with the early style of Euripides: in

[1] *Op. cit.* pp. 230 ff.; cf. Schm.–St. III, 802 n. 2.

Alcestis, for example, I have counted 10 examples in lyric (five times interrogatives), a further five in dialogue (three times interrogatives).[1]

The wide variety of different parts of speech used by Euripides in anaphora, and the diversity of its forms, are demonstrated, for the lyric parts, by Breitenbach's analysis. There is nothing special to note about the particular examples of anaphora in the lyrics of *Rhesus*, all of which are of a quite ordinary kind.

In dialogue the quadruple anaphora of 311 f. may be compared with *Med.* 303 ff., and the content of these lines with *Ph.* 113.

(c) Paregmenon

The figure is not used in the lyric portions of *Rhesus*, but occurs 11 times in dialogue, at 107, 184, 185, 206, 211, 337, 388, 404, 445, 833, 940.

The absence of paregmenon from the lyrics of *Rhesus* is not out of keeping with the style of Euripides, the device being used generally with moderation in his lyric composition; but here again it is somewhat easier to associate the play with his earlier than with his later works. The 104 examples of paregmenon collected by Breitenbach (*op. cit.* pp. 223 ff.) from the lyric parts of Euripides are distributed among the plays and fragments as follows: *Alc.* 1, *Med.* 2, *Hcld.* 2, *Hipp.* 3, *Andr.* 5, *Hec.* 6, *Su.* 7, *El.* 2, *HF* 7, *Tro.* 4, *IT* 6, *Ion* 6, *Hel.* 8, *Ph.* 6, *Or.* 17, *Ba.* 8, *IA* 7, *Cyc.* 2, *frags.* 5. Generally then it is the plays of known early date which make least use of this figure in lyric: in fact, the only examples in these plays are of the most ordinary kind.[2]

---

[1] Anaphora in *Rhesus*, lyric: 11 f., 30 f., 38, 131, 195, 261, 455, 461–3, 527, 681, 692 f., 725, 738 f., 742, 906 f.; dialogue: 116 f., 149–52, 161, 311 f., 847, 915. In *Alcestis*, lyric: 29, 77 f., 108, 132, 275 f., 861, 863 (twice), 912–13, 991–2, (1160); dialogue: 291 f., 530, 834, 942, 961.

[2] All but one of the examples of paregmenon found in the lyrics of *Alcestis*, *Medea*, *Heraclidae*, *Hippolytus* belong to Breitenbach's class (*f*) (*op. cit.* p. 225), i.e. common formulae, used also in prose, involving such words as ἄλλος, πολύς, κτλ.

The total of 11 occurrences of paregmenon in dialogue would be compatible with Euripidean authorship at any date, including an early one (cf. *Alcestis* with 12 examples). The figure is no less common in the other tragedians.

With 184 καὶ μὴν ἐρῶντί γ' ἀντερᾷς ἵππων ἐμοί,
cf. *Alc.* 1103 νικῶντι μέντοι καὶ σὺ συννικᾷς ἐμοί,
also *Hcld.* 26, 27, and Sophocles, *OT* 306.

(d) Alliteration

It has been said that there is a falling-off in alliteration in Euripides as compared with Aeschylus and Sophocles.[1] Nevertheless it is not infrequently met in his work at all dates, and in iambic trimeter, at least, appears to be somewhat more common than it is in Sophocles.[2]

In *Rhesus* alliteration occurs quite often and in several places it is sufficiently striking to arrest the attention. The following are notable:

139 κινοῖτ' ἀκούσας νυκτέρους ἐκκλησίας.
283 πλαγχθεὶς πλατείας πεδιάδος θ' ἁμαξιτοῦ.
286 κλύοντα πλήρη πεδία πολεμίας χερός.
383–4 κλύε καὶ κόμπους κωδωνοκρότους
παρὰ πορπάκων κελαδοῦντας.
393 παῖ τῆς μελῳδοῦ μητέρος Μουσῶν μιᾶς.
545 καιρὸς κλήρου κατὰ μοῖραν.

To these may be added other less prominent examples at 167, 188, 190, 278, 566, 685, 704, 923, 942, 959.[3]

With the notable exception of *vv.* 383–4 it does not appear to be the poet's intention to achieve any special effect by the

---

[1] Schm.–St. III, 802 and 801 n. 4. Breitenbach, *op. cit.* p. 235, quotes this as the finding of Chr. Riedel, *Alliteration bei den drei großen griechischen Tragikern* (Diss. Erlangen, 1900).

[2] Here my observation agrees with the finding of Riedel (Breitenbach, *op. cit.*).

[3] In addition, there are places where two words beginning with the same consonant are juxtaposed: 207, 241, 277, 448, 506, 613, 635, 651, 679, 745, 794: coincidences of this kind are of no account, although they may add slightly to the cumulative effect of alliteration upon the style. Notice also the sigmatism of *v.* 866, a quality characteristic of the style of Euripides, although not peculiar to him (Schm.–St. II, 494 n. 3).

alliteration. It is rather the case that he does not bother to avoid fortuitous collocations of the same consonant. These may sometimes appear to us rather tasteless and to betray a want of refinement in the style. There are however numerous examples of similarly indiscriminate alliteration in Euripides, especially of the very likely coincidences of π and κ.[1] It would certainly appear that he was not very sensitive to any harshness that we might feel in such collocations.

Alliteration is perhaps slightly more frequent in *Rhesus* than is usual in Euripides. But some of his plays have as much or more, the device being especially prominent in the *Supplices*.[2] It may also be observed that the majority of the examples of alliteration in *Rhesus* are in the iambic dialogue, as appears to be usual in Euripides.[3]

Here again therefore there seems to be general conformity with the style of Euripides.

This survey has dealt with some of the essential elements of poetic style. No further discrepancies between the style of *Rhesus* and the ordinary style of Euripides have been brought to light. Rather is there evidence of a general conformity to the habits of style of Euripides. It is indeed not remarkable to find in many respects a closer resemblance in style to Euripides than to Aeschylus and Sophocles, both of whom seek richer poetic effects and greater originality of expression. But the likeness to Euripides extends to those mannerisms which may well be thought the peculiar marks of his style. It now becomes clear that in the matter of style there is a

[1] π: *Alc.* 684, 845, *Hcld.* 125, *Hipp.* 23, 30, 54, etc.; κ: *Med.* 347, *Hcld.* 958–9, *Hipp.* 707, etc. The indiscriminate character of alliteration in the dialogue of Euripides is in contrast with the style of Sophocles, who tends to employ the device for special effects, e.g. *OT* 371, 425, *Aj.* 1112. See Schm.–St. II, 494.

[2] Especially *Su.* 118, 400, 496–7, 498–9; also 247, 341, 452–3, 458–9, 629, 686, 717–18, 748, 880. I have also noticed some striking examples in *Hippolytus* and *Bacchae*.

[3] This is my own observation without detailed study; I note, however, that Riedel's finding (Breitenbach, *op. cit.*) was that alliteration in Euripides is distributed equally between lyric and dialogue. At all events alliteration in dialogue is more extensive in Euripides than in the other tragedians.

quite intimate relationship between *Rhesus* and Euripidean drama, which cannot be obscured by the few superficial differences that have been recorded. It is further apparent, I think, that where a development in the style of Euripides is to be observed, *Rhesus* does not share in tendencies peculiar to his later works, but is in all respects in harmony with his earlier style. Finally, the likeness in style to Euripides is of a kind not easily explained in terms of imitation.

ADDITIONAL MISCELLANEOUS RESEMBLANCES TO THE STYLE OF EURIPIDES

The evidence for similarity of style between *Rhesus* and the works of Euripides has not yet been exhausted. Besides the several striking coincidences of phraseology that were noted earlier there are other detailed resemblances, which, although individually less notable, are not without a collective importance and which help to confirm the impression of the evidence already considered. These may conveniently be assembled under three headings according to their nature.

Resemblances of sentence-structure

In addition to the resemblances of diction already presented there are other passages in *Rhesus* where a striking likeness to Euripides in the form of expression is to be recognized. In these, however, the distinctive feature of the parallel is not so much a verbal similarity, although this is present, as a resemblance in the structure of the sentence or in the arrangement of words within the verse. Most of the parallels in this group have not been noted by previous scholars.[1]

(*a*) 59–61   εἰ γὰρ φαεννοὶ μὴ ξυνέσχον ἡλίου
λαμπτῆρες, οὔταν ἔσχον εὐτυχοῦν δόρυ
πρὶν ναῦς πυρῶσαι καὶ διὰ σκηνῶν μολεῖν.

Alc. 357–62   εἰ δ' Ὀρφέως μοι γλῶσσα καὶ μέλος παρῆν,
. . .
κατῆλθον ἄν, καί μ' οὔθ' ὁ Πλούτωνος κύων

---

[1] In addition to those acknowledged below (*c*) was included in the lists of Hagenbach and Rolfe, but it has little significance as evidence of imitation.

οὔθ' οὑπὶ κώπη ψυχοπομπὸς ἂν Χάρων
ἔσχον πρὶν ἐς φῶς σὸν καταστῆσαι βίον.

Here we may observe the parallel construction of the sentence and the additional coincidence of the main verb, ἔσχον.

(b) 84   ἁπλοῦς ἐπ' ἐχθροῖς μῦθος ὁπλίζειν χέρα.
Alc. 519   διπλοῦς ἐπ' αὐτῇ μῦθος ἔστι μοι λέγειν.

This passage shows a closer resemblance than the two cited by Rolfe:

Aeschylus, Ch. 554   ἁπλοῦς ὁ μῦθος, τήνδε μὲν στείχειν ἔσω,
and Euripides, Ph. 469   ἁπλοῦς ὁ μῦθος τῆς ἀληθείας ἔφυ,

to which we may add:

Euripides, fr. 253   ἁπλοῦς ὁ μῦθος, μὴ λέγ' εὖ.

The parallel in Aeschylus prevents our labelling the turn of phrase as distinctively Euripidean; nevertheless, between the verses in *Rhesus* and *Alcestis* the resemblance extends to the similar use of ἐπί with the dative and the like arrangement of words, and thereby acquires a greater significance.

(c) 403   ποῖον δὲ δώρων κόσμον οὐκ ἐπέμψαμεν;
Hcld. 441   ποῖον δὲ γαίας ἕρκος οὐκ ἀφίγμεθα;

The verbal resemblance is negligible, since this form of question is not confined to Euripides (cf. e.g. Sophocles, *OT* 420–1); but one is struck by the similar rhetorical force of the negative interrogative formula, in both places following another question, and especially by the exact coincidence in the arrangement of words within the verse.

(d) 438–40   οὐχ ὡς σὺ κομπεῖς τὰς ἐμὰς ἀμύστιδας,
                 οὐδ' ἐν ζαχρύσοις δώμασιν κοιμώμενος,
                 ἀλλ' οἷα πόντον Θρήκιον φυσήματα....
Med. 555–9   οὐχ, ᾗ σὺ κνίζῃ, σὸν μὲν ἐχθαίρων λέχος,
                 . . .
                 οὐδ' εἰς ἅμιλλαν πολύτεκνον σπουδὴν ἔχων·
                 . . .
                 ἀλλ' ὡς, τὸ μὲν μέγιστον, οἰκοῖμεν καλῶς.

244

In both places we have a rhetorical formula denying the charges of an opponent and adding the speaker's defence. The sentences are similarly articulated (οὐχ ... οὐδέ ... ἀλλά ...), with the parallel phrases after the first negative, ὡς σὺ κομπεῖς and ἢ σὺ κνίζῃ, imparting to both the same tone of indignation. Similar in effect is *Ba.* 686 f. οὐχ ὡς σὺ φῂς ὠνωμένας κρατῆρι κτλ. The phrase ὡς σὺ κομπεῖς, again in *Rhesus* at 876, is found in Euripides, *Or.* 571.

(*e*) 565–6   Διόμηδες, οὐκ ἤκουσας—ἢ κενὸς ψόφος
             στάζει δι' ὤτων;—τευχέων τινὰ κτύπον;
El. 747–8   φίλαι, βοῆς ἤκούσατ'—ἢ δοκῶ κενὴ
             ὑπῆλθέ μ';—ὥστε νερτέρα βροντὴ Διός;

There is here a quite remarkable similarity of structure, underlined by the coincidence of ἤκουσας: ἠκούσατ' and κενός: κενή. The parenthetical alternative has parallels outside Euripides, e.g. Sophocles, *El.* 352, *Ichn.* 151; cf. also Euripides, *Cyc.* 121. But the same degree of likeness is not found elsewhere.

(*f*) 570–1   Οδ. ὅρα κατ' ὄρφνην μὴ φύλαξιν ἐντύχῃς.
             Δι. φυλάξομαί τοι κἂν σκότῳ τιθεὶς πόδα.
IT 67–8   Ορ. ὅρα, φυλάσσου μή τις ἐν στίβῳ βροτῶν.
             Πυ. ὁρῶ, σκοποῦμαι δ' ὄμμα πανταχῆ στρέφων.

The dramatic situations are similar. There is some resemblance in vocabulary, but not enough to arouse suspicion of imitation. The essence of the similarity is in the form and the tone of the cautious, almost timid, command and the reassuring response.

Between these two scenes there are a few other points of resemblance in expression and sentiment (*IT* 96: *Rh.* 580; *IT* 102–3: *Rh.* 582; *IT* 104–5: *Rh.* 589–90); these amount to little, and certainly do not constitute evidence of imitation, but it is perhaps more likely that the two scenes should be by the same poet than by different poets.

(*g*) 759 f.   λυπρὸν μέν, οἶμαι, τῷ θανόντι· πῶς γὰρ οὔ;
           τοῖς ζῶσι δ' ὄγκος καὶ δόμων εὐδοξία.

Alc. 353 f.   ψυχρὰν μέν, οἶμαι, τέρψιν, ἀλλ' ὅμως βάρος
ψυχῆς ἀπαντλοίην ἄν.

The resemblance is confined to the parenthetical οἶμαι and the arrangement of the words at the beginning of the sentence: this is, however, enough to arrest attention. It may be noted that parenthetical οἶμαι is more common in Euripides than in the other tragedians. Aeschylus has only οἴομαι so used at *Ch.* 958 (the form οἶμαι occurs in Aeschylus only at *Ag.* 321); Sophocles has parenthetical οἶμαι three times (*Ant.* 1051, *Ph.* 498, fr. 583, 4: see Schm.–St. II, 486 n. 4). In Euripides it is found 11 times, and with notable frequency in plays of earlier date (*Alc.* 2, *Med.* 3, *Hcld.* 3, *Hipp.* 1: once each in *Electra* and *Bacchae*).

The following may be added, although they seem to be of less consequence:

(*h*) 105   εἴθ' ἦσθ' ἀνὴρ εὔβουλος ὡς δρᾶσαι χερί.
   Hcld. 731   εἴθ' ἦσθα δυνατὸς δρᾶν ὅσον πρόθυμος εἶ.

This is one of the resemblances listed by Rolfe. The similarity, however, is not in the phraseology but in the structure.

(*i*) 656 f.   ἥκω δ' ἀκούσας οὐ τορῶς, φήμη δέ τις
         φύλαξιν ἐμπέπτωκεν.
   Hcld. 494   κἀμοὶ λέγει μὲν οὐ σαφῶς, λέγει δέ πως.
   Ph. 161   ὁρῶ δῆτ' οὐ σαφῶς, ὁρῶ δέ πως.

There is certainly a similarity of structure and manner here. Pearson, who drew attention to this resemblance, was prepared to attach more importance to it than to any of the coincidences of phrase noted by his predecessors.[1] To others the parallel might seem more tenuous than some of those already cited.

(*j*) 699–701   Θεσσαλὸς ἢ
          παραλίαν Λοκρῶν νεμόμενος πόλιν;
          ἢ νησιώτην σποράδα κέκτηται βίον;
   Tro. 187–9 τίς μ' Ἀργείων ἢ Φθιωτᾶν
          ἢ νησαίαν μ' ἄξει χώραν
          δύστανον πόρσω Τροίας;

_____
[1] *CR*, xxxv (1921), 56.

Ibid. 241–2   αἰαῖ, τίν᾿ ἢ
          Θεσσαλίας πόλιν ἢ
          Φθιάδος εἶπας ἢ Καδμείας χθονός;
With the phraseology of 701 cf. also
    Hcld. 84   οὐ νησιώτην, ὦ ξένοι, τρίβω βίον.

Taken together all these passages seem to contain evidence of an affinity of thought and style. Contempt for the νησιώ-της appears also in *Andr.* 14.

Here we have seen ten instances of a sufficiently distinctive resemblance to the manner of Euripides in the moulding of the sentence or verse. In estimating the significance of this evidence it must be remembered that resemblances of this type to the style of *Rhesus* are met only in Euripides; in Aeschylus or Sophocles or the fragments of the other tragedians there is never to be found more than a superficial resemblance to the expression of our play.[1] The present parallels are of a different character from the coincidences of phrase previously considered; for the point of likeness lies not in a distinctive choice of vocabulary but in the poet's habitual manner of casting his ideas into words, and resemblance of this sort is less easily attributed to imitation. In each separate instance this explanation seems unlikely, and it becomes less and less probable as further examples are added. Imitation of style is not ordinarily so penetrating. The choice thus rests between identity of authorship and coincidence, and if the present parallels do not suffice by themselves to prove the former, they certainly ought to be added to the evidence for authenticity already collected and to the further points of resemblance that are still to be noticed.

Distinctive features of syntax

The few grammatical peculiarities occurring in *Rhesus* were reviewed in the last chapter (pp. 179 ff.), and it was found

---

[1] In the present class of evidence perhaps the most notable parallel to either Aeschylus or Sophocles is *Rh.* 309 f.: *Pers.* 429 f.; but this is easily attributable to coincidence.

that the play is remarkably free from syntactical abnormality and from deviations from Attic usage of the fifth century. Here a different aspect of the evidence of syntax will be considered. To our collection of parallels to the style of Euripides there can be added a few which involve the use of less common, although by no means abnormal, grammatical constructions. These deserve at least passing notice.

(a) 144–5   σάλπιγγος αὐδὴν προσδοκῶν καραδόκει
        ὡς οὐ μενοῦντά μ'.

Editors have noted the parallel construction of *Hcld.* 693 ὡς μὴ μενοῦντα τἄλλα σοι λέγειν πάρα. The accusative absolute with a personal verb after ὡς is not rare (cf. Sophocles, *OT* 101, *OC* 380; Euripides, *Ion* 965, *Ph.* 714; see K.–G. II, 95 *d*), but the further coincidence of the verb makes the parallel worth noting.

(b) 294–5   πρὶν δὴ δι' ὤτων γῆρυν οὐχ Ἑλληνικὴν
        ἐδεξάμεσθα καὶ μετέστημεν φόβου.

The use of πρίν with the indicative here and at 568 was mentioned above (p. 180). There is nothing especially remarkable about the construction, but a close stylistic resemblance to the present passage is seen in *Andr.* 1147

πρὶν δή τις ἀδύτων ἐκ μέσων ἐφθέγξατο

(cf. Denniston, *GP*, p. 220). This is a detailed point of the general resemblance between the narrative styles of *Rhesus* and Euripides.

(c) 467–8   τοιαῦτα μέν σοι τῆς μακρᾶς ἀπουσίας
        πρᾶξαι παρέξω.

The genitive ἀπουσίας is best explained as belonging to the class of genitive of price or exchange, = *in return for*. Precisely parallel is *Med.* 534 f.:

μείζω γε μέντοι τῆς ἐμῆς σωτηρίας
εἴληφας ἢ δέδωκας, ὡς ἐγὼ φράσω.

248

Cf. also Sophocles, *Tr.* 287–8:

εὖτ' ἂν ἁγνὰ θύματα
ῥέξῃ πατρῴῳ Ζηνὶ τῆς ἁλώσεως.

This is the same kind of genitive, but the *Medea* passage bears the closer resemblance in form and style. With the form of *Rh.* 467 cf. also *Med.* 545 τοσαῦτα μέν σοι τῶν ἐμῶν πόνων πέρι | ἔλεξ'.

(*d*) 837 μακροῦ γε δεῖ σε καὶ σοφοῦ λόγου.

δεῖ with accusative of the person and genitive of the thing is a favourite construction of Euripides. With our passage cf. especially

> *Hipp.* 491 οὐ λόγων εὐσχημόνων δεῖ σ',
> *Ibid.* 688 ἀλλὰ δεῖ με δὴ καινῶν λόγων,

also *Hipp.* 23, *Su.* 789, *Ion* 1018, *Ph.* 470, 921, *Hec.* 1021, *HF* 1171, *Hel.* 1424, *IA* 1130.

In tragedy outside Euripides the construction is found only at Aeschylus, *PV* 86; otherwise only in *com. adesp.* 46D.: εὐρυχωρίας σε δεῖ.

(*e*) 932–3 καί σ' ... οὐκ ἐδείμαινον θανεῖν.

The construction of verbs of fearing with the accusative and infinitive is an established poetical usage, nevertheless a quite rare one. In Homer it is found, with the future infinitive, at Ζ 342, χ 40. In tragedy there are the following examples, all with the aorist infinitive as in *Rhesus*:

Aeschylus, *Sept.* 720 ff.	πέφρικα τὰν ὠλεσίοικυν θεὸν ... Ἐρινὺν τελέσαι τὰς περιθύμους κατάρας.
Euripides, *Hec.* 768	πατήρ νιν ἐξέπεμψεν ὀρρωδῶν θανεῖν.
Su. 554–5	ὅ τ' ὄλβιός νιν πνεῦμα δειμαίνων λιπεῖν ὑψηλὸν αἴρει.
	(πνεῦμα is here the subject of λιπεῖν.)
Ion 1564–5	θανεῖν σε δείσας μητρὸς ἐκ βουλευμάτων καὶ τήνδε πρὸς σοῦ, μηχαναῖς ἐρρύσατο.

The force of the construction may be interpreted as 'be afraid at the thought of' (cf. Goodwin, *MT*, § 373), but there is little, if any, practical difference in sense from the construction with μή.

The present parallel with Euripides is enhanced by the recurrence of θανεῖν as the infinitive in two of the Euripidean examples.

The similarities noted in this group are individually of small account, involving nothing that need be thought exclusively Euripidean. Nevertheless, most of these syntactical points are intimately related to style and in each case we find that the construction, in the manner of its use, is most closely paralleled in Euripides. There is here, therefore, yet further illustration of the extent to which the style of *Rhesus* is marked by a Euripidean character.

Formulae of dialogue

Under this heading I wish to note the occurrence in the dialogue of *Rhesus* of certain locutions which may deserve to be thought especially characteristic of the Euripidean style. These are derived from a broad investigation into the treatment of dialogue in such aspects as the forms of address used between characters, the ways in which entrances are announced and leave taken, modes of question and answer, the use of particles, and so on. These things constitute an important part of a dramatist's style. In such matters *Rhesus* is, in fact, found to conform closely to the habits of Euripides, a result which is of some significance in itself. It is, however, also true that there is here some degree of uniformity among the tragedians, who tend to draw the ordinary forms of expression for standard situations from a common stock of tragic diction. It is therefore not easy in this branch of style to point to features that may fairly be called individually Euripidean.

In *Rhesus* we find many of the favourite tricks of style of Euripides, but comparatively few of these are used by him alone among the tragedians. For example, most of the combinations of particles used in the dialogue of *Rhesus* occur not only in Euripides but also in one or both of the other tragedians; so too do such expressions as τοὐπὶ σέ (397), τὸ σὸν μέρος (405), the parenthetical ὡς ἔοικε (631, 807), σὲ τὸν ... λέγω (642), μισῶ introducing a *sententia* (333). These features are strongly reminiscent of the Euripidean manner, but are not exclusively Euripidean. Certain other turns of expression of a similar type do, within the limits of our knowledge, belong peculiarly or predominantly to Euripides: these will serve as further evidence of the Euripidean character of the style of *Rhesus*.[1]

(*a*) Entrance of characters. For noting the approach of a character there are certain stereotyped forms of expression in common use among the tragedians. Nevertheless, the manner in which persons are introduced in *Rhesus* (at 85–6, 627–8, 806–7) is very close to the style of Euripides.[2] In particular, with 85 f.

καὶ μὴν ὅδ' Αἰνέας καὶ μάλα σπουδῇ ποδὸς
στείχει, νέον τι πρᾶγμ' ἔχων φίλοις φράσαι,

cf. *Hec.* 216 f.

καὶ μὴν 'Οδυσσεὺς ἔρχεται σπουδῇ ποδός,
'Εκάβη, νέον τι πρὸς σὲ σημανῶν ἔπος.

Euripides is fond of thus anticipating that the person approaching brings news: cf. also *Med.* 269 f., *IT* 236 f., *Tro.* 230 ff.; Aeschylus, *Sept.* 369–71 and *PV* 943 are similar in this respect.

With the position of the verb of motion at the beginning of the second verse (86 στείχει, 628 στείχοντα, 807 χωρεῖ) cf. Euripides, *Alc.* 612, *Med.* 269, *Or.* 878 (στείχοντα), *Ph.* 445 (χωρεῖ).

(*b*) 52 ἐς καιρὸν ἥκεις.

Euripides often thus combines the phrase ἐς καιρόν with a verb of motion in places where a comment is made upon the

---

[1] With the exception of (*a*) (Hagenbach and others), (*h*) and (*i*) (Sneller, *op. cit.* p. 80), none of these has previously been mentioned.

[2] On the manner in which characters are introduced by the Chorus in Euripides see Arnoldt, *Die chorische Technik des E.* pp. 346 ff.

timely arrival of a character: cf. *Hipp.* 899, *Hec.* 666, *HF* 701, *Tr.* 744, *Hel.* 1081, *Ph.* 106, *Or.* 384. This formula is not exactly paralleled in Aeschylus or Sophocles, although the latter has καιρόν adverbially in similar phrases at *Aj.* 34 (καιρὸν δ᾽ ἐφήκεις) and 1316 (καιρὸν ἵσθ᾽ ἐληλυθώς); cf. *ibid.* 1168 ἐς αὐτὸν καιρὸν ... πάρεισιν. In Aristophanes ἐς καιρόν occurs at *Av.* 1688 (ἐς κ. κατεκόπησαν), but in the present formula it may fairly be called characteristically Euripidean.

(*c*) 87 τί χρῆμα; *Why?*

The fact that this adverbial use of τί χρῆμα; appears to be confined to Euripides is observed by Denniston on *El.* 831, who cites in addition to its occurrence there *Cyc.* 669, *Alc.* 512, *Hec.* 977, *HF* 1179; further examples are *Held.* 633, 646, 709, *Ion* 255, *Or.* 277.

The use of τί χρῆμα; with pronominal force is common to all three tragedians. One may so take it here with νυκτηγοροῦσι, if this is treated as transitive, but the adverbial force is still felt with κεκίνηται.

(*d*) 99 σὺ δ᾽ ὡς τί δράσων πρὸς τάδ᾽ ὁπλίζεις χέρα;
Cf. *Alc.* 537 ὡς δὴ τί δράσων τόνδ᾽ ὑπορράπτεις λόγον;
Med. 682 σὺ δ᾽ ὡς τί χρῄζων τήνδε ναυστολεῖς χθόνα;

For the combination of ὡς with the interrogative one might compare Sophocles, *O T* 1174; the form of expression here is nevertheless distinctive and not closely paralleled elsewhere.

(*e*) 167 σὺ δ᾽ ἀλλά. . . .

Following the rejection of one proposal the speaker puts forward an alternative suggestion. On this locution see Denniston, *GP*, p. 10, who cites several examples from Euripides, others from Aristophanes, Antiphanes, Plato and Xenophon. Euripides is especially fond of this formula, which is not found in Aeschylus or Sophocles.

(*f*) 175   οὐ μὴν τὸν Ἰλέως παῖδά μ᾽ ἐξαιτῇ λαβεῖν;
Cf. *Alc.* 518   οὐ μὴν γυνή γ᾽ ὄλωλεν Ἄλκηστις σέθεν;

See Denniston, *GP*, p. 334: 'οὐ μήν, following a rejected suggestion, introduces, tentatively and half incredulously, an alternative suggestion.' It is only in these two passages that this combination is so used, and it has exactly the same force in both places.

(*g*) 273   παῦσαι λέγων.
Cf. especially *Hipp.* 706 παῦσαι λέγουσα, *Ba.* 809 σὺ δὲ παῦσαι λέγων.

Euripides is particularly fond of using the imperative παῦσαι with a participle in a sharp prohibition: cf. also *Alc.* 707, *Ion* 1410, *IA* 496, *IT* 1437, *Or.* 1625; similarly, with a genitive: παῦσαι λόγων τῶνδε *El.* 1123 and *Ion* 650; cf. *Andr.* 1270, *Med.* 1319, fr. 188, 2.

Neither Aeschylus nor Sophocles has precisely this formula of prohibition, although Sophocles uses absolutely παῦσαι (*Ant.* 280, *Aj.* 483, 1353) and παύσασθε (*OT* 631, *El.* 1428). But παῦσαι with a participle is also found commonly in Aristophanes, e.g. *Ach.* 1107, *Av.* 859, 888, 1382.

(*h*) 762. A narrative ῥῆσις begins with the word ἐπεί.

Sneller (p. 80) observes that this opening is characteristic of the Euripidean narrative style, citing *Cyc.* 382, *Med.* 1136, *Andr.* 1085, *Ion* 1122, *El.* 774, *IT* 940, *Hel.* 1526, *Ph.* 1359, *Hipp.* 1198. To these add *Alc.* 158, *Hcld.* 800. But it must be noted that the beginning of a piece of narrative in this way is not confined to Euripides: ἐπεί is so found also at Sophocles, *Tr.* 900 and Aeschylus, *PV* 829.

(*i*) 281   ἔγνως.

Sneller (*op. cit.*) further notes as typically Euripidean the use of this word, standing alone, to confirm a surmise of the previous speaker. The examples in Euripides are *Andr.* 883, 920, *El.* 617, *Ion* 1115, *Or.* 1131, *Ph.* 983. There is also, however, one similar use of ἔγνως in Sophocles, at *Tr.* 1221.

The beginning of a speech thus with a single word followed by a stop is quite characteristic of the style of Attic tragedy, but Euripides perhaps does it more often than the other tragedians. In this category we may add to our list the following places in *Rhesus*, where the use of a particular word in this way is paralleled more than once in Euripides and not in either Aeschylus or Sophocles.

(*j*) 191 αἰνῶ used absolutely and alone to express assent.

This word is so used alone at the beginning of the verse in fr. 603 (*Peliades*) and *IT* 1486. Essentially similar are *HF* 275, γέροντες, αἰνῶ, and *Alc.* 1093, αἰνῶ μὲν αἰνῶ. Elsewhere αἰνῶ expressing assent has a pronominal object: so in Sophocles, *Ph.* 889, αἰνῶ τάδ', ὦ παῖ, and Euripides, *Med.* 908, *Or.* 786.

(*k*) 201 στείχοιμ' ἂν standing alone and expressing intention to depart.

This formula is common in Euripides, occurring at *Ba.* 515, 845, *El.* 669, *Ion* 668, 981 (cf. 418, στείχοιμ' ἂν εἴσω). The closest parallel outside Euripides is Sophocles, *Ant.* 1108, ὧδ' ὡς ἔχω στείχοιμ' ἄν.

(*l*) 877 λάζυσθ'.

This imperative is used alone in the same way at *Ion* 1266, *Ba.* 503. Cf. also *Ion* 1402, *Ph.* 1660, λάζυσθε τήνδε, and *IA* 622. It was earlier noted that the word λάζυσθαι is not found in Aeschylus or Sophocles.

It must be emphasized again that the above list contains only such points of resemblance between *Rhesus* and Euripides as appear to be especially characteristic of the Euripidean style. In the present category it would be possible to add a great many other resemblances equally close but of a less distinctive quality; these, however, would not add significantly to the present evidence, which gives additional proof of the strongly Euripidean character of the style of *Rhesus*.

'Rhesus' 527–56 and the Parodos of 'Phaethon'

There is one special case of stylistic resemblance between *Rhesus* and Euripides that we have not yet considered. It has often been observed that there are striking similarities in both matter and manner between the song with which the Chorus in *Rhesus* greet the approaching dawn (527–37, 546–56) and the ode on the same theme in *Phaethon* (67–90 Volmer), but the significance of resemblance has been variously interpreted.[1]

The two lyrics have several motives in common: the Pleiads, the nightingale and her song of lamentation, the mountain herdsmen with their pipes. This correspondence of treatment is rather more than can comfortably be attributed to chance. The common elements are not such obviously conventional ornament for this theme that they are likely to have occurred independently to two different poets. The possibility of coincidence is further reduced by the presence of verbal resemblances, not indeed numerous but sufficiently distinctive. Of these certainly the most important is the use of the rare verb ἔγρεσθαι (*Rh.* 532, *Pha.* 77), which is not otherwise found until after the fifth century, and also to be noted is the similar phrasing of *Rh.* 551 f. ἤδη δὲ νέμουσι κατ' Ἴδαν ποίμνια and *Pha.* 79 f. ἤδη δ' εἰς ἔργα κυναγοὶ στείχουσιν.

In spite of the verbal coincidences there is no reason to suppose that the poet of *Rhesus* is imitating *Phaethon*, or *vice versa*. Apart from the places noted there is no verbal resemblance of any account, and it is in fact more remarkable that in the treatment of the common motives there is complete independence of expression. There are, besides, quite sub-

[1] Text of *Phaethon* parodos (Euripides, fr. 773, 19 ff., supplemented by *P. Berol.* 9771): Wilamowitz, *Berl. Kl. T.* v, 2, 81; Volmer, *De Eur. fabula quae* ΦΑΕΘωΝ *inscribitur restituenda* (1930); Pickard-Cambridge, *New Chapters in Greek Literature*, 3rd ser. (1933), pp. 143 f. The resemblance is discussed especially by G. H. Macurdy, *AJP*, LXIV (1943), 408–16. Pohlenz, *Die griechische Tragödie*, 2nd ed. p. 474, thinks that *Rhesus* has borrowed from *Phaethon*, a view apparently shared by Geffcken, *op. cit.* p. 406.

stantial differences, in content and mood, between the two passages, each being admirably suited to its context.

There seem then to be two possible explanations of the resemblances between these two odes. We could suppose that two different poets drew independently upon an earlier treatment of the same theme, each giving fresh and original expression to motives derived from a common source. It is, however, much easier to regard both lyrics as the product of the same mind composing on the same theme at different times and for different settings.

There does not appear to be anything in the nature of the resemblance between these two passages to indicate which is the earlier. The question of the date of *Phaethon* is therefore hardly relevant for us. In fact, its date is disputed, but the metrical evidence, so far as it is possible to judge, suggests that it was not an early work and that it may have been composed later than 420.[1] Acceptance of so late a date for *Phaethon* would not be an obstacle to regarding *Rhesus* as an early work of Euripides.

SUMMARY

This survey has established quite clearly that there is no solid case against the authenticity of *Rhesus* on the grounds of style. The arguments so often brought forward by scholars in the past provide no obstacle to accepting the play as the work of Euripides.

In the first place, it was found that the charge that our poet imitates the diction of the three tragedians is unfounded. There is no proper evidence of any imitation of Sophocles, and reminiscence of Aeschylus is no more extensive than we might expect in a work of Euripides. On the other hand, resemblances of this kind to the diction of Euripides are of an altogether different quality and appear in a number which would be surprising in the work of another playwright.

---

[1] For the different views on the date of *Phaethon* see Macurdy, *op. cit.* p. 414. The metrical evidence for its comparative lateness is fairly substantial.

The remaining allegations of differences in style between *Rhesus* and other works of Euripides are exaggerated. Indulgence in grandiloquent expression occurs only occasionally and to an extent which can be matched in Euripides. Repetition likewise is characteristic of the Euripidean style, although certainly more prominent than usual in *Rhesus*. The paucity of the gnomic element does not constitute an essential difference of style; it can, at all events, be paralleled in other plays of Euripides, and it is notable that the γνῶμαι that do occur in *Rhesus* are expressed in the Euripidean manner. There is possibly more substance in the argument that the terse manner of expression is in contrast to the usual fluency of Euripides' style. Here, perhaps, is a basic cause of the impression of a difference from the familiar style of Euripides; again, however, a similar manner is at times to be detected in his other works.

On the other hand, *Rhesus* has been found to share many leading characteristics of the style of Euripides. In its treatment of the chief ornaments of poetic style, imagery, periphrasis and rhetorical figures, it is fully in keeping with Euripidean practice. Not only is there in all points a general conformity, but there is also identity of manner in certain intimate traits of style.

Finally, various specific points of resemblance have been examined. In selecting these from among many I have sought to focus attention on points where a distinctively Euripidean quality of expression is to be felt. These points may be individually of small account, but cumulatively they bear witness to the strongly Euripidean flavour of the style of *Rhesus*.

Resemblance of style between *Rhesus* and Euripides is far from superficial; indeed, the impress of the Euripidean character upon the fundamental manner of expression of *Rhesus* is undeniable. This essentially Euripidean quality of the style of *Rhesus* has not been sufficiently acknowledged, but it demands an explanation from those who will challenge the play's authenticity. The hypothesis of imitation, which has been so freely put forward, is here totally inadequate. Imitation, however skilled, could hardly be so pervasive. Nor is resemblance of this order easily attributed to coincidence.

It is to be admitted that the style of *Rhesus* has some inelegant features. Most serious among these are the tendency to repetition, the excessive indulgence in a rather empty type of periphrasis and an occasional abruptness of expression. But these are the very faults which mar the style of Euripides: if they appear somewhat more marked in *Rhesus*, the difference of degree is not enough to arouse suspicion.

Could these blemishes of style be taken as evidence that *Rhesus* is an early work of Euripides, written before his style had attained full maturity? It is at least a possible hypothesis, although other explanations might be found. We have indeed observed in this chapter some facts which might support a date for *Rhesus* early in Euripides' career. A development in the style of Euripides is traceable especially in his lyrics, and we have seen that the lyrics of *Rhesus* conform closely to his earlier manner both in their sparing use of certain rhetorical tricks and in their general simplicity and naturalness of expression. It ought also to be noted that in the special points of resemblance to Euripides that have been found a high proportion of parallels are to the earliest plays, *Alcestis*, *Medea*, *Heraclidae* and *Hippolytus*. Moreover the terseness, which is perhaps the most pronounced quality of the style of *Rhesus*, is matched most closely in *Heraclidae*. These are points which must be taken into account in our final assessment of the evidence.

CHAPTER VI

METRE

There has never been a thorough investigation of the metres of *Rhesus* as a potential source of evidence for the question of its authenticity. It is only in certain aspects, such as the treatment of resolution in the iambic trimeter, that a detailed study has been made of the poet's metrical technique. In this important matter we have at our disposal, in statistical form, the results of scholars who have analysed exhaustively the incidence of resolution in the trimeters of Euripides. These statistics provide us with a useful basis of comparison between *Rhesus* and the works of Euripides, and, in view of the development here traceable in Euripides' technique, offer a criterion for dating the play if Euripidean. Besides resolution certain other aspects of the composition of the iambic trimeters call for examination; in particular, statistics have been compiled for the incidence of spondaic feet and for the relative frequency of the various types of caesura, and in both cases evidence has been found against the authenticity of our play.

The other metres of *Rhesus* have received less attention. In the case of the anapaests and the trochaic tetrameters we shall have to consider specific points in which a difference from the metrical technique of Euripides has been alleged. Arguments against authenticity have also been found in particular aspects of the treatment of lyric metres; but this important department deserves a fuller study than it has yet been given. We cannot profitably employ statistical analysis here, but we can hope to discover by comparative study whether the metres of the *Rhesus* lyrics contain any features incompatible with their Euripidean authorship. This inquiry too may yield evidence for the date of the play; for the development of Euripides' metrical technique is no less striking in the lyrics than in the spoken dialogue. In this connection it will be interesting to see whether the indications of the lyric metres and of the iambic trimeters are consistent with one another.

IAMBIC TRIMETER

Resolutions

It is well known that the frequency with which Euripides admits resolved syllables in his iambic trimeters increases steadily as his career progresses. The studies of Zieliński and Ceadel, developing the work of earlier scholars, have demonstrated how the statistical evidence of the percentages of the resolved feet in the trimeters can, if treated with proper discretion, provide a valuable criterion for the dating of his plays.[1] It has further been shown, especially by Zieliński, that the growing frequency of resolution is accompanied by a progressive relaxation of the conditions which govern its admission, so that in applying the evidence of resolutions to the question of chronology it is relevant to consider not only their quantity but also their quality.

Our present task is to inquire whether the treatment of resolution in the trimeters of *Rhesus* is compatible with Euripidean authorship, and, if so, where on the basis of this evidence it is most easily placed among his works. We ought also to consider whether this kind of evidence offers any absolute criterion for dating the play irrespective of its authorship: for this purpose we shall need to look at the treatment of resolution by other tragedians. A survey of the evidence of resolution has been made previously by Sneller, but, as we shall see, his interpretation of it is not altogether acceptable.[2]

---

[1] T. Zieliński, *Tragodumenon Libri Tres* (Cracow, 1925), 133–240 (*De trimetri Euripidei evolutione*); E. B. Ceadel, 'Resolved Feet in the Trimeters of Euripides', *CQ*, xxxv (1941), 66–89. Ceadel (p. 66) summarizes the work of earlier scholars in this field.

[2] Sneller, *De Rheso Tragoedia* (1949), pp. 42–53.

The statistical material which we need for this inquiry has been compiled by Zieliński and Ceadel, both of whom included *Rhesus* in their studies. We must examine first the figures for the overall frequency of resolution in *Rhesus* and the plays of Euripides. Here the significant figures for the purposes of comparison are those giving the proportion of resolved feet to the total number of trimeters in each play, and these are most usefully presented by Ceadel.[1] His statistics differ from Zieliński's in two respects: first, in including first-foot anapaests, which Zieliński reserved for separate consideration; secondly, in excluding resolutions caused by proper names, on the grounds that some plays are clearly affected more than others by the need to use names which cannot be introduced into the trimeter without resolution. This exclusion may perhaps appear a little arbitrary, inasmuch as the poet may sometimes be unable to avoid the repeated use of other words, besides proper names, which involve resolution. Such indeed we shall find to be the case in *Rhesus*. On the other hand, as Ceadel fairly argues, the fact that for proper names anapaests are sometimes allowed in feet from which they are normally excluded indicates that a special licence was felt in their case. In actual practice it does appear that the statistics provide a more reliable basis of comparison when proper names are excluded. It may also be observed that these differences between Ceadel's and Zieliński's calculations do not materially affect the position of *Rhesus* in relation to the plays of Euripides.

In *Rhesus*, according to Ceadel's table, the frequency of resolved feet, proper names excluded, per 100 trimeters is 8·1. The corresponding percentages for the plays of Euripides are as follows: *Alcestis* 6·2, *Medea* 6·6, *Heraclidae* 5·7, *Hippolytus* 4·3, *Andromache* 11·3, *Hecuba* 12·7, *Suppliants* 13·6, *Electra* 16·9, *Heracles* 21·5, *Troades* 21·2, *Iphigenia in Tauris* 23·4, *Ion* 25·8, *Helen* 27·5, *Phoenissae* 25·8, *Orestes* 39·4, *Bacchae* 37·6, *Iphigenia in Aulis* 34·7. The plays appear here in the order

[1] In his Table I (*op. cit.* p. 70).

adopted by Ceadel, which he regards as their probable chronological sequence. Although the only certain dates are those of *Alcestis* (438), *Medea* (431), *Hippolytus* (428), *Troades* (415), *Helen* (412), *Orestes* (408), *Bacchae* and *Iphigenia in Aulis* (406), this order is recommended by the general weight of evidence other than metrical and for most plays is generally accepted. The only real uncertainty is about the exact sequence of some plays in the middle group, notably *Electra* and *Heracles*, *Iphigenia in Tauris* and *Ion*, but this is not sufficient to affect the general picture.[1] From *Andromache* onwards there is a clear tendency for the frequency of resolution to increase, with only minor fluctuations, reaching a peak in *Orestes*, and then falling off slightly. Another notable thing is that the four earliest plays, *Alcestis*, *Medea*, *Heraclidae*, *Hippolytus*, are clearly separated from the rest as a group in which Euripides is sparing in his admission of resolved syllables. Within this group the frequency of resolution varies only slightly, between 4·3 in *Hippolytus* and 6·6 in *Medea*; in the next play, *Andromache*, only three years later than *Hippolytus*, the percentage jumps to 11·3. It is only from *Andromache* onwards that the tendency for resolution to increase is unmistakably defined.

Within the early group Ceadel considers that the frequency of resolution tends to decrease, but this can hardly be asserted on the evidence of four plays. There is in fact a slight increase, though so small as to be negligible, between *Alcestis* and *Medea*. The interval between these two plays, both of known date, is seven years, and the fact that resolution is almost equally frequent in both is an indication that there was no significant development in Euripides' treatment of the tri-

---

[1] Ceadel (*op. cit.* pp. 74–80) presents arguments in support of his arrangement of the plays. We need not add to these, except to note that the commonly accepted dating of the production of *Electra* in 413, by which Ceadel was prepared to abide (while placing its composition earlier), can no longer be upheld in view of the arguments of Zuntz, *The Political Plays of E.* pp. 64–71; the position which Ceadel assigns to *Electra* in his table may well be approximately correct.

meter during this period. From *Medea* to *Heraclidae*, and again from *Heraclidae* to *Hippolytus*, there is a decrease, but it is a very slight one, which may well be attributable to chance. It does not indicate that Euripides was, consciously or unconsciously, becoming stricter. Indeed, the irregular distribution of resolutions within any of these plays and the tendency for a high proportion of them to be due to a few often repeated words ought to warn us against attaching significance to small variations. If, as seems probable, Euripides' treatment of the iambic trimeter remains fairly constant during the early period, the frequency of resolution will not help us to fix the date of a play within this period.

The frequency of resolution in *Rhesus* (8·1) lies between the figures for the early plays of Euripides and that for *Andromache*, the first play of the next group, but is appreciably closer to the former. It would not be possible, however, if *Rhesus* were the work of Euripides, to date it with confidence between *Hippolytus* and *Andromache*. As we have seen, the frequency of resolution does not necessarily begin to increase steadily until *Andromache*. We might indeed expect *Rhesus*, if Euripidean, to be earlier than *Andromache*, since it has a lower frequency of resolution; but this evidence alone will not enable us to date it more precisely.

On the other hand, a closer examination of the type and quality of the resolutions in *Rhesus* shows that there are grounds for associating it with the earlier group of Euripides' works rather than with the later. In the first place, as Ceadel observed, the total number of resolutions is significantly influenced by an accidental factor: the subject of the play makes unavoidable the repeated use of the words πολέμιος and πόλεμος, which between them account for a considerable proportion of the total number of resolved feet. Of the 55 resolutions in *Rhesus* 24 are caused by these two words (πολέμιος 22, πόλεμος 2), including 19 of the 37 third-foot dactyls. Sneller wished to allow for this peculiar circumstance before attempting to relate the figures for *Rhesus* to those for the other plays.[1] His procedure was to deduct 20 from the total number of resolutions, thus reducing the percentage for the frequency of resolution from 8·1 to 5·1. This would bring the play close to *Heraclidae* and *Hippolytus*. But to make so precise an adjustment of the figures is a very arbitrary procedure, which moreover fails to take certain other factors into account. First, the recurrence of these words may have led the poet, consciously or otherwise, to be more sparing in introducing other resolutions. Secondly, other plays may themselves be affected by repeated words in a similar way. In fact they are, although not to the same extent. In *Medea*, for example, of 68 resolved feet nine involve the accusative πατέρα and eight βασιλεύς and derivatives, both words being required by the theme of the play. More striking is *Heraclidae*, in which 12 out of 51 resolutions are caused by the word ἱκέτης (in addition, once ἱκέσιος), another 11 by the words πολέμιος and πόλεμος.

It is therefore difficult to say precisely how much account ought to be taken of this special factor in relating the statistics for *Rhesus* to those for the other plays. It does seem however that in this respect *Rhesus* is affected to an unusual degree and that it is right to make some allowance for it, thereby bringing it closer to the early plays of Euripides than the bare figures would suggest.

When we turn to Ceadel's Table 2, which sets out for the plays of Euripides the relative frequency of the different kinds of resolved feet in the various positions of the trimeter, we find additional grounds for associating *Rhesus* with the group of the four earliest plays. The corresponding statistics for the works of Aeschylus and Sophocles may also be compared (Ceadel's Table 4). The following points are to be noted:

(*a*) Of 55 resolved feet (proper names excluded) in *Rhesus* 37 are third-foot dactyls, i.e. 67 %. This is a higher proportion of the total than in any other tragedy, the nearest being Aeschylus' *Supplices* (62 %) and *Septem* (55 %), and Sophocles'

[1] Sneller, *op. cit.* pp. 44 f.

Trachiniae (58%). The nearest play of Euripides is *Hippolytus* with 52%. The heavy preponderance in *Rhesus* is largely attributable to the repetition of πολέμιος and πόλεμος, which together account for 19 of 37 resolutions in this position, five in all other positions.

Another point, which was observed previously by Harrison,[1] is that dactyls outnumber tribrachs in the third foot by 7 to 1. This proportion is equalled among the works of Euripides only by *Heraclidae*, although *Medea* also approaches it with $5\frac{1}{3}$ to 1. In Sophocles' *Trachiniae*, however, the proportion is 11 to 1.

The third-foot dactyl always remains the commonest type of resolved foot in the tragic trimeter, but in the later plays of Euripides its predominance in proportion to other types tends to decline. If *Rhesus* is Euripidean, both the high proportion of third-foot dactyl in the total of resolved feet and the high proportion of dactyl to tribrach in the third foot favour an early date in his career.

(*b*) *Rhesus* has only one first-foot dactyl (804 ἡνίοχε). Except for proper names (notably Ἱππόλυτε) this type of resolution is generally avoided by Euripides in his four earliest plays, the only exception being in *Alcestis* (802 οὐ βίος).[2] It must however be noted that our fragment of the prologue of *Telephus*, which was produced with *Alcestis* in 438, contains another (10 μητέρα); this is the more remarkable because it closely follows a first-foot dactyl for a proper name (6 Παρθένιον).[3] From *Andromache* onwards the first-foot dactyl appears more than once in every play, and in all plays after *Suppliants* it is firmly established and shows a tendency to become more frequent. In Aeschylus it is very rare (1 in *Septem*, 2 in *Choephori*), and there are not more than two in any play of Sophocles except *Philoctetes* (which has 11). Here then is another link between *Rhesus* and the early works of

---

[1] *CQ*, VIII (1914), 209.
[2] Cf. Zieliński, *op. cit.* pp. 144 f. (see below, p. 268).
[3] *Greek Literary Papyri*, ed. Page, no. 17.

Euripides, in a characteristic which they share with the other tragedians but not with his later plays. We may add, with Zieliński, that ἡνίοχε in *Rhesus* is almost the equivalent of a proper name.

(*c*) *Rhesus* has only three second-foot tribrachs, 5 % of the total number of resolutions. The proportion of resolution in this position is lower than for any play of Euripides, although it is equally rare in most plays of Aeschylus and absent altogether from *PV* and *Eumenides*. Among the works of Euripides the closest are *Hippolytus* (7 %) and *Medea* (9 %). After *Hippolytus* the proportion tends to increase, subject to fluctuation, but not falling below 11 %. Here again *Rhesus* resembles more closely the early plays.

These are the only places where the statistics of Ceadel's Table 2 offer a possible clue to date. The other types of resolution do not show a sufficiently consistent tendency to increase or to decrease, but it can at least be said that *Rhesus* does not in any respect diverge from the early plays. So far then as these figures give any indication of date, they tend to corroborate those for the overall frequency of resolution in placing *Rhesus* close to the four earliest plays of Euripides and separating it from the rest, especially the latest. In some respects *Rhesus* occupies an extreme position in relation to the plays of Euripides, but this may be attributed in part to the accidental factors already observed, and nowhere does it stand so far apart that there is difficulty in associating it with Euripides in his early style. It is also true that some plays of Aeschylus and Sophocles are comparable in respect of these figures.

The investigations of Zieliński into the evolution of the iambic trimeter in Euripides have provided further proof of the affinity between *Rhesus* and the four early plays. Zieliński divided the extant works of Euripides into four groups according to the frequency of resolution in the trimeters (proper names being included). These four groups constitute at the same time four chronologically distinct periods. The first group, comprising plays in which the total frequency of resolution is below 10 %, includes the four plays earlier than 425, *Alcestis*, *Medea*, *Heraclidae* and *Hippolytus*, and, on the basis of these statistics, *Rhesus*. Zieliński's second group, in which the frequency of resolution is between 10 % and 15 %, contains *Andromache*, *Hecuba* and *Supplices*, which he dates between 425 and 416. Seven plays fall within his third period, dated by him from 415 to 409 and comprising plays with a frequency of resolution between 20 % and 30 %; the final period, in which the frequency exceeds 30 %, includes the three latest plays, *Orestes*, *Bacchae* and *Iphigenia in Aulis*. Zieliński errs in setting the beginning of his third period too low in 415, and as a consequence proposes an improbable order for the plays within this period; it is possible, without disturbing the boundaries between his groups, to push back the beginning of the third period to about 420.

Zieliński formulated a series of ten rules governing the admission of resolution in the iambic trimeter by Euripides.[1] In the earliest period these rules are strictly observed and exceptions are rare; in the second period some are still carefully observed but others are violated more often than before; in later plays Euripides progressively relaxes his observance of the rules. *Rhesus* is found to adhere closely to the practice of the earliest group in respect of all the rules and is sometimes the strictest of all in its observance of them. The ten rules are as follows:

1. Only one resolved foot is permitted in a single line. *Rhesus* has one exception to this rule:

286   κλύοντα πλήρη πεδία πολεμίας χερός.

In each of the four early plays there are two exceptions: *Alc.* 159, 802; *Med.* 324, 1322; *Hcld.* 70, 211 (the latter including a proper name); *Hipp.* 1029, 1223. Among these *Med.* 1322 and *Hipp.* 1223 both, like *Rhesus*, have the reso-

---

[1] Zieliński, *op. cit.* pp. 142 ff.

lutions in the third and fourth feet. The former, as it happens, also has a verbal similarity:

δίδωσιν ἡμῖν ἔρυμα πολεμίας χερός.

2. Resolutions of the third foot exceed others in number, and the older the play the greater their proportion.

As we have already seen, this rule holds for Euripides at all stages of his career: it is only in a few of the latest plays (*Phoenissae*, *Orestes*, *Bacchae*, *Iphigenia in Aulis*) that third-foot resolutions account for less than 50 % of the total. Nevertheless, the high preponderance in *Rhesus* again tends to place it early.

3. In the first foot dactyls are not allowed except for proper names; a tribrach in the first foot always consists of a single trisyllabic word.

The first part of the rule was discussed above. Exceptions to it occur in every play from *Andromache* onwards and with increasing frequency. The four earliest plays yield only one exception (*Alc.* 802), to which we must add from the same period *Telephus* 10. *Rhesus* has one exception, 804 ἡνίοχε, which in its context is almost equivalent to a proper name.

The second part of the rule has no exception in *Rhesus* or in the plays of Euripides' first period. In the second period *Hecuba* still has no exception, but there are three in *Andromache* and one in *Suppliants* (excluding proper names: Zieliński, *op. cit.* pp. 155–6). *Electra*, which may be the earliest play of the third group,[1] is again without exception, but in the later plays the rule tends to be observed less strictly and in the four latest it is abandoned.

4. The fifth foot does not admit resolution.

Rhesus has no exception, nor is there one in any play of the first or second period (*ibid.* pp. 146, 157). Later Euripides admits occasional resolution in this position, and it appears in all plays of the third and fourth periods, the greatest

---

[1] See p. 262 n. 1 above.

number being eight (including one proper name) in *Helen*. Resolution of the fifth foot is also very rare in Aeschylus and Sophocles.

5. The arsis of the fourth foot is not resolved unless the thesis of the fifth foot is short.[1] *Rhesus* has no exception to this rule, nor has *Medea*; *Alcestis* and *Hippolytus* have one each, both caused by proper names; *Heraclidae* has one, 70 ἀγοραίου, where, as Zieliński suggests, αι is possibly to be shortened before the following vowel (p. 146). In the next three plays there are eighteen exceptions, but fourteen of these are caused by proper names. It is not until Zieliński's third period that the rule is commonly violated (see his table on p. 173).

6. If the arsis of the second foot is resolved, the thesis of the third foot is more often long than short (although the latter is not uncommon), and there is always caesura after the thesis of the third foot.

Rhesus conforms to both parts of the rule. While, as we have seen, resolution of the second foot increases in frequency in the later plays, the first part of the rule always remains valid. It is in respect of the following caesura that Euripides tends to become more free: in the early period the only exception is in *Hippolytus*; then there are two each in *Hecuba* and *Suppliants*, and in later plays the proportion of exceptions tends to increase (*ibid.* pp. 159, 176, 193).

7. If the arsis of the third foot is resolved, its thesis is more commonly long than short, and there is always a caesura after the thesis of the foot.

The heavy predominance of the third-foot dactyl in *Rhesus* has already been observed. In this position dactyls stand to tribrachs in a proportion of 7:1, and this puts *Rhesus* in line with the plays of Euripides' earliest period. The proportion diminishes in later plays. For this rule the law of caesura is

---

[1] Here and in the subsequent discussion I have followed Zieliński's usage of the terms arsis and thesis; the application of the terms is often, and more logically, reversed.

violated only in late plays (first in *Helen*) and then only rarely (*ibid.* pp. 176, 193). It is strictly observed in *Rhesus*.

8. In all feet except the first a resolved syllable coincides with the beginning of a word.

There is no exception in *Rhesus* and there are only two (*Medea* 375, 505) in a total of 240 resolutions in the early plays. In the next period *Andromache* and *Suppliants* observe the rule absolutely, *Hecuba* breaks it twice. Thereafter exceptions become rather more numerous, totalling 36 in the seven plays of the third group (2 % of all resolutions), 74 in the group of the three latest plays (17 %) (*ibid.* pp. 176 ff., 194 f.).

9. Both syllables of a resolved arsis must be short by nature; *positio debilis* is not admitted.

There is one exception in *Rhesus*:

617 λευκαὶ δέδενται διαπρεπεῖς ἐν εὐφρόνῃ.

This law is observed most strictly in the earlier plays. *Alcestis* has no exception, *Medea* and *Heraclidae* each one, *Hippolytus* four, including two proper names (*ibid.* p. 151). In the next three plays the number of exceptions rises to 20 (including three proper names), which represents an increase in proportion to the total number of resolutions from 2·5 % to 5·3 % (*ibid.* pp. 160–1). The proportion increases further in the next period to 7 % (pp. 179–80); in the latest period there are still 56 exceptions in three plays (two proper names), but this is a slight drop in proportion to the total number of resolutions (5·2 %) (pp. 195–6). Here *Rhesus* fits only in the earliest period.

10. Resolution is admitted only in words of three or more syllables.

There is no exception in *Rhesus*. Among the early plays *Alcestis* has five exceptions, *Medea* two, *Heraclidae* three, *Hippolytus* three. In the second period the law is much more often broken: *Andromache* has 19 exceptions, *Hecuba* 20, *Suppliants* 10. In all later plays the rule is violated in over 20 % of resolutions (pp. 181 ff., 196 ff.).

The position of *Rhesus* in respect of Zieliński's ten rules may be summed up as follows:

(i) Rules 1, 9 and 10 are observed with a strictness matched only in the earliest extant plays of Euripides.

(ii) In its observance of rules 2, 5, 6, 7 and 8 *Rhesus* is as strict as any play of Euripides, but this strictness is not incompatible with his second period (*Andromache, Hecuba, Suppliants*) or in some cases even with a later date. Nevertheless, in respect of rules 2 and 7 *Rhesus* occupies an extreme position, which is more easily associated with an early date in Euripides' career.

(iii) Contrary to the general practice of the early plays of Euripides *Rhesus* has one exception to rule 3, but there is also one in *Alcestis* and in a fragment of *Telephus*. Moreover, the exception in *Rhesus* can almost be regarded as equivalent to a proper name. Otherwise in this rule too *Rhesus* is as strict as any play.

(iv) Rule 4 is observed in *Rhesus* without exception, but this is of no special significance, since, although exceptions occur in each play of Euripides from *Electra* onwards, they are rare even in the latest period.

Altogether *Rhesus* conforms to these ten rules more closely than any play of Euripides; but it agrees generally with the earlier practice of Euripides in the kinds of exception that it admits and the degree to which they are admitted. If in a few respects *Rhesus* is more conservative than the early plays of Euripides, it is at least conservative after the same style, and the difference of degree is never so great as to put it in a class apart.

The studies of Ceadel and Zieliński, which we have examined in their relation to our problem, appear to have dealt with all important aspects of the treatment of resolution in the iambic trimeters of Euripides. The conclusions to which they point in the case of *Rhesus* are clear and unambiguous. In the first place there is no evidence here against its authenticity. Rather have we found remarkably consistent indications of a close affinity with the practice of the four earliest plays of Euripides; with the innovations in the treatment of the trimeter introduced in his later plays *Rhesus* has nothing in common. On the basis of this evidence alone it is surely possible to conclude with some certainty that, if *Rhesus* is the work of Euripides, then (*a*) it cannot belong to the latest period of his composition; (*b*) it is highly improbable that it belongs to a date later than 420; (*c*) it is most likely to have been composed earlier than *Andromache*, that is, before 425. To establish these points the validity of the statistical evidence does not have to be pressed beyond the certain indications of plays of known date, which leave no doubt that from *Andromache* onwards there is a more or less regular increase in the frequency of resolution. Certainly, if we were to place *Rhesus* in this later period of Euripides' career, we should have to suppose that he was deliberately reverting to an earlier metrical style in a manner quite unparalleled in any of his other plays.

Even this limited conclusion has some value in eliminating certain theories that have been advanced about the composition of the play. We can, for example, safely reject Ridgeway's view that *Rhesus* was composed by Euripides in his last years during his sojourn in Macedonia;[1] the trimeters are so completely unlike those of *Bacchae* and *Iphigenia in Aulis* as to rule this out altogether. The theory of Goossens,[2] that *Rhesus* was produced with *Hecuba* in 424, is also contrary to the evidence of the resolutions and would need to be all the more strongly substantiated on other grounds to be acceptable.

The evidence of resolutions cannot be taken beyond this point. It is possible to establish that they contain nothing at variance with the style of Euripides. But we should not

---

[1] *CQ*, xx (1926), 1–19.

[2] *Ant. Class.* I (1932), 93 ff.; supported by Grégoire, *Ant. Class.* II (1933), 91 ff., and by Sneller, *op. cit.*

expect to find here any positive evidence for the authenticity of *Rhesus*, since there is no reason why other poets besides Euripides should not have composed trimeters after the same fashion either at the same or at a different period. In fact, to judge from statistical evidence alone, there are some plays of Aeschylus and Sophocles, for example *Septem* and *Trachiniae*, like enough to *Rhesus* in respect of the frequency and distribution of resolution. When one compares Ceadel's analysis of the resolutions in the works of these two poets, one cannot deny that, on the basis of this evidence, either Aeschylus or Sophocles, or indeed some unknown dramatist, could have written *Rhesus*. This fact in no way weakens the conclusions reached above.

No reliable evidence is to be derived from the figures for resolution in the minor tragedians of the fifth century (Ceadel, Table 5). The fragments are too meagre and their date can seldom be established. With the exception of Neophron, whose fragments may belong to the middle of the century,[1] all these tragedians show a frequency of resolution exceeding that of *Rhesus*. It seems probable that towards the end of the century many poets were composing trimeters with the freedom of Euripides' later style, but we cannot speak for all poets. The influence of Euripides is likely to have been strong, but it need not have been universal.

It is equally difficult to draw any conclusions about the composition of the iambic trimeter by fourth-century tragedians from fragments amounting to only two hundred lines (Ceadel, Table 6). But we may note that they are consistent in one respect: all show a very much higher frequency of resolution than is found in *Rhesus*, a frequency more in keeping with the very late style of Euripides. Again these figures do not speak for all poets or for the whole work of these few poets, but there is at least no support here for the view that *Rhesus* belongs to the fourth century. Even less likely on

---

[1] For the date of Neophron cf. Arg. E. *Med.* (discussed by Page, ed. *Medea*, pp. xxx ff.).

metrical grounds is it that *Rhesus* might be a work of one of the tragedians of the Alexandrian Pleiad, for these, to judge from their remains, avoided resolution altogether.

Verse-weight

It is not only in their treatment of resolution that the trimeters of *Rhesus* can be compared with those of Euripides. Other aspects of their composition can be submitted to statistical analysis for the purpose of comparison. One line of investigation has been to examine the poet's preference for short or long *anceps* in the doubtful positions of the line, or in other words the proportion of iambs to spondees in the first, third and fifth feet. Inquiries of this kind have been undertaken by two scholars, E. Harrison and J. Descroix, both of whom by different methods produced results which seemed to them to reveal a difference of style between *Rhesus* and other works of Euripides.

In an article entitled 'Verse-weight' Harrison observed that the iambic trimeters of *Rhesus* are to an unusual degree spondaic at the beginning and the middle of the line.[1] In proof of this he made an analysis for the three tragedians of the proportion of iambs to spondees in the first, third and fifth feet. He found that in the first and third feet spondees in every play outnumber iambs, as they do also in the total of the three feet, but that in the fifth foot iambs outnumber spondees. *Rhesus* adheres to this rule, but in respect of the first and third feet, as well as in the total of the three feet, it yields a higher proportion of spondees than any other tragedy. Harrison's percentages for *Rhesus* and for the plays which mark the limits of variation among other tragedies are as follows (iambs:spondees):[2]

First foot: *Rh.* 28:70, A. *Prom.* 38:60, E. *Hec.* 28:65.
Third foot: *Rh.* 25:68, A. *Ch.* 40:57, A. *Supp.* 28:66.

---

[1] *CQ*, VIII (1914), 206 ff.
[2] Where the total of the two figures falls below 100, resolved feet make up the remainder.

Fifth foot: *Rh.* 60:40, S. *Tr.* 61:39, E. *Ba.* 50:49.

Total of these three feet: *Rh.* 38:60, A. *Ag.* 45:53, E. *Supp.* 37:58.

Apart from these figures Harrison publishes his results for only a selection of plays (Aeschylus, *Supplices*, *Agamemnon*; Sophocles, *Antigone*, *Philoctetes*; Euripides, *Hippolytus*, *Troades*, *Orestes*, *Cyclops*). I have analysed the proportions also for *Alcestis* and *Heraclidae*, which in some respects approach closer to those of *Rhesus* than those selected by Harrison.

In the first foot *Rhesus* has on an average five more spondees in every hundred verses than *Hecuba* but the same number of iambs. The difference is accounted for by the number of resolved feet; in *Hecuba* the recurrence of several proper names (Ἑκάβη, Ἀγαμέμνων, Πολυμήστωρ, Πολύδωρος, Ταλθύβιος) produces an unusually high frequency of first-foot resolutions. In its total of 58 resolutions in this position are included 44 anapaests and seven dactyls, both of which might be regarded as 'heavier' than an iamb. The difference in first-foot 'weight' between *Hecuba* and *Rhesus* is therefore not very considerable.

Alcestis has fewer resolutions in the first foot than *Hecuba*, so that it may perhaps be more fairly compared with *Rhesus*. By my calculations *Alcestis* has 66·2 % spondees to 31·6 % iambs in the first foot. *Heraclidae* yields very similar figures, a little closer to those of *Rhesus*, 67·4 % to 30·6 %. This is a difference, on an average, of about three spondees in each hundred trimeters, a margin which, even though the percentage of *Heraclidae* may itself be an extreme one, is not too great to be attributed to chance.

In the third foot *Rhesus*' proportion of spondees to iambs (68:25) is affected by the comparatively large number of resolved feet. These total 48, of which 42 are dactyls and six tribrachs, a proportion of 7 to 1, so that their inclusion in the reckoning increases the preponderance of long *anceps* in the third foot. It has already been noted above that *Heraclidae* has the same proportion (7:1) of dactyls to tribrachs among

275

its third-foot resolutions. Checking its proportions of spondees and iambs in the third foot, I find that it has 67·4 % spondees to 29·2 % iambs, resolutions accounting for the other 3·4 %. This is surely so close to *Rhesus* as to make its difference of percentage almost negligible. *Alcestis* in the third foot has a slightly lower percentage of spondees (64 %).

And so, while *Rhesus* lies outside the limits for other tragedies in its proportions of spondees to iambs in both the first and third feet, it is not so far different from some plays of Euripides as to exhibit a dissimilar style. Moreover, although averages are useful for purposes of comparison between plays, they can be rather misleading. For in no play are spondees and iambs regularly distributed, and the percentage in any one part may be very much higher or lower than the average. If, for example, the distribution of the spondees in the first and third feet of *Rhesus* is analysed, it will be found that the proportions in separate sequences of dialogue are as follows:

		Percentage first-foot spondees	Percentage third-foot spondees
52–223	Hector, Aeneas, Dolon	72	65
264–341	Messenger, Hector	65	67
388–526	Rhesus, Hector	78·5	67
565–674	Athena, Odysseus, Diomedes, Paris	71	67
736–819	Chorus, Charioteer, Hector	64⎫62	70⎫72
833–81	Charioteer, Hector	60⎭	75⎭
890–992	Muse, Hector	68	75

The percentage of first-foot spondees varies between 62 and 78·5, of third-foot spondees between 65 and 75.

A similar analysis for *Alcestis* shows the following distribution of spondees:[1]

---

[1] The following small groups of lines, included in the overall count, are omitted from this and the next table: *Alc.* 246 ff., 935–61, *Hcld.* 73–110.

		Percentage first-foot spondees	Percentage third-foot spondees
1–76	Prologue: Apollo, Thanatos	74	68
136–212	Chorus, Woman-servant	67	58
280–434	Alcestis, Admetus	74	73
470–567	Heracles, Admetus	62	63
605–740	Admetus, Pheres	69	58
747–860	Servant, Heracles	61	61
1006–1158	Admetus, Heracles	63	69

Here the percentage of first-foot spondees varies between 61 and 74, of third-foot spondees between 58 and 73.

In *Heraclidae* the percentages of spondees in the various iambic scenes are as follows:

		Percentage first-foot spondees	Percentage third-foot spondees
1–72	Prologue: Iolaus, Herald	67	60
111–287	Herald, Demophon, Iolaus	74	65
297–352	Iolaus, Demophon	75	80
381–473	Iolaus, Demophon	62	71
474–607	Macaria, Iolaus	66	75
630–747	Servant, Alcmene, Iolaus	69	76
784–891	Alcmene, Servant (messenger)	58	55
928–1052	Servant, Alcmene, Eurystheus	66	70

Here the variation of percentage is even greater, between 58 and 75 for first-foot spondees, between 55 and 80 for third-foot spondees.

It is clear that in each of these plays the proportion of iambs to spondees in both the first and third feet varies very much from part to part. In spite of the fact that its overall percentage exceeds the limit for other plays, *Rhesus* has only one scene (388–526) in which the percentage of first-foot spondees (78·5) exceeds the maximum for any scene in *Alcestis* (74) or *Heraclidae* (75), and its maximum percentage for third-foot spondees (75) is equalled in one scene of *Heraclidae* (474–607) and exceeded by a considerable margin in another (297–352). It is therefore difficult to find any one part of *Rhesus* of which it can be said that the percentage of spondees exceeds the limit that might be expected of Euripides. The reason for the overall preponderance of spondees in *Rhesus* is that there tends to be less variation from scene to scene than in the other plays. This is true especially of the third-foot spondees. In both *Alcestis* and *Heraclidae* these drop below 60 % of the total in certain scenes, but in only one scene of *Rhesus* does their proportion fall as low as 65 %. In respect of first-foot spondees *Rhesus* shows a wider variation but not so much as *Heraclidae*. These variations from scene to scene need not in themselves be consciously calculated by the poet, but they may not be unrelated to differences of emotional tone or rhetorical context.[1] We may note, for example, in *Heraclidae* 784–891 how the metre becomes markedly less spondaic in both first and third feet for an excited piece of narrative. In *Alcestis* the farewell scene between Admetus and Alcestis is metrically heavy, the following dialogue between Admetus and Heracles much lighter. In the debate between the Herald and Iolaus, the openings of the lines tend to be heavy.

The same sort of thing can perhaps be detected in *Rhesus*. In the debate and dialogue between Rhesus and Hector there is a similar tendency to weight at the beginning of the line. There is a lightening of the metre in the narrative speech of the Charioteer and the dialogue that follows it, though only at the beginning of the line, perhaps because his speech is slow and laboured. On the other hand, it is to be noticed that the earlier Messenger's speech shows only slight variation of metrical style from the scene which precedes it.

As regards the fifth foot *Rhesus* is not at all unusual. Its proportion of 60 iambs to 40 spondees is, as Harrison notes,

---

[1] This could not be established without the evidence of more plays; the variations observed here could be fortuitous.

very much on a par with those for the early plays of Euripides. *Alcestis* and *Medea* both show a proportion of 60:40, *Heraclidae* and *Hippolytus* both 61:39. Outside Euripides the same proportion is shown, among the plays in Harrison's table, by Aeschylus' *Agamemnon*. But in the later plays of Euripides there is a tendency for the proportion of iambs to decrease, reaching a minimum of 50:49 in *Bacchae*. *Helen*, with a proportion of 58:41, is exceptional among the later works. Here therefore is another point in which *Rhesus* associates itself with the early group of Euripides' works as distinct from the later.

Harrison does not claim for his evidence about 'verse-weight' more than a small contributory importance towards deciding the question whether *Rhesus* is the work of Euripides. On the basis of his overall percentages it looks to have some significance, since *Rhesus* falls outside the limits for Euripides in its proportions of spondee to iamb in both the first and the third feet. But if the analysis of Euripides' practice is extended to separate scenes, it is seen that these proportions may vary greatly in different parts of the same play. Only in one scene does *Rhesus* show a percentage of spondees that is not equalled in some part of the other two plays examined: this is much less striking.

Harrison was probably right in supposing 'preferences for heaviness or lightness in the several parts of the line . . . to have been instinctive and scarcely conscious', but did not consider whether Euripides' instinct guided his preference differently in different dramatic moods or situations. We have seen that in some places he tends to a lightness of metre, so that the proportion of spondees falls far below the average, and that this may perhaps be prompted by the dramatic circumstances. If *Rhesus* has a higher overall percentage of spondees than other plays of Euripides, the reason may be that it lacks the kind of situation which particularly calls for a lightness of metre. The drama maintains an even intensity of tone through the whole course of its action, and in the final scene, when the action is over, the solemnity of the Muse's lament is accompanied by an increased heaviness of metre. Ridgeway may therefore have been near the truth when he attributed the heavy 'weight' of the trimeters in *Rhesus* to the gloomy nature of its subject.[1] The essential point however is that the verse-technique of *Rhesus* is not fundamentally different in this matter from that of Euripides, but merely has less variety from scene to scene. Whether there is or is not some underlying reason for this, the fact itself does not appear to be of major significance.

The work of Descroix in this field can be considered more briefly. In a much more elaborate statistical survey than that of Harrison he analyses all the unresolved iambic trimeters in both the iambic poets and the dramatists into eight classes comprising the various possible combinations of iamb and spondee in the first, third and fifth feet.[2] All lines containing resolution are counted separately as a ninth class. For each poet and each work he gives the number of lines of each class together with the percentage of the total that they represent. On the basis of these statistics he arrives at the following observations about *Rhesus*: 'Sa versification qui ressemble aussi peu que possible à celle d'Euripide — surtout à la seconde et à la troisième manière — copie servilement celle d'Eschyle. . . . Il le dépasse, en effet, pour aller rejoindre les iambographes.'[3] He concludes that it is an archaizing work of the fourth century.

It must first be pointed out that Descroix's statistics do not offer a satisfactory basis of comparison between different works. Because he has included in a separate class all lines containing resolution, there can be no useful comparison in his other classifications between works in which the frequency of resolution differs considerably. For example, a line having a spondee in the first foot, but not in the third and fifth, is not

---

[1] *CQ*, xx (1926), 13.
[2] Descroix, *Le Trimètre iambique* (Paris, 1931), pp. 46-9.
[3] Descroix, *op. cit.* pp. 59-60.

reckoned in the total of such lines if there is a trisyllabic foot in any position in it. It is largely owing to the increasing number of lines containing resolution that Descroix's statistics for the later plays of Euripides appear so strikingly different at all points from those for his early works.

If we confine our attention to the works with which *Rhesus* can reasonably be compared, we shall find little to bear out Descroix's assertion. It seems that he has failed altogether to compare his figures for *Rhesus* with those for the four earliest plays of Euripides, which have a comparable proportion of resolved lines. If he had done so, he would have found that the resemblance is at least as close as it is to his statistics for the plays of Aeschylus and much closer than it is to those for the iambic poets.

The accompanying table incorporates as much of Descroix's results as we need in order to test the validity of his assertions about *Rhesus*. The statistics for the tragedies included here display a remarkable degree of uniformity: in one column (v) there is a difference of 10 % between the extremes, but nowhere else is the range so great. It is hardly possible to make any significant distinction between the three tragedians on the basis of these figures. The statistics for the iambic poets are based in each case on a very small total number of surviving lines, scarcely sufficient to yield any reliable information. In some places they present a greater range of variation than is found in tragedy. There are however two respects in which the figures for the iambic poets tend to differ fairly consistently from those for tragedy: they show a slightly higher proportion of 'pure' iambic lines and a markedly lower proportion of lines containing three spondees. In both respects *Rhesus* aligns itself with the other tragedies.

If we compare *Rhesus* with the four plays of Euripides, we find as follows:

(i) In three classes (vi, vii, viii) the percentage for *Rhesus* falls within the range for the Euripidean plays.

A classification of iambic trimeters according to Descroix

(The figures are his percentages of each class in each poet or work.)

Author and work	I 3 iambs	II 1	III 3	IV 5	V 1, 3	VI 1, 5	VII 3, 5	VIII 3 spondees	IX Resolved lines
		1 spondee			2 spondees				
Iambographers									
Archilochus	12	12	10·3	6·9	31	5·1	5·1	8·6	8·6
Semonides	11·5	17·8	7·4	4·6	28·9	11·5	5·7	9·2	2·9
Others	15·7	15·7	8·7	7	29·8	1·7	3·5	8·7	8·7
Tragedians									
A. *Supp.*	5·9	8·7	13·3	3·3	22	8·7	9·7	18	9·1
Pers.	6	11·9	9·8	3·7	20·5	9·5	9·8	15·9	12·3
Sept.	5·1	10	12·9	3·8	21·9	6·7	9·2	18·6	11·6
Prom.	6·9	10·1	13·4	4·2	21·1	8·6	11·9	17·3	6·2
Agam.	9·1	12·7	12·4	4·7	20·4	8·5	8·5	16·7	6·6
Cho.	8·6	12·1	11·2	6·4	20·2	11·3	8·7	14·6	6·4
Eu.	10·2	11·7	10·7	5·1	22·6	8·2	7·4	18·2	5·5
S. *Aj.*	5·5	11·6	10·7	5·1	23·8	10·3	8·1	17·6	7
Ant.	6	10·3	14	3·7	23·8	9·5	8·3	19	4·8
OT	6	12·6	11·5	4·2	24·5	8·3	8·2	16·7	7·5
El.	7·4	13·2	11·8	3·8	23	9·5	8	18·1	4·7
Tr.	7	13·5	12·3	3·9	24·4	8·4	7·8	15·6	6·6
Ph.	4·7	11·5	11·8	4·2	19·9	7·9	9·8	18·5	11·3
OC	6·3	10·4	12·9	3·1	25·4	7·7	8·6	18·6	6·7
E. *Alc.*	6·4	13	12·4	3·3	24·1	8·9	8·5	16·7	6·3
Med.	6·9	11·6	13·6	3·4	23·3	6·2	9·3	18·5	6·9
Hcld.	5·2	10·8	12	4·3	27	7·7	6·9	17·2	7·4
Hipp.	5·4	13·6	14·2	3·4	23·5	7·8	7·7	17·6	6·4
Rh.	4·9	9·3	10·6	2·9	30·1	7	7·2	18·5	9·3

(ii) In four classes (I, II, III, IV) the percentage for *Rhesus* falls below the minimum for the four plays cited (but in each case there is a lower percentage in at least one other play of Euripides). Only in class IV is the percentage for *Rhesus*, by an insignificant margin, the lowest for all the tragedies cited here.

(iii) In class V the percentage for *Rhesus* (30·1) is appreciably higher than that for any other tragedy. Here alone it is closer to the iambic poets, but Euripides' *Heraclidae* (27 %) is not very far behind.

It is thus only at one place in Descroix's statistics that *Rhesus* diverges at all noticeably from the early plays of Euripides or from earlier tragedy generally. This is not sufficient ground for alleging a reversion to the verse-technique of the iambic poets. Nor is there anywhere apparent a closer resemblance to Aeschylus than to Euripides. Once again statistical analysis shows *Rhesus* in an extreme position in one respect; but the peculiarity is in fact the same one that Harrison's statistics reveal, and, as we have seen, the margin of difference from other plays of Euripides is small.

Caesura

An analysis has been made by Descroix (*Le Trimètre iambique*, pp. 240 ff.) of the incidence of the several varieties of caesura in all the iambic trimeters of Greek literature down to New Comedy. In his tabulation (pp. 262–4) he distinguishes for both the penthemimeral and hephthemimeral caesura between those that coincide with elision and those that do not, and the rarer types of quasi-caesura are also classified, of which only the break coinciding with elision at the end of the third foot concerns us at present. For the various poets and their separate works the total number of each type of caesura is given, together with the percentage of the whole which it represents. There is, as we shall see, some reason to mistrust the absolute accuracy of Descroix's figures, but the margin of error is not likely to be so great as to affect significantly their value for purposes of comparison.

It is clear from a glance at the figures for caesura in the works of Euripides that we shall not find here evidence of a regular chronological development comparable to that shown by the frequency of resolutions. There do appear however certain tendencies, more or less clearly defined, on the one hand for the earlier plays of Euripides to be distinguished from the later, and on the other hand for the practice of Euripides to differ from that of Aeschylus or Sophocles. Moreover, the figures for *Rhesus* are in several respects extreme ones. These facts justify a closer examination of the statistics for caesura.

The first thing to be noticed in Descroix's table is that the ordinary penthemimeral caesura without elision accounts for 84·5 % of the total in *Rhesus*, the highest percentage of any tragedy and indeed of any work included in the table. Descroix has made a serious miscalculation from his own figures in giving the corresponding percentage for *Alcestis* as 82·4: on the basis of his totals it should be 77·4. When this is corrected, there is an appreciable gap between *Rhesus* and any other tragedy. But it is still some of the earlier plays of Euripides which approach it most closely: *Andromache* (78·7), *Suppliants* (78·3), *Medea* (78·2). There is a tendency in Euripides, although not a regular one, for the proportion of this type of caesura to be higher in early plays than in later ones, the minimum percentage being 71·4 in *Troades*. In Aeschylus and Sophocles the percentage tends to be lower, the extremes for Aeschylus being 77·5 in *Eumenides* and 70·8 in *Agamemnon*, for Sophocles 75·3 in *Oedipus Coloneus* and 66·9 in *Trachiniae*.

For the penthemimeral caesura coinciding with elision *Rhesus* shows a lower percentage (5·8) than any play of Euripides, but among his works it is again some of the earlier ones that it approaches most closely. There is, as Descroix observes (p. 269), a tendency for this type of caesura to increase in frequency in Euripides, again not regularly. *Suppliants* with 6·7 % has the lowest proportion, then *Alcestis* with 6·9 % and *Medea* with 7·1 %. On the other hand, the proportion in *Rhesus* is slightly higher than the average for Aeschylus or Sophocles, being exceeded by Aeschylus only in *PV* (6·4 %), and by Sophocles only in *Oedipus Tyrannus* (7·8 %).

Thus for both forms of penthemimeral caesura the total percentage in *Rhesus*, according to Descroix's calculations, is 90·3. This is again by a clear margin the highest proportion in any tragedy, the nearest being 86·3 % in *Andromache*, 85·3 % in *Medea* and *Hippolytus*. These are among the earlier plays of Euripides, and it is notable that the proportion of the penthemimeral caesura tends to decline a little in his later works, although not falling below 80·2 % (in *Bacchae*). For Aeschylus and Sophocles there is nothing approaching the higher proportions of early Euripides, the maximum for Aeschylus being 81·8 % in *Eumenides* and for Sophocles 80·4 % in *Oedipus Coloneus*.

It follows necessarily that *Rhesus* has the lowest total proportion of hephthemimeral caesura. Its 9·3 % is well below the next lowest, 12·5 % in *Andromache*, but is again nearer to early works of Euripides than to any others. Here the early plays of Euripides tend to show a lower proportion (including those that coincide with elision) than the later ones, which are in turn lower than the works of Aeschylus and Sophocles, the minimum for Aeschylus being 17·2 % in *Septem*, for Sophocles 19 % in *Oedipus Tyrannus*. It is worth noting besides that the style of *Rhesus* here diverges from that of fourth-century tragedy, so far as we can infer from the meagre surviving fragments, which yield nearly 26 % of fourth-foot caesura. Descroix finds it difficult to reconcile these figures with his view that *Rhesus* was composed in the fourth century (p. 268), and supposes that its author was archaizing (p. 272).

Only once in *Rhesus* does the hephthemimeral caesura coincide with an elision:

849   ἡμεῖς δ' ἑκὰς τετρώμεθ', οἱ δὲ μειζόνως.

In the earlier plays of Euripides caesura is rarely made with elision at this point: it is found twice each in *Medea* and *Andromache*, four times in *Alcestis*, five in *Hippolytus*, six in *Heraclidae*. In his later plays he has it rather more often. In Aeschylus it is rare in all plays except *PV* (eight times); Sophocles admits it only twice each in *Antigone* and *Trachiniae*, more freely in his other plays.

Elision at the end of the third foot, taking the place of caesura in one of the normal positions, is found only once in *Rhesus*:[1]

986   χωρεῖτε, συμμάχους δ' ὁπλίζεσθαι τάχος.

[1] There is a second example in 208, if, as Murray does, we read νῶτ' ἐνάψομαι (Cobet).

This type occurs more frequently in all other tragedies, but *PV* has only two and *Heraclidae* only three. Its frequency varies in the individual works of each of the tragedians, but in Euripides we can discern a tendency, again not universal, for it to be slightly more common in later than in earlier works.

So far our observations have been based on the statistics presented by Descroix. It seems however that they are not always accurate. An independent analysis for *Rhesus* yields a slightly lower proportion of penthemimeral caesura: 83·6 % without elision and 5·9 % with elision, a total of 89·5 %.[1] On the other hand, for *Andromache*, the only other play checked, my calculations agree closely with those of Descroix. It seems unlikely that any minor adjustments that ought to be made in Descroix's table would affect the extreme position which *Rhesus* occupies among extant tragedies.

Rhesus then, in its sparing admission of the rarer varieties of caesura, is found to be the most conservative of tragedies. In addition, it has an extremely high proportion of penthemimeral caesura, higher than any other tragedy. In both these respects it appears to be closer to the early style of Euripides than to any other of which we have knowledge, but there is nevertheless an appreciable difference in the figures. Ought we to regard this margin of difference as significant? The proportion of penthemimeral caesura in *Rhesus*, 89·5 %, is over 3 % higher than that of *Andromache*, which stands nearest to it. When it is considered that among all the plays of Euripides, *Rhesus* excluded, this percentage varies only between 80·2 and 86·3, a difference of 3 % from the extreme of this range may appear to be one of some magnitude. On the other hand, a difference in three lines of every hundred is not a very great margin to attribute to chance.

Can a difference of this order be said to constitute a perceptible difference of style or to betray the hand of a less

---

[1] My totals for each kind (based on O.C.T. except at *v.* 208) are as follows: penthemimeral, without caesura 572, with caesura 40; hephthemimeral, without caesura 70, with caesura 1; elision after third foot 1; total 684.

sensitive poet? On this point one may refer to Descroix's list of the longest sequences of lines in tragedy showing no variation of caesura.[1] Penthemimeral caesura without elision is found in sequences of up to 26 lines. *Rhesus* is high in the list with 25 consecutive lines (80–104), but there are sequences of 26 in both *Ajax* (1258–83) and *Helen* (1258–83), and of 24 in *Hippolytus* (1051–74). Ten other sequences of 20 to 23 lines are listed, of which one is in Sophocles (*Aj.* 732–51) and the rest in Euripides, including three in *Andromache* alone. Figures of this kind tend to confirm that chance can play a part in the overall proportion of any one variety of caesura. They are also a test of the poet's sensitiveness to monotony, and in this respect *Rhesus* seems not to differ from the plays of Euripides.

Finally, it may be added that the statistics for caesura in *Rhesus* may be influenced to some extent by a special factor which we observed earlier, namely the relatively high number, as compared with the early plays of Euripides, of resolutions which require a caesura in the third foot. These, that is, resolutions of the second and third arsis, occur in 7·2 % of the trimeters of *Rhesus*, as against 4·5 % in *Medea*, 3·6 % in *Hippolytus* and 3·7 % in *Alcestis*.[2] This may contribute somewhat to the difference between *Rhesus* and these other plays in the statistics for caesura, a difference of 5 % in the proportion of penthemimeral caesura between *Rhesus* and *Medea* or *Hippolytus*, of 6 % between *Rhesus* and *Alcestis*. In evaluating metrical statistics we should bear in mind that one peculiar feature may be related to another.

It seems unlikely then that in the treatment of caesura there is any substantial evidence against the Euripidean authorship of *Rhesus*. But it is worth noting that if it is by Euripides, the evidence here is again consistent with an early date in his career.

[1] *Op. cit.* p. 277: the list is not exhaustive.

[2] These percentages are based on Zieliński's totals (*op. cit.* p. 143) and include resolutions due to proper names; *Rhesus* has 49 such resolutions in 682 lines, *Medea* 47 in 1037, *Hippolytus* 36 in 987, *Alcestis* 30 in 802.

Prosody

Before leaving the iambic trimeters we must notice one or two matters of prosody.

(i) *Positio debilis*[1]

In the iambic trimeters of *Rhesus* there are 15 examples of the lengthening of a short vowel in the so-called weak position, or about 1 in 45 lines. This is slightly below the average frequency for Euripides, but well within the limits for his other works (*Alcestis* has about 1 in 47 lines, *Suppliants* 1 in 51 lines, *Iphigenia in Tauris* 1 in 60). This is not a matter in which there is any discernible development in Euripides' style; the frequency fluctuates according to the need for certain words in which lengthening is habitual or necessary to their use in the trimeter. Some of the commonest of such words are not needed in *Rhesus*: e.g. δακρ-, τεκν- (but τἔκν- is found twice). The 15 examples of lengthening in *Rhesus* involve 13 words and nine different stems; of these only one is not found similarly treated elsewhere in Euripides (211 τἔτράπουν). Of the nine stems seven are also found with lengthening in Sophocles. The behaviour of *Rhesus* in this respect is quite consonant with the metrical practice of Euripides, or for that matter of Sophocles; Aeschylus however admits such lengthening less often.

(ii) 494 μηνίων. This cannot be regarded as exceptional. In the present and imperfect Homer has ῐ except in B 769; so too Simonides, fr. 50 Bgk. In tragedy we find μηνίεται in Aeschylus, *Eu.* 101, but μανίω in Euripides, *Hipp.* 1146 (lyr.); the quantity is ambiguous in Sophocles, *OC* 965, 1274.

(iii) 762 Ἑκτόρειᾰ χείρ remains unexplained, but has one certain Attic parallel in Ar. *Eccl.* 1029 καὶ ταῦτ' ἀνάγκη μούστί;–Διομήδειᾰ γε. In view of this we cannot regard it as

---

[1] These observations are based on the material collected by A. Kopp, *Rh. Mus.* XLI (1886), 247–63 and 376–86. My calculations are made from his lists, which have been checked only for *Rhesus* itself.

impossible for Euripides. Other examples of the same phenomenon are doubtful or late: Pi. *O*, xi, 15 Κύκνεια μάχα (Hermann, *metri causa*); *Etym. M.* 461, 44, s.v. θυσία (cf. Cramer, *Anecd. Oxon.* ii, 305, 26), Πολυδεύκεια χείρ, Ἀγαμεμνόνεια; *ibid.* 451, 50 βασίλεια χείρ. We ought perhaps to see here a rare, but established licence.[1]

ANAPAESTS

Rhesus contains several anapaestic passages, amounting to some 75 lines; there are no melic anapaests among these. The kinds of context in which anapaests are used will be considered later. Our present concern is with the treatment of the metre itself, which is in most respects free from anomaly and consonant with the practice of Euripides in his strictest style. One matter however which calls for comment is the admission of ἀντιλαβή, the division of verses between two speakers. The occurrence of this licence in both the anapaests and the trochaic tetrameters of *Rhesus* has been adduced against the view that the play is an early work of Euripides, on the grounds that he rarely admits it in any metre except in his later plays.[2]

The trochaic tetrameters will be treated in the following section. So far as the anapaests are concerned, the ἀντιλαβαί are not numerous: only five verses need to be considered, 15, 16, 17, 540, 561. In *vv.* 15 and 540 the division between speakers is made at the diaeresis of the dimeter. These divisions are certain, but are not evidence either against Euripidean authorship or against an early date in his career, since a change of speaker occurs in this position at *Med.* 1397, 1398, 1402, as well as at Euripides, *El.* 1319 and Sophocles,

---

[1] Despite some confusion in codd. Harrison, *CR*, lvii (1943), 70, was not justified in proposing to substitute Ἕκτορος βία.

[2] Pearson, *CR*, xxxv (1921), 58; Grégoire, *op. cit.* p. 108. Wilamowitz, *Anal. Eur.* pp. 197–9, regarded the occurrence of ἀντιλαβή in anap. dim. as evidence against the authenticity of both *Rhesus* and the anap. prologue of *Iphigenia in Aulis*.

OC 173. It is also found in three places in the anapaestic prologue of *Iphigenia in Aulis*, the authenticity of which has been doubted (*vv.* 2, 16, 140).

A division of speakers within the anapaestic metron is a matter of greater moment, since it is found in tragedy only at Sophocles, *Trach.* 977, 981 and 991, and a few places in the suspect anapaestic prologue of *Iphigenia in Aulis* (*vv.* 2, 3, 149). It is however by no means certain that we have ἀντιλαβή of this kind in *Rhesus*, for in each of three places we have to consider there is some uncertainty about the text.

17 μῶν τις λόχος ἐκ νυκτῶν; [Χο. οὐκ ἔστι. Εκ.] τί σὺ γὰρ
    φυλακὰς προλιπὼν κινεῖς στρατιάν,
    εἰ μή τιν' ἔχων νυκτηγορίαν;

    17 οὐκ ἔστι LP: οὐκέτι VOHaun.: del. Dindorf.

Verse 17 is corrupt and unmetrical. Most editors agree in bracketing οὐκ ἔστι (LP) or οὐκέτι (VOHaun.), which codd. give to the Chorus. This certainly looks like an intrusion, intended to provide an answer to Hector's question. If it is omitted, there is no longer a change of speaker. The verse is also restored metrically, except that it has only an artificial diaeresis between ἐκ and νυκτῶν. The overrunning of the diaeresis in anapaestic dimeter by more than one short syllable is extremely rare,[1] and is not in keeping with the treatment of the metre elsewhere in this play. Perhaps then the correction of the text requires other changes, in which case the question of change of speaker is no less doubtful.

The preceding verse (16) is, as it stands, a single anapaestic metron divided in the middle between speakers:

Χο. θάρσει. Εκ. θαρσῶ.

The manner of this brief exhortation and reply is strikingly like that of the opening verses of the anapaestic prologue of *Iphigenia in Aulis* with their exchanges of στεῖχε –στείχω and

---

[1] For examples see Fraenkel on Aeschylus' *Agam.* 52.

σπεύδεις; –σπεύδω. These moreover are the only places in tragedy where an anapaestic metron is thus centrally divided between speakers. The resemblance is notable, but its significance obscure so long as doubt exists about the authorship of the *Iphigenia in Aulis* anapaests. There is, besides, in *Rhesus* again some reason to suspect the text, although codd. are here unanimous. The line interrupts Hector's series of questions and seems out of place, since Hector, despite his reply of θαρσῶ, is by no means reassured and continues his interrogation in a no less agitated manner than before. Paley on these grounds deleted θαρσῶ, and reconstructed *vv.* 16 and 17 as two dimeters, retaining θάρσει and οὐκ ἔστι and leaving the changes of speaker. But the removal of θαρσῶ only emphasizes the fact that θάρσει is ill accommodated to its surroundings. It is not a satisfactory reply to Hector's preceding question, and without θαρσῶ becomes quite pointless, an impertinent interruption which Hector ignores altogether. If θαρσῶ is deleted, the whole verse should go. This appears to be the most satisfactory solution, and the corruption in this passage may perhaps be more extensive. In *v.* 12 we might have expected a reply to Hector's demand for the password, especially after his sharp imperative θρόει. This has the tone of a general's command and it is strange that it should be ignored: compare ἐνέπειν χρή in *v.* 14, which is followed smartly by an answer. It would be proper for the Chorus to state the password here, and I suspect that in *v.* 12 their reply has been lost, which may have been Φοῖβος· θάρσει. The omission could have been caused by the similarity of θρόει and θάρσει, or else by a scribe's failure to understand the significance of Φοῖβος; if the omission had been noted in the margin, the misplaced attempt at restoration of a later scribe, who may even have recalled the opening of *Iphigenia in Aulis*, could have produced *v.* 16. Whatever the correct solution of the difficulty, there is clearly reason for doubting that *v.* 16 is right as it stands. It would therefore be unwise to use it as evidence of the poet's verse-technique.

In *v.* 561 ἀντιλαβή is introduced only by emendation of the corrupt manuscript text; Murray reads:

ἀλλ᾽ ἦ κρυπτὸν λόχον ἐσπαίσας
διόλωλε; — τάχ᾽ ἄν· φοβερόν μοι.

διόλωλε] διώλεσεν O : ὄλωλε vel ὄλωλεν (V) τάχ᾽ (τύχ᾽) ἂν εἴη codd.: εἴη del. Headlam.

In the unmetrical manuscript text there is no suggestion of change of speaker. The only parallel for ἀντιλαβή in the paroemiac is at *Trach.* 977, and an emendation involving so rare a licence should be treated with caution. The reading adopted by Murray is at best a possible conjecture, and so not to be invoked as evidence of the poet's metrical practice.

Thus the examples of change of speaker within the anapaestic dimeter elsewhere than at the diaeresis all rest upon a doubtful text, and it is highly doubtful whether this licence occurs. These few dubious or corrupt verses ought not to obscure the fact that the treatment of the anapaests in *Rhesus* conforms generally with the practice of Euripides at his strictest.

TROCHAIC TETRAMETER

Rhesus contains a total of 12 verses in trochaic tetrameter: these appear at *vv.* 679, 683–91, where they are used for the encounter between the Chorus and Odysseus, and again very briefly at *vv.* 730–1, at the point where the Charioteer enters and the Chorus prepares to ambush him.

In the use of trochaic tetrameter in *Rhesus*, and especially in the admission of ἀντιλαβή in this metre, evidence has been found against the view that the play is an early work of Euripides.[1] For trochaic tetrameter does not appear in any of his extant works before *Heracles* (*c.* 416?), but thereafter (if we may assume that *Electra*, which has none, is earlier

[1] See p. 289 n. 2 above.

than *Heracles*) is used in all plays, in some extensively.[1]
Further, in the two earliest plays in which this metre occurs,
Heracles and *Troades* (415), it is used without ἀντιλαβή, but
in all subsequent plays, with the exception of *Bacchae*, this
licence is found.

The simple fact that trochaic tetrameter is used in *Rhesus*
but not in the earlier plays of Euripides cannot in itself carry
any weight as evidence that *Rhesus* was not written by
Euripides in the early part of his career. We are not dealing
here with a metre which was apparently new to tragedy when
Euripides employed it in *Heracles*. On the contrary, we are
told by Aristotle that the trochaic tetrameter was the original
metre of tragedy, which later, as tragedy increased in dignity,
gave place to iambic, the metre most closely resembling the
rhythm of ordinary speech.[2] This change, of course, must
belong to a period earlier than our oldest extant tragedies,
but there is no reason to believe that the trochaic metre was
ever discarded as totally unsuitable for the tragic stage.
Indeed we have scattered examples of its use in the period
before 420, by Aeschylus in plays as widely separated in date
as *Persae* (472) and *Agamemnon* (458), by Sophocles in *Oedipus
Tyrannus*, a play whose date is not at all certain but which is
usually placed earlier than 420. There is perhaps even
evidence for the use of trochaic tetrameter by Euripides
before this date. Most of the few Euripidean fragments in
this metre belong to plays whose date is unknown or apparently late, but a single trochaic tetrameter line is cited
from *Phoenix* (fr. 811 N.[2]), which is known from an allusion in
the *Acharnians* (*v.* 421) to have been earlier than 425. This is
slender evidence but, in view of the sporadic occurrence of
trochaic tetrameter in plays earlier than the late period of
tragedy, it would be foolish to assume from its absence from

---

[1] Euripides' use of trochaic tetrameter is analysed by W. Krieg, *Philologus*,
XCI (1936), 42 ff. In view of the uncertain date of some plays Krieg is not
justified in asserting that there is a steady increase in the use of the metre. On
the date of *Electra* see p. 262 n. 1 above.

[2] *Poet.* IV, 18.

Euripides' seven earliest extant plays that he must have avoided it altogether at this period.

The trochaic tetrameters of *Rhesus* are not really to be compared with those in the later plays of Euripides. In the latter trochaic tetrameter is a metre of ordinary spoken dialogue, which is introduced in increasing measure as an alternative to the iambic trimeter, often, it would seem, for the sake of variety in a long scene, sometimes also to underline a change of emotional tone. With internal division between speakers it is effective for rapid exchanges of dialogue, in which use it is often preferred to the less flexible iambic stichomythia.[1]

In *Rhesus*, on the other hand, the tetrameter verses are part of a lyrical composition, in which both the Chorus and actors participate and which is accompanied by lively movement. The opening cries of the Chorus as they enter (675–8) may be defined metrically as a pair of highly resolved dochmiacs followed by an aristophanean clausula; then from 679 onwards the trochaic rhythm is clearly defined, and at 683 we settle down to a series of tetrameters as the Chorus come to grips with Odysseus. We ought probably to think of recitative rather than ordinary speech as the mode of delivery for these lines. In this lyrical context we need not expect the regularity of metre that would be demanded in spoken dialogue, and after the resolved verses with which the scene opens may be prepared for what we meet in *v.* 685: this line is in all probability to be retained as it stands, as the metrical equivalent, highly syncopated, of four trochees. Otherwise the tetrameters are metrically regular, and only two of them (687, 688) contain resolution.[2]

It is true that nowhere else in tragedy do we find a sequence of trochaic tetrameters employed in quite the same circumstances as here. It is possible to compare *Agam.* 1649 ff., where the metre is used for an excited skirmish between

---

[1] Krieg, *op. cit.*
[2] In 683 a harsh synizesis may be avoided by reading εἰδέναι σ' οὐ χρή.

actor and Chorus, but these lines belong to the ordinary spoken dialogue. In *Rhesus* the trochaic tetrameters introduce a lyric composition, the *epiparodos*, which is completed by a pair of strophes alternating with dialogue in lyric iambics. The closest parallel to the design of this whole passage is afforded by the *epiparodos* of *Ajax* (*vv.* 866 ff.). There too the Chorus enter engaged in dialogue, as they search for Ajax, and this is followed by a pair of strophes each succeeded by a passage of iambic dialogue interspersed with dochmiacs. In *Ajax* however the introductory dialogue is in lyric iambics, including some trimeters, a metre suitable to the movement of the Chorus, which is slow and weary. Elsewhere anapaests are commonly associated with the entrance of the Chorus, but theirs is a regular marching rhythm. Here the Chorus enters running, and trochaic metre is obviously appropriate. At *vv.* 730–1 there is a brief recurrence of trochaic tetrameter, no doubt because the guards execute a similar hurried movement at the approach of the Charioteer; but here the trochees are cut short by the Charioteer's anapaestic cries of lamentation, and halted they turn to more sedate iambics.

As for the admission of ἀντιλαβή in these tetrameters one could perhaps plead a special licence in a lyric context of this kind. At least our passage ought not to be put in the same class as the trochaic tetrameters of spoken dialogue in the later plays of Euripides. The poet's attitude to the division of verses between speakers in ordinary dialogue is to be judged solely from his treatment of the iambic trimeter, in which it does not occur at all. It is however questionable whether in Euripides the occurrence of ἀντιλαβή in either the iambic trimeter or the trochaic tetrameter is of any relevance for purposes of dating. In the iambic trimeter he uses it sparingly at all periods. There are some examples in the four early plays which we have found to be generally strict in their treatment of this metre (*Alc.* 390, 391, 1119; *Med.* 1009; *Hipp.* 310, 352, 724, 1325; nine in *Heraclidae*). Except in *Phoenissae* (18 verses) and *Orestes* (24 verses) it is hardly more frequent in any of the later plays (there is no instance in *Troades* and only one in *Helen*).[1] In trochaic tetrameters, as we have seen, ἀντιλαβή occurs in all but the first two of the Euripidean plays which use the metre; the trochaic passage in *Heracles* contains, in fact, only three changes of speaker and that in *Troades* has none. It would be exceedingly rash to look here for evidence of a development in the technique of Euripides. It may be added that Sophocles introduces ἀντιλαβή in the iambic trimeter in his earliest play, *Ajax*, and in all others except *Antigone*; it is also found in two of the three passages of trochaic tetrameter in his plays (*OT* 1515–23, *Phil.* 1402–8).

THE LYRIC METRES

In all the controversy about the authorship of *Rhesus* very little consideration has been given to the evidence to be derived from the lyrics and their metres. Some scholars of the last century asserted that the lyrics showed in their metrical forms the influence of Aeschylus, but they did not elaborate this view.[2] Of more recent critics few have dealt with the lyrics at all, although Murray recognized their merit and his praise was echoed by Pearson.[3] Only Wilamowitz has discussed the lyric metres of *Rhesus* in any detail; he found in them further evidence to support his view that the play is not by Euripides but a work of the fourth century.[4] Apart from this some studies of Greek lyric metre have treated particular aspects of the *Rhesus* lyrics without touching on the question of their authorship.[5]

[1] Totals for other plays (excluding trimeters in lyric contexts) are: *Andromache* 1, *Hecuba* 3, *Suppliants* 3, *Electra* 4, *Heracles* 5, *Ion* 1, *Iphigenia in Tauris* 2, *Bacchae* 5, *Iphigenia in Aulis* 8.
[2] Gruppe, *Ariadne*, p. 337; Hagenbach, *De Rheso Tragoedia*, p. 26 (citing the view of Lachmann).
[3] Murray, *Rhesus* transl. p. x; Pearson, *op. cit.* p. 59.
[4] *Griechische Verskunst* (Berlin, 1921), esp. pp. 583–9.
[5] Especially important is A. M. Dale, *The Lyric Metres of Greek Drama* (Cambridge, 1948); see also E. Fraenkel, 'Lyrische Daktylen', in *Rh. Mus.* LXXII (1917), 161–97 and 321–52.

It is proposed here to analyse the lyrics strophe by strophe, examining the treatment of the various metres and the ways in which they are associated with one another in composition. In this study we must first try to judge whether the metrical technique of the lyrics is like that of Euripides or not, giving special attention to alleged anomalies, especially those noted by Wilamowitz. We must also consider whether it is possible to fix the position of *Rhesus* in relation to the clearly defined development in Euripides' handling of the lyric metres, and so to find a further criterion for its dating if Euripidean.

The parodos

23–33 = 41–51

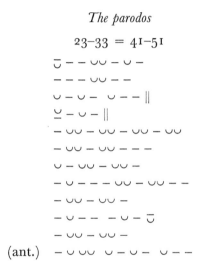

(ant.)

Textual uncertainties affect the metre in two places. At 25 = 43 strophe and antistrophe do not correspond in codd. In 25 ὄτρυνον must certainly be read, and the rest is a matter of choice between variant spellings. The scheme given here follows the text adopted by Murray, who restores response by reading αἴρειν in 25, ναῶν in 41, both the more likely forms for tragic lyric. The metre is then iambic, and the shape of the line requires a pause after αἴρειν and ναῶν to give a dimeter followed by a single iambic metron.

297

The other difficulty is in the final line, where codd. again fail to respond. If, with Murray, we accept Bothe's re-arrangement of words in 51 to agree with the traditional text for the strophe, we have – ∪ ∪ ∪ ∪ ∪ ∪ – ∪ – –. This could be interpreted as an alcaic decasyllable with its second long resolved. The alcaic decasyllable is found in tragedy as a clausula to dactylic and dactylo-epitrite sequences, but nowhere else with resolution. A colon so resolved is the less easy to accept, if it be regarded as continuing the dactylic rhythm of the preceding hemiepes. In dactylic metre resolution is exceedingly rare, and perhaps unexampled in tragedy, nor is the hemiepes of dactylo-epitrite resolved.[1] The other possible interpretation of this colon is as a trimeter comprising two resolved cretics + bacchiac. It is however by no means necessary to accept the text of the strophe. The reading of codd. in the antistrophe (μήποτέ τινα μέμψιν εἰς ἔμ᾽ εἴπῃς) is itself unexceptionable and metrically very plausible, a straightforward iambic line. If it is accepted, we must add one short syllable in 33: τά could have dropped out before κερόδετα, but it is impossible to guess. Whatever correction is required in the strophe, it seems right to start from the antistrophe, in which case there is no metrical anomaly.

The composition of the strophe is simple. It opens with a glyconic followed by a pherecratean; then by way of iambic the metre passes into dactyls, thence to dactylo-epitrite, which is sustained until the last line. The elements combined here are found similarly associated, though in different proportions, in the first strophe of the second stasimon (342–50 = 351–9). Consideration of the metrical structure of the present lyric will be reserved until that strophe is discussed.

---

[1] On resolution in dactylic metre see Dale, *op. cit.* p. 25 n. *Andr.* 1032 = 1042, a resolved line in a dactylo-epitrite context, may be interpreted as iambic; in *Phoen.* 1513, possibly a hemiepes in view of the preceding colon, we may scan ἄχεα.

131–6 = 195–200

⏑ ⏑ ⏑ – ⏑ ⏑ ⏑ ⏑ ⏑ ⏑ – ⏑ –
⏑ ⏑ ⏑ – ⏑ – ⏑ – – ⏑ –
⏑ ⏑ ⏑ – ⏑ –
⏑ ⏑ ⏑ – ⏑ – ⏑ – – ⏑ –
⏑ ⏑ ⏑ ⏑ ⏑ ⏑ ⏑ – ⏑ –
⏑ ⏑ ⏑ – ⏑ – ⏑ – ⏑ – – ⏑ –

The metre is a straightforward combination of dochmiac and iambic. If the first line is scanned as a dochmiac dimeter, the normal diaeresis is lacking in the strophe; there are comparable divisions in the lyrics of Euripides, that is, where the first dochmiac of a dimeter ends with a short syllable which is the initial syllable of a word (*HF* 1070, *Tro.* 244). In the present case, however, the line may also be scanned as iambic (cretic + lecythion). The penultimate verse is an iambic dimeter with the first metron fully resolved, and the last verse is best divided as cretic + iambic + dochmiac. A quite similar clausula to a dochmiac lyric occurs at *Med.* 1281: ⏑ ⏑ ⏑ ⏑ ⏑ ⏑ ⏑ – ⏑ – ⏑ – – ⏑ –.

The metrical composition is simple and needs no special discussion. But the strictness of treatment is notable. Exact responsion is preserved throughout (provided Nauck's πόνος ὅδ᾽ for πόνος δ᾽ is accepted in 197), and only the two commonest forms of dochmiac are employed. Such simplicity of metrical form in a dochmiac context is seldom to be associated with the later style of Euripides, but is comparable with the manner of his earliest extant plays.

There are many parallels to this use of dochmiacs for brief choral utterances interposed in passages of dialogue. In Euripides we may compare *Hipp.* 362 = 669, 1268, *Hec.* 1024, *El.* 585, *IT* 644. Aeschylus has short dochmiac lyrics of a similar kind, for example at *Sept.* 417 = 452, 481 = 521, 563 = 626, *PV* 687, *Agam.* 1407 = 1426, *Ch.* 152. In Sophocles the spoken dialogue is not so often punctuated by brief lyrics of this kind, but there is a comparable pair of responding strophes in *Philoctetes* (391 = 507): these provide internal divisions in a long iambic scene, and are mainly iambic with some admixture of dochmiac.

First stasimon

Strophe α', 224–32 = 233–41

$$\overline{\cup} - \cup - \ - \cup \cup - \cup \cup -$$
$$- \cup - \ \cup - - \parallel$$
$$\cup \ - \cup - \ - \ - \cup \cup - \cup \cup - \ - \ - \cup \cup - \cup \cup -$$
$$- \cup - \ - \ - \cup \cup - \cup \cup - \ -$$
$$- \cup - \ - \ - \cup \cup - \cup \cup -$$
$$- \ - \cup \cup - \cup \cup -$$
$$- \ - \cup - \cup - -$$

The text is free from complications.

The metre is dactylo-epitrite throughout. Strophes wholly composed of this metre are not uncommon in tragedy, occurring in Aeschylus, *PV* (two); Sophocles, *Ajax*, *Trachiniae*; Euripides, *Medea* (five), *Andromache* (two), *Troades*, *Electra*.

The ithyphallic clausula is paralleled in dactylo-epitrite strophes at *PV* 535 = 544, *Med.* 420 = 430, 634 = 642, *Andr.* 776 = 787, also at *Hec.* 932 = 942, where the closing passage of the strophe is dactylo-epitrite.[1]

With the appearance of the ithyphallic earlier in the strophe, after the opening sequence, it is possible to compare *Andr.* 1030, since there also the opening dactylo-epitrite verses are rounded off by an ithyphallic, after which the same metre is continued, with variations, to the end of the strophe. There is therefore little ground for thinking that this might be evidence for a post-Euripidean date.[2]

[1] On the use of the ithyphallic clausula in the dactylo-epitrite of tragedy see Dale, *op. cit.* p. 170.

[2] A view expressed, but not elaborated, by Hagenbach, *op. cit.*

First stasimon

Strophe β', 242–52 = 253–63

This strophe presents rather more difficulty. Wilamowitz offers the following analysis:[1]

∪ – ∪ – – ∪ ∪ – ∪ – ∪ –	(3 ia.)
– ∪ ∪ – ∪ ∪ – ∪ ∪ –	(4 dact.)
– ∪ ∪ – ∪ ∪ – –	(dact.-ep.)
– ∪ ∪ – ∪ ∪ – ∪ – ∪ ∪ – ∪ ∪ –	
– ∪ – – ‖	
∪ ∪ – ∪ ∪ – ∪ – ∪	(enopl.)
– ∪ ∪ ∪ ∪ ∪ ∪ ∪ ∪ ∪͡∪	(5 chor.)
– ∪ ∪ – – ∪ ∪ –	
– ∪ ∪ – ∪ – –	

With the first half of the strophe there is no real difficulty. The only line about which there is uncertainty is the third; 245 λήματος· ἢ σπανία (σπάνις LP) is one syllable shorter than 256 μῖμον ἔχων ἐπὶ γαῖαν (γαίας LP). Responsion can be restored simply by reading γᾶν (Dindorf), but the unanimity of codd. for the other form does not recommend this solution. It is perhaps more likely that the corruption is in the strophe: the form σπανία is not otherwise known before Diodorus Siculus, but σπάνις is common in tragedy. The latter is perhaps to be restored from LP, with ἐστίν or ἀεί (Wilamowitz) or some other word to complete the metre. The point does not vitally affect the metre, the line being a hemiepes with or without a pendant long syllable.

We have then in the first half of the strophe an iambochoriambic trimeter followed by dactyls, which lead into a brief repetition of the dactylo-epitrite of the first strophe. From 250 = 260 the analysis is more difficult. Wilamowitz's scheme has first a dicolon comprising an enoplion together with a

---

[1] Wilamowitz, *op. cit.* p. 583. The differences between his text and Murray's are not significant for the metre, but Murray adopts a different colometry. Wecklein's text varies slightly from these, but without producing better metrical sense.

highly resolved colon, which he takes, in view of what follows, to represent two choriambs (or a choriamb + iambus); then come a pair of choriambs and an aristophanean clausula.

In this Wilamowitz himself finds more than one abnormal feature. In the first place he regards the resolution of the two choriambs, or choriamb and its iambic substitute, as unparalleled. It certainly does not seem possible to find elsewhere in the lyrics of tragedy a resolved colon which the context requires us to interpret as a pair of choriambs, and it is not easy even to quote certain examples of the resolution of a choriamb. Instances of a resolved metron ᴗ ᴗ ᴗ ᴗ – responding to an unresolved choriamb are doubtful: Aeschylus, *Pers.* 1007, a possible case, is one of several places where the scansion of δια- as a long syllable seems to be called for; at Euripides, *Supp.* 614 the irregular responsion is rendered uncertain by corruption in the strophe (604).[1] There are however a few places where a resolved metron might justifiably be interpreted in its context as a choriamb, although there is naturally a certain ambiguity: among these might be included *Ion* 123 = 139 (where a resolved glyconic precedes), *Aj.* 1185 = 1192 and *IA* 1036–7. It is relevant to compare also *Alc.* 120 = 130 and 971 = 981: in each of these places the resolution again results in ambiguity, but the context suggests interpretation as an aeolic colon with its choriambic element resolved.[2] Although the evidence is not abundant, it seems likely that the resolution of choriambs was occasionally admitted in tragic lyric. But it must be conceded that in the present case the resolution would be bolder than any of those we have mentioned.

A second anomaly which Wilamowitz finds here is the coupling of an enoplion with this resolved choriambic colon to form a dicolon. The enoplion appears inevitable here if the resolved choriambs are accepted. The division of this

---

[1] These might also be regarded as examples of the irregular responsion of an iamb to a choriamb, of which possible examples, all uncertain, are collected by Denniston, 'Lyric Iambics', in *Greek Poetry and Life*, p. 142.

[2] See Dale, *Alcestis*, pp. 63–4, 120.

colon from the preceding period is clearly defined by the hiatus after ἐνέγκοι. Musgrave's ἐνέγκοιθ' would remove the hiatus and might make possible a continuation of the preceding dactylo-epitrite movement, but it is difficult to justify the middle here.

The enoplion ∪ ∪ – ∪ ∪ – ∪ – ⌣̱ (with initial ∪ ∪ as distinct from – – ∪ ∪ – ∪ – –) is an element familiar enough in Euripidean lyric. It is at home in a variety of contexts, appearing both as an independent colon (e.g. at *Alc.* 255, 457, *Hec.* 652, *El.* 732; also probably Sophocles, *Trach.* 879) and as the first part of a dicolon (e.g. *Hipp.* 755 f., *Med.* 645, *Andr.* 1014). The last two examples are of particular relevance to the present case. In *Med.* 645 the enoplion is joined with an ithyphallic and the dicolon follows an opening choriambic period (2 chor., aristophanean) comparable to the closing passage of our strophe. In *Andr.* 1014 it is combined with a hemiepes to provide a slight variation of rhythm after a passage of dactylo-epitrite.[1] The context at *Hec.* 652 is also akin to dactylo-epitrite. In itself then the enoplion appears to be appropriately placed in the present strophe, where it makes a transition from dactylo-epitrite to choriambic, having a rhythmical affinity with both. For Euripides it is often a transitional element and he uses it in association with both metres.

There still remains the difficulty presented by the dicolon, of which according to Wilamowitz's analysis the enoplion is here an inseparable part. The combination is not as easy a one as the other dicola in which this enoplion is found and, while in view of its varied rhythmical affinities its conjunction with choriambs cannot be deemed impossible, there is certainly no parallel to it.

There is a third point made about this strophe by Wilamowitz. He sees as a departure from the older practice the pair of dactylo-epitrite verses, in which the first strophe is echoed, interposed between the iambic and choriambic passages. It is

---

[1] Dale, *Lyric Metres*, p. 183.

not explained in what respect this is to be regarded as an innovation, and it is difficult to find anything unusual here. Indeed, the second stasimon of *Medea* (627 ff.) displays a quite similar metrical technique. The first strophe is, as here, dactylo-epitrite. The second, which was discussed above, opens with choriambs followed, as we have seen, by a di-colon consisting of enoplion and ithyphallic; after this there is in all probability a hemiepes, followed by the colon ∪ ∪ – ∪ ∪ – ∪ – ∪ – –, a clearly recognizable echo of the metre of the preceding strophe; then there is a return to choriambic rhythm with two choriambic dimeters and a hipponactean clausula. This combination of elements is not unlike that of our strophe, in which opening and close, iambic and choriambic, are related in character, and the middle element echoes the dactylo-epitrite of the first strophe. The other three stasima of *Medea* show a comparable technique. In each the first strophe is wholly dactylo-epitrite and the second a composition of more varied character, which nevertheless contains a reminiscence of the insistent rhythm of the first, either in a repetition of the same metre or in a purely dactylic passage. The same technique is used in the second stasimon of *Troades*, and the other two Euripidean stasima in which the first strophe is wholly dactylo-epitrite, *Andr.* 766 ff. and 1009 ff., also have a repetition of the metre together with iambic elements in the second strophe (or epode).

In this last respect then we cannot agree with Wilamowitz that our strophe departs from the technique of Euripides as it is exemplified in some of his earlier works. But in the resolved choriambs and the abnormal form of dicolon his analysis of the metre does present us with phenomena which cannot be precisely paralleled. We are not however committed to Wilamowitz's interpretation here, and indeed it appears somewhat artificial; Murray's colometry, which accords more closely with the division of words, gives the following scheme:

250   ∪ ∪ − ∪ ∪ − ∪ − ∪ − ∪ − ‖

∪ ∪ ∪ ∪ ∪ ∪ ‿‿

− ∪ ∪ −   − ∪ ∪ −

− ∪ ∪ −   ∪ − −

Here 250 becomes enoplion (or telesilleion) + iambic, alternatively 'iambo-anapaest', quite appropriate as a transitional colon.[1] The strophe ends with a choriambic sequence. The intervening resolved verse is still metrically ill-defined: it could be interpreted as a dochmiac or as a resolved aeolic colon (∪ ∪ ⌒ ∪ ∪ ‿‿). For the latter one might compare again the resolved elements occurring at *Alc.* 120 = 130 and 971 = 981.

The proper interpretation of the metre in the second half of this strophe must remain uncertain. But while there exists a more satisfactory alternative analysis to that which Wilamowitz has proposed, we ought not to attach too much weight as evidence to the metrical anomalies that he has found. The existence of variant readings in these lines in both strophe and antistrophe must also be kept in mind. Although it is doubtful whether other readings can be made to yield better metrical sense, we cannot feel absolute confidence in the text upon which our analysis has been based.

Second stasimon

Strophe α′, 342–50 = 351–9

− − − ∪ ∪ − ∪ −

− − − ∪ ∪ − ∪ −

∪̲ − − ∪ ∪ − −

− − − ∪ ∪ − ∪ − −

∪̄ − − ∪ ∪ − − ‖

− − ∪ −   − ∪ ∪ −   ∪ − −

− − ∪ ∪ − ∪ ∪ −

− ∪ − −   − ∪ ∪ − ∪ ∪ −

− ∪ ∪ − ∪ − −

---

[1] For cola of this type cf. Dale, *op. cit.* pp. 181 ff.

There is no difficulty in the text and the scheme is straight-forward.[1] The opening sequence comprises five aeolic cola ending with a pherecratean. Then follows an iambic trimeter whose central choriamb links it rhythmically with what precedes. For the last three lines I have followed the colometry adopted by Wecklein and Porter. It can be regarded simply as a brief echo of the dactylo-epitrite metre, which was dominant in the preceding stasimon, followed by an aristophaneus as clausula to the whole strophe. Wilamowitz divides (after Πιερὶς and θεῷ) into two verses, describing them as prosodiacs joined once with one and once with two iambic metra, the latter in a common clausula form. Whatever name we adopt, the metre seems to be a recollection of the rhythm of preceding lyrics.

This strophe in its composition has something in common with the lyric of the parodos. The same elements, glyconic, iambic, dactylo-epitrite, appear in both in the same order. In the parodos strophe the dactylo-epitrite element is of longer duration and is introduced by pure dactyls: here the glyconic part is sustained longer. Similar combinations are not uncommon in Euripides. At *Tro.* 1060 = 1071 we find a strophe compounded of similar elements to those of the present strophe, arranged in the same order and in much the same proportions. At *Med.* 431 = 439 the elements are an iambic trimeter (identical with the one in this strophe), dactyls and glyconics in that order. In a strophe of *Hecuba*, 905 = 914, glyconic and dactylo-epitrite are again associated in the same strophe; in the following strophe the sequence is iambic, glyconic, iambic, dactylo-epitrite, and the epode of this stasimon has the same elements. At *Ion* 1048 = 1061 dactylo-epitrite introduces a strophe, the remainder of which is built of glyconic and iambic elements. *El.* 452 = 462 differs only in having a purely dactylic opening.

It appears then that these elements of diverse type are not uncommonly found in association with one another and that

---

[1] The strophe is treated by Wilamowitz, *op. cit.* pp. 584 f.

the composition of these two strophes of *Rhesus* is quite in keeping with the metrical technique of Euripides.

Second stasimon

Strophe β′, 360–9 = 370–9

– ∪ ∪ – ∪ – ∪ – – ∪ ∪ –

– ∪ ∪ – ∪ – ∪ –

  – ∪ ∪ – ∪ – – ‖

– – ∪ – ∪ ∪ – – ∪ ∪ – –

∪ ∪ – ∪ – ∪ – –

∪ ∪ – ∪ ∪ – –

– – – ∪ ∪ – – ∪ ∪ – ∪ – – ‖

– ∪ ∪ – ∪ –

– ∪ ∪ – – ∪ ∪ – – ∪ ∪ – ∪ – –

The few uncertainties of text in this strophe do not affect the metre. The scheme given here is that adopted by both Wilamowitz and Dale;[1] it is recommended by its simplicity and by the coincidence in most places of colon-end with word-division.

Beginning and ending are alike iambic and choriambic, the closing passage admitting the element – ∪ ∪ – ∪ –, which appears in various contexts and is clearly at home among choriambic cola. In the middle of the strophe there is a change to ionics, the sequence including the anaclastic dimeter, a syncopated dimeter and a tetrameter. Dale has remarked upon the ambiguous character of *v.* 363, which can be otherwise analysed as a typical aeolic colon with a central pair of choriambs.[2] Similarly, the ionic tetrameter of 366–7 is very similar in shape to an asclepiad. The transition from iambo-choriambic to ionics and back again is thus effected very smoothly and skilfully. We may regard the combination of metres in this strophe as a very natural one; iambic, choriambic and ionic are in fact found together from the

---

[1] Wilamowitz, *op. cit.* pp. 586 f.; Dale, *op. cit.* p. 123.
[2] Dale, *op. cit.* p. 137.

time of Aeschylus. Wilamowitz cites examples to illustrate the tendency of ionics to be associated with these other metres; apposite parallels to the metrical structure of this strophe are also cited by Dale.[1]

Within the range of extant tragedy ionics are much more prominent in the lyrics of Aeschylus than in those of the younger tragedians. Euripides' only extensive use of the metre is in the parodos of *Supplices* and in the parodos and first two stasima of *Bacchae*, where we find strophes composed wholly in ionics as well as others which combine ionic with aeolic cola. But there are places in some other plays where, as in *Rhesus*, we may recognize a brief appearance of ionics, although some of these may be otherwise interpreted: e.g. *Alc.* 256, 908–10; *Hipp.* 732 f.; *Ph.* 1516 f., 1527; *IA* 171–5.

There is nothing in the metrical composition of either strophe of this stasimon to suggest that Euripides might not have been its author.

Separated strophe and antistrophe

454–66 = 820–32

The metrical analysis of this pair of strophes presents difficulty in several places, but the perplexities are never dissociated from a doubtful text.[2] Corruption has occurred in both strophe and antistrophe, sometimes disturbing responsion. Although there remains much uncertainty in the restoration of the text, there are comparatively few places where both strophe and antistrophe are manifestly unsound. The metre can therefore be established in its main lines. The following is a tentative scheme:

454 = 820   ∪ – ∪ –
∪ ∪ ∪ – ∪ – ∪ ∪ ∪ – ∪ –
∪ ∪ ∪ ∪ ∪ ∪ – ‖

---

[1] Wilamowitz, *op. cit.* p. 343; Dale, *op. cit.* pp. 123–5.
[2] For discussion see Wilamowitz, *op. cit.* pp. 587 f.

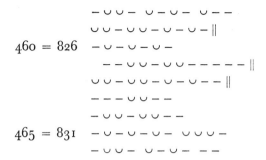

455 = 821. The beginning of the antistrophe (821–2) is corrupt. The manuscripts give μέγας ἐμοὶ μέγας ὦ πολιοῦχον κράτος τότ᾽ ἄρ᾽ ἔμολον (ἔμολ᾽ LP). Attempts to restore sense and responsion are unsatisfactory. Porter accepts from Wilamowitz μέγα σύ μοι, μέγ᾽, ὦ πολίοχον κράτος, τότ᾽ ἄρ᾽ ἔμολον: but this gives a curiously involved apostrophe, and it is difficult to have to understand κατάσκοποι as the subject of ἔμολον from as far back as 814, especially as with no subject expressed we might more naturally understand the verb as first person singular. Verrall's μετὰ σέ, μή, μετὰ σέ, . . ., τότ᾽ ἄρ᾽ ἔμολον, which Murray adopts with ναί instead of μή, is also open to the latter objection. Wilamowitz[1] further proposed μέγας ἐγώ, μέγας, πολίοχον κράτος, τότ᾽ ἄρ᾽ ἔμολον, understanding μέγας in the sense of 'gewichtig, glaubwürdig', for which he compared Sophocles, _OT_ 441, 653; but these parallels are not convincing. In view of LP's ἔμολ᾽ we cannot be absolutely certain of ἔμολον; it is possible that corruption involves the loss of a noun, agreeing with μέγας or μέγα and subject of ἔμολ᾽. There can at least be no reliance on the antistrophe in establishing the metre here.

The strophe, on the other hand, looks sound enough in 455, which is a dochmiac dimeter.

456 = 822. Provided that we accept the traditional text in the antistrophe, a metrical pause is clearly marked by the hiatus after σοι. The resulting colon, consisting in both

---

[1] _Loc. cit._

strophe and antistrophe of seven shorts and a long, is too long by one short syllable to be the metrical equivalent of a dochmiac. It can however be precisely paralleled in other dochmiac passages (cf. Aeschylus, *Sept.* 789, *Eum.* 158 and Euripides, *HF* 1057). Dale treats it as a form of 'long' dochmiac, the resolved equivalent of ∪ ∪ – – ∪ –, which itself has a claim to recognition as a possible unit of dochmiac composition.[1] We cannot however rely on the antistrophe at this point, and the strophe too, though apparently sound, may be corrupt.

457 = 823. The text of the strophe is sound and responsion is restored in the antistrophe by reading ἀμφὶ ναῦς πῦρ' αἴθειν. The line is readily divisible as a trimeter made up of choriamb, iamb and bacchiac. Wilamowitz treats it as another dochmiac dimeter, in which ∪ – ∪ – – is an irregular substitute for a dochmiac, but this is unnecessary. As often in this kind of context, the dochmiac rhythm is carried into an iambic verse.

824. 'Αργείων στρατόν corresponds to nothing in the strophe and is almost certainly an interpolation; its removal does not disturb the sense.

459 = 825. The text is undisputed and colon-end is again defined by hiatus. The colon is of a form found occasionally in dochmiac contexts in Euripides, notably at *El.* 586 and 588 and *Phaethon* fr. 781, 66, possibly also at *Ion* 1448; in Sophocles it occurs, also among dochmiacs, at *Aj.* 399.[2] It might possibly be analysed as a dimeter consisting of anapaest and iambus, an interpretation which finds some support in the appearance among dochmiacs of such cola as *Hec.* 1068 ∪ ∪ – ∪ ∪ – ∪ ∪ ∪ – ∪ – and *Hipp.* 1270 ∪ – ∪ – ∪ ∪ – ∪ ∪ –. It is however probably better regarded as an indivisible unit, with which besides the cola already mentioned one may also

---

[1] Dale, *op. cit.* p. 113; cf. Koster, *Traité de métrique grecque*, XII, 3.
[2] This colon is discussed by Dale, *op. cit.* p. 161, who treats it as a form of enoplion; Denniston, *op. cit.* pp. 135 f., interprets it as a dimeter composed of anapaest and iambus; cf. Wilamowitz, *op. cit.* p. 385.

compare *Andr.* 861 ⏑⏑ − ⏑⏑ − ⏑ − − −.[1] Whatever name we give it, the colon has several Euripidean parallels.

460 = 826. The antistrophe appears sound here; I have accordingly accepted Nauck's rearrangement in the strophe. An alternative might be οὔτε πρίν < ποτ' > οὔτε νῦν τιν', with ἔβριξα | μά in the antistrophe (initial anceps in the following enoplion). It is a lecythion or trochaic dimeter as the case may be.

461–2 = 827–8. The colometry given above is based on the manuscript text for the strophe: if this is accepted, the division between cola is fixed by the hiatus after μοι. Alternatively, it may seem preferable to adopt Wilamowitz's transposition in 462 (τὸ σὸν ἔγχος 'Αχιλλεὺς ἂν δύναιτο) and then to divide at the natural rhetorical pause in both strophe and antistrophe, beginning the second line with μή μοι and πῶς μοι respectively. In either case both cola can be assigned to the family of prosodiacs and enoplia. In the scheme presented here 461 could be divided as an anapaestic dimeter + spondee, but is best classed as an enoplion with a 'dragged' close and ⏑ ⏑ twice contracted to −. Similar enoplia, without contraction, are found in Euripides at *Andr.* 480, *Ion* 716 f., 1442, *Ph.* 184, the last three in close association with dochmiacs.[2] In 462 we then have another colon of the enoplion class, which recurs in later lyrics of this play (531, 900–1) and has several Euripidean parallels (see on 900–1).

The text proposed by Wilamowitz would give us

461   − − ⏑ ⏑ − ⏑ ⏑ − − −
462   − − ⏑ ⏑ − ⏑ ⏑ − − − ⏑ − −

Wilamowitz, seeing in this and the following lines a recurrence of the dactylo-epitrite metre of the earlier odes, regarded as strange the combination of dactylo-epitrite with

---

[1] Dale, *op. cit.*, adds other examples in Euripides; cf. Denniston, *op. cit.* p. 137.

[2] Dale, *op. cit.* pp. 159 f.

dochmiac in the same strophe.[1] It may be true that we do not find anywhere else a dochmiac period and a dactylo-epitrite period juxtaposed in the same strophe. On the other hand isolated cola of a dactylo-epitrite character are to be found in predominantly dochmiac contexts, e.g. at *Hipp.* 1274, 1280–1; and the colon known as iambelegus ($\underset{\smile}{-} - \smile - \underset{\smile}{-} - \smile \smile - \smile \smile -$), which is akin to dactylo-epitrite, appears occasionally among dochmiacs, e.g. at *Alc.* 876, and several times in Euripides' later plays.[2]

But even with this colometry we are not bound to take the metre as dactylo-epitrite. The interpretation of 462 is obscured by textual uncertainty, but 461 may perhaps be seen as an initially contracted version of $\smile \smile - \smile \smile - \smile \smile - - -$, a form of enoplion which Euripides has among dochmiacs at *Andr.* 296 and 298, and at *Hypsipyle* fr. 64, 81.

463 = 829. There is hopeless corruption in the antistrophe, but the text of the strophe is probably sound. The line is pherecratean in form but in this context may be regarded as a pendant hemiepes with − for $\smile \smile$ in its first half. The same form is found at 535 = 554. If in either place the metre is really dactylo-epitrite, we have in the contraction an example of an occasional licence in this metre in both tragedy and choral lyric: Euripidean instances are *Med.* 980 = 987, *Andr.* 774 = 785.[3] In this strophe however we may regard it simply as a dactylic colon occurring as an element among dochmiacs. The hemiepes is sometimes met among dochmiacs, e.g. at Aeschylus, *Sept.* 778 ff.; Sophocles, *Aj.* 879 ff.; Euripides, *Tro.* 239 ff. Here the transition from dochmiacs to dactyls is easily made by way of the preceding cola. A colon of the same shape appears among iambic and choriambic elements at *Alc.* 117 = 127.

464–5 = 830–1. The metre can be analysed in two ways, according as we choose to take as our basis the text of 464

---

[1] Wilamowitz, *op. cit.* p. 587.
[2] E.g. *Hel.* 686 (cf. Wilamowitz, *op. cit.* p. 564), *Ba.* 1018, 1155, 1179 f.
[3] Others are cited by Fraenkel, *op. cit.* p. 339.

εἰ γὰρ ἐγὼ τόδ' ἦμαρ or that of 830 εἰ δὲ χρόνῳ παράκαιρον. It is easy enough to emend 464 by accepting Hermann's τόδε γ' or Dindorf's τόδ' ἔτ', but neither is anything more than a stopgap. We ought not to overlook the possibility that the antistrophe is corrupt; Headlam may have been on the right lines in proposing πάρωρον for παρὰ καιρόν codd. (cf. Hesych. πάρωρον· παρὰ καιρόν).[1]

The analysis given above is based on the text of the antistrophe: 830 is a pendant hemiepes, an uncontracted repetition of the preceding colon, and 831 a lecythion + resolved cretic. The text of the strophe is best divided thus:

$$464 \quad - \cup \cup - \; \cup - \cup - \; \cup - \cup -$$
$$465 \quad \cup - \cup \cup \cup -$$

In 464 we have an iambic trimeter with initial choriamb, which may be compared with 458 and the final colon of the strophe; 465 is a resolved dochmiac.

466 = 832. The text of this final verse is uncertain in the strophe, but the antistrophe is apparently sound. As at 457 Wilamowitz interprets it as a dochmiac dimeter, the second irregularly syncopated, but it is more easily divided as choriamb + iamb + spondee. An identical colon is found, also among dochmiacs, at *HF* 1022.

The problems of metrical analysis presented by this lyric are largely attributable to corruption of the text. There does not appear to be anything abnormal about its composition. The metre is predominantly dochmiac and iambic, but contains an admixture of other cola which are associated with dochmiacs elsewhere in Euripides. In these combinations there is nothing inconsistent with his metrical technique. The lyric contains no strong evidence of date, but could certainly be accepted as belonging to the early period of Euripides' career.

---

[1] *CR*, xv (1901), 103.

527–37 = 546–56

∪∪ – ∪∪ – ∪∪ – –
– ∪ – – – ‖
– ∪ – – – ∪∪ – ∪∪ –
– ∪∪ – ∪∪ –
∪∪ – ∪∪ – ∪ – ∪ – – ‖
∪̆ – ∪∪ – ∪∪ – –
– ∪∪ – ∪∪ –
– – ∪∪ – ∪∪ – –
– – – ∪∪ – –
– ∪ – – – ∪∪ – ∪∪ – ∪ – –

This strophe and antistrophe are part of the lyric composition preceding the departure of the Chorus from the orchestra, which occupies the place of a regular stasimon. The lyric strophes alternate with anapaests in dialogue between members of the Chorus, but there is no need for the internal changes of speaker which Murray marks within the strophes.

The metrical scheme given here differs very little from that presented by Dale, more strongly from that of Wilamowitz.[1] The colometry adopted pays regard to coincidences of word-ending in strophe and antistrophe. The only textual problem of significance for the metre is in 533, where ἔγρεσθε πρὸς φυλακάν does not correspond to the hemiepes of 552; the text in the latter place looks sound, and it is probable that ἔγρεσθε has intruded from the previous line, displacing an imperative of dactylic shape, perhaps ἔξιτε (Hartung).

The metre is akin to dactylo-epitrite, but is varied in one or two places by the introduction, besides the normal elements of that metre, of other closely related cola. The closest parallel to this metrical design is seen in the second stasimon of *Alcestis*, particularly in its second strophe (588–96 = 597–605). There too the metre bears a resemblance to dactylo-epitrite, especially in its opening lines,

---

[1] Dale, *op. cit.* p. 171; Wilamowitz, *op. cit.* pp. 588 f.

two of which have the same form as 528 = 547 ($- \cup - -$ $- \cup \cup - \cup \cup -$), but it expands into longer dactylic and prosodiac elements of varied character with cretics towards the close. Our strophe, although it shows rather less variation from the normal dactylo-epitrite forms, is composed on essentially the same principle. For the variation of the ordinary dactylo-epitrite structure with other related cola there are additional Euripidean parallels in *Med.* 991–5 = 996–1001, *Andr.* 1009–18 = 1019–26, and *Tro.* 799–808 = 809–18.[1]

The second line of our strophe, which closes a period, is of unusual form. Wilamowitz describes it as a syncopated ithyphallic, but cites no parallel. Dale, who treats the strophe as dactylo-epitrite, points out that the spondee is a rare but recognizable element in this metre, and gives instances from Pindar and Simonides.[2] But no example is forthcoming from an ordinary dactylo-epitrite context in tragedy. Perhaps, however, we may compare, in the strophe of *Alcestis* already mentioned, 595 = 604, where one of two possible readings gives $- \cup - - - - \cup - -$.

531 = 550 $\cup \cup - \cup \cup - \cup - \cup - -$. The division of words allows us to treat this as a separate colon, although it may also be taken together with the preceding line as a dactylic sequence ending with an ithyphallic. We have already observed this colon as a possible unit in the strophe last treated. It will be discussed further below (on 900–1).

The epiparodos

692–703 = 710–21

$\cup - - \cup -$

$\cup \cup \cup \vee \cup \cup \quad \cup - \cup -$

$\cup \cup \cup - \cup -$

$\cup - - \quad \cup - -$

---

[1] Cf. Fraenkel, *op. cit.* p. 342.
[2] Dale, *op. cit.* p. 171. At *OT* 1097 $- \cup - - - -$ is clausula to the strophe, but does not form part of the dactylo-epitrite period, which ends two lines earlier.

315

∪ ∪ ∪ − ∪ −
‾∪ − ∪ − − − ∪ − − − ∪ −
∪ ∪ ∪ − ∪ − ‾∪ ∪ ∪ − ∪ −
− ∪ ∪ −
∪ ∪ ∪ − ∪ − ∪ ∪‾∪ − ∪ −
‾∪ − ∪ − ‾∪ ∪‾∪ ∪ − ‾∪ − ∪ −
∪ − ∪ − ‾∪ − ∪ −
‾∪ ‾∪∪ − ∪ − ∪ ∪ ∪ − ∪ −

Here again each strophe is followed by a passage of choral dialogue, this time in iambics and bacchiacs. Although exactly corresponding, these dialogue passages may be regarded as separate from the strophes.

The text of the strophe is corrupt in the last two lines (702–3). The metre is established clearly from the antistrophe, and the scheme presented here follows Murray's text for the strophe.

It is a dochmiac-iambic lyric without complications. In metrical style it is similar to the earlier strophe in this metre (131 = 195), permitting a little more freedom in the responsion of the dochmiacs. There are still not more than four different forms introduced, all common, the variations being confined to the opening syllables. In this respect the treatment is rather stricter than, for example, in the dochmiac-iambic lyric at *Hipp.* 362 = 669, and has none of the freedom of the later Euripidean technique.

Other elements appearing here are at home among dochmiacs: with the bacchiac dimeter (695 = 713) we may compare *HF* 879 and *Ion* 1447, and with the single choriamb (699 = 717) *Hcld.* 91. There is nothing here that is not readily admissible in a dochmiac context.

The Muse's monody

895–903 = 906–14

∪ − ∪ ∪ − ∪ ∪ −
∪ − ∪ ∪ − ∪ ∪ −

$$- \cup - \cup - -$$
$$\cup - \cup \cup - \cup \cup - - \parallel$$
$$- - - \cup \cup - \cup \cup -$$
$$\cup \cup - \cup \cup - \cup - \cup - -$$
$$\cup \cup - \cup \cup - \cup - \cup - -$$
$$- \cup \cup - \cup \cup - \cup \cup -$$
$$\underline{\cup \cup} - \cup \cup - \cup \cup - -$$

The text is uncertain in 912, but the strophe is sound at this point and the metre not in doubt. The colometry is clearly defined and presents no problems; in both strophe and antistrophe the metrical divisions coincide with word-divisions throughout.[1]

The lyric is composed of related cola belonging to the general class of prosodiac and enoplion, the opening pair being separated off by means of an ithyphallic. The constituent cola are to be regarded as metrical units which do not require further analysis. At the beginning of the strophe and again later the character of the metre is clearly defined by the appearance of pairs of identical cola. In the former case the colon ($\overset{\smile}{-} - \cup \cup - \cup \cup -$), which is labelled prosodiac by Wilamowitz and enoplian by Dale, is one found quite often in the lyrics of tragedy. Aeschylus has it in two strophes (*Sept.* 750, *Supp.* 524), in both places in association with iambics. In both Sophocles and Euripides it is used to begin a strophe: at Sophocles, *Ant.* 354 the opening movement is, as in our strophe, a pair of prosodiacs of this shape, the opening period being rounded off by a longer colon of the same class, after which the metre changes to iambic; at Euripides, *Med.* 846 a single colon introduces a strophe composed of enoplia of the form $- - \cup \cup - \cup - -$ and related types; at *Hel.* 1479 a lengthened version of the same colon ($\cup - \cup \cup - \cup \cup - -$) opens a strophe which continues with a series of choriambic dimeters. Euripides also has it in other positions in the strophe: at *El.* 482 it is among dactyls

---

[1] Dale, *op. cit.* p. 164; cf. Wilamowitz, *op. cit.* p. 392.

and iambics; at *Alc.* 90 and 438 it appears among other cola of its own class.

The other repeated colon of the strophe (∪ ∪ – ∪ ∪ – ∪ – ∪ – –) has already been noticed at *vv.* 462 and 531. It appears in several places in Euripides, notably at *Alc.* 437, 442, 460, *Med.* 648, *HF* 1080, *Ion* 457, *IT* 1275. The last two of these are in a clearly glyconic context, where the interpretation as glyconic + bacchiac is admissible, as it might also be at *Alc.* 460 and *Med.* 648. But the other two occurrences in *Alcestis* are in a context comparable to that of the present strophe in *Rhesus*.[1] Perhaps the only example in tragic lyric outside Euripides is at Sophocles, *Trach.* 648 = 656, where it follows ∪ ∪ – ∪ ∪ – ∪ – – –.[2] Whether it occurs elsewhere or not, the significant fact for our purposes is that a colon of this shape is readily associated with the style of Euripides.

It is to be observed that the two cola we have been considering are found again in close association in a strophe of *Alcestis*. This strophe (435 ff.) certainly provides the closest parallel in extant Greek tragedy to the metrical technique of the Muse's monody.[3] Its scheme is as follows:

$$– \cup \cup – \cup \cup –$$
$$– – \cup \cup – \cup \cup – \cup \cup –$$
$$\cup \cup – \cup \cup – \cup – \cup – –$$
$$– – \cup \cup – \cup \cup –$$
$$– – \cup \cup – \cup \cup – –$$
$$– \cup \cup – \cup \cup –$$
$$– \cup – \cup – –$$
$$\cup \cup – \cup \cup – \cup – \cup – –$$
$$– – \cup \cup – \cup – \cup –$$
$$– \cup \cup – \cup – –$$

Both strophes are composed wholly of various cola belonging to the prosodiac and enoplion class, with the ithyphallic

---

[1] The colon is described as dactylic by Fraenkel, *op. cit.* pp. 331 f., as enoplian by Dale, *op. cit.* p. 162.

[2] It occurs also in Ar. *Av.* 1411, 1415 (a parody).

[3] The two strophes are compared by Dale, *op. cit.* pp. 163 f.; in her view however the *Rhesus* strophe is 'of an almost un-Euripidean simplicity'.

used as an internal clausula within the strophe. Prosodiacs of the form ⏑̱ – ⏑ ⏑ – ⏑ ⏑ – (–) occur in both strophes and, twice in each, the colon ⏑ ⏑ – ⏑ ⏑ – ⏑ – ⏑ – –; the other elements are closely akin. The resemblance between the two odes is sufficiently distinctive; for although the many varieties of prosodiac and enoplion are by no means uncommon in tragedy, there is nowhere else a strophe composed exclusively of elements of this class.

SUMMARY OF METRES USED IN THE LYRICS

From our analysis it appears that the lyric metres of *Rhesus* contain very few features which it is at all difficult to parallel in the lyrics of Euripides. At this point it may be useful to give a summary of the various classes of lyric metre used in *Rhesus* and to consider how the treatment of each compares in its salient features with the technique of Euripides.

Aeolic metres

Under this heading we might include the passages in which sequences of choriambs, or choriambs and iambics, occur, notably in the second strophes of the first and second stasima. In the former of these strophes there is the difficult resolved colon, which is possibly to be interpreted as choriambic. This is certainly the most curious metrical anomaly in the play, but it may not be entirely without parallel in Euripides.

The principal aeolic cola are the glyconic and its immediate relatives; these constitute one of the commonest lyric types in both Sophocles and Euripides, assuming in many plays a dominant role. In *Rhesus* the glyconic varieties appear only in the strophe of the parodos and the first strophe of the second stasimon, and in the former they are used only briefly. For a comparably restricted use of glyconics in plays of Euripides we may compare *Andromache*, where they are used for a single whole strophe, and *Troades*, in which, except for isolated cola, they are used for only the first half of one strophe.

The treatment of the aeolic cola in *Rhesus* is characterized by conservatism. There is no resolution of either of the opening syllables and no irregular lengthening of a normally short syllable following the choriambic element. In both these respects we find a similarly strict treatment in *Alcestis*, *Medea* and *Heraclidae*, the earliest extant plays of Euripides, but a growing freedom in all his plays from *Hippolytus* onwards, with the exception of *Troades*, where glyconics are little used. Sophocles admits these licences occasionally even in his earliest works and in his later composition rather more freely.[1] In Aeschylus, except in the *Oresteia*, the aeolic metres are sparingly used and no licence is found in their treatment.

Here we must notice too the absence from *Rhesus* of a metrical type closely related to the glyconic and often associated with it, the polyschematist choriambic dimeter. In Euripides cola of this class appear first in *Medea* and *Hippolytus*, in both plays very briefly; they are subsequently found in all plays except *Andromache* and *Troades*, and in combination with freely built glyconics become one of the most characteristic lyric forms in his late plays. The two latest plays of Sophocles, especially *Philoctetes*, show a comparable partiality for this type of lyric composition; in his earlier plays, with the exception of *Ajax*, choriambic dimeters are found, but only sporadically.

In respect of these characteristics *Rhesus*, if it is to be attributed to Euripides, is much more easily associated with his earliest plays than with the later ones.

Dactylo-epitrite

Dactylo-epitrite is especially prominent among the lyric metres of *Rhesus*. One whole strophe is composed in this metre, and it appears in at least four others. The predi-

---

[1] E.g. among the earlier plays, *Aj.* 199–200, *Ant.* 104, 1122, *Trach.* 844–5, 848–9, *OT* 1198.

lection for dactylo-epitrite is by no means incompatible with the tastes of Euripides. In two plays, both among the earlier extant works, we find it in even greater proportion than here: in *Medea* (431) there are five wholly dactylo-epitrite strophes, and in *Andromache* (probably 425) it is used for two whole strophes and parts of two others.

There is of course nothing peculiarly Euripidean about this metre nor any strong reason for associating it with a particular date. It is a common metre of choral lyric, found first in Stesichorus and often in Pindar and Bacchylides, and we might therefore be prepared to find it in tragedy from an early date. In extant plays it appears first in *Prometheus* and *Ajax*, and its latest significant occurrences are in the *Troades* (415) and *Electra* (probably earlier) of Euripides.[1] It does not appear to be characteristic of the latest style of Euripidean lyric.

In dactylo-epitrite composition of the normal type we are not likely to detect any features peculiarly characteristic of one poet or period. The treatment of the metre in *Rhesus* appears to be free from any notable irregularities. The clausula at 33 = 51, as we saw above, need not be an irregularly resolved alcaic decasyllable. If there are instances of – for ◡ ◡ in the first half of the hemiepes (463, 535), this is done also by Euripides.

The composition of the strophe 527 = 546, in which the basic dactylo-epitrite structure is varied by the inclusion of other closely related cola, is of a somewhat more distinctive character. This is a technique which has its closest parallels in Euripides; the strophe most like ours in its design is *Alc.* 588 = 597.

Dactyls

Apart from their use as an ingredient of dactylo-epitrite composition dactyls occur briefly here and there in the lyrics of *Rhesus*, notably in the parodos, in the second strophe of the

[1] On the date of *Electra* see p. 262 n. 1 above.

first stasimon and in the strophe 454 = 820. The dactylic elements vary in shape: there is no long sequence of dactylic lyric in regular cola. These brief admixtures of dactylic metre with other types are quite in keeping with the metrical technique of Euripides.

Prosodiac and enoplion

The strophe of the Muse's monody is composed of a variety of cola belonging to this category; we have already noticed that there is a strophe of *Alcestis* composed in a very similar style and containing similar elements. In the strophe 454 = 820 we find cola of this class combined with dochmiacs in a manner which is best paralleled in the lyrics of Euripides.

Dochmiac

This metre occurs in three strophes of *Rhesus*, also probably in *vv.* 675–6. According to Wilamowitz's analysis the strophe 454 = 820 would have irregular forms of dochmiac at 458, 466, but, as we have seen, these cola are more simply interpreted as iambic of a perfectly regular type. The only remarkable feature is the apparent resolved 'long' dochmiac in 456 = 822; this is not without a Euripidean parallel. The total number of varieties of normal dochmiac in *Rhesus*, if we include the two resolved forms of 675–6, is not more than five or six. There is a heavy preponderance of the two commonest forms, and the varieties do not include any with a long penultimate syllable.

The extremely simple composition of the dochmiac-iambic strophes 131 ff. and 692 ff. is reminiscent of the strict metrical style of Aeschylus, but is also comparable to the treatment of dochmiac by Euripides in *Medea* (1251 ff.) and *Heraclidae* (parodos, 75 ff.), both early works. In Euripidean dochmiac lyric we can perhaps discern a development of technique, which first appears in *Hippolytus*: in this play, where dochmiacs are used extensively, many more varieties are used within the same strophe, responsion is freer, and the long penultimate syllable, already an occasional phenomenon in Aeschylus and Sophocles, now first appears noticeably in Euripides. The succeeding plays of Euripides generally adopt and extend this freer technique. Although a quite simply composed dochmiac lyric can occur in a later play (e.g. *El.* 585 ff.), the wholly straightforward treatment of the metre found in *Rhesus* is more in keeping with the technique of the earlier plays.

On the other hand, Sophocles' treatment of dochmiacs varies much from play to play. *Ajax*, while admitting a long penultimate syllable, is almost as simple as *Rhesus*; so too in *Oedipus Tyrannus* and even, for the most part, in *Oedipus Coloneus*, the latest play, the dochmiacs are straightforward. *Antigone* however shows a somewhat more elaborate treatment. There is thus no absolute criterion for date in the style of the dochmiacs in *Rhesus*; but if the play is Euripidean, we may have here further evidence that it belongs to an early stage of his career.

Iambic

Iambic metre plays some part in most of the lyrical compositions of *Rhesus*, but there is no wholly iambic strophe like those often found in Aeschylus and occasionally in the other tragic poets. It has rather a subordinate role in composition, appearing briefly among other types of metre, several times in the form of a trimeter. Cola in which iambs and choriambs are combined are not uncommon: these tend to show the influence of their surroundings (e.g. 347 = 356, 457 = 823, 466 = 832).

Such a treatment is quite in keeping with Euripidean technique; but in view of the widespread and varied use of iambics in the lyrics of tragedy, it would be unwise to look here for distinctively Euripidean traits. All we need say is that there is nothing in the iambic elements of the *Rhesus* lyrics that we should hesitate to associate with Euripides.

Ionics

There is only one certainly ionic period, in the second strophe of the second stasimon. The treatment of the metre there has already been discussed. The style of composition, which makes an easy transition between iambs, ionics and choriambs, can be compared to that of some Euripidean lyrics, but is not of an especially distinctive character.

In this survey of the lyrics of *Rhesus* their metrical structure has been analysed and the treatment of each of the various classes of metre has been separately considered. The primary question before us has been whether these lyrics, so far as their metrical form is concerned, could or could not have been written by Euripides. Of the answer to this question there can, I think, be no doubt: there is nothing at all in the lyric metres of *Rhesus* that we should have any real difficulty in attributing to Euripides. This result is clearly established and, even if a negative one, is nevertheless of significance for the present inquiry.

It might perhaps be argued that this result was only to be expected and is therefore unimportant; for, on the one hand, the metrical style of *Rhesus* is generally conservative, and on the other hand we possess a quite considerable quantity of Euripidean lyric, of great variety, so that it is not surprising that we are able to find somewhere or other in Euripides a parallel for each separate feature of the lyric metres of our play. Against this it may be said that the lyric composition of *Rhesus*, while comparatively free from complexity, is by no means artless, and that the treatment of lyric metres has in several particulars a quite distinctive character. It is in some of the less common characteristics of the lyric metres of *Rhesus* that we have been able to trace an especially close resemblance to the style of Euripides and to him alone of the tragedians. The following are the most striking points of similarity:

(i) The strophe 895 ff. is composed of varieties of prosodiac and enoplion of distinctive shape. This particular type of strophic composition is not common, but one other strophe, *Alc.* 435 ff., is composed in a very similar manner, incorporating some of the same cola and others of a like kind.

(ii) The metrical structure of the strophe 527 ff., in which the dactylo-epitrite pattern is slightly varied by the introduction of other related cola, is one favoured particularly by Euripides. Of comparable strophes the one most like this is *Alc.* 588 ff.; others showing some affinity of style are *Med.* 991 ff., *Andr.* 1009 ff., *Tro.* 799 ff.

(iii) In these two strophes of *Rhesus* the colon $\cup\cup-\cup\cup$ $-\cup-\cup--$ is found thrice (531 = 550, 900 = 911, 901 = 912; cf. also 462 = 828). A separable colon of exactly this shape occurs several times in Euripidean lyric, there being three examples in *Alcestis*, one in *Medea* and a total of three in other plays. It is certainly recognizable only once in other tragic lyric. The context of its use in the Muse's monody is precisely similar to that of *Alc.* 435 ff.

(iv) The metrical design of the first stasimon, in which the first strophe is wholly dactylo-epitrite and the second echoes this metre briefly among other things, is similar in these respects to that of all four stasima in *Medea* and one in *Troades*. In the case of the second stasimon of *Medea* the resemblance extends a little further, since the second strophes of both odes have similar component elements arranged in a similar way.

And so the metrical technique of the *Rhesus* lyrics, besides being in no way uncharacteristic of Euripides, bears certain individual marks of his style. It is remarkable that these special resemblances are principally to the earlier plays, notably *Alcestis* and *Medea*, and especially the former. This agrees with our general findings about the treatment of lyric metres in *Rhesus*: in particular, the aeolic cola and dochmiacs are treated with a conservatism matched in the earliest plays of Euripides, but not in *Hippolytus* and most subsequent plays. In all respects in which an evolution is discernible in Euripides' handling of lyric metres *Rhesus* is close to the earliest works and has none of the features which only begin to appear later.

Our survey of the lyric metres leads therefore to the following conclusions: first, that they contain no evidence against the authenticity of the play; secondly, that they show some notable resemblances to Euripidean lyric metres and especially to those of the earliest plays, *Alcestis* and *Medea*; thirdly, that if *Rhesus* is to be attributed to Euripides, the lyric metres will provide significant evidence in favour of assigning it to an early date in his career. It is to be noted that these conclusions are in complete accord with those suggested by our analysis of the treatment of the iambic trimeter.

In the present state of our knowledge we cannot expect to go beyond these conclusions. We have, it is true, a representative selection of the lyric composition of Euripides, with which we can compare the lyrics of our play; but we have comparatively little non-Euripidean tragic lyric, so that it is difficult to measure the significance of such likeness as may be observed between the lyrics of *Rhesus* and those of Euripides. Although we may say that in certain respects *Rhesus* resembles Euripides more closely than either Aeschylus or Sophocles, it has to be remembered that we possess a smaller amount of the work of these two poets and that both have highly individual styles. The gaps in our knowledge are here no less baffling than they are elsewhere. How are we to say that there were not other poets, either in the fifth century or later, whose style was much more like that of Euripides? We know next to nothing of the lyric styles of other fifth-century tragedians and just as little of the character of lyrics composed in the fourth century. It might however be a reasonable guess that the developments in lyric style that are traceable in Euripides were not confined to him but were fairly general in the late fifth century. Such might be inferred from Aristophanes' criticisms, from the little we know of the style of Agathon and even from developments seen in the late works of Sophocles. *Rhesus* has nothing in common with any of the later tendencies, and if it belonged to the late fifth or to the fourth century, it would mean either that these tendencies were not so universal as is usually thought or else that our poet was making a quite astonishing reversion to an earlier style.

CHAPTER VII

STRUCTURE OF THE LYRIC PARTS

We have examined the metrical style of the lyrics of *Rhesus* but have still to consider the characteristics of their form and structure. It is important that we should also look at this aspect of the lyrical composition, and inquire whether it differs in any way from the practice of fifth-century tragedy and in particular from the technique of Euripides. Further, since the lyrics of tragedy, and especially those of Euripides, show in several ways a quite marked formal development, it may be useful to consider whether the form and structure of the lyrics of *Rhesus* contribute any evidence for its date.

Consideration must be given first to two unusual features of the lyrical composition, each of which has been adduced as evidence against the authenticity of the play.

SEPARATED RESPONSION

It is a very remarkable feature of the design of the lyrics in *Rhesus* that twice in the play metrically corresponding strophes are separated from one another by a considerable interval. This happens in the following places:

(i) 131–6 = 195–200. In these two brief dochmiac and iambic lyrics, both in the same scene, the Chorus excitedly expresses its feelings at important stages in the action. The strophe, following Aeneas' speech, greets with approval his advice that a spy be sent out; in the antistrophe, which comes after Dolon has obtained Hector's agreement to his reward and just before he takes his leave, the Chorus praises him and offers a prayer for his success.

(ii) 454–66 = 820–32. Here the interval between strophe and antistrophe is very much greater; in it there occur the departure of the Chorus from the scene of action and its return, and the choral odes which accompany both these movements. In the strophe, which follows Rhesus' reply to Hector's censure, the Chorus praises him and expresses its confidence of victory with his aid; in the antistrophe, after the Charioteer has reported the slaying of Rhesus, they defend themselves against Hector's charge of negligence.

The remains of Greek tragedy yield no more than a handful of examples of a comparable separation of strophe and antistrophe. These occur in all three tragedians in plays widely separated in date. They are as follows:

(i) Aeschylus, *Sept.* 417–21 = 451–6, 481–5 = 521–5, 563–7 = 626–30. Here six short lyrics, comprising three successive pairs of strophe and antistrophe, all predominantly dochmiac and iambic, are separately interposed by the Chorus in the iambic dialogue between Eteocles and the Messenger. The whole scene is composed to a symmetrical pattern: each strophe follows a passage of spoken dialogue in which the Messenger names the assailant at one of the gates of Thebes and Eteocles replies appointing a defender; in each the Chorus prays for the success of the chosen warrior.

(ii) Aeschylus, *Agam.* 1407–11 = 1426–30. A strophe and antistrophe of the Chorus, dochmiac and iambic, punctuate Clytemnestra's speech in iambic trimeters, being separated from each other by fourteen lines. Clytemnestra speaks a further seventeen lines after the antistrophe, so that the structure is nearly, but not exactly, symmetrical.

(iii) Sophocles, *Ph.* 391–402 = 507–18. By means of this pair of strophes Sophocles provides internal divisions in an extremely long iambic scene. At the same time the lyrical expression, in dochmiac and iambic metre, is appropriate to the heightened emotion of the Chorus in both places.

(iv) Sophocles, *OC* 833–43 = 876–86. At two places within the same scene, some thirty lines apart, dochmiac lines are interposed among the iambic trimeters. The two passages, both in dialogue between the Chorus and actors, correspond exactly and have corresponding changes of speaker. The former occurs at the point where Creon tries to seize Antigone, the latter where he lays hands on Oedipus.

(v) Euripides, *Hipp.* 362–72 = 669–79. This dochmiac strophe and antistrophe occur in successive scenes; in the interval between them there is a stasimon, of dissimilar metrical character, and a passage in which dochmiacs of the Chorus without responsion are interposed among Phaedra's iambic trimeters (569 ff.). A curious feature here is that the strophe is delivered by the Chorus and the antistrophe by Phaedra. The strophe follows Phaedra's admission of her love and expresses the distress of the Chorus at the news; the antistrophe is an utterance of despair by Phaedra after Hippolytus has rejected her.

(vi) Euripides, *Or.* 1353–65 = 1537–48. This strophe and antistrophe of the Chorus, again dochmiac and iambic, open and close the lyric scene in which the Phrygian slave appears. The intervening scene comprises the Phrygian's long astrophic monody, which is interrupted at intervals by iambic trimeters of the Chorus, and a passage of dialogue in trochaic tetrameters. In this case the function of the responding strophes is to enclose a complete scene, separating it from its surroundings.

There are, besides, many places where a separated strophe and antistrophe form part of a balanced 'epirrhematic' composition together with iambics or anapaests. These belong to a different class, which is not to be compared here. Even the two Aeschylean examples included above are almost of this kind, since in *Septem* the lyrics alternate with iambic passages of parallel design, though of unequal length, and in *Agamemnon* the strophes are followed by iambic passages of almost the same length. But in the former passage anyway the distance between the responding lyrics is greater than in the strictly epirrhematic compositions of tragedy: here perhaps we may see a stage in the process by which the wider separation of responding strophes evolved. In neither of the *Rhesus* examples is there a balanced design of this kind.

The total number of cases of separated responsion is therefore very small, and the second of the two examples in *Rhesus* may appear to be stranger than any other. The two Euripidean examples are the only other ones in which lyric intervenes between strophe and antistrophe, and only in *Hippolytus* is the design at all closely comparable. But the attendant circumstances in *Rhesus* seemed to Wilamowitz to put it beyond comparison even with *Hippolytus*; for the interval between strophe and antistrophe is greater, and it contains not one but two choral odes, as well as the temporary removal of the Chorus from the scene.[1] On the other hand, there are also some very curious features in *Hippolytus*: the strophe is sung by the Chorus, the antistrophe by Phaedra, and other dochmiac verses of the Chorus, which are without responsion, intervene. On balance the licence in both plays may appear to be equally extraordinary; certainly the demand on the memory of the hearer is no less severe in *Hippolytus* than in *Rhesus*.

It has been argued however that the effect which the poet intends to produce by the distant responsion is more readily perceptible in *Hippolytus* than in *Rhesus*.[2] For in the former play the strophe comes at a critical point in the action, where Phaedra admits her love for Hippolytus, and the antistrophe is reserved for the subsequent catastrophe, when Hippolytus rejects this love. But in *Rhesus* the lyrics do not so happily correspond in their relation to the plot: the strophe expresses the Chorus's hopes in Rhesus, but in the antistrophe, instead of recurring to these hopes now lost, they merely defend themselves against Hector's sudden accusation. This argument does not deal with equal justice with the two plays, for it is the position of the lyrics in *Rhesus* rather than their actual sentiments which should be compared. The antistrophe comes at the point where the hopes expressed in the strophe have been shattered. This fact does not need to be made explicit in the words of the Chorus; the reminiscence of the earlier

---

[1] Wilamowitz, *Griechische Verskunst*, p. 587.   [2] *Ibid.* p. 443 n.

ode is enough in itself to underline the contrast between the former confidence and the present confusion and despair.

There is perhaps little point in arguing from a subjective interpretation of the poet's intention but, while we are so engaged, it is possible to suggest another reason for the introduction of this pair of strophes in *Rhesus*. The removal of the Chorus in the middle of the play might be regarded as disturbing the continuity of the action. The strophe which they sing after their return corresponding to one sung before their departure helps to bridge the interval of their absence; it further confirms, both in its words and in its metre, that these are the same Guards who left the scene with the intention of summoning their relief. Thus there might be a connection between one peculiar feature of the play and another. But it must be conceded that no such device is found in any of the other plays in which the Chorus temporarily vacates the scene.

The other instance of separated response in *Rhesus*, 131 = 195, falls into a different class, since both strophes are contained within the same scene and there is no intervening lyric. It is thus more closely to be compared with the examples cited above from Aeschylus and Sophocles. It is a much less striking phenomenon than the responsion of 454 = 820 and does not need special discussion. Euripides in several places inserts short dochmiac lyrics in the middle of iambic dialogue, but usually (e.g. at *Hipp.* 811–16, 852–5, *Hec.* 1024–34, *El.* 585–95, *Ph.* 291–300) these are without responsion. It is not unnatural that two such lyrics occurring in the same scene should be made to correspond metrically.

In view of the extremely bold separation of responding lyrics in *Hippolytus* it can hardly be denied that Euripides was capable of employing the same device in either of the forms in which it is found in *Rhesus*. On the other hand the total number of instances of separated response in Greek tragedy is extremely small and, apart from the one in *Hippolytus*, there is only one other to be found in the whole of

Euripides. It is therefore very striking that we should find it employed twice in the one play, once with an unusual boldness. With *Hippolytus* before us we may find it very much less difficult to associate this licence with Euripides than we otherwise should. Nevertheless it must be noted among the peculiar features of the play, which may in their cumulative effect tell against its authenticity.

VIOLATION OF THE INTERNAL UNITY OF THE STROPHE

At *Rh.* 351 the division between strophe and antistrophe is made in the middle of a sentence:

346 (str.) ἥκεις, ὦ ποταμοῦ παῖ,
ἥκεις, ἐπλάθης Φιλίου πρὸς αὐλὰν
ἀσπαστός, ἐπεί σε χρόνῳ
Πιερὶς μάτηρ ὅ τε καλλιγέφυρος ποταμὸς πορεύει

351 (ant.) Στρυμών, ὅς ποτε τᾶς μελῳδοῦ Μούσας δι' ἀκηράτων
δινηθεὶς ὑδροειδὴς
κόλπων σὰν ἐφύτευσεν ἥβαν.

The choral lyric poets quite often allow a sentence to run over the division between strophes, but this is contrary to the normal practice of the tragedians, who as a rule prefer to make each strophe an independent grammatical unit. Although the division of a sentence between strophes is by no means unknown in tragedy, it is usual in such cases for the break to coincide with a clear division between syntactical units. Thus a strophe may open with a clause that is grammatically subordinate to the previous strophe, for example, with a relative or ἐπεί or ὅτι. *Rh.* 242 ff. (ἐπεὶ πρό τ' οἴκων πρό τε γᾶς ἔτλα μόνος) is one of a number of examples of this class.[1] In such cases the essential grammatical unity of the strophe is preserved.

---

[1] Cf. Aeschylus, *Supp.* 49; Sophocles, *Ant.* 1137, *OT* 179, 1197, *El.* 1070; Euripides, *Hcld.* 362, 777.

Examples of a more violent transgression of the boundaries of the strophe are very rare in tragedy, but there are a few places where a phrase is carried over into a following strophe, although it belongs with what precedes and is divorced from what follows. At Aeschylus, *Supp.* 582, for example, the phrase δι' αἰῶνος μακροῦ πάνολβον, which belongs syntactically with the strophe, stands at the beginning of the antistrophe, where it is separated by a major stop from the following clause. Similarly, in *Agam.* 238 the words βίᾳ χαλινῶν τ' ἀναύδῳ μένει are carried over into a new strophe, where they are detached from what follows.[1] In this case the enjambement is the more remarkable because the sentence flows over the division between an antistrophe and a following strophe.[2]

Euripides very occasionally allows a sentence to overrun the division between stanzas. In *Hec.* 647, where the words ἐπὶ δορὶ καὶ φόνῳ καὶ ἐμῶν μελάθρων λώβᾳ are carried over, it is only the dividing line between antistrophe and epode that is neglected, possibly a less serious transgression, because it is less likely to obscure the metrical structure of the ode. At *v.* 943 of the same play a sentence again runs over from antistrophe into epode, but there is a stronger syntactical break at the strophic division, so that the effect is less harsh. In *Supp.* 48 and *El.* 157 it is a participial clause which is carried over into the antistrophe; and in *Hipp.* 131 the antistrophe opens with the clause τειρομέναν νοσερᾷ κοίτᾳ δέμας ἐντὸς ἔχειν οἴκων, which is dependent on φάτις ἦλθε in the strophe.

In the present passage of *Rhesus* it is the single word Στρυμών that is carried over from its own clause to stand alone at the head of the antistrophe, and to this extent the licence is of a unique form for tragedy.[3] Kranz indeed was

---

[1] See Fraenkel, *ad loc.*

[2] Sophocles, *Ant.* 1137 is the only other example of this kind, but there the new strophe simply adds a relative clause.

[3] Aeschylus, *Supp.* 1026 is different: the antistrophe begins a new sentence, in which the verb has to be understood from the preceding strophe.

prepared to assert that this verse alone would be enough to cause the rejection of *Rhesus* as a work of one of the three great tragedians.[1] Nowhere else, he says, in the choral lyric of tragedy is there such a remarkable violation of the internal unity of the strophe. It is difficult to share this view; for although there is no parallel in tragedy to the carrying-over of a single word of a clause into a following stanza, it does not really result here in a serious disturbance of the unity of the strophes. The strophe is complete in sense and syntax without the addition of Στρυμών in apposition to ποταμός. In the antistrophe Στρυμών coheres closely with the relative clause that follows it. We have already noted that a new strophe sometimes subjoins a relative clause to what precedes.[2] Is it so much more violent to open with Στρυμών, ὅς than with the relative alone?

Kranz rightly points out that the carrying-over of a single proper name, in order to give a heavy opening to the following strophe, is a device of the choral lyric poets; but the two examples that he compares (Pi. *Ol.* II, 95 and Bacchyl. v, 151), while somewhat similar in effect to our passage, differ essentially in having a strong stop following the proper name, after which the strophe continues with a new and independent sentence. In these places one cannot preserve the natural break between stanzas without leaving a word in isolation from the construction to which it belongs. In *Rhesus*, however, Στρυμών belongs as much with what follows as with what precedes, and the unity of the antistrophe is not disturbed by its presence. One can in fact make a pause between the two strophes without either becoming unintelligible. Such is not the case with some of the other examples cited from tragedy: in particular, the strophes beginning at Aeschylus, *Supp.* 582, *Agam.* 238 and Euripides, *Hec.* 647 have no independent unity.

It does not seem then that there is evidence here against

---

[1] *Stasimon* (Berlin, 1933), p. 263.
[2] Euripidean examples include *Hcld.* 362, *Hipp.* 764, *Hel.* 1353, *Ba.* 88, 997.

the authenticity of the play. It is in fact only very slightly, if at all, bolder to begin the antistrophe thus than to begin it with the simple relative; and the opening with Στρυμών is undeniably effective.

No other arguments against the Euripidean authorship of *Rhesus* have been found in the structure of its lyrics. In fact, this aspect of the play's composition has received little attention. It is nevertheless worth while to consider briefly how the poet's technique in this department compares with that of Euripides. We may note especially the following characteristics of the formal structure of the lyrics, which are possibly relevant to the questions of authenticity and date.[1]

Responsion

It has already been noticed that in respect of metre the responsion between strophe and antistrophe admits no striking licence. From the point of view of structure it is to be observed how strictly the poet adheres to the principle of antistrophic composition. With the exception of the brief passage introducing the epiparodos (675–82) there is no astrophic lyric in *Rhesus*, and the fact that strophes separated by a considerable interval are made to correspond is a sign of the strong feeling for balance in the lyrical composition. This quality is noteworthy in view of the marked trend in the later plays of Euripides towards a freer lyric structure, in which strophic responsion is often abandoned. A limited use of astrophic lyric is found in some of his earlier works, for example *Medea* and *Hippolytus*, but only for brief passages.[2] Responsion is abandoned in Polymestor's long monody in *Hecuba* (1056 ff.); but it is especially in the last fifteen years of his career, from *Supplices* (about 420) onwards, that Euripides' growing favour for astrophic composition is

---

[1] The best account of the formal evolution of the lyrics of tragedy is that of W. Kranz, *Stasimon*; the following observations owe much to that work.

[2] *Med.* 131 ff., 204 ff.; *Hipp.* 1268 ff. Cf. Kranz, *op. cit.* pp. 177, 202.

apparent.[1] In this respect *Rhesus* clearly resembles the works of Euripides of earlier date.

Length of strophe

Along with the increasing use of astrophic composition in the later Euripidean lyric there is a tendency, where the antistrophic form is retained, for the strophes to become longer and more loosely articulated in their internal structure, with the result that the rhythmical balance of the ode is felt less strongly. This lengthening of the strophe goes hand in hand with Euripides' growing predilection for the polyschematist choriambic dimeter, although the longer unit is also employed for composition in other metres. The development is apparent in some places in *Heracles* (637 = 655, 673 = 687, 781 = 798), and even before this in the monody of *Supplices* (990 = 1012).[2] These plays also have some more compact strophes, but in all plays from *Troades* (415) onwards the strophes are consistently longer than any in *Rhesus*.

In *Rhesus* the strophes are uniformly short, longer indeed than those sometimes employed by Aeschylus, but commensurate in length with those of works of Euripides earlier than 420, and particularly with the earliest of these.

The stasima

The two stasima of *Rhesus* both consist of two pairs of strophe and antistrophe, which is indeed the predominant form in post-Aeschylean tragedy.[3] There is however a clearly defined trend in the later works of Euripides, and even of Sophocles, towards a less evenly balanced form, in which a single pair of responding strophes is followed by a long, often straggling, epode.[4] These neatly balanced stasima with their compact strophes resemble those of Euripides' earlier works.

---

[1] Kranz, *op. cit.* p. 229.
[2] Kranz, *op. cit.* p. 181, cites esp. *HF* 781 ff. as transitional to the freer style.
[3] *Ibid.* pp. 175f.
[4] *Ibid.* p. 230 (and table, pp. 124 f.).

It is interesting to consider the treatment of the stasima in relation to their context. Especially remarkable is the way in which the first stasimon (224 ff.), a hymn to Apollo praying for the success of Dolon's enterprise, is largely composed of sentiments repeated, with many verbal echoes, from the preceding dialogue (cf. especially 233–5: 216; 236–41: 182–8; 244: 150, 155; 255 f.: 211 ff.; 257–63: 219–23). A very similar technique is to be observed in some stasima of early Euripidean works.[1] The best examples are *Alc.* 435 ff. and *Hcld.* 353 ff.: these stasima are in great part a repetition of ideas already expressed in the preceding dialogue, sometimes with hardly more verbal alteration than is needed to accommodate them to the lyric metre. The same method of composition, less extensively employed, is to be seen elsewhere, for example in *Alc.* 568 ff., where echoes of the prologue are found, and in some stasima of *Medea*. The technique of Sophocles, as Kranz has pointed out, is somewhat different: although his odes too quite often recur to the ideas of the preceding scene, it is usually to remould them and to present the dramatic situation in a new light. The method of close repetition, which we find in this stasimon of *Rhesus*, is particularly characteristic of the early style of Euripides.

We may notice also in passing how in the two stasima *Rh.* 224 ff. and *Alc.* 435 ff. a similarity of theme, admiration for a selfless action, is accompanied by verbal likeness: with *Rh.* 242 ἔτλα μόνος compare *Alc.* 460–2 μόνα . . . ἔτλας, and with *Rh.* 245 f. σπάνις . . . τῶν ἀγαθῶν compare *Alc.* 474 σπάνιον μέρος.

The second stasimon (342 ff.) is given up to the praise of Rhesus, expressing feelings aroused by the preceding dialogue and at the same time looking forward with high hopes. This is again in keeping with the technique of Euripides, who not seldom takes as the theme of an ode the praise of a character,

---

[1] Cf. Kranz, *op. cit.* p. 212: 'Es gibt sogar Stasima, namentlich euripideische der früheren Zeit, deren Gedanken man fast alle hintereinander bezeichnen kann als Wiederholung des auf der Skene Gesagten.'

usually inspired by the events immediately preceding. Examples are again forthcoming from the early plays: here too *Alc.* 435 ff. may be compared, also *ibid.* 962 ff., *Hcld.* 608 ff. and *Andr.* 766 ff. Common to these and other Euripidean odes is the direct address to a character either present or absent, which Kranz has noted as a special mark of the lyric style of Euripides in his earlier period.[1] The several addresses to Rhesus in the second stasimon (346, 355, 368, 370, 375) are quite in the Euripidean manner.

The monody[2]

Of the three tragedians it is Euripides who shows a particular fondness for the actor's monody. In his extant plays, *Rhesus* excluded, there are eighteen lyric passages that may be assigned to this class.[3] Only five plays, including *Cyclops*, lack a monody, while some have more than one. On the other hand, the extant works of Aeschylus contain only one monody, that of Io in *PV* 574 ff.; and in the seven plays of Sophocles there are two: *El.* 86–120, if this anapaestic passage is properly so described, and *OC* 237–53, a lyric without responsion.

The Muse's monody in *Rhesus* is structurally of a type common in Euripidean tragedy. It consists of a brief strophe and antistrophe, separated from each other by two iambic trimeters spoken by the Chorus. Monodies of this form are found at *Alc.* 393 ff., *Hipp.* 817 ff., *Andr.* 1173 ff. and *Supp.* 990 ff. In each of these there is a single strophe and antistrophe, between which two (or in *Supplices* three) trimeters are interposed. The monody of Aeschylus, *PV*, a composition on a more elaborate scale, differs in having a fully epirrhematic

---

[1] *Ibid.* pp. 206 f., where several examples are cited.

[2] On Euripides' treatment of the actor's monody see P. Masqueray, *Formes lyriques de la tragédie grecque*, pp. 259 ff.; P. Decharme, *E. et l'esprit de son théâtre*, pp. 353 ff.

[3] *Alc.* 393, *Hipp.* 817, *Andr.* 103, 1173, *Hec.* 1056, *Supp.* 990, *El.* 112, *Tro.* 122 (anap.), 308, *Ion* 112, 859 (anap.), *Hel.* 229, *Ph.* 182, 301, 1485, *Or.* 960, 1369, *IA* 1279.

structure, strophe and antistrophe each being followed by a speech of Prometheus in four iambic trimeters.

Here again there is a particular resemblance to the form found in the earlier extant works of Euripides, down to about 420. Within this period, which ends with *Supplices*, there are only two monodies which do not belong to the type just described. These are the elegiac monody in the prologue of *Andromache*, which is metrically unique, and Polymestor's monody in *Hecuba* (1056–1106), a long lyric without responsion, which is nevertheless divided into two unequal parts by a pair of trimeters spoken by the Chorus (1085–6). In the plays later than *Supplices* Euripides constructs his monodies without interrupting spoken lines, and there is also a tendency for the strophic form to be abandoned. Although there are a few monodies in the later plays of a wholly or partly responding form, there is nothing that resembles the compact brevity of the Muse's lament.[1]

The monody of *Rhesus* is unique in its position in the drama. In no other surviving tragedy do we find a monody in the exodos and in the mouth of a *deus ex machina*. But this ought not to make us doubt its Euripidean authorship. In fact, Euripides introduces his monodies in a variety of places in the drama. Here, of course, it is proper for the bereaved mother to sing a dirge, and especially appropriate that we should have song from the lips of a Muse. The way in which the Muse passes directly from spoken iambics into lyric (895), and back again from lyric into iambics (915), is unusual and without parallel in Euripides.[2] But it is dramatically effective, and there is no reason why he should have avoided such a transition.

---

[1] Cf. *El.* 112 ff., *Or.* 960 ff.

[2] Masqueray, *op. cit.* pp. 273 f., notes this peculiarity, which he regards as contrary to the practice of the tragedians.

Epirrhematic structure

A structure of epirrhematic type, in which lyric strophe and antistrophe alternate with spoken or recitative passages in other metres, is used in *Rhesus* for the parodos (1–51) and for the later passages (527–64, 675–727) where the departure and return of the Chorus provide occasion for the replacement of formal stasima with lyric compositions of a special kind.

In the parodos an actor participates. There is anapaestic dialogue, at first among the Chorus, then between the Chorus and Hector; this is followed by a strophe and antistrophe of the Chorus, between which are interposed further anapaests spoken by Hector. There is no correspondence between the anapaestic passages. In the other two passages no actor takes part. At 527 ff. the strophe and antistrophe are probably sung by the whole Chorus in unison, each being followed by a passage of dialogue in anapaests between the two halves of the Chorus or among individual members. The anapaestic passages (538–45 and 557–64), in the present state of the text at least, do not exactly correspond. In the epiparodos (675 ff.), after the trochaic dialogue between the Chorus and Odysseus, there is a rather similar arrangement. Here strophe (692–703) and antistrophe (710–21) are each followed by choral dialogue in iambic trimeters and syncopated iambics (bacchiacs); the two passages of dialogue, which are perhaps spoken rather than sung, correspond exactly.

The epirrhematic structure, in which lyric strophes are combined with spoken passages in an alternating scheme, is rightly regarded as characteristic of earlier tragedy.[1] Composition of this form is quite common in the works of Aeschylus, but becomes rarer in the course of the fifth century, as tragedy moves towards a sharper separation of the choral and the spoken parts. In Euripides lyric composition

---

[1] Kranz, *op. cit.* pp. 20 ff.; Schm.–St. III, p. 815 n., cf. II, p. 145 n.

of the epirrhematic type belongs particularly to the earlier extant works. Examples are to be found in *Alcestis*, *Medea* and *Andromache*, the only later occurrence being in *Electra*.[1] Sophocles, on the other hand, has passages of epirrhematic form both in his two earliest plays, *Ajax* and *Antigone*, and again in his two latest, *Philoctetes* and *Oedipus Coloneus*.[2]

We have already seen reason to suppose that an iambic prologue originally preceded the present opening of *Rhesus*. The opening passage of the play as we have it (1–51) is therefore to be regarded, not as prologue and parodos combined, but simply as parodos. As such it resembles in structure the parodoi of some other tragedies. The parodos in which anapaests and lyrics are found in epirrhematic arrangement is met again in Aeschylus, *PV*; Euripides, *Alcestis* and *Medea*; and Sophocles, *Antigone*, *Philoctetes* and *Oedipus Coloneus*. In *PV* and *Medea*, and also in *Philoctetes* and *Oedipus Coloneus*, the anapaests are delivered by actors and the lyrics by the Chorus, the two Sophoclean plays having besides a further strophe and antistrophe which are internally divided between stage and Chorus. In *Alcestis* and *Antigone* both anapaests and lyric are delivered by the Chorus; in *Alcestis* however the anapaestic parts are in dialogue with rapid changes of speaker in a style similar to that of the *Rhesus* parodos.

The parodos of *Rhesus* in form and style most closely resembles that of *Alcestis*, although this differs in having a second pair of strophes without intervening anapaests. The parodos of *Medea* is like that of *Rhesus* in having only one pair of strophes, but its anapaestic parts are a little longer. These two passages, together with *Alc.* 861 ff., provide the best Euripidean parallels to the form of epirrhematic composition found in the parodos and other passages of *Rhesus*. Again therefore there is reason to associate *Rhesus* with the early plays of Euripides.

[1] *Alc.* 86 ff., 244 ff., 861 ff.; *Med.* 131 ff.; *Andr.* 501 ff.; *El.* 859 ff.
[2] *Aj.* 201 ff., 866 ff.; *Ant.* 100 ff., 1261 ff.; *Ph.* 135 ff.; *OC* 117 ff., 1447 ff.

In the structural aspects of lyric composition which we have been considering, it is possible to distinguish some marked differences between the earlier and the later technique of Euripides. The change of style is not abrupt, nor does it always follow a regular development, but it provides none the less a useful secondary criterion for the dating of his plays within broad limits. A few of the formal features of Euripides' later lyric style are to be seen developing as early as *Hippolytus* (428) and *Hecuba* (probably 424), but the late characteristics do not become prominent until after *Supplices*, that is, about 420. The structure of the lyrics of *Rhesus* has nothing at all in common with the style of Euripides in the years after this date. In all the formal aspects of its lyric style *Rhesus* belongs with the earlier works of Euripides, and in its complete freedom from later characteristics it is to be compared especially with the earliest extant plays, *Alcestis* and *Medea*.

It is less easy to decide how far this evidence of lyric structure offers us an absolute criterion for dating the play irrespective of its authorship. Too little of fifth-century tragedy survives. In the seven extant plays of Sophocles, although they are spread over the same period as Euripides' extant works, there is not so marked a development in the formal structure of the lyrics. There is however some change, and his two latest plays especially show to some extent the same late tendencies seen in Euripides. In respect of structure *Rhesus* does not belong with these, but rather with *Ajax* and *Antigone*, almost certainly the two earliest of our Sophoclean plays. So far then as our evidence goes, *Rhesus* appears to have most in common with the plays of both Euripides and Sophocles that belong, or are generally thought to belong, between the years 450 and 430.

It is apparent that on the basis of the present evidence *Rhesus* is not easily associated with the manner of the late fifth century. And so it would have to be argued by the champions of a fourth-century date that the poet was archaizing in the design of his lyrics.[1] One has to reckon with this possibility, and the case might be supported by pointing to tendencies shown here and there in the last plays of Sophocles to revert to older forms of lyric structure, for example the epirrhematic parodos. But in these plays the use of an old technique is only occasional. *Rhesus* in the manner of its lyrics is consistent throughout with the early practice of Euripides, a strong argument against its being a late imitation.

The evidence of the structure of the lyrics is thus strikingly in harmony with the evidence of their metres and of the metre of dialogue. In all respects *Rhesus* shares the essential characteristics of Euripides' earliest known style and has no mark of lateness. The clear indication then is that, if *Rhesus* is the work of Euripides, it is an early work.

---

[1] This was the conclusion of Kranz, *op. cit.* pp. 263 ff.

CHAPTER VIII

CONCLUSION:
THE DATE OF COMPOSITION

In the foregoing chapters the aim has been to make an impartial survey of the evidence relating to the authorship of *Rhesus*, and in the light of this evidence to assess the worth of the many arguments which have been brought forward both for and against its attribution to Euripides. The investigation has now been pursued in all fields which seem likely to contribute useful material. It remains to review briefly the significant results of the inquiry, to decide what conclusion they justify, and to consider whether any further grounds remain for not accepting this conclusion as final.

Since the findings of the various parts of the investigation have been summarized at the end of each chapter, only a brief recapitulation of the salient points is needed. The important findings are as follows:

EXTERNAL EVIDENCE

(1) It is established beyond reasonable doubt that Euripides was the author of a play called *Rhesus*, which was a work of his youth.

(2) Our own *Rhesus* was known to Dicaearchus about 300 B.C. as the work of Euripides. It seems certain that by this time it had at least two different forms of opening, and so had been produced more than once on the stage; and that it had for some time been regarded as Euripidean.

(3) It is not wholly impossible that our play has been mistakenly identified as the work of Euripides, but, since such an error could only happen after the play had lain forgotten for some considerable length of time, its composition cannot on any reasonable hypothesis be placed later

345

than the early fourth century. The evidence provided by the variant forms of prologue for our play's popularity before it reached the Alexandrian scholars makes it less easy to suppose that it could have been forgotten long enough for a mistake to have been made.

(4) The single reference in the Argument is our only indication that the authenticity of *Rhesus* was suspected in antiquity. The only explanation offered there suggests that the unnamed persons who took this view did so for subjective reasons. We cannot tell who they were or when they lived; but the suspicion cannot have been widely held, for there is evidence that the leading scholars of both Alexandria and Pergamum accepted the play as the work of Euripides. The question of its authenticity is most likely to have been considered by the earliest Alexandrian scholars, and it may have been at this period that the suspicion was expressed.

External sources yield no evidence against the authenticity of *Rhesus*. Indeed we possess more positive testimony in support of its genuineness than we do for some other works of Euripides.

INTERNAL EVIDENCE

The case against Euripidean authorship

The arguments brought forward to prove *Rhesus* spurious are of great variety. Those which have to do with the poet's methods of composition and dramatic presentation are divisible into two .classes, one kind being concerned with supposed differences from the ordinary manner of Euripides or of the fifth-century tragedians in general, the other kind being aesthetic arguments involving allegations of inferior craftsmanship. In respect of the former it has been possible to find adequate parallels in the works of Euripides or the other fifth-century tragedians, while the aesthetic arguments, which are necessarily of doubtful relevance for the question of authorship, are often open to challenge and not seldom founded on misinterpretation of the poet's intention.

Of much greater importance is the evidence furnished by the vocabulary, phraseology, style and metre of the play, in which a fundamental dissimilarity could not easily be attributed to accident. Here the case against Euripidean authorship is decisively refuted by a detailed comparison with his other works. Of the peculiarities that *Rhesus* is alleged to show the majority are found to have a parallel in Euripides; the few strange elements that remain are no more than we should expect to find in any play of Euripides.

In addition it is to be noted that many of the reasons given for dating *Rhesus* specifically in the fourth century have been discounted. These include the charges that the poet is an imitator of the great tragedians, that he violates the conventions of the fifth-century tragic stage and that the characters are types unknown before the fourth century. There are some further arguments for a late date which will be mentioned below.

Positive arguments for authenticity

It is to be expected that positive evidence that Euripides is the author of *Rhesus* will be limited in quantity. Resemblances to the style and methods of Euripides are easily found, but our knowledge of Greek tragedy is not sufficient to enable us often to decide with confidence whether these are significant. We have always to reckon with the possibility of imitation and in individual instances this can seldom be discarded. There is however in certain aspects of style a degree of likeness between *Rhesus* and the works of Euripides which cannot easily be so explained. In this class we have observed a large common stock of ordinary vocabulary, which includes many words that are the peculiar favourites of Euripides, several distinctive coincidences of phrase and a number of common habits of expression, as well as a closely similar metrical technique. Such intimate characteristics of the style of Euripides we should hardly expect to be reproduced by an imitator.

Specific resemblance to the earlier works
of Euripides

Not only has it appeared that *Rhesus* is stylistically like the works of Euripides, but it is consistently associated with his early plays in all aspects of composition in which a development of Euripides' style is to be discerned. The evidence of both the iambic trimeter and the lyric metres has indicated a close affinity with the earlier works, and this impression has been confirmed by an examination of the formal structure of the lyric parts.

On the other hand *Rhesus* shares no feature which belongs peculiarly to Euripides' later style or technique. Various arguments against a date early in his career have been considered and rejected. These include the use of the θεολογεῖον (p. 122) and the *deus ex machina* (pp. 132 ff.) and the occurrence of *antilabe* in the anapaestic dimeter and trochaic tetrameter (pp. 289–96). A further argument against the early date has been given prominence by some scholars, notably by Murray and Pearson,[1] but may also now be discarded. It is argued that supposed peculiarities in the style of *Rhesus* are not shared by the fragments of *Peliades*, Euripides' earliest work. But we have found the stylistic differences in question to be of minor importance. The reference is particularly to the lack of sententious utterances in *Rhesus*, the few surviving fragments of *Peliades* (about 23 lines) containing a high proportion of this kind. It has, however, already been demonstrated that the deficiency of this element in *Rhesus* is not significant. There can be no further objection here to an early date for *Rhesus*. In fact the style of *Peliades* seems to have something of the terseness and brevity noted as characteristic of our play. But it is impossible to judge distinctive qualities of style from such meagre fragments, especially when they are nearly all of the gnomic kind.

[1] Murray, *Rhesus* (transl.), p. viii; Pearson, *CR*, xxxv (1921), 54; Hagenbach, *De Rheso Tragoedia*, p. 27; Nestle, *Euripides*, p. 381 n. 28.

The internal evidence is thus consistent with the testimony of Crates, enabling us to draw a conclusion with confidence from the evidence that has been considered: *Rhesus* is the work of Euripides and it was written at a date early in his career.

To this it must be added that it is highly probable that the play has lost an iambic prologue with which Euripides originally provided it. It is likely that this prologue was of a type familiar in other works of Euripides, an introductory dialogue between two deities, of the kind found in *Troades* or *Alcestis*, or possibly a monologue spoken by a single god, as in *Hippolytus* for example. Apart from the loss of this opening there is no reason to believe that we do not have the play substantially as Euripides wrote it. There is, as we saw (pp. 290 ff.), probably some corruption of the text in the opening anapaests, and there are inevitably some places, especially in the lyrics, where the text is damaged beyond repair, but the suspicion nowhere arises of deliberate interpolation. The style of *Rhesus* is homogeneous, and no passage bears marks of interference by a later hand. If actors were responsible for removing the prologue written by Euripides, as our evidence suggests, they appear to have left the rest of the play intact.

It has been decided on the basis of an examination of its style, structure and technique that *Rhesus* is the work of Euripides. Since these are the aspects of the dramatist's art which can be analysed and compared, it is from these sources that those who deem the play spurious must derive the material evidence to support their contention. Such evidence has been found to be totally lacking, and without its support it is scarcely possible to establish a convincing case against the authenticity of the play. The opponents of authenticity nevertheless have left a few arguments, which have not yet been fully treated because they do not fall into the classes of evidence examined in the previous chapters.

These further arguments have in common the assertion that *Rhesus* is totally unlike the kind of drama we otherwise know Euripides to have written, even unlike any other fifth-century Attic tragedy. It is not to be denied that the play does strike us as different in character from our other specimens of fifth-century tragedy. This difference, which is readily felt but not so easily defined, lies at the root of the suspicion that *Rhesus* is spurious. Now that it has been established that in the essential fabric of its style and composition *Rhesus* has a close affinity with the other works of Euripides, we may turn to consider wherein the difference lies, and in seeking to define it we shall take account of the few remaining points of the case against authenticity.

At the outset it may be said that even if *Rhesus* were a fundamentally different type of drama from any other written by Euripides, it would hardly be possible on these grounds alone to deny that he was its author, and it would certainly be difficult to maintain this against the weight of the stylistic evidence. For, whereas a poet does not easily change his basic equipment of vocabulary, forms of expression and metrical technique, he may at will vary the type of drama that he writes. There could only reasonably be grounds for suspicion if *Rhesus* seemed not to fall within the limits of the kind of drama proper to the tragic stage in fifth-century Athens. Such indeed is the underlying contention of the critics whose arguments we are now to consider.

One argument is that *Rhesus* is essentially comic in character and therefore unsuitable for the tragic stage. Geffcken puts the case as follows: 'Man hat immer wieder mit Recht das Wesen des Dramas sehr "untragisch" gefunden. Auch darum gehört das Stück allerletzten Grundes ins 4. Jahrhundert, in die Zeit von Anaxandrides' Κωμωιδοτραγωιδία, in die Periode des Amphitruo, dessen Prolog das Stück als eine *tragicomoedia* bezeichnet.'[1]

By so fantastic a comparison Geffcken betrays a complete misconception of the dramatic spirit of *Rhesus*. Of the kind of comedy exemplified in *Amphitryo*, namely burlesque of myth, *Rhesus* has nothing. The most superficial comparison

---

[1] *Hermes*, LXXI (1936), 407.

of the drama with its epic source will show that the dramatist has treated the myth in no spirit of burlesque or parody. In fact the element of comedy in *Rhesus* has been absurdly exaggerated. As we have already seen (above, pp. 96 ff.) there is nothing comic in the treatment of the chief characters, nor even of Dolon, although here perhaps the epic version provided scope for it. The only scenes containing any elements that might be described in a very broad sense as comic are those involving Odysseus and Paris, but even here the poet does no more than represent traditional elements in their characters. A comic treatment of minor characters, if this can properly be so called, is not contrary to the spirit of fifth-century tragedy, and does not make the play a κωμῳδοτραγῳδία. A drama which ends in the death of the hero and the grief of his bereaved mother answers to no definition of comedy either ancient or modern.

Others, while not venturing to label *Rhesus* comic, nevertheless maintain that it lacks qualities essential to fifth-century tragedy. Of this view, which is shared by most of those who hold *Rhesus* spurious, the judgement of Pohlenz may be quoted as representative: 'Von der tragischen Atmosphäre der alten Zeit, vom tragischen Gehalt des Geschehens, von einem tragischen Lebensgefühl des Dichters ist nichts zu finden. Die Tragödie ist zum "Drama" geworden.'[1] Wilamowitz in condemning the play on similar grounds makes the substance of the charge more explicit. After referring to the rhetorical tragedy of the fourth century he adds: 'Daneben steht dies in der Form archaistische Stück, das doch im übrigen von seinen Vorbildern so stark abweicht, daß man es kaum eine Tragödie nennen kann. Wenigstens Theoretiker, die eine Peripetie, einen Helden, eine κάθαρσις τῶν παθημάτων δι' ἐλέου καὶ φόβου verlangen, finden hier nichts davon.'[2]

Expressed in this form the criticism is, as Wilamowitz concedes, an unfair one, because it judges the play in terms

---

[1] *Griechische Tragödie*, 2nd ed. p. 475.   [2] *Hermes*, LXI (1926), 286.

of a theory of the tragedian's art which was not yet known when it was written. But if this criticism is to be formulated at all, it is bound to be put in such terms. It is in fact the Aristotelian standards which those critics are applying who state that *Rhesus* is untragic.

Although the validity of this kind of argument is thus questionable, it is not inappropriate to take Aristotle's aesthetic principles as a standard against which to measure the tragic quality of *Rhesus*. If we do so, it is immediately apparent that Wilamowitz has overstated his case. The drama most conspicuously contains *peripeteia* in the full Aristotelian sense of the term. Surely the death of Rhesus is a reversal of fortune that answers to Aristotle's definition, one which the dramatist reinforces by making Rhesus die by the guile of the very man whom, in the last words he speaks on the stage, he has resolved to kill. This is a *peripeteia* which involves not only the hero but the Chorus and the other chief characters of the drama.

The kernel of the criticism, however, is that the death of Rhesus fails to be tragic because it does not follow as a result of his own ἁμαρτία, but is caused entirely by an external agency. It would be idle to deny the truth of this, and it is a valid aesthetic criticism of the drama if one agrees with Aristotle's view that the best kind of tragic plot is that in which a man suffers a change from good fortune to bad through some ἁμαρτία of his own.[1] But Aristotle nowhere says that all the tragedies written in the fifth century possessed plots of the kind he deems best. There is no need to enumerate the extant tragedies that are not of this kind. Indeed Aristotle's own observation is that poets at first chose τοὺς τυχόντας μύθους and only in his own day came to prefer those legends which provided the type of plot he regards as most tragic.[2] And yet our critics would place *Rhesus* in the fourth century rather than the fifth!

If the plot of *Rhesus* is not by Aristotelian standards of the

---

[1] *Poetics* xiii, 3. [2] *Ibid.* xiii, 7.

best kind, it does not follow that the drama is wholly lacking in tragic spirit. This is far from the case. In the catastrophe and the expressions of grief that it occasions there is surely an appeal to the emotions of pity and fear, in the evocation of which Aristotle finds the essence of the tragic pleasure.[1] Wilamowitz complains that the play fails to arouse these feelings, and others have been in agreement with him. If this is so, it may be that the dramatist has not succeeded in his object, but it is certainly not true that he was seeking an emotional response of a kind foreign to the spirit of fifth-century tragedy. It is the dramatist's intention which we should consider here, and not the degree of his success or failure, although we may more readily attribute the impression formed by these critics to their own prejudice than to the defect of the poet, who does nothing to obscure his meaning.

A further argument in the same class, which is advanced by both Pohlenz and Geffcken,[2] is that *Rhesus* is out of harmony with the religious spirit of Euripidean tragedy. In this connection, as we saw (pp. 120–5, 132–5), there is specific reference to the epiphanies of Athena and the Muse, which are held to be unlike those of Euripidean drama. It has already been demonstrated that this argument is groundless. The Muse in the closing scene performs functions corresponding to those of the common Euripidean *deus ex machina*; and the epiphany of the hero's divine mother has a precedent in the drama of Aeschylus. The earlier epiphany has a parallel, in both form and function, in Euripides' *Heracles*. Nor does a broader view of the religious ideas embodied in *Rhesus* reveal anything which might be thought to be at variance with the spirit of Euripidean tragedy. We have already seen (p. 124) that the dramatist makes explicit in the Muse's speech his conception of the relation between men and gods. There the gods are held ultimately responsible for the events that have taken place; the action on the human plane is seen as the consequence of conflict among the gods,

---

[1] *Ibid.* VI, 2.   [2] Pohlenz, *op. cit.*; Geffcken, *Hermes*, LXXI (1936), 405 f.

who arbitrarily inflict sufferings upon men in furtherance of their quarrels with one another. There is nothing novel about this conception of the gods: it is essentially the Homeric theology which the dramatist has adopted unchanged from the epic version of the myth. It would be a mistake to think that such a treatment of the gods is opposed to the spirit of Euripidean tragedy. In several of his plays the divine role is similarly represented. It is made explicit in the prologue and epilogue of *Hippolytus*, spoken respectively by Aphrodite and Artemis, and in the dialogue between Poseidon and Athena which forms the prologue of *Troades*; the same conception of the divine causation of the human tragedy is presented equally clearly in the intervention of Iris and Lyssa in *Heracles*. In all these places the gods are shown cruelly and capriciously inflicting undeserved evil upon men. In one respect *Troades* offers the closest parallel; for there too the gods are seen in control of the fortunes of war, and the individual humans who suffer as the result of actions divinely willed are as far removed from personal moral responsibility as they are in *Rhesus*.

As recent critics have shown, it is a mistake to look in the works of Euripides for any systematic theology.[1] In spite of the spirit of scepticism with which he often approaches the myths, criticism of the traditional religious beliefs is not for him an end in itself, and he has no positive doctrine to preach. He is primarily a dramatist, for whom the treatment of the gods in each play is dictated by artistic considerations. In those plays in which he dramatizes the myth with its traditional divine elements, he admits in the mouths of his characters more or less censure, as the circumstances warrant, of the cruelty of the gods. In this respect *Rhesus* is quite consistent with his dramatic methods: although Athena is taken straight from the epic tradition, she does not escape reproach in the speech of the Muse.

[1] See especially F. Chapouthier, 'Eur. et l'accueil du divin', in *Entretiens de la Fondation Hardt*, I (1954), 205 ff.

The critics whose view we have just been considering commit the error of expecting a dramatist to be a consistent thinker. While there are perhaps few who would maintain that Euripides is consistent in his views, it is nevertheless common to regard him as essentially a thinker. Such a belief is implied in the argument that *Rhesus* cannot be by Euripides because, to use the phrase of one recent critic, it is 'intellectually null'.[1] It is obvious what is meant by this. Euripides is noted for his critical attitude towards traditional beliefs and for an interest in the ethical, social and political ideas current among his contemporaries; he is given to philosophical reflection and is a master of subtle rhetoric. In *Rhesus* these qualities are missed: the drama is treated objectively, the interest is concentrated upon the plot with no emphasis on its deeper significance.

Although this is certainly an overstatement of the case, it is true that there is here an appreciable difference between *Rhesus* and the general run of Euripidean tragedy. But those who assert on these grounds that Euripides could not have written the play make the mistake of treating as essential an element which is properly incidental and subordinate in drama. We have already seen that in *Rhesus* elaborate rhetorical embellishment would be neither in character nor appropriate to the dramatic situation (see above, pp. 91 f.), and that the limited amount of sententious reflection, in which *Rhesus* is not unique among the plays of Euripides, is explicable on the same grounds (pp. 225 ff.). If the alleged intellectual poverty goes beyond this, it is probably for the same reason that the plot is not of the kind that gives scope for indulgence in philosophy. It is a false idea that the Attic dramatists were in any way primarily concerned with imparting moral instruction to their audience.

It appears then that the differences of treatment which have been noticed between *Rhesus* and other tragedies of

[1] D. W. Lucas, *The Greek Tragic Poets*, 1st ed. (1950), p. 226, and *CR*, 1 (1951), 20.

Euripides may simply be a consequence of the difference of its subject-matter. If this is after all the essential difference, it cannot give cause for doubting that Euripides is the author of the play. There is clearly no reason why a dramatist should not choose to treat a plot which in its matter or setting is unlike his others. Yet it has been put forward as a serious argument against the authenticity of *Rhesus* that Euripides could not have written a play whose background is a military camp and whose theme is an episode of war. Geffcken refused to believe that Euripides, who so often shows himself a lover of peace, could have written such a drama μεστόν "Αρεως.[1] The argument would only carry weight if it could be shown that the subject-matter of the play lay outside the range of fifth-century tragedy. But this is quite certainly not the case. Even among the extant plays of Euripides *Heraclidae*, *Supplices* and *Phoenissae* are set amidst battle and bloodshed. Lost tragedies probably presented a closer parallel. As we saw earlier (see above, pp. 79 ff.), Aeschylus had already dramatized the closely similar myths of Memnon and Cycnus, both likewise set against a background of battle, so that Euripides at any date of his career had ample precedent for a drama on the theme of the death of a warrior. The limits of the subject-matter of tragedy were not thus narrowly defined. A poet surely had the right to choose his plot from the whole range of heroic myth. It was only necessary that it could be treated in the serious spirit proper to the tragic stage, and *Rhesus* as we have seen satisfied in this respect.

But the intention of Geffcken's argument is clear. Would Euripides, whose attitude to war is one of loathing, have chosen to dramatize an actual exploit of war, one involving bloodshed, and to present in such vivid detail the life of the camp? This objection betrays a failure to appreciate the spirit of the drama. It is true that *Rhesus* is full of tactical details, but these merely belong to a realistic presentation of the

[1] *Op. cit.* p. 399.

background against which the drama takes place. The real spirit of the tragedy is in no way at variance with the usual attitude of Euripides to war. What Geffcken and other critics have failed to observe is that the central interest of *Rhesus* is very different from that of the *Doloneia*, and that the moral standpoint of the dramatist is very different from that of the epic poet. Unlike the epic version the drama shows no delight in bloodshed, but dwells upon the pathos of untimely death in a spirit of pity which we can well associate with Euripides.[1] There is nothing either in the theme or in the sentiments of the play which might lead to doubt of its authenticity.

The differences between *Rhesus* and other tragedies of Euripides are superficial and not of a kind to disturb the conclusion we have already reached. These differences should not blind us to the close affinity in essential character between *Rhesus* and the rest of Euripidean drama. Analysis of the various aspects of style and technique has shown that *Rhesus* conforms closely to the ordinary manner of Euripides. But the qualities of his dramatic art are more obviously apparent. The narrative speeches of the Shepherd and the Charioteer are worthy specimens of Euripides' genius for descriptive narrative. The lyrics have the simplicity and grace of his early style. The debate of Rhesus and Hector, despite its lack of rhetorical ornament, and the speech of the Muse are also fully imbued with the spirit of Euripidean tragedy.

The date of 'Rhesus'

Our conclusion that *Rhesus* is an early work of Euripides raises the further question whether its date can be more precisely determined. The evidence that has so far occurred for the date of the play is as follows:

(*a*) Crates states clearly that Euripides was νέος when he produced *Rhesus*. The limits of age within which a man may

---

[1] On the difference of spirit between *Rhesus* and the *Doloneia* see G. H. Macurdy, *The Quality of Mercy* (1940), pp. 28–36.

be called νέος will be relative to the particular circumstances. Here the purpose is to excuse Euripides for showing ignorance of astronomy, and we should not expect to find the error condoned on the grounds of his youth if he were over forty. Now the date of Euripides' birth is unknown, but according to different traditions it was either 484 or 480. It is not certain that either is correct nor which Crates was following, but even if he reckoned from the later date, he would hardly have described Euripides as νέος at a date later than 440. He would certainly not have written thus of a play belonging to the 420's or later. If he was thinking in terms of Euripides' dramatic career, which is known to have begun in 455, the year 440 would still be a conservative late limit for the use of the adjective νέος. It would more naturally be used of a somewhat earlier date.

(*b*) The evidence of resolution in the iambic trimeter puts *Rhesus* with the earliest group of Euripides' works, *Alcestis* (438), *Medea* (431), *Heraclidae* and *Hippolytus* (428). Its extreme conservatism in respect of the rules formulated by Zieliński and the extreme position which it sometimes shows in the statistical analysis of Euripides' resolutions suggest that the play might possibly be even earlier than *Alcestis*. But this is uncertain, especially as it is not possible to discern clearly a regular development of metrical style within the plays of the early group.

(*c*) The evidence of lyric metre and structure agrees closely with that of the iambic trimeter. On the basis of this evidence it seems inconceivable that *Rhesus* could be later than 420, and it is not easy to suppose it later than *Hippolytus* (428). The closest resemblance is to the earliest plays, especially to *Alcestis*.

The consistent tendency of this evidence makes it possible to eliminate altogether the possibility that *Rhesus* might be later than *Hippolytus*, and gives some reason for preferring to place it earlier than any other extant work of Euripides, that is, before 438.

Further evidence for the date of *Rhesus* is not easily found. The subject-matter of the play shows that it belongs to a period when the Athenians were interested in Thrace and reasonably well acquainted with Thracian institutions. But this would have been the case at any date within Euripides' career, which began in 455. Although we have only limited information about Athenian activity in Thrace in the early fifth century, it need not be thought that it was only intermittent during this period. The connection of Athens with the mines of Pangaeum goes back to the time of the Pisistratids,[1] and the attempt to establish a colony at Ennea Hodoi in 465–4 certainly proves more than a passing interest in the region. There is no reason to think that there was any relaxation of this interest between the failure of 464 and the successful colonization by Hagnon in 437. We may therefore believe that a drama with a Thracian background could have been presented before an Athenian audience at any date within the period of Euripides' career to which our play has already been assigned.

The description of the river Strymon as καλλιγέφυρος (*v.* 349) has been cited in connection with the dating of the play, but it does not help us.[2] Thucydides writes of a bridge existing there in 424, and this may have been the same one that Xerxes had built, for his bridge was perhaps a permanent structure and not merely a temporary one.[3] If so, the epithet might have been used by Euripides at any date.

The allegorical interpretation of the drama, which seeks to identify Rhesus with Sitalces and hence to place the play in the 420's, has already been discredited (see above, pp. 82–3). Apart from the fact that there is no parallel for this sort of allegory in Attic tragedy and no convincing

---

[1] Aristotle, *Ath. Pol.* 15, 2; cf. Hdt. 1, 64; Adcock, *CAH*, iv, 64 f.

[2] Wilamowitz, *Griechische Verskunst*, pp. 585 ff., included this among his evidence for a fourth-century date. He is answered by Buchwald, *Stud. zur Chronologie der att. Trag.* pp. 50 ff.

[3] Thuc. iv, 103; Hdt. vii, 24; cf. 114. The fact that it was prepared in advance of Xerxes' march by the engineers of the Athos canal suggests that it was a permanent structure. Aeschylus, *Pers.* 495 ff. may not be historical.

evidence for it in this play, we can now see clearly that it is incompatible with the other evidence for the date of the play. Euripides does not indulge in elaborate political allegory, but he does like to point out a connection between the events of his drama and institutions existing in his own day. In many plays, as we have seen (p. 135), this is introduced in a prophetic statement by the *deus ex machina*. So in *Rhesus* 962 ff. the Muse prophesies the future existence of Rhesus as an ἀνθρωποδαίμων in a cave of Mount Pangaeum. Here there is clearly a reference to a contemporary institution, which was evidently familiar to Euripides' Athenian audience. In connection with these lines we have to consider a passage of Polyaenus, the relevance of which for the dating of *Rhesus* is disputed.[1] Polyaenus relates that at the time of the foundation of Amphipolis, in 437, the Athenian general Hagnon, at the bidding of an oracle, had the bones of Rhesus brought back from his tomb at Troy for burial in Thracian soil. Prevented by the Thracians from crossing the Strymon, he concluded a truce with them for three days; then, observing it to the letter, he crossed the river at night, buried the bones beside it and fortified the place. Thus the Athenians secured the ground of Amphipolis. This episode is not mentioned by Thucydides, but is not necessarily to be rejected as a fiction on that account, for the historian alludes only briefly to the founding of Amphipolis. On the other hand, Polyaenus is an unreliable authority, and the inherent improbabilities of this story are enough to cast serious doubt upon it.[2] We must at least regard it with suspicion.

Those who have accepted the substance of Polyaenus' account have variously interpreted its significance for the dating of *Rhesus*. Goossens, following Leaf and others, regards it as fixing the year 437 as *terminus post quem* for the play.[3] But if the story is compared with the Muse's words in

[1] *Strateg.* VI, 53.
[2] J. Rempe, *De Rheso Thracum heroe* (1927), pp. 13 ff.; cf. Sinko, *Ant. Class.* III (1934), 414.
[3] Goossens, *Ant. Class.* I (1932), 97; Leaf, *JHS*, xxxv (1915), 6.

Rhesus, it is apparent that, far from the two having any connection, they are indeed incompatible. Not only does Polyaenus place the burial παρὰ τὸν ποταμόν, while Euripides makes Rhesus dwell ἐν ἄντροις on Mount Pangaeum, but it is also quite clearly ordained in the play that the body of Rhesus is not to be buried at all in Trojan soil but is immediately to be transported back to Thrace. We cannot believe that Euripides, or anyone else, would have been so careless in alluding to an historical event. If the episode related by Polyaenus really took place in 437, it would have been famous at Athens, and Euripides was unlikely thereafter to have written a play which by presenting a contradictory version exposed Hagnon's action, and the oracle which prompted it, as fraudulent. The idea that *Rhesus* refers to this event may be discounted.

If then Polyaenus is to be accepted, we must regard 437 rather as the *terminus ante quem* for *Rhesus*.[1] Polyaenus' account is then compatible with the play. The action of Hagnon is not to be interpreted as an attempt to found a cult of Rhesus, but implies that he was already honoured as a hero by the Thracians of the Strymon region, which was clearly the case when *Rhesus* was written.

If the authority of Polyaenus is rejected, it is still possible to associate *Rhesus* with the foundation of Amphipolis. But there is nothing in the content of the play to connect it particularly with this occasion. If the event had been recent, we should have expected a clearly recognizable allusion to it in the Muse's prophetic speech.

The sum of the evidence leaves us with a strong preference for dating *Rhesus* as the earliest of Euripides' extant works. There are good grounds for placing its composition between 455 and 440, with a preference, in view of the testimony of Crates, for an earlier date within this period.

---

[1] This view was taken by Richards, *CQ*, x (1916), 192; Buchwald, *op. cit.*; also by Hartung, *Eur. rest.* pp. 6 f.

SELECT BIBLIOGRAPHY

This list, which is arranged in chronological order, includes only works which either discuss the problem of the authorship of *Rhesus* or present evidence relevant to this problem.

I. WORKS EARLIER THAN 1850

A fuller bibliography for this period is given by C. B. Sneller, *De Rheso Tragoedia* (1949), pp. 1 f.

J. Scaliger, *Prolegomena ad Manilium* (Leiden, 1600), pp. 6 f.

J. Hardion, *Dissertation sur la tragédie de Rhésos*, Mém. Acad. des Inscr. x (1731), 323 ff.

L. C. Valckenaer, *Diatribe in Euripidis dramatum perditorum reliquias* (Leiden, 1768), chs. IX and X.

A. Boeckh, *Graecae tragoediae principum Aeschyli Sophoclis Euripidis num ea quae supersunt genuina omnia sint* (Heidelberg, 1808), ch. XVIII.

C. D. Beck, *Diatribe critica de Rheso supposititio Euripidis dramate* (Leipzig, 1824).

R. Morstadt, *Beitrag zur Kritik der dem Euripides zugeschriebenen Tragödie Rhesos* (Heidelberg, 1827).

G. Hermann, *De Rheso Tragoedia dissertatio, Opuscula*, III (Leipzig, 1828), pp. 262–310.

O. F. Gruppe, *Ariadne* (Berlin, 1834), chs. VII–X.

F. G. Welcker, 'Der Rhesos', *Zeitschr. für Altertumswiss.* 76 (1834), 629 ff. (= *Die griechischen Tragödien mit Rücksicht auf den epischen Cyclus geordnet*, vol. III, Bonn, 1841, pp. 1101 ff.).

F. Vater, *Vindiciae*, in his edition of *Rhesus* (Berlin, 1837).

J. A. Hartung, *Euripides restitutus* (Hamburg, 1843), I, 11 ff.

II. WORKS PUBLISHED BETWEEN 1850 AND 1900

(a) Dissertations, articles, etc.

R. Spengler, *De Rheso Tragoedia* (Progr. Gymn. Düren, 1857).

F. Hagenbach, *De Rheso Tragoedia* (Diss. Basle, 1863).

O. Menzer, *De Rheso Tragoedia* (Diss. Berlin, 1867).

F. A. Paley, Introduction to *Rhesus* in his edition of Euripides, 2nd ed. (London, 1872), I, 5 ff.

P. Albert, *De Rheso Tragoedia* (Diss. Halle, 1876).

362

SELECT BIBLIOGRAPHY

W. Nöldeke, *De Rhesi fabulae aetate et forma* (Progr. Realsch. Schwerin, 1877).
U. von Wilamowitz-Moellendorff, *De Rhesi Scholiis* (Diss. Greifswald, 1877).
L. Eysert, *Rhesus im Lichte des euripideischen Sprachgebrauches*, Progr. Böhm-Leipa, I (1891), and II (1893).
N. Wecklein, *Berl. phil. Woch.* (19/12/1891), coll. 1613 f.
J. C. Rolfe, 'The Tragedy Rhesus', *Harv. Stud. Cl. Phil.* IV (1893), 61 ff.

(b) Reference in literary histories, handbooks, etc.

Th. Bergk, *Griechische Literaturgeschichte*, III (1884), 613 ff.
U. von Wilamowitz-Moellendorff, *Einleitung in die griechische Tragödie* (Berlin, 1889), p. 41.
H. J. G. Patin, *Euripide*, 7th ed. (Paris, 1894), II, 148 ff.
A. E. Haigh, *Tragic Drama of the Greeks* (Oxford, 1896), pp. 284 f.

III. WORKS PUBLISHED SINCE 1900

(a) Dissertations, articles, etc.

E. Walda, *Zur Rhesosfrage* (Progr. Prachatitz, 1908).
W. H. Porter, 'The Euripidean *Rhesus* in the Light of Recent Criticism', *Hermathena*, XVII (1913), 348 ff.
G. Murray, *The Rhesus of Euripides* (translation) (1913), pp. v ff.
E. Harrison, 'Verse-Weight', *CQ*, VIII (1914), 206 ff.
W. Leaf, 'Rhesus of Thrace', *JHS*, XXXV (1915), 1 ff.
W. N. Bates, 'Notes on the *Rhesus*', *TAPA*, XLVII (1916), 5 ff.
G. C. Richards, 'The Problem of the *Rhesus*', *CQ*, x (1916), 192 ff.
P. Fabbri, 'De nonnullis Rhesi tragoediae locis discrepantibus', *Riv. di fil.* XLVIII (1920), 192 ff.
A. C. Pearson, 'The *Rhesus*', *CR*, XXXV (1921), 52–61 (also other articles in *CR*, XXXI (1917), 25–7, and *CQ*, XX (1926), 80).
M. Maykowska, 'De Rhesi compositione', *Eos*, XXVI (1923), 52 ff.
W. Ridgeway, 'Euripides in Macedon', *CQ*, XX (1926), 1 ff., and *ibid.* p. 81.
U. von Wilamowitz-Moellendorff, 'Lesefrüchte', *Hermes*, LXI (1926), 284–9.
H. E. Mierow, 'The Sophoclean Character of the *Rhesus*', *AJP*, XLIX (1928), 375 ff.
C. W. Keyes, 'Apollo and Athena in the *Rhesus*', *TAPA*, LIX (1928), 28 ff.

W. H. Porter, *The Rhesus of Euripides*, 2nd ed. (Cambridge, 1929), Introduction, pp. xxx–liv.

A. D. Nock, *CR*, XLIV (1930), 173 (review of Porter's 2nd ed.).

R. Goossens, 'La date du Rhèsos', *Ant. Class.* I (1932), 93 ff.

H. Grégoire, 'L'authenticité du Rhésus d'Euripide', *Ant. Class.* II (1933), 91 ff.

R. Goossens, 'Rhésos et Sitalkès', *Bull. Assoc. Budé*, XLI (1933), 11 ff.

C. Gallavotti, 'Nuove hypotheseis di drammi euripidei', *Riv. di fil.* LXI (1933), 177 ff.

W. Morel, *Bursians Jahresbericht*, 238 (1933), 153, and *ibid.* 259 (1938), 61.

Th. Sinko, 'De causae Rhesi novissima defensione', *Ant. Class.* III (1934), 223 ff., 411 ff.

H. Grégoire and R. Goossens, 'Sitalkès et Athènes dans le Rhésos d'Euripide', *ibid.* pp. 431 ff.

P. Perdrizet, *Le Pont d'Amphipolis et la date du Rhésos*. Mélanges in mem. A. Parvan (Bucharest, 1934), pp. 284–90.

J. Geffcken, 'Der Rhesos', *Hermes*, LXXI (1936), 394 ff.

W. Buchwald, *Studien zur Chronologie der attischen Tragödie 455 bis 431* (Diss. Königsberg, 1939), pp. 50 ff.

G. H. Macurdy, 'The Dawn Songs in *Rhesus* (527–36) and in the Parodos of *Phaethon*', *AJP*, LXIV (1943), 408 ff.

C. B. Sneller, *De Rheso Tragoedia* (Diss. Utrecht, Amsterdam, 1949). [This work is reviewed by J. C. Kamerbeek, *Mnemosyne*, III (1950), 347–9; R. Goossens, *RBP*, XXIX (1951), 1209–13; A. Lesky, *Gnomon*, XXIII (1951), 141–4; D. W. Lucas, *CR*, n.s. I (1951), 18–20; G. M. A. Grube, *CP*, XLVII (1952), 56.]

G. Björck, 'Rhesos', *Arctos*, n.s. I (1954), 16–18.

G. Björck, 'The Authenticity of *Rhesus*', *Eranos*, LV (1957), 7–17.

H. Strohm, 'Beobachtungen zum "Rhesos"', *Hermes*, LXXXVII (1959), 257–74.

(b) Reference in literary histories, handbooks, etc.

W. Nestle, *Euripides* (Stuttgart, 1901), pp. 380 f.

W. Ridgeway, *The Origin of Tragedy* (Cambridge, 1910), pp. 147 ff.

H. Steiger, *Euripides, seine Dichtung und seine Persönlichkeit* (Leipzig, 1912), pp. 90 ff.

A. and M. Croiset, *Histoire de la littérature grecque*, III, 3rd ed. (Paris, 1913), pp. 404 ff.

U. von Wilamowitz-Moellendorff, *Die griechische Verskunst* (Berlin, 1921), pp. 583 ff.

SELECT BIBLIOGRAPHY

M. Pohlenz, *Die griechische Tragödie* (Leipzig, 1930), pp. 507 ff., and 2nd ed. (Göttingen, 1954), pp. 470 ff.

W. Kranz, *Stasimon* (Berlin, 1933), pp. 263 ff.

W. Schmid, *Geschichte der griechischen Literatur*, I, 3 (1940), 838.

G. H. Macurdy, *The Quality of Mercy* (New Haven, 1940), pp. 33 ff.

G. M. A. Grube, *The Drama of Euripides* (London, 1941), pp. 439–47.

P. W. Harsh, *A Handbook of Classical Drama* (Stanford, 1944), pp. 250–3.

G. Norwood, *Greek Tragedy*, 4th ed. (London, 1948), pp. 291 ff.

A. Lesky, *Die tragische Dichtung der Hellenen* (Göttingen, 1956), pp. 218–19.

T. B. L. Webster, *Art and Literature in Fourth-Century Athens* (London, 1956), p. 31.

INDEX OF PASSAGES CITED

A. 'RHESUS'

1–51	64 f., 341f.	144 f.	248
4	181, 234	149	113–15
5 (schol.)	48 f., 51, 53	149–223	67 f.
7	205	150	338
8	213	151 f.	115
12	291	154 f.	206
15	289	155	338
16	209, 290 f.	159	105
17	290 f.	162 f.	199
22	201	164	206
23–51	297 f.	165 (schol.)	48
36	174	167	252
41 (schol.)	49, 53	168	201
42	181	175	253
46	182	179–80	199
50	178	182–8	338
52	251	183	201
52–84	65	184	161, 241
54	199	191	254
55	201	195–200	299, 328, 332
56–64	98	195–263	115–18
59–61	243	201	201, 254
63	234	206	227
73	214	208	285 n.
80	205	208 ff.	68
80–104	287	210 (schol.)	48, 51
82	202	211	288
84	244	211 ff.	338
85	234	216	338
85 f.	251	219–23	338
85–148	66	224–41	300
87	252	224–63	338
99	252	239 (schol.)	48 f., 51
100–4	98	242	333
105	246	242–63	301–5
105 (schol.)	51	245	178
106 f.	227	249	201 f.
111	214	251 (schol.)	49, 51, 53
115	181	256	161
116	211	257	179
122	206, 232	257 ff.	214
125	105	260 (schol.)	52
126	199	263	178
131–6	299, 322, 328, 332	264–526	68 f.
139	241	268	182

565 f.	245	758–60	227
566	216, 233	759 f.	245 f.
570	238	762	253, 288 f.
570 f.	245	780–6	75 f.
580	245	783	174, 216
582	245	783 f.	70
589 f.	245	785	174, 216, 233
592 f.	76, 88	789	77
595	182	790 f.	77
600–4	64, 97	794	77
608–26	71 f.	796	211, 233
617	270	804	265, 268
626	127	806 f.	251
627 f.	251	807	251
630	127	811	178
631	251	819	202
639	209	820–32	308–13, 322, 328–33
642	251	824	50
642 ff.	126–9	828	178, 325
647	127	833 ff.	94
656 f.	246	837	249
660	178	849	285
668–74	72	855	212
669	233	863	200
674	233	864	181
675	239	865	181
675 ff.	2 f., 294	866	203
675–82	336	875	233
675–91	129 f.	876	245
675–727	72–4, 341	877	254
677	182	878	130–2
679	292, 294	882–4	203
682 ff.	76	882–982	77 f.
683–91	292–6	885 ff.	132–5
686	73 f.	893–4	88
692–703	315 f., 322	895–903	316–19, 325
699–701	246 f.	895–914	339 f.
708	179	900	80, 325
710 ff.	77, 88	901	325
710–21	315 f.	906–9	88
711	233	906–14	316–19
715	202	911	325
716 (schol.)	49, 51 f.	912	325
720	181, 239	913	176 f.
721	209, 234	917 ff.	62
728 ff.	3	932 f.	249
728–881	74–7	934	201
730	210	957	91
730 f.	292, 295	962 ff.	80, 360 f.
737	135, 210	965 f.	203
742–4	210	970–3	81
751	211	972	181

B. OTHER WORKS

INDEX OF PASSAGES CITED

INDEX OF SELECTED WORDS

SUBJECT INDEX

B. GENERAL

INDEX OF SCHOLARS CITED

The references are principally to discussion of the various arguments advanced by the scholars whose works are included in the Bibliography. A few other names have been added, but it is not a complete list of all scholars referred to.

INDEX OF SCHOLARS CITED